DALIT STUDIES

DALIT STUDIES

RAMNARAYAN S. RAWAT & K. SATYANARAYANA, EDITORS

Duke University Press · Durham and London · 2016

© 2016 Duke University Press

All rights reserved. Designed by Courtney Leigh Baker and Typeset
in Scala, Scala Sans, and Minion Pro by Westchester Publishing Services

Library of Congress Cataloging-in-Publication Data
Names: Rawat, Ramnarayan S., editor. | Satyanarayana, K., editor.
Title: Dalit studies / Ramnarayan S. Rawat and K. Satyanarayana, editors. Description:
Durham : Duke University Press, 2016. |
Includes bibliographical references and index.
Identifiers: LCCN 2015040886|
ISBN 9780822361138 (hardcover) |
ISBN 9780822361329 (pbk.) |
ISBN 9780822374312 (e-book)
Subjects: LCSH: Dalits—India. | Caste—India.
Classification: LCC DS422.C3 D2016 | DDC 305.5/688—dc23
LC recordavailableathttp:// lccn.loc.gov/2015040886

Cover art: Courtesy of Laxman Aelay, *Secular Song*, 2013. Acrylic on canvas, 72" × 48".
Laxman Aelay is a contemporary artist from Telangana.

To Dalit men and women who have dedicated their lives
to the pursuit of human dignity

CONTENTS

Acknowledgments • ix

INTRODUCTION. Dalit Studies: New Perspectives on
Indian History and Society • 1
RAMNARAYAN S. RAWAT AND K. SATYANARAYANA

1   The Indian Nation in Its Egalitarian Conception • 31
GOPAL GURU

PART I. Probing the Historical

2   Colonial Archive versus Colonial Sociology: Writing
Dalit History • 53
RAMNARAYAN S. RAWAT

3   Social Space, Civil Society, and Dalit Agency in
Twentieth-Century Kerala • 74
P. SANAL MOHAN

4   Dilemmas of Dalit Agendas: Political Subjugation and
Self-Emancipation in Telugu Country, 1910–50 • 104
CHINNAIAH JANGAM

5   Making Sense of Dalit Sikh History • 131
RAJ KUMAR HANS

PART II. Probing the Present

6   The Dalit Reconfiguration of Modernity: Citizens and Castes in the Telugu Public Sphere • 155
     K. SATYANARAYANA

7   Questions of Representation in Dalit Critical Discourse: Premchand and Dalit Feminism • 180
     LAURA BRUECK

8   Social Justice and the Question of Categorization of Scheduled Caste Reservations: The Dandora Debate in Andhra Pradesh • 202
     SAMBAIAH GUNDIMEDA

9   Caste and Class among the Dalits • 233
     D. SHYAM BABU

10   From *Zaat* to *Qaum*: Fluid Contours of the Ravi Dasi Identity in Punjab • 248
     SURINDER S. JODHKA

     Bibliography • 271   Contributors • 293   Index • 295

ACKNOWLEDGMENTS

Dalit studies has recently emerged as a new field of study in India. As we explain in the introduction to this volume, a number of factors have contributed to the rise of this exciting field. Perhaps the most striking is the entry of Dalit intellectuals into academic institutions. Since the late nineteenth century there has been a long tradition of Dalit activist-scholars outside academia. This volume brings a new group of scholars and activist-scholars to academic attention in North America and the West more generally. The rise of the field of Dalit studies has been propelled by the emergence of a new generation of Dalit activists and intellectuals since the 1990s. This development coincided with the discussions of caste inequities in the Indian media and academia. In Indian—or, more broadly, South Asian—academia, historical and anthropological research in the first two decades of the twenty-first century yielded information about previously unacknowledged struggles by Dalit groups, tribal people, women, and other marginal sections of Indian society. This period also coincided with new research in the disciplines of religious and literary studies and in historical and contemporary fields, which further highlighted the role of marginal social groups in sustaining different forms of devotion and protest. The exciting new research in the past two decades, especially the rise of Dalit studies and new attention paid to B. R. Ambedkar, also coincided with the formal end of the subaltern studies collective. It is in this new exciting moment that *Dalit Studies* raises a new set of questions, focusing on Dalits as subjects of study and on Dalit studies as a location of marginality to be studied in Indian history. The book seeks to draw attention to the persistence of practices that sustain caste inequality and its relationship with the unraveling of modernity in India. The last two hundred years of Indian history seems to suggest, as several essays in this volume argue, that commitments to equality can not only coexist, but can be made coeval, with regimes of caste inequality. This volume explores many of these themes.

A distinctive feature of the volume is that the contributors to the volume did additional new research and substantially rewrote their essays after presenting them as papers at the Dalit studies conference at the University of Pennsylvania in December 2008. The discussants, chairs of sessions, and audience at the conference played a crucial role in asking the right questions and enabling the contributors to further develop their research. The anonymous referees at Duke University Press provided solid feedback to all the contributors by asking insightful questions, which were specific but also addressed the overall theme of the volume. The volume introduces a new group of scholars who have addressed the concerns of Dalit studies in different regions of India. Most contributors to the volume belong to the marginal social groups in India. Indeed, many of us were deeply influenced by the political and academic debates in the 1990s following the Mandal commission report controversy in 1990. These debates were also shaped by the rapid rise of right-wing Hindu groups following the demolition of the Babri *masjid* (mosque) in December 1992. We have addressed these concerns in the introduction to the volume.

Our objective in writing a definitive introduction was to introduce Dalit studies to a diverse audience. It also provided us with a valuable opportunity to formulate the idea of Dalit studies as a critical location that allows the study of Dalits as marginalized subjects but also offers a perspective for reinterpreting Indian society and history. We wrote the introduction together in the fall of 2010 when K. Satyanarayana was a visiting fellow at the Center for the Advanced Study of India (CASI) at the University of Pennsylvania. The introduction eventually became a bold statement on our part, motivating us to engage a variety of topics from several disciplines. Recognizing the merit of the introduction, the two anonymous referees of the book's manuscript for Duke University Press became the most valuable interlocutors with their incisive comments and suggestions. Feedback from them has helped us considerably revise and rework parts of the introduction, making it sharper and clearer. Most of the comments by the two referees dealt with the introduction.

We would like to thank the participants at the Dalit studies conference, where this volume began its journey. Nearly three hundred people submitted proposals for papers to be delivered at the conference. The conference brought together a new group of scholars and was instrumental in creating new friendships and collaborations. We are grateful to those who presented papers at the conference, who in the order of presentation there are Narendra Jadhav, Chinnaiah Jangam, Gopal Guru, Sanal Mohan, Raj Kumar

Hans, Rupa Viswanath, Sukdeo Thorat, Shailaja Paik, Laura Brueck, Jebroja Singh, Hugo Gorringe, M. S. S. Pandian, Sambaiah Gundimeda, Shyam Babu, Surinder Jodhka, Chandrabhan Prasad and Devesh Kapur, Karthik Muralidharan, Katherine Newman, and Paul Attewell. We are especially thankful to the discussants at the conference for their valuable time and suggestions: Douglas Haynes, Lucinda Ramberg, Mrinalini Sinha, Sudipto Kaviraj, Steven Wilkinson, and Lant Pritchett. We are also grateful to the chairs at the conference: Priya Joshi, Jamal Elias, Ania Loomba, Atul Kohli, and Gail Omvedt. We are extremely grateful to Barbara Savage and Tufuku Zuberi for participating in the African American and Dalit studies roundtable. This roundtable was another highlight of the conference because it attracted a large audience, nearly ninety people. CASI provided substantial financial support for the conference, enabling us to invite a large number of scholars from India. In addition, it provided a small research grant to all contributors. Additional support was provided by the South Asia Center, the Department of South Asian Studies, and the Center for Africana Studies, at the University of Pennsylvania.

Over the years we have accumulated boundless debts to friends, colleagues, and institutions, and we made new friends during the course of producing this volume. Most of all, we acknowledge our deep gratitude to Devesh Kapur, director of CASI, for his support to the conference and the volume. The conference was his idea. The remarkably professional but kind staff at CASI made the conference and the book possible. Their commitment to the conference turned it into a choreographed festival of ideas. Our heartfelt thanks go to Juliana Di Giustini, deputy director of CASI and a dynamic leader and person of ideas, who planned and executed the entire conference when Ramnarayan Rawat was in India on sabbatical. We are also very grateful to Tanya Carey, administrative coordinator, for managing the conference with so much ease and a smile. Alan Atchison, the online editor and expert, was always around and ready with answers to our numerous questions. Our thanks go to Tanmaya Nanda. Several Penn undergraduates who worked part-time at CASI contributed immensely to the success of the conference. They include Katherine Maughan, Rahul Reddy, and Yashas Vaidya, all of the class of 2009. Thanks are also due to Maisha Philips and Paola Campos at South Asia Center.

In the Department of South Asian Studies and at the South Asia Center at Penn, our heartfelt thanks go to Kathy Hall, who was director of the center; the late Aditya Behl, who supported the conference plan; and Jody Chavez, assistant director of the center. The graduate students in the Department of South Asian studies provided support in various ways. Christian Novtzke and Sunila Kale, Ramnarayan Rawat's colleagues at Penn at the time, played a crucial role in conceptualizing and planning the conference—thank you both. A special thanks to Deven Patel and Jamal Elias.

Over the years Ramnarayan Rawat has greatly benefited from conversations with his colleagues at the University of Delaware, not just in history but also in anthropology, English, political science, foreign languages, and area studies. They have all been very supportive of his various projects. He is grateful for the camaraderie of his colleagues in the Asian studies program. The Dean's Office, the Center for Global and Area Studies, and the Institute of Global Studies have been generous with their support.

Susie Tharu, Madhava Prasad, Satish Poduval, Uma Bhrugubanda, Parthasarathi, and Sujit—K. Satyanarayana's colleagues and friends in the Department of Cultural Studies at the English and Foreign Language University, in Hyderabad—encouraged and contributed to teaching of Dalit studies. This intellectual collaboration has made it possible to conceive of Dalit studies as a location of critical intervention. Our conversations with Lisa Mitchell gave clarity and sharpness to our introduction to this volume. Lisa read drafts of the introduction, and her comments and criticisms helped us revise it and make a bold and sharp statement.

Devesh Kapur and Gopal Guru have been coeditors of this volume. They proposed the idea that we should organize a series of conferences on Dalit agendas and produce solid academic scholarship to create an impact in the intellectual arena. Their support was critical to creating the Dalit studies editorial collective. We wish to expand the collective and plan how to forward the Dalit studies project of alternative knowledge production. The present volume is a first step in that direction.

Ramnarayan Rawat's two brothers, Ved and Yogesh, and their wonderful families in Delhi have always been a source of emotional strength and support. Thanks to them for taking care of father. Sara and Larry Mitchell, thank you for your endless enthusiasm at all times. A special thanks to the neighbors on Beaumont Avenue, Philadelphia, who have been the most reliable of friends and well-wishers. Leela (age ten) and Rohan (age three) bring joys every day to our lives. Of course, thanks also to Lisa Mitchell for her deep wisdom, thoughtful suggestions, and boundless affection. K. Satyanarayana's wife Pavana and daughter Taara (age four) were a great source of support and love while he was working on this volume.

Dalit Studies: New Perspectives on Indian History and Society

RAMNARAYAN S. RAWAT AND K. SATYANARAYANA

These privileged young Indians [studying in England] during English rule [*gulami*, or slavery] in India had to suffer humiliation [*apaman*] at every step of their stay in England, unable, for example, to travel by first class even though they had a first-class railway ticket. They could not enter some hotels. They had to listen to the humiliating [*apaman-janak*] English term "Indian dog." Such humiliation [*apaman*] enraged them. These elite Indians didn't know that Dalits in India had to suffer the worst kind of humiliation. . . . Among the foreign returned [Indians] were Gandhi-ji, Jawaharlal Nehru, Subhas Chandra Bose, Dr. Rajendra Prasad, Lala Lajpat Rai and others. When these people experienced humiliation and loss of dignity [in England] they then became conscious of the need for independence.

—MATA PRASAD, *Jhompri se Rajbhavan*

―――――――――

The Contemporary Context

Mata Prasad's 2002 autobiography attributes the emergence of Indian nationalism to the everyday humiliation experienced by the English-educated Indian elite under colonial rule. Like earlier Dalit authors, Prasad argues that the origins of Indian nationalism must be located in the nationalist leaders' personal experiences of colonial humiliation, during which they were treated as second-class citizens both in India and England. Furthermore, Dalit writers like Prasad insist that Indian nationalism cannot be explained merely as an outcome of economic inequity; rather, they argue that colonial conditions of social and cultural exclusion motivated middle-class Indians to launch a nationalist struggle. Prasad illustrates the question of humiliation by discussing at length Mahatma Gandhi's experience on a train in South Africa in 1893, which was a formative incident in his politics. Gandhi was evicted from the first-class compartment, despite his English attire, his education in England, his status as a lawyer, and his legal right to be in the compartment because he had bought a first-class ticket. Prasad further argues that the Dalit struggle is against caste Hindu discriminatory practices that have humiliated Dalits for centuries. Using experiences of racism and exclusion as the main lenses for understanding the emergence of Indian nationalism, Prasad draws parallels between Indian elite experiences of humiliation at the hands of the British and Dalit experiences of humiliation at the hands of caste Hindus. As Prasad shows, experiences of humiliation similarly form a crucial explanatory role in fights for dignity in Dalit narratives.

In descriptions of struggles for dignity and against caste inequality, the term "Dalit" is today widely used to describe India's former untouchables. Beginning with the Dalit Panthers' movement in the 1970s, the term acquired a radical new meaning of self-identification and signified a new oppositional consciousness.[1] The Congress Party and several other organizations, following Gandhi, adopted the term "Harijan" (children of god), a term that continues to be used by members of these groups even today. But from the 1970s onward the term "Dalit" has been widely used in academic writings following its adoption by Dalit activists and writers—especially in the vernacular literary sphere.

Dalit vernacular narratives in the twentieth century have conceptualized the category of humiliation not merely as personal but also as informing social and political processes like nationalism and Dalit struggles for personal and political dignity. Drawing from their own individual and collective struggles and activist backgrounds, Prasad and other Dalit authors writing in Indian languages offer an analysis of human dignity, and they echo Charles Taylor by insisting that they are engaged not only in a political project but also in a historiographical one.[2] Gopal Guru offers us a theoretical engagement with the contentious histories of humiliation and dignity present in both Western and Indian contexts. As he argues, in colonial India the caste Hindu "traditional elite develop an insight into humiliation not because they have an innate moral capacity" but because the "colonial configuration of power,

produced by western modernity, necessarily disrupts their feudal compla-
cency and awakens them to their own subordination within this framework
of power."[3] He has emphasized the privileged location of the colonial Indian
elite in defining the intellectual and cultural agendas of anti-colonial struggles.
It has maintained dominant position after independence within social, political, and academic contexts. The categories of humiliation and dignity, salient
in Dalit vernacular writings, have entered South Asian academic discourse
because Dalit intellectuals, consciously retaining an activist sensibility, have
entered academia in a significant fashion since the 1990s. Once almost completely absent from the academy, Dalit academics are now beginning to bring
vernacular histories of these two categories to bear on debates in the study
of India.

This volume represents the beginning of a qualitative transformation of Indian academia, both in terms of debates and in its recognition of the entry of
new social groups into academia after the 1990s. A number of developments
after the 1990s (discussed below) contributed to the emergence of Dalit studies as a significant intervention to reassess the study of Indian society and
history. Dalit academics and activist-intellectuals outside of formal institutions contributed a significant number of essays to this volume, with eleven
of the original nineteen papers at the conference presented by Dalit scholars.[4]
It would be more accurate to describe these scholars as belonging to nonelite social and educational backgrounds. The conference acknowledged the
emergence of a new generation of scholars—both Dalit and non-Dalit—who
do not belong to the traditional elite of India. They do not belong to the elite
landed and bureaucratic Indian families. They did not study at elite colleges
in India such as the St. Stephen's, the Lady Shri Ram, or the Presidency, and
they do not have PhDs from English institutions such as Oxford and Cambridge, which is characteristic of Indian academia. Another crucial feature of
this group is that for the majority of them English is not their first language;
they learned it in college. The entry of social groups who have often been
the subject matter of academic scholarship rather than actors in the production of that knowledge is perhaps the most significant recent development in
India. In that sense, this volume's contribution goes well beyond simply paying attention to the study of Dalit society and history and enables a significant reconsideration of many of the core assumptions in Indian academia.
All of this is also an indication of the rapid changes taking place in India in
recent decades, visible especially after 1989–90.

The project of this volume must be located in the context of post-1990
political and intellectual developments. According to Partha Chatterjee,

this period marks the rise of autonomous Dalit politics and regional political formations in India that have decisively replaced the Congress Party, which dominated Indian politics until the 1990s, "as the central active force."[5] Five broad trends have made the rise of Dalit studies possible: (a) the political and intellectual controversy in the 1990s over implementation of the recommendations of the 1980 Mandal commission report (named after B. P. Mandal, chairman of the Second Backward Classes Commission, 1979–80) that expanded the constitutionally mandated reservations in public education and employment for "lower-caste" Hindu groups;[6] (b) the rise of new Dalit activism in southern India; (c) political and electoral interventions by new Dalit political parties such as the Bahujan Samaj Party (BSP); (d) the rise of Dalit feminism in India; and (e) global discussions of caste, race, and social exclusions, such as those at the 2001 Durban conference (the World Conference Against Racism, Racial Discrimination, Xenophobia and Racial Intolerance) in South Africa. Rajni Kothari suggests that the new Dalit movement in the 1990s has forced a "detailed consideration of the theoretical and political issues involved in the whole debate on caste and its role in social transformation."[7] It has challenged structural injustices and hierarchical practices by demanding "education, employment and special rights."[8]

First, questions of dignity and the stereotypes associated with Dalit communities culminated in critical discussions in the 1990s. In August 1990 the Indian government decided to accept the recommendations in the Mandal commission's report, expanding statutory reservation (or affirmative action) policies from Dalits to other backward classes (or "lower-castes"). Considered a feature of rural India, caste became extremely visible in urban India during student protests in Delhi, Mumbai, Kolkatta, Hyderabad, and Bengaluru. The caste Hindu students in urban centers protested the extension of affirmative action from scheduled castes and tribes to other historically disadvantaged "lower-caste" groups. Several commentators at the time, such as K. Balagopal and Gail Omvedt, noted that the vast majority of the Indian intelligentsia opposed implementation of the recommendations in the Mandal commission report, arguing that such policies would tear the national fabric apart.[9] Perhaps the most productive contribution of the debate was to bring into focus the dominance of Indian academia by caste Hindu intellectuals from relatively homogeneous economic, cultural, and educational backgrounds. Most important, caste became a recognized legitimate political category and a modern and living one, as opposed to its prior representations as primordial, backward, and reactionary. Yet at the same time, the continued visible exclusion of Dalits from formal academic institutions, the media, and the private sector has further validated the primacy of caste in institutional exclusions. The controversy over the Mandal commission report also deeply affected the Dalit intelligentsia, especially the younger generation, many of whom had previously identified primarily with Marxist ideas. For example, in the 1990s, Dalit groups questioned the dominance of Brahmins and caste Hindus in leadership positions in Marxist and Naxalite organizations. The past decade has seen the emergence of Dalit student organizations in universities and Ambedkar Youth Forums throughout India and the expansion of Dalit political organizations into new regions of the country.[10] The conception of caste as a form of inequality and discrimination emerged on the center stage of the Indian political scene for the first time in independent India, creating intense discussions in the public domain.

Second, in the 1990s, South India witnessed the rise of the new Dalit activism. The phenomenon of mass killings of Dalits in southern India and the failure of both parliamentary parties and Marxist organizations to satisfactorily address this challenge led to new discussions of caste-based violence in India. In the southern state of Andhra Pradesh, a large number of Dalit activists discarded Marxist-Leninist (Maoist or Naxalite) ideological frameworks and embraced a Dalit identity as a more effective way of engaging with mainstream political discourse.[11] The declining ideological appeal and legitimacy of socialism and communism in India, especially among Dalit activists, has also played a major role in catalyzing identity-based Dalit struggles in Kerala. Class-based activism is no longer the dominant and legitimate mode of activism in India today, as it was prior to the 1990s. This ideological realignment also led to the resurrection since the 1990s of Indian leader and jurist B. R. Ambekar, born in a Dalit family, as an important social philosopher and icon.[12] In Tamil Nadu, Dalit organizations and activists have questioned the legacy of Periyar (E. V. Ramasamy) and the Dravidian movement.[13] Autonomous Dalit organizations such as the Dalit Sangarsh Samiti in Karnataka, Dalit Panthers of India in Tamil Nadu, and Dalit Mahasabha in Andhra Pradesh and many other caste-specific Dalit forums such as the Madiga Reservation Porata Samiti in Andhra Pradesh and Adi Tamilzhar Peravai in Tamil Nadu were all established in the 1990s. The consolidation of Dalit identities and their increased presence in the public domain is a hallmark of the 1990s.[14]

Third, one of the significant contemporary developments in Indian politics is the remarkable electoral success of the BSP in northern India. The BSP was founded in the Punjab in 1984 as an all-India party, but its electoral success has been most striking in the northern Indian state of Uttar Pradesh after 1990. The controversy over the implementation of the Mandal commission report's recommendations in 1990 played an important role in the BSP's success by realigning the political and electoral map in India. The BSP entered into a pre-election alliance with the Samajwadi Party, representing "lower-caste" interests (particularly those of the Yadavs), and the coalition stunned political pundits by winning the 1993 state assembly elections. Since then, the BSP's increasing political and social strength has continued to surprise the mainstream establishment.[15] By building a formidable alliance of Dalits, poor backward communities, Muslims, and Brahmins, the BSP won a majority in the 2006 elections in Uttar Pradesh. This electoral and political success in the last two decades in northern India has inspired and motivated a cross-section of Dalit groups in different parts of India, reflected in the BSP's presence in almost all of the southern states, including Dalit parties such as the Dalit Panthers of India and the Pudiya Tamilazham.

Fourth, the post-1990s context, defined by the mobilization of groups that supported and those that opposed the Mandal commission's report and the rise of Dalit movements, also marked the emergence of Dalit women's forums as a distinct political formation that enabled a new inquiry into the foundational paradigm of liberal and Marxist Indian feminist ideologies. The implementation of the Mandal commission report's recommendations in 1990 motivated sections of caste Hindu women to participate in anti-Mandal political forums. The centrality of caste in women's lives was illustrated by the caste Hindu women who took to the streets to protest the implementation of the Mandal commission's recommendations and who displayed placards expressing their anxiety about finding a good caste Hindu husband in light of the new reservation policies. Such a public display of caste arrogance and upper-caste identity by sections of Hindu women also revealed the social divide between Dalit and upper-caste women.[16] Institutionally, the formation of the National Federation of Dalit Women in 1995 signaled a new political intervention within the women's movement in India.[17] Describing mainstream Indian feminism as Brahmanical for its failure to recognize caste as a crucial element of social and political life, informing norms that shape even the most intimate and sexual domains, Dalit women's organizations challenged upper-caste Indian feminists' right to speak on behalf of all women. Dalit feminist organizations have emphasized three distinct modes of subjugation. These are patriarchy (male domination of females in the family and society, and the exclusion of Dalit women from Dalit male–dominated political and cultural organizations), caste inequities (exclusion of Dalits by caste Hindu men and women), and sexual violence (especially used by caste Hindu men to enforce their domination over Dalits, but also used at times by Dalit men in the family context). Gopal Guru's 1995 essay, "Dalit Women Talk Differently," emphasized the crucial role of caste identity in instituting forms of domination, exclusion, and violence. Citing testimonies of Dalit women activists at a 1995 conference, Guru argued that caste identity plays a significant role in the humiliation and violation of Dalit women's bodies and takes on a severe and intense form that cannot be explained by existing frameworks of patriarchy, class, and psychological factors. By foregrounding the centrality of caste inequities against Dalit women and articulating the complex connections between caste and patriarchy and between caste and class, the emergence of a Dalit feminist movement after the 1990s has posed new questions for interrogating a feminist history of India. The 2003 *Gender and Caste* reader edited by Anupama Rao contains many articles published after the 1990s that reflect this shift.[18]

Fifth, with Indian economic liberalization in the 1990s, new institutional and formal public spaces have become available as sites of debate. The new political economy has created new opportunities for Dalit writers and activists. The rise of the Internet, an explosion in vernacular media, and the growing availability of resources outside the state framework have all helped Dalits gain public attention through literary productions, print media, and social media mobilization.[19] Global communication, transportation networks, and access to international forums have enabled new dialogues and alliances. For example, a large contingent of Dalit activists and scholars participated in the "World Conference against Racism, Racial Discrimination, Xenophobia and Related Intolerance" held in Durban, South Africa, in September 2001. Dalit participants demanded that caste be included as a form of racial discrimination in the conference agenda. This reconceptualization of caste discrimination allowed Dalit activists to declare the rights of their community to be legitimate human rights.[20] The reinvigoration of the study of India in the United States over the past two decades and the increasing exchange of scholars between the two countries gave additional impetus to the emergence of Dalit studies. The African American civil rights movement and the presence of black studies departments in the United States have provided a forum for comparative analysis and exchange. This global circulation of Dalit issues, the rise of a Dalit diaspora, and an engagement with questions of diversity and race have all helped enrich and expand the debate on caste. In this context, the University Grants Commission, a federal institution of higher education in India, established centers for the study of "Social Exclusion and Inclusion Policy" in several Indian universities to examine caste-based and other forms of exclusion.[21]

The increasing visibility of Dalits in contemporary India and abroad has been accompanied by the rise of the Dalit intelligentsia. In the 1990s, Dalit activists and intellectuals began to enter Indian academe, marking the arrival of a new social group in the mainstream Indian public sphere.[22] For the first time questions were raised about the domination of Indian academia by intellectuals belonging to the caste Hindu groups. There is no doubt that the protests and counterprotests in 1990 over the implementation of the recommendations of the Mandal commission, along with the rise of Dalit movements all over India, brought the question of caste discrimination into the center of academic and political debates.[23] This is a historic development that has largely gone unnoticed, even as it has made possible a reconsideration of Indian history and politics.

Interrogating the Prevailing Paradigms

There has been a general absence of research into and engagement with the perspectives of twentieth-century Dalit intellectuals like Swami Achhutanand, Bhagya Reddy Varma, Kusuma Dharmanna, and Iyothee Thass, and their critiques of untouchability and caste inequality are not widely known. Until the 1990s, even Ambedkar's critique of Indian society and the Gandhian national movement remained on the margins.[24] In Indian historiography, Dalit struggles against untouchability and upper-caste domination were frequently regarded as sectarian and pro-British, and therefore as antinational. The prominent Marxist historian of India, Sumit Sarkar, suggests in a self-critical essay in 2002 that "it has proved difficult to accommodate within this framework [colonialism versus nationalism] sympathetic evaluations of many movements for women's rights and "lower caste" protests, for these often utilized aspects of colonial policies and Western ideologies as resources."[25] In the context of his work on Tamil Dalits in 1998, G. Aloysius points out that "social crises in subaltern life had begun to throw up organized activities as early as the middle of the 19th century," though such actors "still await the historiographers and social scientists to unearth and install them in their legitimate niches of history."[26] A notable shift since the 1990s has been the recognition of Dalits as actors in India's history. New attention has been devoted to the contributions of Dalits to the shaping of modern India, both in terms of their political struggle and in the recognition of their key leaders. This is in marked contrast to the absence of attention to Dalit struggles and intellectual agendas in English-language publications and mainstream academic writings in the long twentieth century.

In this section we discuss dominant frameworks in Indian academic scholarship on Dalits. These include (a) the Gandhian Harijan ideology; (b) the primacy of the colonialist historiographical framework over the nationalist one to study modern India; (c) the nationalist idea of Indian civilization; and (d) the Nehruvian model of modern developmentalism. Each of these prevailing notions excluded Dalits and their perspectives from academic debates. The latter half of this section traces the noticeable shift in the tone and content of academic writings on Dalits from the 1960s to the 1990s. The perceptible transition is from a general study of Dalit society and movements to the positioning Dalits as actors with a distinct ideological agenda, recovering their active role in shaping debates in India.

The hegemony of the Harijan perspective is one explanation that helps account for the absence of systematic engagement with Dalits as political and historical actors. It represents Dalits through the powerful stereotype of the *bhangi* (scavenger) figure and stigmatized victim in need of reform from above.[27] Removing other more prominent forms of Dalit lives from discussion, the scavenger figure became the dominant trope through which questions related to Dalits were discussed and debated in the nationalist discourse. Gandhi played a prominent role in creating this discourse when he idealized the scavenger figure and sought to ennoble the occupation of scavenging. Gandhian discussions of reforming Hindu society relied heavily on the reform of untouchables' impure occupation of scavenging. "An ideal Bhangi," Gandhi claimed, would be an expert who "would know the quality of night soil and urine" because of his scientific education.[28] In the Gandhian agenda the reform of untouchables became intricately linked to the reform and modernization of the profession of scavenging. Gandhi maintained that the *varna* model of social division consisting of four orders (Brahmin, Kshatriya, Vaishya, and Shudra) is an ideal system because the "callings of a Brahmin—spiritual teacher—and a scavenger are equal, and their due performance carries equal merit before God."[29] Harijan perspective denies any notion of liberty and freedom to the scavenging community. Following Gandhi, the manual scavenger was romanticized in early Indian classics such as Mulk Raj Anand's 1935 novel, *Untouchable*, and Sivasankara Pillai's 1947 novel, *Tottiyute Makan* (Scavenger's son), both of which reinforced the stereotype of the scavenger figure and stigmatized victim as the normative figure of the Dalit.[30]

Gandhism, or the Harijan perspective, became the normative framework for representing Dalits in modern India. Ambedkar argued in his 1945 book, *What Congress and Gandhi Have Done to the Untouchables*, that Gandhi organized campaigns in the 1930s against untouchability to reform the practice by elevating the traditional occupations of Dalit communities. Gandhian campaigns also perpetuated the notion that untouchables were victims and objects of reform. Ambedkar argued in his critique of Gandhism that it will render Dalits the eternal scavengers of modern India.[31] Such a perspective did not promote Dalits as active political actors. Indeed, during his lifetime Gandhi refused to engage with Dalit political movements. Ambedkar's predictions have been borne out by Indian historiography, which continued to be informed by the Harijan perspective even fifty years after independence. In an insightful essay in 1993, Guru argued that existing studies of caste and untouchability in modern India have only further reinforced the Harijan perspective.[32] According to Guru, caste studies have emphasized the role of Gandhi-led campaigns against untouchability in which untouchables were represented as victims, scavengers, and objects of reform. The caste studies informed by the Harijan perspective have focused on the elite-led initiatives in instituting social and political reform practices among the Dalits. The prominent Indian sociologist M. N. Srinivas's Sanskritization model, which assumes that Dalit groups and individuals imitate religious and cultural practices of caste Hindus, formed an important conceptual tool for studying Dalit struggles as initiatives for social mobility in modern India.[33] The model of Sanskritization or emulation denies agency and autonomous consciousness to Dalits and also prevents us from recognizing their role in initiating social struggles against caste hierarchy.

Another reason for the absence of Dalit actors and their agendas in Indian academic knowledge production is the dominant conceptual framework defined by the binary of colonialism versus nationalism.[34] Indian historiography views colonialism as marking a decisive break in Indian history by constituting a single and unified discourse of power. Colonialism, in the dominant Marxist and nationalist understanding, was conceptualized as the single most important cause of India's social and economic backwardness, and the colonial state was the instrument of exploitation and subjugation. This view discouraged the study of Dalit social and religious reform movements that invoked the promise and possibilities of colonial modernity. Anti-untouchability agitations, temple entry movements, and struggles for access to public spaces and representation in colonial institutions were neither concerned with anticolonial agendas nor nationalist in motivation.

Rather, these struggles emphasized caste discrimination in the social and cultural arenas and lack of representation in the political sphere.[35] Dalit groups used the colonial state and its institutional framework to articulate their rights, and therefore a total rejection of the colonial state was never on their agenda. Dalit histories remain untold in modern Indian history because autonomous Dalit organizations and groups could not easily be assimilated into the anticolonial nationalist narrative. Instead, Dalit histories, as Neeladri Bhattacharya has argued, were appropriated into the nationalist narratives for their opposition to colonialism, in much the same way as that of peasant and working classes.[36]

Sociologists like G. S. Ghurye and M. N. Srinivas were inspired by nationalist notions of India as a civilization that has been sustained by its inherent cultural unity since ancient times.[37] The idea of Indian civilization was conceptualized essentially in the caste Hindu framework by nationalist leaders such as Gandhi, Rabindranath Tagore, and Jawaharlal Nehru.[38] A generation of scholars demonstrated the unity of the nation in terms of its religion, culture, and social institutions primarily by focusing on the caste system.[39] That system was conceptualized as a social structure that encouraged consensus by emphasizing the principles of reciprocity and interdependence among various caste groups. Particularly instructive here is Srinivas's model of Sanskritization, which valorized consensus over conflicts and, as noted above, interpreted Dalit protests as mere aspirational imitations of caste Hindu practices.[40] They did not pay attention to anti-untouchability protests that were also anti-Hindu. This focus on the caste system and its antiquity acquired canonical status in the work of Louis Dumont, who located the system in Hindu religious values and ritual status linked to purity and pollution.[41] This view, derived from Indological and anthropological studies (discussed below), largely obliterated Dalit life and social protest from sociological studies. Dalits and other subordinated caste groups challenged the Sanskritization model in the 1990s. The pro-reservation agitations and autonomous Dalit movements in the social and electoral domains posited new identities (Dalit, Dalit-Bahujan, Madiga, and so on) for subordinated caste groups.[42]

The dominant representation of Dalit society prior to the 1990s stemmed from colonial sociology. Its objective was to understand untouchability and discrimination against Dalit communities in terms of their "impure" religious and social customs. Representing Dalits as objects of study, these sociological works nevertheless opened up discussions of the practice of untouchability in India. Colonial volumes on castes and tribes published between the 1890s and 1930s offered the first extensive descriptions of Dalit societies in modern

India. These volumes—for example, on Malas, Madigas, Paraiyars, Mahars, Namasudras, Chamars, and Pasis—contained extensive details about specific Dalit communities.[43] Such descriptions also associated each of these castes with an occupation that was considered impure by Brahmin textual sources like *Manusmriti* and dominant-caste Hindu groups in each locality. These volumes paid attention to the religious and social ideas and practices of Dalit groups to understand their relationship with Hindu society. Anthropological studies from the 1960s on used extensive ethnographic field work to address the question of Dalits' social and cultural practices in relationship to Hindu society. Studies of Chamars and Doms of northern India and of Paraiyans and Pallans in southern India examined social customs, economic structures, and political practices to distinguish those groups from caste Hindus. Another set of studies focused on what was perceived of as the re-creation of hierarchical practices in Dalit neighborhoods.[44] Until the 1990s the dominant focus was on identifying the impure practices of Dalit communities that set them apart from Hindu society.

Given the Dalits' stigmatized status, another leading trend from the 1960s onward has been to view Dalit protest as "a necessary and inevitable response to, and outcome of, an obscurantist Hindu tradition."[45] This tendency promoted a new theoretical framework, including the concepts of social mobility and relative deprivation, which were used extensively by sociologists and anthropologists. These concepts constrained the scholars to imagine a future based on autonomous life and values. Attaining the status of the caste Hindus was posited as the goal of Dalits and other subordinated castes. In other words, the normative reference group used to assess mobility and deprivation in these studies remained the dominant-caste Hindus. The 1972 collection of essays titled *The Untouchables in Contemporary India* examined two broad themes.[46] The first concerned strategies adopted by Dalits to overcome deprivation and the second outlined restrictions created by upper-caste groups, who were also regarded as the reference point for normative behavior. Bernard Cohn's essays on the Chamars of northern India tracked avenues of social mobility created by electoral politics and new work opportunities outside of the village.[47] Departing from the framework of social mobility, a new body of work from the 1970s on focused on Dalit protests. The unique feature of this body of literature on Dalits was to identify Dalit movements and focus on the ways that their localized initiatives challenged dominant groups. These issues were elaborated in the context of western India by Eleanor Zelliot's work on Ambedkar, Dalit activism, and Dalit saints and by Rosalind O'Hanlon's history of Jotirao Phule's movement and his intellectual world in the 1860s–1900s.[48] In northern India, Owen Lynch's study of Dalit (Chamar) activism in the city of Agra, R. S. Khare's significant discussion of Swami Achhutanand as an Indic ascetic who crafted an alternative history of Dalits, and Mark Jurgensmeyer's discussion of Mangoo Ram's ideological agenda of Adi-Dharma in Punjab drew attention to Dalit actors who challenged caste Hindu practices of domination and exclusion.[49] According to Guru, these writings from the 1970s onward demonstrated for the first time the role of caste inequalities in shaping the cultural and political protests of Dalits in modern India.[50]

It is through the state-led developmentism that the Nehruvian idea of an Indian nation was postulated as an inclusive space of casteless and secular citizens. The Nehruvian era produced a pan-Indian elite "exclusively of upper caste [Hindus] and middle class . . . from a very select cultural background and a specific set of regions." This national elite "spoke in the modernist idiom of secular nationalism, scientific technology, and economic development; by adopting this idiom, the elite was able to render invisible its own ascriptive markers."[51] It is the ideological project of national modernity that suppressed and made invisible "ascriptive markers" such as caste in the public sphere. Studies of Indian society in the 1960s and 1970s, in the context of post-independence liberal democracy, reinforced the dominant political agenda by demonstrating that the nationalist modernity has transformed the "traditional institution of caste" into a secular "para community."[52] Lloyd Rudolph and Susanne Rudolph argued that caste-based mobilization in the context of liberal democracy and elections led to secularization and democratization of the caste order.[53] The thesis of modernization of caste still shares the assumption that "caste is a traditional system, its central principle is ritual hierarchy and its known structure is vertical."[54] Based on the empirical sociological criteria (vertical or horizontal groups, mobility, modernization of tradition, and so forth), it was argued that caste identities have declined and transformed in modern India. Invoking modern developmentalism and the constitutional abolition of caste-based discrimination, some social scientists and commentators—such as Srinivas, A. M. Shah, B. S. Baviskar, Andre Beteille, and Veena Das—maintained that caste is an anachronism in modern India and caste-based quotas are a legacy of colonial policies of divide and rule. They actively opposed the extension of caste-based reservation through the implementation of the recommendations of the Mandal commission in 1990.[55]

The subaltern studies project didn't develop a systematic engagement with questions of caste inequality, even though caste continues to be the primary form through which hierarchical discrimination is practiced even today. However, both Ranajit Guha and Partha Chatterjee have pointed to the significant role of caste consciousness and hierarchical practices in constituting subaltern radicalism and political struggles, describing them as modern rather than traditional. Chatterjee has argued that caste and subaltern consciousness were specifically concerned with questions of bodily and ritual purity and sought to challenge the dominant social groups' use of dharma to claim authority.[56] Questions of caste discrimination were (and are) a crucial part of everyday life in modern India, but they remained on the margins because of the way the category of the subaltern subject was formulated. The unqualified use of the term "subaltern" to mean peasant has tended to ignore the world of Dalit peasants and laborers within agrarian society and their exploitation and subjugation by the landlords and the subaltern peasants. In the subaltern studies project, the subaltern was an unmarked subject, and caste inequity was not the core feature of its cultural and political formation. The subaltern peasant in most cases belonged to "lower-caste" groups (but not to the untouchable castes), who were culturally committed to forms of Hinduism and values of caste inequality. The subaltern was rarely either a Dalit peasant who was involved in struggles with other caste groups over land and segregation or a laborer in the cities dealing with exclusionary practices of workforce consisting primarily of people from "lower-caste" backgrounds. Indeed the question of caste or *jati* (regionally defined social group) in the formulation of subaltern consciousness did not receive much critical attention in any of the volumes of the subaltern studies project. There are a number of essays in the series that failed to recognize Dalit subalterns as actors in rural peasant mobilizations (volume 1) or criticized Dalit struggles for their failure to recognize the class character of their politics while refusing to engage with their political agendas (volume 10).[57] It is hard to theorize the subaltern subject, in its protest against the colonial state or against the local elites, or in postcolonial democratic struggles, as untainted by caste markings.[58] Consisting of a new generation of scholars, the authors of the penultimate volume of the subaltern studies project (published in 2005) sought to address the question of caste inequality.[59] The volume represented an attempt to engage with the recent political transformation in India after the 1990s, when debate and research on caste inequality took over the public sphere.

Since the 1990s a number of authors have shed light on numerous Dalit initiatives about which little was previously known. From the literary accounts of the Namasudras in Bengal between the 1880s and the 1930s to the new religious practices created by Satnamis in central India, there is substantial evidence of a long history of Dalit efforts to envision new social and po-litical structures free from caste Hindu domination.[60] Aloysius's 1998 study draws our attention to Iyothee Thass and his organizational efforts between 1890 and 1914 in claiming that Buddhism is the original religion of Tamil Dalits.[61] Thass's work on the 1900s has enabled the recognition of the emer-gence of an autonomous Dalit movement that used the language of south-ern Indian indigeneity well before the mature Dravidian movement of the 1930s.[62] Anupama Rao's 2009 book discusses the strategies of emancipation advocated by "caste subalterns" in questioning caste inequality as "forms of civic and political exclusion" and their efforts to rewrite history, rename identity, and challenge Brahmanical knowledge production.[63] Rao further argues that the liberal state's policies of affirmative action also created new sites of violence against the Dalits. More recently, Ramnarayan Rawat's 2011 study recovers the role of Dalit actors in intervening in and reshaping politi-cal practice in northern India from 1922 onward, providing new models not just for Dalits but for all political actors.[64]

The rise of Dalit feminism has interrogated existing stereotypical as-sumptions of Indian feminist historiography, especially its representation of Dalit women as liberated.[65] Urmila Pawar and Gopal Guru have urged an investigation into Dalit patriarchy and representations of Dalit women in mainstream historiography as liberated subjects.[66] Dalit women, Pawar has argued, have had to deal with "caste based atrocities . . . the threat of rape, [and] in the family . . . tolerate physical violence and other atrocities of men."[67] Guru's influential essay has emphasized the social location and experience of the woman intellectual-activist in articulating a distinctly Dalit feminist standpoint that is markedly different from the experience of caste Hindu women. Sharmila Rege has expanded on this point by arguing that the feminist movement in India did not analyze the formative influence of Brahmanism in shaping the cultural and political practices of caste Hindus, both men and women.[68] The visibility of Dalit women in work and social roles and their increased political activism after 1990 has elicited violent re-prisals against them.[69]

One of the more systematic efforts to rethink colonial modernity and offer a conceptual framework for the study of colonial and postcolonial India has been provided by Guru. He asks a historiographical question that is ex-tremely important for the study of India when he writes, "what are those nor-mative grounds on which the struggle for rejection of rejection is carried out by the subaltern masses?"[70] He goes on to suggest that the normative grounds are created by the politics of recognition, emancipation, and education of the subject. At the same time we must recognize that these modern principles, along with modern institutions, bureaucracy, industrialization, and the public sphere, have also created new conditions for the perpetuation of humiliation. Modernity, argues Guru, creates new shared moral and ethical commitments to egalitarian values among dominant and subordinate groups, yet it also creates new practices that contribute to the latter's exclusion. D. R. Nagaraj has emphasized the long history in Dalit neighborhoods of Dalit cultural memory of saints and yogis who have challenged caste hierarchy. The efforts of indigenous rebels and radicals to fight caste discrimination "has been one of the spiritual requirements of their tradition."[71] It is important to note the continued popularity of an alternative tradition built by the followers of saints like Ravi Das in northern India, Chokhemala in western India, and Basavanna and Nandanar in southern India in shaping struggles for dignity. At the same time, Dalit intellectuals and activists are wary of Nagaraj's suggestion of a civilizational connection between Dalit and caste Hindu societies and his criticism of Dalit social and literary movements' faith in the project of modernity. Instead, what we are emphasizing is that the Dalit groups were particularly attentive in appropriating cultural practices and using them to engage with the modern liberal context to transform their self-identities to fight caste inequality. Departing from the subaltern studies project, this volume seeks to emphasize struggles related to dignity that successfully engage with colonial liberalism to interrogate religiously sanctioned caste discrimination that has shaped the politics of nationalism and continues to inform democratic practices today.

By writing histories of struggles for human dignity and recovering histories of struggles against caste discrimination, this volume seeks to outline a new historiographical agenda for the study of India. Dominant scholarly frameworks have elaborated aspects of exclusion and deprivation faced by caste subalterns through the paradigms of social mobility and Sanskritization. However, because of the overwhelming concern with movements against colonialism and a commitment to the cultural unity of Indic civilization, until recently Indian historiography has paid little attention to Dalit thought and activism. The pedagogical projects of nationalist elites identified Dalits' activities, including their social and political struggles, as occupying the domain of tradition, as primordial and backward, or as a product of the colonial state's patronage politics. Yet Dalits found colonial modernity, including colonial liberal thought, useful in addressing concrete questions of representation for minorities, which offered new opportunities for engaging with caste Hindus. Most Dalit organizations engaged with the colonial state over issues concerning affirmative action to secure representation in legislative assemblies and schools and colleges. The longer history of Dalit struggles related to questions of self-esteem and self-worth deserves serious academic attention today.

Notes for New Scholarship on India

One of the most important objectives of this volume is to offer a new perspective for the study of India. Some of the key interventions the authors in this volume offer include (a) foregrounding issues of human dignity as central to the study of Indian history, (b) examining discursive practices that have allowed caste discrimination to persist, and (c) moving beyond the conceptual obsession with the framework of colonialism versus nationalism. The long quote with which this introduction opened offered Mata Prasad's interpretation of India's freedom struggle. He examined it not through the dyad of colonialism versus nationalism that has dominated Indian historiography but through a framework of human dignity. Prasad insists that the Indian elites' experience of the loss of dignity was central to their struggle against colonial domination. Humiliation and dignity are the prominent themes that permeate the Dalit vernacular literary and political sphere in provinces throughout India.

This volume is conceived of as an academic intervention that can connect activists and writers with scholars to investigate the untold narratives of Dalits as active participants in the project of imagining new visions of modern India. It aims to move beyond the nationalist historiographical framework of colonialism versus nationalism and recover struggles related to dignity. In the process, we reexamine prevailing conceptions of colonial rule and colonial knowledge. In the nationalist narrative, colonial rule is seen only as exploitative, repressive, and therefore anti-Indian.[72] This view of colonialism as a homogeneous and singular structure of oppression does not adequately explain the complex transformations of the colonial period or the diverse responses of different social groups within society. Yet this uniform view of colonialism has helped a caste Hindu nationalist elite appropriate both history and power in modern India. In contrast, we demonstrate that protocols of colonial public space and its normative categories enabled Dalits and other subordinated caste groups to use modern juridical practices.[73] Prominent Dalit leaders and intellectuals in the twentieth century like Ambedkar, Swami Achhutanand, Mangoo Ram, Bhagya Reddy Varma, Jagjivan Ram, and Iyothee Thass viewed the colonial state as offering new legal structures, which guaranteed Dalits new access to public space and provided employment in new professions. A small section of the Dalit community benefited from colonial education, employment, and political representation. This group of educated rural and urban Dalits fashioned counter-ideologies to challenge organizations such as the Congress Party and caste Hindu organizations. They swiftly embraced new opportunities, establishing local organizations, setting up printing presses, launching newspapers, and opening schools and hostels to mobilize their community and take advantage of opportunities for engaging in the new public space. Chapters 2, 3, 4, and 5 in this volume demonstrate that Dalit groups deployed the language of rights, social equality, and affirmative action to challenge caste Hindu organizations' refusal to discuss issues relating to caste inequalities.

Research over the past three decades has revised the nationalist and Marxist representations of the colonial state as a purely secular and external entity. Such research has drawn attention to the colonial state's role in consolidating Hindu society and nationalizing Hinduism as a unified Indian tradition.[74] Caste Hindu dominance—particularly by Brahmans—in the colonial bureaucracy, education, and middle-class professions has been well demonstrated. Practices that helped produce colonial knowledge like the census and caste and tribe surveys in the nineteenth century classified and organized Indian society on the four-fold varna model of social division, based on Brahmanical texts like the *Manusmriti* (one of the most cited texts in colonial sources), with Brahmans at the top and untouchables at the bottom of the census table. The varna ideal in the Brahmanical texts excluded untouchables from the social order by describing them as *avarna*—literally, "out of caste" or outside of society. Furthermore, the colonial state enumerated and identified impure occupations as a unique feature of Dalit communities. By equating Dalit groups with traditional impure occupations, the colonial state ignored its own evidence of Dalit groups' other occupations in the nineteenth century, including work as agricultural peasants, stonemasons, and weavers. Stereotypes of Dalit occupations also shaped the colonial state's land tenure policies, which favored caste Hindus and "lower-caste" groups but worked to the disadvantage of Dalits. In many provinces, colonial tenancy laws barred Dalits from buying and selling agricultural land because of occupational stereotypes that defined them as nonagriculturalists and limited the buying and selling of land to those groups explicitly defined as agriculturalists. Colonial policies reinforced caste Hindu notions of Indian society, which also ensured caste Hindus' domination of the modern institutional apparatus.

Religious and social values associated with untouchability have continued to shape the evolution of modern India and contributed to new exclusionary practices. Historical and anthropological studies have documented caste Hindu attitudes that consider agricultural work, urban and rural sanitation work, and forms of industrial work like the leather industry as unfit occupations.[75] These attitudes also affect the occupations available to women in Indian society. For example, "lower-caste" and Dalit women worked in the fields and elsewhere as laborers, whereas caste Hindu women were frequently prevented from working in the fields.[76] Recognizing the formative role of caste Hindu attitudes to work and space, recent debates on the ideological inheritances of the Indian working classes have highlighted the role of religion and caste in shaping their politics.[77] In rural India, spatial configurations have played a significant role in the perpetuation of inequality. Dalit groups typically live in separate villages that are normally situated at some distance away from the main caste Hindu village. Dalits' autobiographies have underlined spatial exclusion as a prominent method through which discrimination is practiced in rural India.[78] Hindu temples occupy a canonical place as a particularly compelling symbol through which exclusionary regimes have been perpetuated and also challenged. Not surprisingly, one of the earliest forms of Dalit protest in the early twentieth century was about the exclusion of Dalits from temples. Modernity has reinforced caste Hindu society's commitment to exclusionary regimes that rely on religion and the social values of Hinduism.

The continued practice of untouchability in explicit forms and the ways in which these sustain ongoing strategies of exclusion illustrate the urgency of this volume and bring home the importance of investigating everyday struggles related to questions of dignity, which have been central to Dalits and other marginalized groups. In pursing this agenda we must bear in mind that in both public and private domains vast numbers of caste Hindus have continued to embrace practices of caste inequity in modern India. Rege has argued that the production of social sciences knowledge in India was shaped by nationalist agendas in ways that normalized elite caste Hindu perspectives on Indian society as academic knowledge. Rege has convincingly demonstrated that the social sciences knowledge produced in India has also systematically obscured and erased Dalit actors and agendas.[79] This volume provides a new framework for rethinking the agendas of Indian social sciences and humanities from a Dalit perspective. This has several implications. First, the field of Dalit studies seeks the inclusion of the study of Dalits in the

Indian context and in the global diasporic context within broader trends of knowledge production and pedagogy. Second, it offers a framework to compare Dalits with related social groups in other national contexts, including African American struggles, with which Dalits have forged long-standing connections; the Burakumin protests in Japan; and the anti-apartheid protests in South Africa. Third, with the upsurge of Dalit political and cultural movements in the 1990s and the renewed national and international debate on caste, efforts like this project have emerged as sites of new scholarship being produced by both Dalits and other like-minded scholars that reframe the analysis of society from the structural position. The project provides a new perspective for the study of Indian society and has the potential to redefine existing models of scholarship in both the Indian humanities and social sciences.[80]

Critical Questions in the Study of India

This volume, whose authors include a large number of Dalit scholars, intervenes in the study of India in three distinct ways. First, the essays in this collection draw attention to practices of caste exclusion in ways that seek to refocus Indian historiography and social sciences. Second, in contrast to earlier ideological positions that viewed Dalits only as passive victims or as objects of reform (as illustrated by Gandhi's Harijan discourse or Arya Samaj's embrace of temple entry movements), this volume recognizes Dalits as intellectuals, leaders, and active participants in processes of social transformation, highlighting their interventions in shaping debates in modern India. Third, the essays demonstrate that Dalits were not passive imitators of dominant discourses and practices; rather, they actively articulated their own agendas for advancing struggles against caste discrimination.

Dalit writings in Indian languages have praised the arrival of colonial modernity for introducing new principles and institutions that enabled Dalits and other marginal groups to participate in the public space. This is a widely shared theoretical framework that informs many Dalit writings. Arjun Dangle's review of Dalit literature associates the arrival of the British with "new knowledge, technology and production processes" and, more importantly, with "a new codified legal system" that enabled Dalits to challenge Hindu religious- and scriptural-based systems.[81] Baburao Bagul associates colonial modernity with "the rise of new literary expression" based on "self-critical thinking" that made possible for the first time an expression of "social themes rather than the metaphysical, transcendental or religious."[82] Essays in this volume develop and expand on this view of colonial modernity in the contexts of Kerala, Andhra Pradesh, Uttar Pradesh, and Punjab. As one method of building a movement and claiming a space in modern institutions, Dalit organizations and activists relied on colonial laws and appropriated the political language of equality and representation.

The essays in this collection highlight struggles related to dignity in the colonial and postcolonial periods to move beyond the mainstream preoccupation with anticolonial struggles. Guru's essay alerts us to the dominant framework of Indian historiography within which Dalit histories have been examined. He outlines at length the theoretical flaws of Indian historiography and concludes that "mainstream scholars of history direct their acrimony toward colonial racism but refuse to contribute any criticism on the question of caste outside of a rhetorical accommodation in the nationalist agenda." Ambedkar had argued in the Constituent Assembly debates of 1946–48 that Indian nationalism as led by the Congress Party had developed the doctrine of "the divine right of the majority to rule the minorities," and "any claim for the sharing of power by the minority is called communalism while the monopolizing of the whole power by the majority is called nationalism."[83] This was a widely shared view among Dalit activists and intellectuals in much of the twentieth century. In 1949, the Dalit Hindi author Nandlal Viyougi argued that the unique feature of caste discrimination in Hindu society is the absence of a cultural and religious commitment to equality in Hindu religion. It is therefore easy, he wrote, for a radical Indian nationalist like Gandhi to be socially conservative and yet claim a revolutionary image by being an anticolonial nationalist.[84]

In contrast to Indian historiography's stereotypes of Dalit activism as a product of the Congress Party and British patronage or enlightenment, this collection of essays highlights Dalits not only as engaged participants but as actors who effectively intervened in political and cultural debates in modern India. Sanal Mohan's chapter outlines a history of Dalits' engagement with questions of modernity in late nineteenth- and early twentieth-century Kerala. From 1898 onward, the Dalit activist Ayyankali and his organization, the Sadhu Jana Paripalana Sangham, organized protests to demand access to public schools and spaces like roads and markets in the Travancore region of southern Kerala. These Dalit struggles created what Mohan rightly describes as a "modern social space" in Kerala. Chinnaiah Jangam reveals the active role of Bhagya Reddy Varma in creating a Dalit public space in the Hyderabad region through the mobilization of Dalit groups, the opening of schools, the publication of newspapers and books, the organization of conferences, and ongoing engagements with leaders of dominant groups on the question of Dalit rights. Bhagya Reddy established the Central Adi-Hindu Social Service League in Hyderabad in 1922 to address issues of inequity and discrimination that Dalits faced in public spaces. Ramnarayan Rawat's chapter similarly uncovers the history of Dalit activism in Uttar Pradesh during the 1920s, highlighting the role of Chamar organizations in intervening in public discourse. Rawat outlines Swami Achhutanand's role in creating and mobilizing a Dalit public in Uttar Pradesh through the organization of conferences and demonstrations that challenged the failure of the Congress Party to address questions of untouchability and caste discrimination.

Essays in this collection further demonstrate Dalit engagements with the question of representation that helped expand the language of democratic politics from the early decades of the twentieth century. Nationalist historiography interpreted Dalit commitments to liberal ideas as a product of the colonial state's policy of divide and rule or as a deliberate strategy on the part of colonial officials to weaken the Congress-led nationalist struggle. Particularly relevant here are Dalit groups' demands for constitutionally mandated provisions that would guarantee specific rights within representative bodies. Mohan's essay documents the initiatives of Dalit organizations in Kerala that used the courts and the language of minority rights to gain access to public spaces between 1898 and 1910. Jangam's essay argues that members of the Adi-Hindu Mahasabha in Hyderabad played a significant role in debates over constitutional and political rights for Indians by passing resolutions in 1937 to seek affirmative rights for Dalits. Rawat demonstrates that in Uttar Pradesh Dalit groups appropriated the language of affirmative action in the 1920s, most spectacularly by organizing an all-India conference in 1928 in Allahabad.

The search for alternative religious identities has become a crucial aspect of Dalit activism in the past hundred years. The appropriation of Buddhism by Dalits in Maharashtra in the 1950s has been well documented. Focusing on equality and a critique of caste hierarchies in the contexts of Christianity in Kerala and Sikhism in Punjab, essays in this volume tell us about less well known aspects of this search for new religious identities. According to Surinder Jodhka, the search for a new religion is most visible in the continued transition of the Adi-Dharmis into the Ravi Dasi community in Punjab. This became more pronounced in the 1940s when its leaders, including Mangoo Ram, began to adopt the teachings of northern Indian Nirgun saint Sant Ravi Das, whose teachings are part of the Sikh text, the *Guru Granth Sahib* and his followers are known as Ravi Dasis. Adi-Dharmis, primarily Chamars, have patronized Ravi Das *deras* (places of worship) and following their teachings to distance their religion from Sikhism, but also to build a conscious Ravi Dasi community. Members of the Punjabi Dalit diaspora in England (who accounts for around 10 percent of the total Punjabi population in the United Kingdom) have played a key role in sustaining the deras in Punjab as an alternative to the Sikh Gurudwaras. Similarly, several Dalit Christian organizations have led struggles against inequality in the Christian denominations. These organizations sought, for example, to distinguish Dalit Christians from Syrian Christians by expanding the meaning of salvation and revelation with ideas drawn from Dalit lives to build what Mohan calls a new "emancipatory discourse." Borrowing from the biblical notion of salvation, the Dalit Christian leader Poikayil Yohannan has emphasized the role of a Dalit messiah in liberating their community.

By providing evidence of Dalit activism in social, political, and religious spheres from the early decades of the twentieth century, these essays sift through modern Indian history to recover Dalit agency. Raj Kumar Hans's essay traces the critical role of Dalit activists in Sikh history from the era of Guru Gobind Singh in the seventeenth century to their role in the Singh Sabha movement in Punjab in the late nineteenth and early twentieth centuries. Hans's essay captures the visible tensions in Sikh religion and its history, including contestations over its theological claim of equality, its criticism of caste oppression, and the continued persistence of untouchability. The resultant fractures evident in Sikhism are well described by Hans, who accepts the Sikh theological standpoint but accuses Jatt Sikhs, who came to dominate Sikh religious organizations and political economy in the past two centuries, of introducing exclusionary practices directed against Dalit groups. Do we describe the leading role of Jatt Sikhs as a Brahmanization of Sikhism? Hans also explains why Dalit Sikhs have begun to create alternative religious sites for their community, the Dalit Sikh deras. Hans's essay reveals a typical pattern in which such debates are frequently present in Indian-language literature but do not exist in English-language academic writings, and it alerts us to the importance of ensuring that such debates and narratives are included in mainstream English-language scholarship. Hans demonstrates that despite the claims in Sikh history of an absence of caste, Dalit Sikh activists from the seventeenth century onward have carefully documented ongoing discrimination against untouchables.

Dalits' visibility as agents of change in the postcolonial Indian social and cultural domain, especially since the 1980s, marks a remarkably new development (even if their activity is not new). K. Satyanarayana argues that it was the phenomenon of mass killings of Dalits and the controversy over the implementation of the Mandal commission's recommendations in 1990, with its implication for an extended system of affirmative action, that created the necessary social and political conditions for caste to begin to be debated as a national question. Caste has emerged as a key category of political, social, and cultural mobilization in Indian politics in the 1990s. During this period it has also challenged dominant Marxist and nationalist paradigms of class-based politics. Laura Brueck's and Satyanarayana's essays demonstrate that this debate has taken place most intensely and productively in the Hindi and Telugu literary spheres. Discussing the absence of Dalits and other marginal groups as literary writers and poets, Dalit writers have challenged the dominant canons associated with writers like Munshi Premchand in Hindi and Sri Sri in Telugu to displace class as the most important category for understanding Indian society. In contrast to Indian historiography's focus on anti-imperialist, nationalist, and peasant struggles, these two essays shine light on Dalit writers' efforts to challenge the dominant construction of modern secular and class-based citizenship by emphasizing the continuing power of caste identity.

Reflecting on political and cultural debates in the Dalit community, the essays by Brueck, Sambaiah Gundimeda, and Shyam Babu address the question of inequity in Dalit groups, including gender inequity. Brueck's essay focuses on Dalit women activists' criticisms of male-dominated Dalit organizations and their inability to practice gender equality. Brueck critiques the feminist assertion of "a Dalit feminist standpoint" that hinges on understanding gendered violence as constitutive of Dalit women's experience and their womanhood. Such an assumption, she argues, can reduce Dalit women to a hypersymbolic state of victimhood to defend the collective masculine community identity. Brueck demonstrates that Hindi Dalit feminist writers have sought to move beyond mainstream Dalit male writers' representations of a "Dalit rape script" that has been employed to serve and mobilize the Dalit community. Recent Hindi Dalit feminist writers have made claims for a literature of dignity that brings core issues of education, labor, and women's rights into the discussion.

Gundimeda's essay examines the recent rise of the Dandora movement among the Madigas of Andhra Pradesh, which questions the overwhelming dominance of Malas in the state's educational, administrative, and economic spheres. This recognition has galvanized Madiga youth to demand a caste-based categorization in existing reservation policies to ensure more equitable admissions into educational institutions and employment opportunities in the federal and state government. Such a policy, Madiga groups argue, would enable a more equitable distribution of resources among the scheduled caste communities. In describing the history of the debate over reservation policies in Andhra Pradesh over the past two decades, Gundimeda compares the demands made by Dandora activists with Dalit demands for affirmative action in the Constituent Assembly debates in 1947–48, claiming that in many instances the arguments made by Malas against Madigas are similar to those offered by caste Hindu leaders. Babu argues that the recent emergence of a Dalit bourgeoisie, a promising development, has posed new challenges. Many Dalits in this position have been unable to resolve the dilemma posed by their status and find themselves confronting the question of whether their caste or their class is more fundamental to their situation. Babu's essay captures this post-1990 phenomenon by arguing that affirmative action has created contradictory challenges. On the one hand, the Dalit middle classes want to be a part of the consuming Indian middle class, and on the other hand, they continue to recognize the role that caste plays in Indian society and politics and in their own lives.

Conclusion

In his 1938 foreword to G. R. Pradhan's *Untouchable Workers of Bombay City*, Ambedkar pointed out that this study would have been "of greater value if it had been a comparative study contrasting the social condition of the Untouchables with that of the Caste Hindus."[85] He urged foregrounding the role of untouchability in shaping the choices available to Dalits and caste Hindus in the modern "competitive society." Ambedkar cautioned against studying Dalits in isolation, removed from their wider social and political context. From the 1920s through the 1990s, Indian scholarship, both sociological and historical, that centered on Dalits focused exclusively on their stigmatized conditions and the exclusionary practices of untouchability. Scholars emphasized processes like social mobility and Sanskritization as central objectives of Dalit struggles in the twentieth century. In contrast, building on Ambedkar's insight, essays in this volume restore agency to Dalit activists and organizations and critically engage with the persistence of caste inequalities in Indian society.

With essays by Dalit and nonelite scholars, most of whom have been educated at nonelite institutions not usually associated with mainstream Indian academia, this volume is a product of the post-1990s reconfiguration of power in India. The authors in this volume represent the post-1989 Mandal generation,

whose members recognize caste inequality and hierarchy as important political, social, and ethical questions of our time and see the pressing need
for a more thorough inquiry into these topics. It is insufficient to suggest
that struggles against caste inequality emerged in response to the practices of
colonial governmentality or to the demand for affirmative action. Questions
of humiliation, dignity, and struggles against caste inequality have a longer
history, which has been reshaped and reframed by Dalit organizations in the
context of colonialism. Dalit engagements with colonial modernity, along
with longer histories of struggles related to questions of self-esteem and self-
worth deserve serious academic attention today. The essays in this volume
pose these questions to recover actors who engaged in initiatives that sought
to protect the human dignity of all Indians.

NOTES

1. Guru, "The Politics of Naming."

2. Taylor, "The Politics of Recognition," 37–50.

3. Guru, "Introduction," 3.

4. Recognizing the emergence of Dalit studies as a significant field of study and
a perspective to use in reassessing Indian society and history, a conference on this
theme was held at the University of Pennsylvania in December 2008, as noted in the
acknowledgments. Organized by the Center for the Advanced Study of India, this
conference was the first of its kind in the United States and marked the culmination of
a series of conversations that had started the previous year. See Babu and Prasad, "Six
Dalit Paradoxes."

5. Chatterjee, "Introduction," 38–39.

6. The Indian government introduced the policies of positive discrimination for
the backward groups in India because of historic social and educational barriers
imposed by the dominant Hindu groups. The Indian constitution of 1950 provided
the scheduled castes (formerly known as untouchables) and the scheduled tribes with
15 percent and 7 percent, respectively, of the seats in representative institutions such
as the Indian Parliament and state legislative assemblies and of jobs in public education and employment. The Mandal commission report recommended expanding this
reservation to the other backward classes in admissions to centers of public education
and in employment, to total 27 percent. The category of other backward classes is
made up of a cluster of "lower-caste" Hindu groups identified on the basis of the constitutional principles of social and education marginalization.

7. Kothari, "Rise of the Dalits and the Renewed Debate on Caste," 441.

8. Ibid., 450.

9. Balagopal's "This Anti-Mandal Mania" captures the spectrum of responses to the
government's decision to implement the recommendations in the Mandal commission
report. See also Omvedt, "'Twice-Born' Riot against Democracy."

10. The B. R. Ambedkar Students' Association and Dalit Students Forum at the University of Hyderabad and the United Dalit Students' Forum at JNU, Delhi, came into existence in the 1990s.

11. Srinivasulu, "Caste, Class and Social Articulation in Andhra Pradesh."

12. Kothari, "Rise of the Dalits and the Renewed Debate on Caste," 450–52.

13. Ravikumar, "Re-Reading Periyar."

14. See Pendse, *At Crossroads*. This collection of essays provides a detailed discussion of the Dalit movement in independent India. See also Gorringe, *Untouchable Citizens*.

15. Pai, *Dalit Assertion and the Unfinished Democratic Revolution*; Pushpendra, "Dalit Assertion through Electoral Politics."

16. Chakravarti, *Gendering Caste*, chapter 1.

17. Guru, "Dalit Women Talk Differently," 2548–49.

18. A. Rao, *Gender and Caste*.

19. The 2001 World Conference against Racism, Racial Discrimination, Xenophobia and Racial Intolerance, Durban (South Africa), and the International Dalit conference at Vancouver, BC, in 2003 brought together representatives of Dalit diasporic nonprofit organizations and other international agencies to debate caste discrimination in the global context. A significant group of Dalit scholars and activists attended these conferences. The international French literary festival "Les Belles Etrangères" (Beautiful foreigners) honored the Dalit writers Bama (Faustina Mary Fatima Rani) and Narendra Jadhav in Paris 2009. Two academic conferences were held in the United States: the Dalit studies conference in December 2008 organized by the Center for the Advanced Study of India at the University of Pennsylvania, mentioned above; and "Caste and Contemporary India," a conference held in October 2009 at Columbia University, in honor of its alumnus B. R. Ambedkar.

20. For an extensive discussion on race, caste, and the 2001 Durban conference see D. Reddy, "The Ethnicity of Caste."

21. See "Guidelines for Establishment of Centres in Universities for Study of Social Exclusion and Inclusive Policy," http://www.ugc.ac.in/pdfnews/2118716_social -exclusion-colleges.pdf, accessed September 15, 2015 (also on March 26, 2011).

22. Guru organized a small but significant group of scholars under the banner of the Dalit Intellectual Collective. A major outcome of Dalit activism in the 1990s was the "Bhopal Conference: Charting a New Course for Dalits for the 21st Century" in January 2002 which brought together Dalit scholars, activists, and nongovernmental organizations to demand a share in the development in a globalized economy.

23. Such debates were most evident in the Dalit vernacular writings; some are recently translated, including Dangle, *Poisoned Bread*; K. Satyanarayana and Tharu, *No Alphabet in Sight*. A large number of Dalit vernacular writings are being translated into English.

24. Since the 1990s Ambedkar has attracted considerable academic attention, but his theoretical contributions have not yet been sufficiently appreciated in the mainstream social science disciplines.

25. Sarkar, *Writing Social History*, 359.

26. Aloysius, *Religion as Emancipatory Identity*, 49. However, some of these issues were addressed in Tamil-language writings in the early 1990s (see Ravikumar, *Venomous Touch*).

27. Human Rights Watch, *Broken People*. See also the Dalit commentator Chandrabhan Prasad's critique of this report in the Indian English daily *Pioneer*, February 21, 2001.

28. Gandhi, "The Ideal Bhangi," in *Collected Works of Mahatma Gandhi*, 70:127.

29. *Ambedkar Writings and Speeches*, 1:83. The vedic conception of the varna model excludes the untouchable castes as avarnas who perform "impure" menial services to the four varnas. The varna order is an ideal imagined in classical Hindu literature which resonates with the real and lived caste order. When Ambedkar and others argued against caste and untouchability, Gandhi was forced to take a public position. Ambedkar explains how Gandhi opposes the practice of untouchability but justifies birth-based social division and hierarchy in his interpretation of the varna model. In Ambedkar's view, Gandhi's ideal of vedic varna model and the lived caste system theoretically fix the social position of the individual based on birth in a particular varna or caste. Gandhi's endorsement of the vedic varna model does not question the imposition of scavenging on certain untouchable castes based on birth, in the past, and even today (92–94).

30. Anand, *Untouchable*; Pillai, *Tottiyute Makan*.

31. Ambedkar, *What Congress and Gandhi Have Done to the Untouchables*, 306.

32. Guru, "Dalit Movement in Mainstream Sociology," 570.

33. Srinivas, *Caste in Modern India*, chapter 2. Srinivas popularized Sanskritization as a conceptual model in the 1950s to assess social change among the "lower-caste" groups in Indian society. "Sanskritization" was defined as a social process by which castes placed at the bottom in the caste hierarchy seek upward mobility by emulating the rituals and practices of the upper or dominant castes.

34. Sumit Sarkar observes that the "dominant historiographical assumption here, cutting across many otherwise widely varied approaches, has been that of a single, colonial/anti-colonial binary, setting both narrative pattern and standards of evaluation" ("The Limits of Nationalism"). For a more elaborate discussion, see Rawat, *Reconsidering Untouchability*, introduction.

35. See the chapters in this volume by Sanal Mohan, Chinnaiah Jangam, Rajkumar Hans, and Surinder Jodhka.

36. Bhattacharya, "The Problem."

37. Upadhya, "The Idea of Indian Society."

38. Sabyasachi Bhattacharya, "Kosambi and the Discourse of Civilization," *Hindu*, July 31, 2008, accessed June 27, 2015, http://www.thehindu.com/todays-paper/tp -opinion/kosambi-and-the-discourse-of-civilization/article1303866.ece.

39. Uberoi, Deshpande, and Sundar, "Introduction."

40. For a critical analysis of Srinivas, see Deshpande, "Fashioning a Postcolonial Discipline." See also Rodrigues, "Dalit Struggle for Recognition within India."

41. Dumont, *Homo Hierarchicus: The Caste System and Its Implications*.

42. The Indian sociologists Srinivas, A. M. Shah, and B. S. Baviskar opposed caste-based reservations for other backward classes recommended by the Mandal commission and described the caste system as divisive and premodern. See Kothari, "Rise of the Dalits and the Renewed Debate on Caste," 444.

43. Thurston and Rangachari, *Castes and Tribes of Southern India*, 4:292–325 ("Madigas") and 329–87 ("Malas"), and 6:77–140 ("Paraiyan or Pariahs"); Crooke, *The Tribes and Castes of the North-Western Provinces and Oudh*, 2:168–94 ("Chamars") and 4:138–52 ("Pasis").

44. Moffatt, *An Untouchable Community of South India*.

45. Guru, "Dalit Movement in Mainstream Sociology," 570.

46. Mahar, *The Untouchables in Contemporary India*.

47. Cohn, *An Anthropologist among the Historians*, chapters 11–14.

48. Zelliot, *Doctor Bahasaheb Ambedkar*; O'Hanlon, *Caste, Conflict, Ideology*.

49. Lynch, *The Politics of Untouchability*; Khare, *The Untouchable as Himself*; Juergensmeyer, *Religious Rebels in the Punjab*.

50. Guru, "Dalit Movement in Mainstream Sociology," 571.

51. S. Deshpande, *Contemporary India*, 71.

52. Rudolph and Rudolph, *The Modernity of Tradition*, 29–36.

53. Ibid., 64–87.

54. K. Satyanarayana, "Dalit Reconfiguration of Caste," 51.

55. Kothari, "Rise of the Dalits and the Renewed Debate on Caste," 443; Dirks, *Castes of Mind*, 286–88.

56. Chatterjee, "Caste and Subaltern Consciousness."

57. This theme is discussed in Rawat, *Reconsidering Untouchability*, 12–18.

58. Chakrabarty, *Provincializing Europe*, 10–11.

59. Mayaram et al., *Subaltern Studies XII*.

60. Bandyopadhyay, *Caste, Protest and Identity in Colonial India*.

61. Aloysius, *Religion as Emancipatory Identity*, especially chapters 3 and 4.

62. Satyanarayana and Tharu, *No Alphabet in Sight*, 119.

63. A. Rao, *The Caste Question*, 2.

64. Rawat, *Reconsidering Untouchability*, chapters 4 and 5.

65. Liddle and Joshi, *Daughters of Independence*, 85–94 and 65–69; Ilaiah, *Why I Am Not a Hindu*, chapter 2.

66. Pawar, "What Has the Dalit Movement Offered to Women?," 84–85; Guru, "Dalit Women Talk Differently." See also Pawar and Moon, *We Also Made History*, chapter 9. For a brief discussion of Dalit feminist arguments, see "The Dalit Woman Question," in Satyanarayana and Tharu, *Steel Nibs Are Sprouting*, 36–43.

67. Pawar, "What Has the Dalit Movement Offered to Women?," 84–85.

68. Rege, *Writing Caste/Writing Gender*, 3–7.

69. A. Rao, introduction.

70. Guru, "Rejection of Rejection," 219.

71. Nagaraj, *The Flaming Feet and Other Essays*, 25.

72. David Ludden writes incisively that in Ranajit Guha's "accumulated writings, colonialism appears to be a single, unified, discursive structure of power inside a vast ethnographic present; and state institutions, texts, personnel, and discourse, including those of the nationalist movement, stand in stark opposition to subaltern India and its indigenous culture from the first day of British rule down to the rupture of Subaltern Studies. Ranajit Guha might be said to be the Louis Dumont of colonialism, which

in his writing attains a comprehensive power like that of caste in *Homo Hierarchicus*" ("Introduction," 14).

73. See the chapters in this volume by Sanal Mohan and Chinnaiah Jangam.

74. See Dirks, *Castes of Mind*, chapter 11; Dalmia, *The Nationalization of Hindu Traditions*, introduction.

75. On sanitation, see Prashad, *Untouchable Freedom*, chapters 3 and 6. On land and caste, see D. Kumar, *Land and Caste in South India*. On labor, see R. Gupta, *Labour and Working Class in Eastern India*.

76. Chowdhry, *The Veiled Women*. See also R. Kumar, *The History of Doing*, chapters 2 and 3.

77. On this point, see the review article by Sarkar, "The Return of Labour to South Asian History." See also Chakrabarty, *Rethinking Working-Class History*; Chandavarkar, *The Origins of Industrial Captialism in India*.

78. Namishray, *Apne-Apne Pinjare*; Moon, *Growing Up Untouchable in India*; Omprakash Valmiki, *Joothan: An Untouchable's Life*.

79. Rege's essay on Dalit studies may be one of the first attempts to conceptualize Dalit studies (*Dalit Studies as Pedagogical Practice*, 10–51).

80. K. Satyanarayana, "Dalit Studies as a New Perspective in the Indian Academia," 87.

81. Dangle, "Dalit Literature: Past, Present and Future."

82. Bagul, "Dalit Literature is but Human Literature," 278. In recent years Chandrabhan Prasad, a Dalit writer and public commentator, has started celebrating Lord Macaulay's birthday in Delhi every year to applaud his role in establishing colonial modernity by formulating a uniform rule of law from which groups like Dalits benefited.

83. Ambedkar, *States and Minorities*, 427.

84. Viyougi, *Ambedkar ki Awaz Arthat Achhutoin ka Federation*, 33.

85. Ambedkar, foreword, iii–iv.

I

The Indian Nation in
Its Egalitarian Conception

GOPAL GURU

The public imagination in India seems to be increasingly gripped with Dalit issues and concerns. This is evident in the writings of both Dalits and non-Dalits, who have focused on a variety of Dalit issues ranging from theory to poetry. Books on Dalit themes now find nominal accommodation in some of the leading publishing houses in India. Dalit issues previously did not receive much recognition from those who had complete control over the sphere of critical public inquiry, but that group has now found the issues worthy of scholarly attention.[1] Prior to the 1990s, continuous marginalization and ghettoization implicitly suggested that the so-called Dalit question failed to attract any serious attention from the intellectual mainstream. Thus it is rather gratifying to note that Dalit studies, though previously present at various levels, are now ending this silence and have begun receiving far more serious intellectual attention from the national and international scholarly communities. However, one of the distinguishing characteristics of such writings is that they claim to have found for Dalits a clear intellectual vision and efficacious political framework within which Dalits can realize their emancipatory aspirations.[2] According to the writings of these scholars, Indian nationalism, electoral politics, and globalization are the three sequential spaces that provide the necessary framework for the realization of a Dalit vision. Moreover, in these spaces Dalits are represented as budding nationalists with sterling qualities and triumphant modernists. The scholars who claim to have found this vision for Dalits unquestioningly accept the validity of these claims. The faith and force in their assertions leave no room for any ambiguity or confusion that Dalits may have in understanding nationalism, electoral politics, or globalization. That is, these writers suggest that nationalism, electoral politics, and globalization are the spaces that tend to clarify the Dalit vision of any kind of confusion. These are the spheres, so the writers would argue, that provide an opportunity for Dalits to acquire a generic identity as Indian nationalists. This would mean that Dalits could appear in different spheres with secular but national identities. For example, someone might argue that in the sphere of nationalism a Dalit could change from an untouchable to a citizen; or in the realm of electoral politics a Dalit could shed the culturally attributed identity of *dhed* and, through the dynamics of electoral power, acquire a secular identity, possibly even as head of a political institution.[3] However, at the other end of the spectrum, there are scholars among the Dalit community who seem to have developed a new set of aspirations for their social constituency. According to these scholars, Dalits need to aspire to become consumers of commodities.[4] In the context of globalization, such scholars would further argue, Dalits have a unique opportunity to become part of a more homogeneous social space of global consumers. Constructing Dalits in terms of enlightened consumers in the global cultural sphere pushes them beyond the boundaries of nationalism. Imagining Dalits as global consumers also contests the intellectual claim that there is a particular construction of Dalits as nationalists.

In fact, scholars tend to claim that they have discovered a space for Dalits in Indian nationalism (Badri Narayan and Charu Gupta), electoral democracy (Kanchan Chandra), and globalization (Gail Omvedt). It is interesting to note that writers who are looking for nationalists among the Dalits are taking a nonlinear route that exists outside B. R. Ambedkar's conception of nationalism and its implication for Dalits.[5] Claiming radical intellectual agency by writing on Dalits and attesting to the presence of a nationalist space for them, the nationalist scholars' claim is at odds with the Dalit articulation of these agendas, which contests whether Dalits have any space in nationalism, electoral democracy, and globalization.[6]

These writers, claiming originality for their discovery of Dalits as nationalists, seem to be arguing that scholarship on Indian nationalism has neglected the role played by the Dalits in India's struggle for independence. It is fine if they criticize mainstream writing about the history of nationalism for its failure to recognize the contribution that the Dalits have made to India's freedom. One might even see some merit in writings that can claim to have led to recognition for Dalits as nationalist. However, in claiming to have recovered the Dalits as nationalist subjects, they seem to be suggesting that nationalism is the only sphere that can help Dalits gain some importance in the life of the nation. The writers also suggest that it is this historical recovery of the Dalits as nationalist subjects that give them a good reason to feel associated with Indian nationalism. Indeed, the claim to have delivered justice to Dalits by writing about their contribution to nationalist history also speaks of an ideological distance between the scholars and the passive objects of their historical narrative. Furthermore, such efforts end up insulating the idea of nationalism from the point of view of its Dalit critique. It seems that these scholars fail to detect the obvious contradiction associated with this recovery: that it makes nationalism a discursive space containing intersecting purposes and tendencies. For example, nationalism becomes available to different social forces for mutually exclusive purposes. The industrial classes had an interest in nationalism because it was expected to help them acquire benefits without any colonial constraints. On the one hand, workers put faith in nationalism for the reason that it would help them to gain a better deal from the industrialists. On the other hand, the Hindutva forces (right-wing Hindu organizations) had a stake in nationalism because it was expected to help Hinduize India. Naturally, the minorities and the "lower castes" were skeptical about nationalism because they rightly assumed that it would bring back the dominance of the upper-caste Hindus. Finally, I would like to argue that these scholars fail to subject the normative strength of concepts like nationalism to rigorous epistemological and methodological scrutiny. As a result, they end up producing the kind of writing that they sought to critique in the first place. To use the category of exclusion or silence as a rhetorical device or tool for critiquing mainstream historical writing is one thing, but interpreting people's perceptions and using them to uphold the value of a concept (in the present case, nationalism) is quite another thing.

But I believe that there exists a fundamental contradiction between Dalits' existential place, their segregated dwellings and obnoxious occupations like rag picking and scavenging, and nationalist spaces both symbolic (the national flag) and material (parliament buildings and big dams). The Indian state that gives concrete meaning to nationalism by transforming the existential conditions of the people on the margins has not been able to effectively resolve this contradiction. Similarly, electoral democracy and globalization have not been able to address it. For example, electoral democracy has not been able to create a positive sense of citizenship among the Dalits. In fact, they feel as if they are the passive recipients of fringe benefits that trickle down from this kind of democracy. Globalization also has not led to any structural transformation in the lives of the Dalits, many of whom continue to lead degraded lives in the villages and urban slums. According to Ambedkar, India as a modern nation no doubt attempts to organize society based on egalitarian principles, but it is helpless to enforce these principles as a part of social practice.[7] The modern nation vehemently asserts its geographical boundaries without dissolving the pernicious boundaries that exist between, for example, the main village and the Dalit *vadas* (quarters or neighborhoods). National boundaries invoke respect and pride, while the boundaries that divide society perpetuate a deep sense of contempt for the Dalit vadas. Ambedkar argued that in India there are two nations: Puruskrut Bharat (ideal, pure India) and Bahiskrut Bharat (actual, polluting India). Ambedkar articulated many of his ideas relating to the two Indias in the fortnightly newspaper, *Bahiskrut Bharat* which he started in 1924. According to Ambedkar, the Puruskrut Bharat represents the twice-born castes who are spatially, socially, and culturally different from the Bahiskrut Bharat, the untouchables who occupy separate spatial and cultural spaces. He proposed an alternative idea of the nation, which he called Prabuddha Bharat (enlightened and inclusive India).[8] Jotirao Phule, the nineteenth-century non-Brahman thinker, imagines the Indian nation in terms of the mythical King Bali who was the most egalitarian peasant ruler but was portrayed as a demon in Brahmanical narratives.[9] These portrayals suggest that any subjective imagination of the nation that does not talk of the existence of two nations—the Puruskrut and the Bahiskrut Bharats—necessarily involves an acceptance of nationalist rhetoric of equality and unity. In the context of this reading of nationalism by both Phule and Ambedkar, it is important to examine whether the scholarship on nationalism shows any sensitivity to, or sense of urgency about recognizing and interrogating, this spatial and ideological contradiction between Puruskrut and Bahiskrut Bharats.

Ambedkar's conception of the Indian nation consisting of Puruskrut and Bahiskrut Bharats helps us comprehend the riddle of nationalism and its ideological framework—which makes a rhetorical claim for social equality but sustains the spatial practices of exclusion. It also helps us question the recent efforts by radical Indian scholars to include Dalits into the nationalist narrative of the 1857 rebellion.[10] In addition, this ideological formulation provides us with a valuable resource to explain why some Dalit writers find the idea of nation deeply problematic, while others do not. This is one of the main issues that I would like to address in the first half of this essay. In the second half

I would like to draw on a set of writers—both Dalit and non-Dalit—who, I would like to argue, knowingly or unknowingly gloss over the Ambedkarite critique of the dominant conception of India that is internal to Dalit politics, including politics in the northern Indian state of Uttar Pradesh. It is democratic politics that provides a necessary foundation for the concrete realization of nationalism. A sense of belonging to the nation emerges from the thick socially interactive and democratically associational life of the different classes that inhabit the nation. Democratic politics is supposed to forge these bonds and overcome internal divisions. It is also expected to generate equal self-worth among the citizens, who can then participate in all the issues that are nationally important. It is supposed to help Dalits gain value because they are not passive recipients of the dominant classes' commands, but possess the moral as well as the political capacity to force others to take them seriously on matters that have a bearing on the national interests. Indian scholars sense that the Dalits matter in the national life due to their participation in the deliberative processes of the democracy. If they are not considered—or do not consider themselves—to be part of these processes, then they do not feel that they are part of the nation. The nation can forget them, and they can forget the nation.

How much do the Dalits matter in terms of the nationalist questions that are debated in the deliberative processes? Dalits should participate because of their capacity to contribute, and in the process they could develop further democratic practices. Through associational life they could also demonstrate their moral ability to produce normative values like friendship, love, and equality that would help the nation acquire a decent reputation. *Sarvajan*—the ideal model of inclusion referring to the equality of all individuals without caste barriers, used by the Dalit political party, the Bahujan Samaj Party (BSP)—must be evaluated against the normative need to engage in honest conversations about the intention to use this concept. Founded in 1984, the BSP fashioned itself as exclusively a party of Dalit-Bahujan—literally, "the oppressed majority," or the Dalits, tribal people, members of "lower castes," and Muslims—which had enabled the party to acquire political power, but only through coalitions with other parties. Ideological commitment to Dalit-Bahujan necessarily limited the BSP's electoral base and political possibilities. The party became more ambitious in the electoral and political arena, seeking to represent all Indians, which led it to become more national in its character. In 2007 the BSP consciously shifted its ideological agenda from Dalit-Bahujan to sarvajan, to build political and electoral alliances. Diluting its ethical commitment to fighting on behalf of Dalit-Bahujan, the BSP's appropriation of the sarvajan model enabled ideologically opposed groups to form political alliances. The ideal of sarvajan should be separated from its instrumental value. The Brahmans in Uttar Pradesh have supported the BSP not because of their commitment to equality or opposition to untouchability but purely out of self-interest—to oust a "lower-caste" political party, the Samajwadi Party, from political power because it was viewed as anti-Brahman. Furthermore, as longtime supporters of the right-wing Hindu political party, the Bharatiya Janata Party, they were acutely aware that it is no longer capable of winning elections in Uttar Pradesh. Hence, the Brahmans who provided electoral backing to the Dalits found the ideal of sarvajan useful.

One needs to develop the critique of the BSP's sarvajan model of politics which disregards caste domination and oppression. As a Dalit political party, the BSP relies on the moral legitimacy of Dalit struggles but also ignores it for the sake of caste Hindus votes. The sarvajan model will only produce unethical norms and support hierarchical societal norms. The Dalit politicians focus their attention only on the existential question, seeking to win elections to remain relevant in the narrow sphere of state politics. Therefore I intend to look at Dalit politics in general and the BSP's politics in Uttar Pradesh in particular to detect the contradictions within two formations. In this sense, identifying the paradoxes between the two can be a useful and enabling resource for Dalit politics, offering possibilities of emancipation.

AS I said above, I will begin by discussing to what extent the element of paradox is inherent in the idea of India. The privileging of Puruskrut and Bahiskrut Bharat is built around the notion of hierarchy that is spatially and socially regulated. The exclusionary nature of nationalism is rooted in the simultaneous hypothetical elevation of people and their real reduction to insignificance. That is, the discourse of nationalism constructs the people as an abstract category. It demands the people's complete allegiance to nationalist interests, which in turn seek to subordinate people's existential questions to nationalist questions. Even the question of social emancipation for Dalits through the annihilation of caste has to wait for the resolution of the nationalist concerns like the fight against colonialism. This totalizing reason makes nation a god, and people are expected to worship this nation. This devotional mode suggests that the nation is something that is not the embodiment of the people; rather, it stands outside them as a godlike entity. Thus, it is through the nation that people are expected to feel elevated; however symbolic this elevation may be. "Mera bharat mahan" (my India is great)—this slogan, which has become popular in India and is frequently used in the mass media, indicates the elevation of people in the devotional mode to the nation, but only at the abstract level. Through their devotion and nationalist rhetoric, people virtually write the hagiography of the nation. In this regard, it is interesting to note that several nationalist leaders and thinkers have actually written hagiographies of India. The foremost among them is that of Jawaharlal Nehru. This idealization of India is clearly evident in his seminal work, *The Discovery of India*.[11] The idealization of nationalism was justified because of the normative promises of democracy, freedom, fraternity, and dignity that it held out to people during the struggle for freedom. But these promises came to fruition only for the members of Puruskrut Bharat. For the members of Bahiskrut Bharat, the vast majority of the Indian population, the promises remained unfulfilled. This glorified concept of the nation was deployed to attract the devotion—and thus the political support—of those who remained marginalized with respect to access to the promised rights and freedoms.

In contrast, it is interesting to note that Gandhi's approach to nationalism was quite cautious, even though Gandhian hagiography elevates it to the sacred status by comparing it with Gandhi's notion of Ram Rajya (Lord Rama's perfect rule). Sarker has argued that the Gandhian-initiated nationalist program incorporated promises regarding democracy only with great reluctance.[12] A leading scholar in Gandhian studies, Bhiku Parekh, has convincingly demonstrated Gandhi's deep skepticism of nationalism. According to Parekh, Gandhi saw in Indian nationalism an element that sought to frighten Muslims, other minorities, and even the "lower castes."[13] The minorities were frightened because of the Brahman and caste Hindus' domination in the Congress Party. Arguably Gandhi's notion of India as Ram Rajya would not be intimidating to either minorities or the "lower castes." Ultimately Gandhi does provide a vision for India. In that vision, the independent Indian nation is imagined as a Rama Rajya, promising to flatten social hierarchies and enabling equality.[14] In the Gandhian vision of India, villages would dissolve all forms of hierarchy as they expanded outward. Ashish Nandy calls this a "shudraization of India," or the entry of "lower-caste" and Dalit groups into mainstream politics.[15]

The Gandhian hagiography expressed a new perception of the Indian nation, but it also undermined the more substantive aspects of daily interaction and social practices that produce the sense of belonging to a nation. Hagiography does not provide space for concrete expressions of nationhood through processes of interaction and dissolution of cultural boundaries. The democratic dimension of the nation provides a much-needed interactive element for social groups belonging to Bahiskrut Bharat, and it has the capacity to overcome their sense of alienation, produced through civilizational violence by the twice born. Civilizational violence in the Indian context renders the untouchable also as unseeable, unapproachable, and incapable of communicating.

Freedom to engage in social and cultural communication in everyday life plays an important role in the realization of the nation as concrete entity. To put this differently, the everydayness of nationalism has to be interactive rather than celebrated as an abstract form that is accessible only through devotion. In India, a large portion of civil society (or Puruskrut Bharat) arouses sentiments of patriotism by deploying rhetoric and cultural symbols. Yet, these sections of civil society actively refuse to promote interaction with the untouchables or adopt measures to extricate Dalits' wretched levels of human existence. The upper-caste imposition of a social boycott on the untouchables bears out this antinational and illiberal tendency. Caste Hindu groups belonging to Puruskrut Bharat even permit the social diminution of Dalits and members of "lower castes" who take part in wars to defend the nation. For example, many Dalit soldiers fight for the nation on the front line, but after retirement they find themselves pushed to the ghettos. Many Dalit soldiers who return to their hometown after retiring from the defense services cannot live in upper-caste areas even if they can afford to buy houses there. Dalit soldiers had to buy houses in the Dalit vadas in the village of Mundgaon, in the *taluka* (administrative district) of Akot, Akola District, Maharashtra. Similarly, villagers might put portraits of Dalit soldiers in little hotels in semi-urban towns but would hesitate to accommodate Dalits in an upper-caste area. This was the experience of Dalit soldiers from Gadhinglaj, in Kolhapur District, Maharashtra. Civil society ridden with caste consciousness continues to ostracize them and continuously push them to the Bahiskrut Bharat. The articulation of this pernicious caste consciousness was evident in the wall of separation that was erected by members of the upper caste of Tamil Nadu so they did not have to look at Dalits.[16] Thus, the upper-caste conception of nation is constitutive of social practices regulated by the ideology of purity and pollution, and this ideology—as Ambedkar very rightly pointed out—characterized Indian villages as the den of ignorance and the sink of casteism.[17] Thus for a Dalit or an outcaste, the Indian nation is based on fragmentation, which is not only physical but ethically repulsive. The majority of the population defines the nation through war and opposition, but they simultaneously articulate its fragmentation by practicing segregation based on untouchability. The caste Hindus can easily relate to the nation even from the sphere of civil society without necessarily participating in war. The hagiographic efforts to create an ideal nation rely on rather than resolving the issue of India's existence as Puruskrut Bharat and Bahiskrut Bharat. This paradoxical nature of the conception of nation mediated through its hagiography has been overlooked both by mainstream nationalist writers and those who claim to be the historians of the Dalits.

In India the writing of history and intellectual practice have failed to interrogate the persistence of hierarchical practices that endow the world of Bahiskrut Bharat. This is evident from the caste Hindus' differential vision of their demand from those of the minorities and the Dalits. For example, they pursued a clear vision of self-rule in the colonial period, assuming that the realization of self-rule was contingent on the clarity of their vision. The primacy of political concerns (independence or patriotism) in the upper-caste nationalist agenda obscures the existence of any underlying contradiction. They see everything very clearly. What they do not see, however, is their own contradictory role in violating the principle of self-respect in the local configuration of power. This configuration consists of two social forces, capitalism and Brahmanism. Dalits saw in capitalism a source of material exploitation, while in Brahmanism they saw the source of what would destroy their dignity and self-respect. The nationalists' failure to apply the logic of their broad political agendas to local situations by addressing the concerns of Bahiskrut Bharat illustrates their exclusive attitude. The contradiction in the nationalist goal of self-rule has been rightly detected by Ambedkar, who saw this particularly in Gandhism. For him, "Gandhism is a paradox, because it stands for freedom from foreign domination, which means the destruction of existing political structure of the country. At the same time it seeks to maintain the social structure which permits the domination of one class over another."[18]

Mainstream scholars of history direct their acrimony toward colonial racism but refuse to contribute any criticism on the question of caste outside of a rhetorical accommodation in the nationalist agenda. This approach seeks to subordinate the caste question to the more abstract question of national freedom. Similarly, the hagiography of the nation subordinates the normative question of self-respect to self-rule. Those who defend the idea that hagiography has contributed to the development of the nation tend to overlook this dichotomy, which plays a key role in forming a strong basis for both the imagination of nation and the politics of nationalism. Taking their cue from this hagiographic construction of the Indian nation and the contribution made by Dalits from northern India, some scholars and commentators argue that Dalits, particularly women heroes who also participated in the

1857 rebellion, have been exemplars in contemporary Dalit politics, at least in northern India. How radical is postcolonial theory? These scholars argue that the common Dalit women in contemporary Uttar Pradesh would like to conceptualize the state's Dalit leaders in the form of Dalit heroes of 1857.[19] This naïve perspective on Dalits' relationship with the 1857 rebellion aims to demonstrate their role in contributing to the hagiography of Indian nation and of self-rule but ignores the key question of self-respect. Recent writings demonstrating Dalits' stellar role in the 1857 rebellion outline a new nationalist position for them. The writings seemingly suggest that a nationalist resolution of the caste question is possible without resolving the paradox inherent in nationalism—that is, that Indian nationalists deliberately ignored questions about and struggles against caste inequality.

Indeed, the rhetorical accommodation of the question of social hierarchy can be extended to examine the sarvajan model of casteless and inclusive politics introduced in Uttar Pradesh in the 1990s by the Dalit political party, the BSP. Sarvajan, a Sanskrit and Hindi term and literally, "all people," seeks to highlight the unmarked, universal identity of all Hindus and actively denies the caste hierarchies that continue to subjugate Dalits and "lower castes." The BSP is the only Dalit political party that has formed a state government in independent India, which it did three times (in 1993, 1997, and 2002) with allied parties and then on its own in 2007. In fact, the sarvajan idea is an inversion of the nationalist resolution of caste. Sarvajan literally means "all individuals," but in the context of Uttar Pradesh politics it is used to suggest those who are beyond the pale of caste identity or casteless, and it is used in this way by the BSP to mobilize all sections of Indian society in contrast to its earlier slogan of Dalit-Bahujan. Indeed, this shift is considered as a major ideological shift in the long history of the Dalit movement. Let us see how the politics of sarvajan, instead of dissolving the social hierarchies, tends to accommodate them.

INDEED, THE concept of sarvajan makes it possible to gloss over the differences between Puruskrut and Bahiskrut Bharat, central to the politics of nationalism, electoral politics, and globalization. Because the nationalist framework allows for the rhetorical accommodation of the critique of social hierarchy, it enables us to recognize that sarvajan politics obscures the essentialist character of both Dalits and members of upper castes. Sarvajan's projected political persona must be somewhat vague and ambiguous to provide space for erasure. My aim in this essay is to foreground this intentional ambiguity and explain the durability of the concept of sarvajan in the context of Uttar Pradesh politics. This reading is contrary to mainstream understandings—that is, many commentators on Uttar Pradesh politics do not see any inherent contradiction in the politics of sarvajan. In fact, some of the writings on Dalit politics in Uttar Pradesh suggest that the politics of sarvajan there has given Dalits the perfect vision to use in pursuing their emancipatory project.[20] In their enthusiasm, they suggest that this is the perfect vision of empowerment that needs to be adopted by people in other parts of the country. These writings characterize Dalit politics in Uttar Pradesh as a model to be replicated elsewhere. This also holds out the promise that Dalits in other parts of the country might also be able to avoid the inherent flaw in the philosophies of other dominant parties. Now the BSP is on the move to disseminate the clear vision of emancipation to Dalits in other states, and among these scholars there is more celebration than skepticism about this sarvajan model. It is interesting to note that even the Marxists find no contradiction in the sarvajan model politics of the BSP. This is evident from their readiness to support the BSP's president for prime minister of India. In other words, it is being claimed that sarvajan propositions are free of any kind of paradox. The question that needs to be answered is, to what extent could the claims of sarvajan politics be defended? But before we address this question, it is necessary to offer some clarification here.

Dalit politics is not the source of the sarvajan model because the model has already been produced for Dalits. First, there are objective conditions such as the failure on the part of the main political parties, like the Bharatiya Janata Party and Congress, to accommodate the material aspiration of the upper castes that provide the necessary context for this model to become a possibility. The sarvajan model emerges primarily in the post facto situation. It is a product of an imperfect world; such a situation can exist only when structures of inequality and asymmetry are firmly established. Its success also suggests the self-reflective capacity of the establishment. It is the existing structures of Indian politics that have produced this model through the efficient use of ideology. Dalits carry secondary responsibility for producing this model through ideological interpellation. Thus Dalits play a far greater role than caste Hindus in terms of performing an ideological function and looking for this supposedly clear, egalitarian vision where it does not exist. In fact, Dalit politics provides the formative context. Dalits and their power politics become the medium through which the sarvajan model and hagiography of Indian nationalism becomes rooted in society, as well as in the minds of succeeding generations of Dalits. As I mentioned in the opening pages of this essay, rhetorical accommodation of a critique of social hierarchy is endemic to the concept of Indian nation and nationalism; it is also endemic to Dalit politics as well. Ironically, in the changing configuration of power, those who get to the top need egalitarian rhetoric to remain in power. The Dalit political leaders therefore need to produce the necessary conditions to reproduce the nationalist rhetoric of social equality.

The sarvajan model is a product of conditions that are produced and reproduced through the dynamic configuration of power. That is, social groups like Dalits, especially in Uttar Pradesh, who acquire political power through elections to enter the power structure, ironically rely substantially on Indian nationalist rhetoric, reproducing it for their own advantage even though their ancestors fought against it. The BSP's critique of Congress Party politics may be justified because the latter sought to trap the Dalits in the nationalist rhetoric of social inequality. It is justified on the ground that Congress politics denied Dalit autonomy and agency. Congress, through its control of the structures that provide opportunities and its readiness to dole out fringe benefits, produced an enduring nationalist rhetoric of social equality among the Dalits. The reproduction of this situation becomes necessary for the survival of those who control the strings of power and those who benefit from the power seepage. The seepage is deliberate in the sense that it releases the pressure that would otherwise accumulate to the point of becoming dangerous. This element of deliberateness suggests that those who have the capacity to detect the nationalist doublespeak avoid articulating it, since they are enmeshed in the system. Deliberate design plays an important role in giving the marginalized a feeling of ownership and a sense that they too are stakeholders in the system. The marginalized groups as stakeholders begin to see the seepage of fringe benefits as reassurance of a continued systemic resource.[21] Thus, a symbiotic relationship is formed between nationalist rhetoric and power, and even in the changing configurations of power, the latter becomes almost endemic in the system, as we see in the case of Uttar Pradesh through the BSP's articulation of the sarvajan model.

I would like to argue that the egalitarian claims of social inclusion in the sarvajan model have enabled caste Hindus to perpetuate the separate worlds of Puruskrut and Bahiskrut Bharat and that it has also enabled them, Brahmans in particular in Uttar Pradesh, to support the sarvajan politics of the BSP. Since 2007 the politics of sarvajan has promised the Brahmans of Uttar Pradesh some kind of a respite—at least for the moment—from the possible humiliation that would have seemed imminent except for the model of sarvajan. The fear of being humiliated at the hands of Dalits was felt to be imminent during the first phase of BSP rule in Uttar Pradesh in the 1990s. During this phase many upper-caste officers and politicians did face a threat of possible humiliation. The goal of Brahman politics, among other things, was to eliminate the possibility of such humiliation from the Dalit power structure, and the sarvajan model provided a politically valuable tool for the Brahmans to use in enaging with the BSP. Given the new political configurations after the 1990s marked by the rise of Dalit politics, the caste Hindus in India today have found a way to deflect the irresolvable tension between rhetorical and substantial recognition of Dalits and their cultural symbols. For example, at the rhetorical level, the caste Hindus assign so much respect to Ambedkar's *pratima* (image) that they may carry it on their heads, but at the substantive level of recognition they would trample under their feet his *pratibha* (genius)—his intellectual and philosophical writings and his role in drafting India's constitution (1947–50). Let me further explain the irresolvable tension in the cultural practices of orthodox Hindus or in the Hindutva politics. The right-wing National Democratic Alliance government in India (1999–2004) had established a commission in 2000 to review the Indian constitution. This move was seen as an attempt on the part of right-wing Hindutva groups to violate the secular and democratic norms and provisions of the constitution written by Ambedkar, the Dalit thinker and activist who fought for the rights of minorities. Similarly, the caste Hindus would show respect to the larger-than-life size images of Dalit leaders such as Ambedkar, or respectfully address the president of the BSP and three-time Chief Minister of Uttar Pradish Mayawati as *bahenji* (elder sister), but they have little or no respect for ordinary Dalits.[22] The politics of sarvajan, I further argue, provides the background condition for a paradox to successfully sustain itself in the public imagination of Dalits by seemingly resolving the irresolvable tension between rhetorical and substantial recognition of Dalits.

It is impossible to resolve the tension between the Puruskrut and the Bahiskrut Bharat, but the nationalist rhetoric of social equality and the sarvajan model mask the contradiction and become a source of power in two major senses. First, through making promises, an essential element of the sarvajan model, the model provides an initial condition in which people begin to offer allegiance to the most powerful. Simply put, if no promises are made to the people, there is no sarvajan model. Not all promises generate people's allegiance, particularly since only less spectacular promises could be partially realized. Second, to make such promises, one has to possess political power. That is, no one would take seriously promises made, for example, by a pauper. One has to make promises that are not completely empty but at least partially realizable. Thus, these promises assume a donor. Those who are a part of power structures (whether at the center or on the margins) can make false promises only if they look realistic in the beginning to the potential recipients. However, over time, promises lose their hold on the public imagination, thus paving way for the articulation of the sarvajan model, which begins to surface due to a growing sense of discontent, while inability or a sense of incapacity grows among those who made the promises. The more one aspires to remain in power, the more the sarvajan model accelerates the degeneration of promises into vacuity. As mentioned above, the sarvajan model looks almost endemic in the structures, irrespective of its social base in power, which makes it increasingly difficult to contain the growing frustration among social groups such as Dalits or even Brahmans. Thus, public articulation of the sarvajan model depends on the widening gap between hope and despair. However, it has to be mentioned that the sarvajan model does not choose the condition of its own articulation. This insight into the sarvajan model can be vitiated by several factors.

First, the expression of the sarvajan model depends on those who have acquired moral power to not only resist but also to critique the paradox. Moral power becomes important in contexts where many political observers and scholars recognize the limits of the sarvajan model but for some reason choose not to expose it. On moral and ethical grounds, it is the middle-class Dalits who are supposed to develop an insight into Dalit politics and expose the limits of the sarvajan model of BSP politics in Uttar Pradesh. But the Dalit middle class does not seem to take the moral lead in developing an internal critique of the sarvajan politics of the BSP. Why? There may be two interrelated reasons. First, upwardly mobile middle-class Dalits aspire to benefit from the structures of opportunities and patronage that flow from the Dalit leaders who control state institutions. Second, middle-class Dalits view the ascendance of Dalit leaders to political power as a weapon, with which they can avoid upper-caste domination and discrimination at the work place. These twin factors prevent them from criticizing the Dalit leaders' paradoxical politics of sarvajan. The middle class is only a tiny part of the Dalit community, but it plays an important role in making this model salient. This is done through deploying certain pedagogical devises. This class would thus argue that the existing structures are full of opportunity and that it is possible to convert these opportunities into an asset. Individual efforts are warranted to acquire this asset. This pedagogy also entails the moral message that those who do not take risk (both by making material efforts and by losing their dignity) can expect to gain entry into the system in the future. Thus, the message is conveyed that it is natural that structures do not solve the problem of everybody all at once, but gradually. Thus, these beneficiaries of state patronage keep advocating the virtue of patience, repeating the popular refrain, "today it is somebody else's chance, tomorrow it will be yours." This suggests that those who are missing out today have something to lose tomorrow if they step out of line. This effectively prevents the widespread expression of discontent. This rhetoric succeeds in naturalizing the sarvajan model, a fact that continues to escape the critical attention of those who have been legitimately ambitious in their life plans.

Second, the sarvajan model becomes durable precisely because those who took the lead in detecting the contradiction tend to reproduce it depending on where the middle class fall in the power structure. Progressive accommodation into opportunity structure, which emerges as a part of the self-reflectivity as mentioned above, makes the middle class part of the system. Thus, those who originally stood outside the contradiction ironically now become complicit in its reproduction.

Third, the sarvajan model provides a constitutive condition. When the state fails to provide opportunities, those who might withhold their allegiance to the state do not, as they still think that there is a possibility that the state will offer them some opportunity. If the state has provided accommodations to people whose sociological background is similar to those to whom it has made promises, this decreases the possibility that the latter group will criticize the state. In the case of Uttar Pradesh, having a Dalit government replaces the need for detecting the paradox that defines only the rhetoric of truth, not the truth itself. The elimination of the possibility for subversive action happens through what could be termed ethical relativism. Ethical relativism tends to make morally objectionable practices appear acceptable to those under their sway, which becomes evident as the paradox loses its ideological potency. In the act to produce a balanced impact on all people, the supporters of particular leaders (such as Mayawati) then would ask, why single out only the Dalit leaders when leaders of other political parties are on this moral slippery slope? The supporters of such Dalit leaders tend to defuse criticism by spreading the position of ethical relativism within their organization and affiliated groups who form the core of the morally depleted society. In addition to this ethical relativism, Dalits use caste identity as a powerful defense mechanism to disarm any legitimate criticism that seeks to expose the paradox that lies at the heart of their politics. Ethical relativism used in this way acts to perpetuate this sarvajan model. Ethical relativism acts against those who seek to criticize the moral practice or cultural lifestyle of some of the contemporary Dalit leaders. In fact, Dalit leaders often use this language of relativism to consolidate support for their paradoxical past and present as well as to propose that they know the truth. In contrast, our exemplar (Ambedkar) is produced through a continuous process of moral editing, or examining oneself for paradoxical behavior. Ambedkar followed this form of moral editing, which is why he could see the contradiction in the rhetoric of social equality in nationalist and electoral politics and why he offered a conceptual framework to understand the audience of this message, the people belonging to Puruskrut Bharat but not those who belong to Bahiskrut Bharat. His famous speech in the Constituent Assembly is a testimony to his creative capacity and moral ability to detect the paradox in the system.[23]

Fourth, developing an insight into the sarvajan model depends on the moral ability to militate against what could be called the designated power structure. The power structure adversely affects the cognitive capacity of Dalits, and they refuse to detect the paradox. For example, several Dalit women tend to celebrate the expensive clothes of their leader while they themselves are in rags or tattered clothing. Similarly, Dalits celebrate the palatial mansions of their leaders while they continue to live in wretched huts. Those who are caught in the framework of designated power somehow refuse to recognize the contradiction or articulate their critique of the sarvajan model. With the help of a common saying, let me explain this statement. In Marathi, the seductive quality of this designated power structure is very well captured in the saying "patalache ghode, maharala bhusahn," which means "taking care of Patil's (the landlord's) horse, is a privilege and an honor for the Mahar (Dalit) family." The Mahar family is responsible for maintaining the landlord's horse in the village. Those who see the irony in this situation would say that there cannot be any pride for the Mahar family in feeding Patil's horse; rather it should create a sense of moral anger at their predicament. Dalits should rediscover worth in themselves rather than basking in the glory of the master. They should develop critical consciousness about the hegemonic power of the master and restrain from participating in it. It is in this sense they should use anger as a moral resource to sustain the critical consciousness against upper caste hegemony.

These four factors should help us to understand the BSP's appropriation of the sarvajan model but also the support it has received among Dalit and non-Dalit groups. Its popularity has also tempered the radical potential of Dalit politics and making it subservient to the nationalist rhetoric of caste equality.

Instead of embracing the sarvajan model of inclusion, it is incumbent on the Dalit middle-class intelligentsia to expose the limits of this model.

IN CONCLUSION, I must say that whether or not one recognizes the nationalist rhetoric of social equality that actually perpetuates social hierarchy by actively ignoring the spatial contradiction between those who belong to the Puruskrut and the Bahiskrut Bharats depends on one's location in time and space. Those who are continuously on the margin or outside the opportunity structures and belong to the Bahiskrut Bharat are potentially ready to develop this insight. However, that insight is not automatically apparent—in fact, it is much more difficult to sustain continuous and critical opposition to nationalist rhetoric. As has happened with the Dalit consciousness in India, those who raised their voices against the rhetoric of nationalism were pacified and drawn into these structures. The Dalit Panthers of Maharashtra are a case in point. These Dalit leaders, who used their social vigilance to publicly reveal the paradoxical political relationship between the Republican Party of India (established by Ambedkar in Maharashtra) and the dominant Congress Party in Maharashtra, at some point began to see promise in the Congress Party. This shift in approach happened after their incorporation into power hierarchies, though they were not given a central place of power. Ruling parties belonging to the Puruskrut Bharat in Maharashtra carried out this co-option with a remarkable degree of success. Today one does not require non-Dalit ruling parties to perpetuate nationalist rhetoric because Dalits have their own parties that can do this job. Members and groups belonging to the Puruskrut Bharat now argue that Dalit political parties have the potential to win the highest political position. What they often ignore, however, is that this desirable shift in power will actively sustain the nationalist rhetoric, reducing adversity in the political realm without necessarily diminishing the hardship that many Dalits face in the social realm. For example, the upper caste in the BSP may be politically subservient to the BSP's supreme leader, but in their social interactions they may be overtly anti-Dalit. Yet the BSP's sarvajan model serves to diminish the historical political adversity of Dalit groups and exclusionary practices experienced by people who live in the Puruskrut Bharat.

Indeed, as mentioned in the last section, challenging the sarvajan model depends on people who have the necessary moral power to expose it but choose to ignore for personal benefits. Whether a person understands the contradiction depends on his or her capacity to develop insights into such matters. As discussed above, the Dalit self has to take the moral responsibility to detect the contradiction. The moral stamina alone, however, is not sufficient for detecting the contradiction in the sarvajan model. In addition, one must have a background characterized by deprivation or underprivilege; this creates the potential for state intervention and the manipulation of disproportionate populism by the state. If the state starts acting honestly and accepts its limitations in terms of the needs it is able to satisfy, there will no longer be a need for the sarvajan model or rhetoric of social equality. In a liberal framework, it is impossible to imagine this kind of a moral state. Hence, this leads to positive conditions in which those who are part of the counterpublic must take the lead in exposing the contradictions.

NOTES

1. The best example is D. R. Nagaraj's book, *The Flaming Feet*. The first edition was published by a small press in Bangalore and was not even reviewed in most journals, but the second revised edition was published by Permanent Black in 2011.

2. Bose, *Bahenji*; Chandra, *Why Ethnic Parties Succeed*; C. Gupta, "Dalit Virangana and Reinvention of 1875"; Narayan, "Reactivating the Past, Memories of 1857"; Omvedt, "The Great Globalization Debate."

3. The Dalit caste name, "dhed," has been used only in a derogatory sense for the Dalits of Gujarat, Madhya Pradesh, and Maharashtra.

4. Omvedt, "Capitalism and Globalization, and Dalits and Adivasi." See also Chandrabhan Prasad's numerous articles on this subject in the Delhi *Sunday Pioneer*.

5. Khairmode, *Babasaheb Ambedkaranche Charitra*, 89.

6. Bagul, *Dalit Sahitya ajache Kranti Vidynana*, 70; Teltumbde, "Reverting to the Original Vision of Reservation" and "State Market and Development of Dalits"; S. Thorat, *Givan Marge*, a Marathi language monthly, Mumbai, May 2008.

7. More, *The Social Context for an Ideology*, 314.

8. The concept of *Prabhudha Bharat* was developed by Ambedkar through a fortnightly newspaper started by Ambedkar in the 1950s.

9. Wangmay, *Mahatma Jotirao Phule*, 190.

10. See C. Gupta, "Dalit Virangana and Reinvention of 1875"; Narayan, "Reactivating the Past, Memories of 1857."

11. Nehru, *The Discovery of India*.

12. Sarkar, "Indian Democracy," 30.

13. Parekh, *Gandhi's Political Philosophy*, 193.

14. Tendulkar, *Mahatma*, 6:67.

15. Personal conversation with the author.

16. There are several examples of caste walls, separating Dalits from caste Hindu (or, at times, from "lower-caste") neighborhoods, in the districts of Salem, Coimbatore, and Madurai in Tamil Nadu. See "Uthapuram Wall Is No Berlin Wall," *Hindu*, March 21, 2012; "Caste Fence Pulled Down in Tamil Nadu," *Times of India*, October 18, 2010.

17. Ambedkar, *Babasaheb Ambedkar*, 6:290.

18. Ibid.

19. C. Gupta, "Dalit Virangana and Reinvention of 1875"; Narayan, "Reactivating the Past, Memories of 1857."

20. This and other points developed in this section of the essay are a response to the normative understanding of Dalit politics by the mainstream India establishment, and this is best represented in Bose, *Bahenji*.

21. Bose, *Bahenji*.

22. The op-ed article in *The Times of India*, Delhi, October 5, 2008.

23. In this speech Ambedkar made it clear that on "26 January 1950 [when Indian constitution was adopted] we are going to enter into a life of contradictions. In politics we will have equality, and in social and economic life we will have inequality" ("On the Adoption of Constitution," 219).

PART I. Probing the Historical

2

Colonial Archive versus
Colonial Sociology: Writing Dalit History

RAMNARAYAN S. RAWAT

More than three-quarters [of Jatavs] work in agriculture and less than a quarter [of Jatavs] work in artisanal and other kinds of occupations.

Skills: Except their knowledge of agriculture and artisanal industry, the Jatav community does not have skills in other professions. Their livelihood is dependent on artisanal [industry], agriculture, and day wages, and they [the Jatavs] have lost the business of leather work that has been usurped by Muslims, Kayastha Khatri communities.

—PANDIT SUNDERLAL SAGAR, *Yadav Jivan*

Outlining his community's conditions in 1929, Pandit Sunderlal Sagar, a major Jatav publicist from Agra and founding member of Jatav Mahasabha, an untouchable community association established in 1917, stated that more than 75 percent of Jatavs (untouchables) were engaged in *krishi karya* (agricultural work). Indeed, on the next page he lamented the unfortunate condition of Jatavs because they knew no other occupation except agriculture (*krishi vidhya*). During my fieldwork in the northern Indian state of Uttar Pradesh (UP), many Dalit activists, belonging to a prominent Chamar untouchable community that consists of several regional communities such as Jatavs, Jatiyas, and Kurils, made similar claims about their community, indicating that this is still a widely shared sense among sections of Dalits. Sagar of course was drawing on his personal experience in representing the Chamar community of Jatavs as cultivators, but census data support his claim. According to the 1911 census, 96 percent of Chamars were agriculturists, and of these, 40 percent were occupancy tenants with legal rights to the land, 40 percent were rent-paying nonoccupancy tenants at will with customary rights, and 14 percent were landless laborers. By 1961 the percentage of occupancy tenants had increased to 50 percent.[1] In UP the majority of Chamars belong to two prominent castes, the Jatavs in the western part of the state and the Jatiyas in the eastern part of the state.

Sagar's 1929 book and scores of other Hindi-language Dalit publications dating back to the early decades of the twentieth century have proved to be a valuable source of information that I collected during the course of my fieldwork spanning the past fifteen years. The Hindi-language books by Dalit writers that I found in the personal collections of activist families have been the most useful in providing both a perspective and information that is generally absent in historical and archival sources. In contrast to the dominant assumption that Dalits in the early part of the twentieth century did not write histories of their community, it would be more accurate to say that their works are not available in the traditional sites such as libraries and archives. Dalit activists in small towns in northern India have collected and proudly maintained personal collections in their homes. One Dalit activist, Mr. J. Kanaria, from Gawalior, a small town in northern India, explained the reason to me on March 3, 2009. On that pleasant morning, he told me Chamars, like Brahmans, earn income to read and write books and consider themselves as an intellectual class in India.[2] The personal collections of Dalit activists in small towns in northern India have played a crucial role in my research, emphasizing the value of local, nonmetropolitan sources.

Writing the history of Dalits in northern India was made possible by recognizing the differences between the regional or local archives and the more centralized all-India archival collections. This distinction offers an important corrective to the way we think about the project of colonial sociology and its relationship to different types of colonial-period archives. My research and interactions with Dalit groups in Lucknow, Kanpur, Agra, Etawah, Allahabad, and Mainpuri raised new questions for my project, which I took to the provincial- and district-level archives for further study. This approach yielded extensive material that illuminates the regional character of the Dalit struggle in UP. It also meant that I did not need to focus on the more commonly used National Archives of India or the British Library collections located in metropolitan centers. This methodology provided me with material to consider a new approach to Dalit history, offering a striking corrective to stereotypes about Chamars that are found in the kinds of projects of colonial sociology produced with an emphasis on all-India framework (including the all-India Census, the imperial gazetteers, and caste and tribe surveys). The land revenue records became the most significant body of evidence to offer a contrasting representation of Chamars and their lives in different parts of UP. These sources have been used to write agrarian history, typically of dominant groups in a locality, but rarely to write Dalit histories. This essay draws attention to the role of settlement and land tenure surveys as crucial sources for writing Dalit history. Recognizing local- and district-level archival sources was an enabling and productive alternative to the argument of a hegemonic colonial sociology of the last two decades that has deemphasized the conflict, dissension, and debate evident in the colonial archive and adopted the perspective of the metropolitan centers of Delhi and London.

A key assumption relating to the colonial archive underscores the role of colonial sociology, particularly influential documents such as the census and caste and tribe surveys, in producing dominant representations of Indian society and history around the *varna* model of social division, consisting of four castes (Brahmin, Kshatriya, Vaishya, and Shudra), and the untouchables, who were outside the varna. In 1987, Bernard Cohn demonstrated the role of the census in "classifying and making objective to the Indians themselves their culture and society," in which the category of "caste in terms of social precedence" played a key role.[3] By the 1870s "the ethnographic state," taking "caste as the primary object of social classification and understanding," created a new archive "from miscellaneous collections and volumes, office manuals and gazetteers, to the census."[4] Such accounts of colonial sociology draw considerably, if not primarily, from caste and tribe surveys and all-India decennial reports, but rarely from district settlement reports. In *Castes of Mind*, Nicholas Dirks has argued that caste emerges as an organizing principle of colonial knowledge in the late nineteenth century when the colonial state transitioned into "an ethnographic state." Dirks contrasts this with the absence of caste in any "kind of systematic and autonomous sense" in early colonial practices, and to support this he discusses at length Colin Mackenzie's ethnographic survey from 1799 to 1809.[5] This survey was part of the larger concern of the early colonial state with questions of land tenure, as the state sought to maximize and stabilize its revenue base and understand the rural society for purposes of taxes. By the late nineteenth century, especially after the 1857 rebellion, the colonial state had shifted its attention to caste because several ethnographic surveys and the census increasingly began to rely on caste to tabulate and regulate Indian society. In organizing the vast data, the colonial state paid particular attention to the varna model.[6] There is no doubt that a focus on colonial sociology has informed our current understanding of what Dirks has described as the "modernization of caste" by historicizing the impact of the colonial encounter in producing the practices and politics of caste identities.

An undue focus on colonial sociology has reduced the diversity of colonial archives to a single imperial monolith. I intend to substantially modify this postcolonial understanding of the archive, and by extension the new representation of caste located in the caste and tribe surveys (colonial sociology). We might want to emphasize the distinctive qualities of local archives in contrast to colonial sociology to highlight the role of locally embedded ethnographic investigations in constituting the former. By distinguishing colonial knowledge from the sources of local knowledge we can problematize the homogeneous assumption about the colonial archive implicit in postcolonial studies. It may be more productive to underline the unique strengths of district and provincial repositories in contrast to imperial archives based in the metropolitan centers of Delhi and London. Documents of local conditions, such as the land revenue surveys, often contained details that were not concerned with sustaining the objectives of all-India colonial sociology and provided strikingly contrasting perspectives on caste and Dalits. According to Dirks, caste as a category was absent in colonial archives of the early nineteenth century, but he acknowledges that it "was important in relation to debates over historical forms of land tenure." As he writes, "many learned Orientalists made major contributions to this debate, as for example in the substantial treatise by Francis Ellis on *mirasi* [land tenure] rights in southern India."[7] Ellis discusses the proprietary rights of the Vellar community near Madras to locate their role in the revenue regime being instituted by the incipient colonial state. To be sure, the relationship between land revenue and regimes of proprietary tenures relied substantially on the role of dominant local caste groups, or *jatis*. Revenue reports in the late nineteenth century for the first time recognized the role of jati kinship connections in the collection and distribution of rent and revenue. Jatis acquired importance not because of the varna model of the census but because they were so deeply implicated in the land revenue regime. It is this aspect of the late colonial archives, I would insist, that provides a very heterogeneous and at times contradictory representation of Indian society that stands in contrast to the homogeneous portrayal of that society in colonial sociology.

The locally embedded (district-level) revenue reports offer a representation of caste (and Indian society) that may in turn offer a different representation of caste and untouchable histories (as I will show) than the normative varna model that the colonial sociology seeks to construct. The meticulously detailed land revenue records contain details about the rich social and cultural history of a district precisely because the district office had to tabulate and assign the rent and revenue obligations of various social groups. In his introduction to William Crooke's 1879 glossary of northern Indian agricultural life, Shahid Amin has emphasized the importance of Crooke's glossary in providing a "compendium of agricultural and rural terms" and "offer[ing] a meticulous report on the rural society." Addressing the reason for issuing a new edition of the glossary in 1989, Amin claims that it "will aid a fuller understanding of rural North India, past and present," because it "contains a wealth of very useful information."[8] Comparable to this is the well-known Dufferin Report of 1888 (*Inquiry in the Conditions of Lower Classes of Population*), which collected information about peasant households belonging to different social groups from district officers and others such as Crooke, who wrote a detailed report of nearly a hundred pages from his district in Etah. This enquiry provides valuable information about Dalit peasants in northern India.[9] It identifies Chamars in four categories—peasants with occupancy and nonoccupancy rights, agricultural laborers, and artisans—but never mentions them as leatherworkers. The report discusses thirty-one Chamar families, eleven of which are identified as occupancy peasants, eleven as nonoccupancy peasants, five as weavers, and four as agricultural laborers and part-time leatherworkers. Such repositories of local knowledge, especially the settlement and revenue reports, created opportunities for district-level officers to contradict and challenge dominant frameworks and conventions that might not accurately represent their local society. Attention to these sources made it possible to write a different Chamar history, highlighting their nuanced but solid position within agrarian society as occupancy and nonoccupancy peasants in UP. Such a perspective endow us to document their relationship with significant events in northern Indian history, such as the history of the Awadh Kisan Sabha movement. Chamars' participation in the peasant movement was one example of their sustained engagement with mainstream politics in the first four decades of the twentieth century.

Instead of assuming that the colonial archive is an imperial monolith, it might be more productive to recognize it, to use Ann Stoler's term, as an "archival form" that contains "genres of documentation" generated by a diversity of motives.[10] In considering the colonial archives as the site of "surplus production," Stoler acknowledges the infinite possibilities contained in the supporting documents that formed part of *Mailrapporten*, the mail report generated by the governor-general of Batavia.[11] The mail report was an official request for information on a particular issue, generated from the office of the minister of colonies. Similarly, Carolyn Steedman has warned us about thinking of any archive as a source of power, particularly the colonial archive.[12] In the context of colonial Peru, Kathryn Burns has suggested that an emphasis on the "centripetal movement: the bureaucrats' data-gathering impetus, and their tendency to draw things in toward imperial institution" or "the Foucauldian panopticon writ large" prevents us from recognizing the fact that the colonial state "not only couldn't oversee all instances; it never tried to."[13] Burns's study historicizes and reconstructs the practices and local stories of colonial *escribanos* (notaries) and the archives they constructed in the colonial context. Given these cautionary notes on colonial archives in diverse contexts, we should recognize that the imperial archive contains genres of documents motivated by multiple, and often contradictory, objectives and concerns. We can recover and interpret Dalit histories by discriminating between all-India sources such as the census and local sources, which represent district-level society very differently. The varna or occupational representation of Dalit groups in colonial sociology can be contrasted with the spatially distinct jati or caste neighborhood, or *jati mohalla*, in the district-level settlement and revenue sources. The motivations and compulsions of the latter body of sources are starkly different from those of the all-India census.

A unique feature of the local revenue reports is the attention given to local space and village clusters or jati villages—for instance, detailed discussions of varieties of land ownership rights and acreage of cultivated and uncultivated land—because they affect the revenue projections. This attention to space and the spatial distribution of various jatis is also very helpful in thinking about caste. Dalits' autobiographies pay particular attention to the role of jati experience in localities. Indeed, Vasant Moon and Mohan Dass Namishray underscore the spatial character of Dalit jati mohallas or *vastis* and *bastis* (neighborhoods or villages) as crucial to the formation of Dalit consciousness. Emphasizing the lived experience of growing up untouchable in the Dalit jati mohallas of Nagpur in Maharashtra and Meerut in UP, Moon and Namishray help us grasp the role of space as a crucial signifier in understanding untouchability and exclusion as opposed to the determining role assigned to occupation in the varna model of studying caste in South Asia.[14] I have developed this point centrally elsewhere, and here I want merely to suggest possible conversations between the two contrasting sets of sources, conversations that may not be possible with sources of colonial sociology.[15]

Attention to local level sources and the likely conversations with the jati mohalla experience should also take into account the promise of vernacular sources as the third node of local archives. Prachi Deshpande has argued that "an analysis of colonial discourse and colonial policy regarding 'Maratha' [caste] indicates that colonial sociology was not homogeneous"; rather, regional motivations from diverse localities influenced the accounts of colonial officers and members of the Maratha elite in explaining the latters' identity formation.[16] In particular, Deshpande demonstrates that the continued relevance of numerous Maratha *bhakhars* (chronicles) in shaping the discussion around the identity of the Rajputs and the military. Similarly, Sagar's 1929 book along with several other Hindi-language Dalit books, local colonial sources, and an ethnographic engagement with active agendas of Dalit activists enable us to question academic assumptions about Dalit history. Dalits' Hindi-language writings are one form of evidence of their stoic activism over the past century, which has become visible to us in the political and electoral success of the Bahujan Samaj Party in the past two decades.

Settlement Reports and New Perspectives on Dalit Histories

District settlement reports, *tehsil* (revenue block) assessment reports, and land tenure enquiries are the new promising sources for writing Dalit history. The first of these detailed reports from the 1870s and 1880s, and revised reports from the 1910s and 1930s, provide a representation of Chamar society and culture that is largely absent in the more homogeneous sources like the census and the caste and tribe surveys. Many of these settlement reports stand out as fine enthographic surveys with details that you can correlate with contemporary research and fieldwork. The questions relating to Chamars' peasant status were first articulated during my conversations with activists in the cities of Lucknow, Kanpur, Agra, Meerut, and Allahabad and in comparatively small towns like Etawah, Mainpuri, Gawalior, and in the revenue reports—but not in mainstream academic accounts. In the 1891 *Report of the Settlement of the Basti District*, J. Hooper argued that Chamars should be recognized as one of the chief cultivating castes in the district. He wrote, "Many of the Chamars are genuine cultivators, that is to say, they earn their subsistence entirely by farming on their own account, but a great many are ploughmen or labourers depending chiefly for their living on wages."[17] He noted that 49,728 Chamar peasants owned 74,280 acres of land, and he commented on the presence of twenty-nine Chamar proprietors in Bansi *Pargana* (administrative unit) of the district. These sentiments were echoed in the settlement reports of Aligarh, Shahjahanpur, Etawah, Kanpur, Bharaich, Azamgarh, and Gorakhpur. The Etawah settlement report expressed its authors' unease with a classificatory regime in the census that created confusion about the position of Chamars by classifying them as "non-agricultural."[18] On the basis of this data generated by the settlement reports, we can make a few general statements about Chamars as cultivators: (a) in most districts of UP they held land as occupancy and nonoccupancy tenants, and many were also plowmen and laborers; (b) depending on whether the zamindari and the *bhayachara* (coparcenary) land tenure system was in place (explained below), in most cases Chamars either maintained or increased their share of land; (c) in very few cases they had proprietary rights; and (d) they were unanimously recognized for their skills as one of the best groups of cultivators. Revenue inquiries in the nineteenth century into the status and rights of peasants of UP show evidence of Chamars' presence and claims of occupancy and nonoccupancy tenure rights.[19]

The Chamar peasants of Moradabad District paid an annual rent of about Rs (rupees) 324,571 in 1909. Out of the total rent of Rs 3,021,394, Chamars' payment in 1909 represented the highest rent paid by any caste in the district. In the same year the Jat tenants paid Rs 281,268 in rent, while the Sheikhs paid Rs 313,733, the Thakurs paid Rs 164,419, and the Brahmans paid Rs 142,597. Given their 107,525 acres of land, the Chamars were the third largest peasant caste after the Jats and Sheikhs.[20] Many settlement reports in western UP, like those from Saharanpur and Bareilly Districts, noted Chamars' excellent skills as cultivators of sugar, basmati rice, and wheat. In Saharanpur they were the sixth largest community of occupancy tenants, and their annual rent of Rs 263,260 in 1921 put them in the fourth position—after Gujars, Garas, and Malis or Sainis, but ahead of well-known peasant groups like Jats, Ahirs, and Rajputs.[21] They controlled a good percentage of land both as tenants and as proprietors. By the beginning of the twentieth century, Chamars held 7 percent (49,506 acres) of the land in Bareilly, and they paid an annual rent of Rs 209,905.[22] In the 1880s the Chamars of Agra District held 60,286 acres of land, amounting to 7.1 percent of the total land under cultivation. By the 1930s they had managed to increase their land to 65,000 acres, out of which 40,000 acres were held under occupancy rights and the rest (25,000) under nonoccupancy rights. Their gain of 5,000 acres was the highest among all the castes.[23] Their strongest position as tenants in the western part of UP was in the Bulandshahr District, where they held 81,179 acres. Most Chamar cultivators also owned a pair of bullocks.[24] These examples are representative of the strength of Chamars as one of the largest rent-paying caste in much of western UP and in the central and eastern districts of the state. Furthermore, they were among the top six rent-paying social groups, a point reiterated in many settlement reports of various districts of UP.

The rights of Chamars over land were shaped and conditioned centrally by the nature of proprietary tenures. This was particularly the case under the bhayachara tenure, in which the dominant peasant groups belonging to a shared lineage were recognized as proprietors of land, and responsible for the collection and payment of revenue to the state because they were also actively engaged in the management and cultivation of land. Peasant proprietors in the bhayachara tenure valued skilled occupancy tenants such as Chamars who contributed centrally to sustaining the revenue obligations. In the bhayachara region of western UP, from Jhansi in the south to Saharanpur in the north and west of Kanpur, Chamar peasants not only possessed occupancy rights but also acquired, in very small percentages, proprietary rights. The settlement officer of Jhansi District in the Bundelkhand region noted in 1893 that the Chamar peasants were the most sought cosharers by the peasant proprietary groups.[25] By 1921, the Chamars in Saharanpur District had gained more land under bhayachara tenure as well as a bit of proprietary share, because the proprietors considered them good tenants.[26] In Agra District, too, bhayachara tenure enabled Chamars to acquire occupancy rights, because the proprietary bodies "are always slower to move, and have not sufficient unanimity to carry out any sustained measures for preventing the acquisition of occupancy rights."[27] The settlement officer of Muzaffarnagar District succinctly observed in 1896 that because of their skills, the Chamar peasants gained proprietary rights, living alongside the dominant cultivating castes, which included Jats and other groups.[28]

The settlement reports of the 1870s and 1880s from central UP (the Awadh region) draw our attention to the presence of Chamar and Pasi peasants in the area. These reports also help us rethink the social history of the region, especially from a Dalit perspective. For instance, the dominant historical perception of the Awadh Kisan Sabha movement is that it was a "lower-caste" peasant struggle, against landlords' illegal and excessive rent demands, in which Dalits' participation was always relegated to the role of looters and rioters. It was assumed, because of the Dalit occupational caste stereotype that they were landless laborers, and their participation was therefore viewed as marginal or exploitative of the situation (thus the charges of looting). In

Rae Bareli, for example, the key theater of the Awadh Kisan Sabha movement, we can see that Chamars paid an annual rent of Rs 75,820 in 1898 for 19,005 *bighas* (7,602 acres) of land held under occupancy rights.[29] Similarly, members of the Dalit Pasi caste paid an annual rent of Rs 198,546 and cultivated 49,729 bighas (19,891.60 acres) of land. Compared with the Kurmis' 42,380 bighas (16,952 acres) and the Muraos' 45,574 bighas (18,229.60 acres), the Chamars' cultivation of 19,005 bighas and the Pasis' of 49,729 bighas is impressive and attests to their position in the area as cultivating peasants, rather than simply landless laborers. Even the 1867 inquiry into the rights of the nonproprietary tenants of Awadh (in central UP) documents the claims made by Chamars and Pasis of their right to the land they cultivated, similar to claims made by "lower-caste" peasants like Kurmis, Muraos, and Ahirs.[30] The settlement officers of all the districts in the Awadh region, who wrote reports for this inquiry, recorded claims made by Dalit peasants (Chamars and Pasis) of the right to cultivate their land and contested the right of anyone else to dispossess them from their holdings. Despite the two Oudh Rent Acts of 1868 and 1886, only 1 percent of the vast body of tenants held rights of occupancy, with the rest only provided with security of tenure for a period of seven years.[31] These figures also indicate that many Dalit groups had very good reasons for joining the Awadh Kisan Sabha movement not just as looters taking advantage of a disruptive situation, but as invested members of the movement with much at stake. In the famous police firing on Kisan Sabha activists in the Rae Bareli District in January 1921, the majority of the peasants killed were Dalits. The battle between protestors and the state took place in the town of Rae Bareli at the Fursatganj bazaar and led to a police action that resulted in the deaths of twenty-five peasants.[32] Eighteen of the dead were Chamars and Pasis, suggesting that groups regarded as untouchable made up a large, rather than a marginal, percentage of the overall participants.

Baba Ramachandra, the renowned peasant leader of the Awadh Kisan Sabha movement, mentions the role of Chamar and Pasi peasants in his accounts of the movement in his diaries. In his diary on the movement, Ramachandra notes the presence of Chamars and Pasis prominently in the Kisan Sabha committee meetings at Rure Village in Partabgarh, suggesting that they were part of the movement from the very beginning in 1919 and not just from 1921, when other scholars have claimed that they first appear.[33] The names of thirty-five participating castes are mentioned in the following order by Baba Ramachandra in his diary: "Brahman, Thakur, Baniya, Chauhan, Kurmi, Koeri, Teli, Pasi, Chamar, Barhi, Kahar, Ahir."[34] By listing them alongside other peasant groups, he underlines the important position that the Pasis and the Chamars occupied in the region. He also notes their contribution to the movement in the form of provisions. Baba Ramachandra's description of peasant groups is in sharp contrast to Gyanendra Pandey's description of the Kisan Sabha movement as a movement of Kurmis, Muraos, and Ahirs. Baba Ramachandra stresses the role of Chamars and Pasis not because he sees them as landless laborers whose interests converge with those of peasants, but because he recognizes them as important peasant groups in Awadh region. The settlement reports of Rae Bareli District, the key theater of the Kisan Sabha struggle, attest to the substantive position of Chamars and Pasis as cultivating peasants in the area rather than simply as landless laborers.

It should not surprise us that sections of the Chamar elite that claimed Jatav status (pure Kshatriya identity) and established Jatav organizations in the western UP in the first two decades of the twentieth century belonged to well-off agrarian families. Ramnarain Yadvendu's 1942 book *Yaduvansh ka Aitihas* provides short biographies of dozens of Jatav Mahasabha activists based in Agra and the surrounding region and mentions that many of them, such as Seth Jivan Ram of Mainpuri, were zamindars. Equally notable is that almost all the fifty-nine activists mentioned in the book were high-school graduates who belonged to diverse occupations. The most prominent of these Agra-based activists were "building contractors" and state and federal employees. These activists led the Chamar movement for a Jatav identity during the first four decades of the twentieth century. Seth Sitaram Mansingh, who belonged to "a family of contractors," established the first Jatav organization in Agra City in 1889.[35] He also became a zamindar of the villages Milavda, Agra, and Pingri in Mathura District. The Jatavs of Agra take particular pride in having played an important role in the building of Delhi as the new capital by the British during the first decade of the twentieth century. In the words of one Jatav, "we supplied them with labor and stones."[36] Ram Dayal Jatav, a Chamar contractor of labor and red Jaipuri stones, provided financial support and also chaired the first meeting of the Adi-Hindu Mahasabha (movement to claim Dalits as the original [Adi] inhabitants of India), held in the town of Etawah on October 16, 1923, under the leadership of Swami Achhutanand.[37] We can take this date—thus far unknown in Indian history—as the founding date of Adi-Hindu Mahsabha in UP.[38] The Chamar elite that emerged in the first two decades of the twentieth century in Agra were contractors who acquired wealth by supplying labor to the construction sites in Calcutta and Delhi.[39] These vernacular-language local sources allow us to rethink the dominant explanation of the emergence of an educated and prosperous Chamar elite in the first two decades of the twentieth century to the leather industry.[40] The Jatav literature on the subject offers a starkly different representation of the social origins of the Chamar elite in Agra City and outlines several reasons for Jatavs' investment in claiming a Kshatriya Yadava identity.

The Jatavs of western UP and Jatiyas of eastern UP—along with thirteen other major jatis like the Azamgarihiyas, Aharwars, and Jhusiyas—were categorized as part of the Chamar caste. Given that the category Chamar covered diverse groups of communities who primarily were peasant and, according to the 1911 census, less than 4 percent of whom were leatherworkers, it is unclear on what principle these diverse groups of people were incorporated within the generic term. Despite the Jatavs' preference for a name that identifies their distinctive geographical location, the official classification grouped them with the generic Chamar occupational category. Perhaps equally if not more important was the centrality of village as marker of their identity, producing names like Chamrauli or Chamrauti that gave residents of the village a way to enter the official classificatory regime. We should be cautious in associating these village names with leather work because of the prefix *cham-* as a derivative of *charma* (hides/skins). For instance, it is assumed that the term *Chamrai* refers to a tax on leather, but according to B. T. Stoker, it referred to a range of agricultural taxes on Chamars' plows, land, irrigation, and crops. A seasoned civil service officer who retired as secretary of the UP government, Stoker, in his 1889 assessment report of block Khurja in Bulandshahr District, noted that Chamrai, one of the nine important taxes, was levied at the rate of 1 rupee per plow from tenants who did not render unpaid labor.[41] It is district-level settlement reports like Stoker's that provide detailed information about Dalits that challenge a simplistic understanding of their status and position.[42]

A reliance on colonial sociological sources has reinforced the Hindu textual representation of Chamars as leatherworkers. By emphasizing the role of census and colonial classificatory regimes, the field of postcolonial studies has, unwittingly, reinforced the image of the colonial archive as an imperial monolith. In addition, this understanding has also mapped caste centrally on the varna status. In striking contrast, the district-level revenue reports, embedded in local relationships, offer new ways of thinking about caste and untouchability—especially in spatial, economic, and political terms. Chamars emerge in these reports not as leatherworkers but as peasants who also participated in UP's major peasant movement of the early twentieth century.

Chamars and Dalit Agenda:
Vernacular Narratives and Police Reports

Prioritizing land revenue records over typical caste history sources of colonial sociology—such as the caste and tribe surveys—paid handsome dividends in enabling me to understand claims made in Chamar publications of the 1920s and 1930s and their activism as noted in the police reports of the period. Such an approach empowered me to move beyond the stereotypical representation of Chamars as leatherworkers, demonstrating their substantive relationship to agricultural production and their role in the rural political economy. The issues raised in Dalit publications resonated, quite remarkably, with official descriptions of Chamar political activities recorded in Criminal Intelligence Department reports from 1922 through the 1940s. The land revenue records were important in my understanding of trajectories of Chamar and Dalit histories in northern India, drawing my attention to the groups' agrarian context and their distinctive tenure position in UP. Jatavs' claim for Kshatriya status was not unique but rather was comparable to similar assertions by the "lower-caste" peasant groups such as the Gujars, Jats, Ahirs, and Kurmis in the 1920s.

The 1883 *Statistical, Descriptive and Historical Account of the North-Western Provinces of India* noted that the Chamars of Shahjahanpur District of UP traced their genealogy to the noble Kshatriya Raghubansia family belonging to "the race of Raghu, mythical King of the Solar race."[43] Explaining the context for such claims, Robert Currie noted in 1874 that most of the 101,227 Chamar tenants who possessed occupancy rights were well located in a cultural scenario for asserting a noble Kshatriya identity.[44] These themes were also addressed in four Chamar histories published in northern India in early decades of the twentieth century: the anonymous *Suryavansh Kshatriya Jaiswar Sabha* and works by U. B. S. Raghuvanshi, Pandit Sunderlal Sagar, and Ramnarain Yadvendu.[45]

Most recently, *Chamar Jati ka Gauravshali Aitihas* (A glorious history of the Chamar community) by Satnam Singh rehearsed the stories and accounts mentioned in those histories.[46] The objective of the histories was to engage and challenge Hindu and colonial histories available in the census reports and caste and tribe volumes. Instead of viewing these Chamar jati histories or *vanshavalis* as obscure, representing autonomous voices of subalterns produced in isolation, we should view them as offering us evidence of Chamars' engagement with caste Hindu agendas. The histories' methodological and ideological agendas enlighten us about Chamars' solid engagement with northern Indian literary history.

Claiming a Kshatriya status for Chamars, authors of the Chamar histories were borrowing from the popular *itihasa-puranic* tradition (a collection of genealogical, myth, and historical narratives in Sanskrit); that is, viewing the *Puranas* as historical narratives of writing history, used in numerous caste histories by various social groups around the beginning of the twentieth century. A recognized mode of historical writing employed in Puranic literature, the itihasa-puranic tradition has been described as "embedded histories" used by non-Kshatriya groups to acquire ideological legitimacy by seeking Kshatriya status "embodied in the *itihasa-puranic* tradition."[47] The northern Indian middle-class urban Hindu literati based in towns such as Lahore, Kanpur, Allahabad, and Benares drew from the itihasa-puranic tradition, folklore, and colonial ethnography to question colonial interpretations of the Hindu past.[48] Bharatendu Harischandra, the founder of the modern Hindi language and a leading Hindu notable of Benares, wrote several caste histories in Hindi by borrowing from puranic sources.[49] In terms of their methodology and agendas, the four Chamar histories drew heavily from the itihasa-puranic tradition of writing caste histories. Such a methodology also helps us question the dominant stereotype created by much of anthropological and historical literature that Dalit groups like Chamars were isolated and living on the margins.

In "Khatriyon ki Utpatti" (Origins of the Khattris), Harischandra laid out evidence to uphold claims made by the Khattri community of the Punjab of upper-caste Kshatriya status to challenge the 1871 census classification as Shudras. As an ethnographer, Harischandra borrowed from popular folklore, puranic sources, and Orientalist accounts to claim that even though the Punjabi Khattris were not occupationally Kshatriyas, they were nevertheless still Kshatriyas.[50] He borrowed from colonial accounts to argue that Punjab was the original home of the Aryans and that the Khattris were their descendants, recounting many popular stories to strengthen his claim. Second, Harischandra argued that by adopting the Shudra practices, such as eating meat and taking up menial occupations, Khattris escaped the persecution against Kshatriyas launched in the third century BCE, by the Mauryan Emperor Chandragupta, who was of Shudra or "lower-caste" origin.[51] According to the third story, when Prashuram, the sixth incarnation of Lord Vishnu, launched the war to eliminate the Kshatriyas, the Punjabi Kshatriyas went underground, so to speak—protecting their lives by taking the name Khattri and taking up impure artisan occupations of the "lower castes" and adopting their customs.[52] Harischandra also wrote a history of his caste, a trading community titled "Aggarwaloin ki Utpatti" (Origins of the Aggarwal caste) in which he used a similar methodology to claim that the Aggarwals gave up their Kshatriya status to protect their community from annihilation.[53]

There are noticeable similarities in the methodology employed in Harishchandra's histories of the Khattris and Aggarwals and the histories written by Chamar publicists three decades later. Raghuvanshi used the discovery of a new Chanvar Purana to claim a *suryavanshi* (royal) past by creating a story from the familiar tropes of Hindu epics like the Ramayana and the Mahabharta: the birth of a son, a sage's prediction of the threat to the royal lineage from the son, a maid's sacrifice of her own son to protect the son of the queen, the son's penance (in this case, after he became King Chamunda Rai), penance to achieve *moksha* (salvation), the curse of Lord Vishnu (that in this case led to the loss of the Chamars' Kshatriya status and the recovery of that status in the *kaliyuga* [present time]). In the context of the Ramayana, Sheldon Pollock has described these narratives as "offering us an established constellation of mythological components."[54]

The Chamars claimed in their accounts that they had lost their true Kshatriya status because of persecution or punishment. Sagar innovatively draws evidence from contemporary sources and strengthens his claim by borrowing from the Puranas and folklore. He quotes from an 1882 work by the well-known colonial ethnographer J. C. Nesfield, *Brief View of the Caste System of the North-Western Provinces and Oudh*, which states that Jatavs "may be an occupational off-shoot from the Yadu tribe from which Krishna came," thereby elevating their status through association with the god Krishna.[55] He also quotes from volume 4 of the 1881 *Statistical Descriptive and Historical Accounts of the North-Western Provinces of India* which discusses the Jatavs' claims of a superior status. By claiming a pure Kshatriya status, Chamar publicists were also contesting the colonial formulation of their history that defined them as defiled and unclean. The urban-based caste Hindu literati like Harischandra were writing within a framework that drew from the Puranas and folklore. In their efforts to contest dominant colonial and Hindu narratives of their past, Chamars used the same puranic and oral myths to offer an alternative interpretation of their past, with the immediate political objective of convincing the colonial state of their Kshatriya upper-caste status. The methodology evident in the Chamar literary histories enables us to recognize that they were embedded in an established genre of writing Hindi-language caste histories. In claiming a pure and noble historical past, these histories represent the Chamars' intellectual engagement with a prominent theme of the time.

The weekly police intelligence reports from 1922 to 1949 have been used for writing histories of the anticolonial nationalist movement, and peasant movements, but not for writing the history of the Dalits' struggle for dignity and equality. More than any other colonial source, the police reports provide the most valuable notes on the Dalit movement. By documenting Chamar protests and meetings, these reports provide sociological evidence for claims of noble or Kshatriya status made in Chamar histories. These protests were first noticed in 1921–22 in the western districts of UP, but by 1924 such protests had extended to central and eastern districts as well.[56] I have discussed these protests extensively elsewhere, but here I will give a few examples.[57] For instance, at a vast meeting of four thousand Chamars in the town of Mowane, Meerut District, in November 1922, a series of resolutions was passed claiming a Kshatriya status and vowing to purify their lifestyle.[58] In Mainpuri City, a Chamar association was formed in May 1924 explicitly to claim Kshatriya status for Chamars.[59] Similar meetings were organized by Chamars in different parts of western UP between 1922 and 1932 to assert a noble identity and adopt a pure and clean lifestyle. In addition, other demands were also outlined. From early on, Chamars were eager to show their loyalty to the British government, a fact reflected in the nature of resolutions passed at these meetings. Access to education, the opening of municipal schools for their children by the colonial government, and the starting of their own independent private schools constituted a very important part of their struggle. The agrarian context of the lives of Chamars, which I discussed above, played a very important role in their desire to acquire a new noble identity because the "lower castes," such as the Jats, Ahirs, Gujjars, and Kurmis, were also making similar assertions in UP in the 1920s.

By engaging with puranic and the colonial forms of writing history, and by articulating agendas of social reform, Chamar organizations were involved in debates with various sections of Indian society. One example was the organizations' engagement with Arya Samaj's agenda of Hindu religious reform. In this respect Jatavs' concerns were similar to those of "lower-caste" peasant groups whose members were also involved in religious and social reform activities, in which Arya Samaj played an active role. Arya Samaj addressed the Chamars' agendas of reform and activism. The methodology of Jatav claims for a clean Kshatriya status provided what David Hardiman has called a "meeting point" between Chamar agendas and reformist Hindu organizations such as the Arya Samaj.[60] In his study of *adivasi* (tribal) protest in Gujarat, Hardiman argued that the advasi sought to deprive the dominant Hindu classes "of their power of domination" by appropriating their value systems instead of rejecting them outright.[61] In UP the Arya Samaj facilitated the creation of such a "meeting point" with the Chamar protestors. From the Chamars' point of view, the Arya Samaj certainly played a crucial role, because it criticized Hindu practices like untouchability and organized efforts to open temples and wells to Chamars.

Chamar organizations had first raised two issues of reform—temple entry and access to public wells—between 1917 and 1924, and the Arya Samaj responded to their agenda of social religious reform.[62] Mainstream Hindi nationalist newspapers like *Pratap* and *Abhyudaya* in UP began to report the Arya Samaj's *shuddhi* (purification of untouchables using Hindu religious ceremonies) activism–related activities in March 1924, as did the weekly police reports.[63] A typical Arya Samaj drive would involve purifying Chamars through a shuddhi ceremony, which would be followed by a procession of Chamars to the public well to proclaim their rights to use it and enter a temple. Such initiatives were undertaken in most districts of western UP, from Pilibhit and Dehradun in the north to Jhansi in the south, Meerut in the east, and Mainpuri in the west.[64] Northern India's two recognized liberal newspapers, *Pratap* and *Chand*, published editorials congratulating Arya Samaj for its agenda of reforming the Hindu religion and putting untouchability on the agenda of caste Hindu society.[65] The right to enter temples and bathe in the Yamuna River during the Garhmukteshwar fair was first demanded in March 1923, in Meerut City. In Benares, Chamars demanded access to the Vishwanath temple and to the Dashavmegha ghat for bathing.[66] In Allahabad, Purshottam Das Tandon and Madan Mohan Malaviya led Chamars to the temples of Alopi Devi in Prayag. Both temples were later purified by priests. The Arya Samaj also used the Hindu festivals of Holi and Dussehra to incorporate Chamars into an imagined Hindu community of equals. Such functions were organized in Meerut City, Bulandshahr, Agra, Moradabad, Pilibhit, Bijnor, and Muthra, where Hindus were urged to embrace Chamars in the festivals.[67]

The agenda of the Arya Samaj found a very receptive audience among Chamars, a relationship that was further cemented by opposition from orthodox Hindus that put the Arya Samaj and Chamar reformers on the same radical plane. The first and second generations of activists belonging to the Jatav community were educated in schools run by the Arya Samaj. The early Chamar advocates Pandit Sunderlal Sagar and Ramnarain Yadvendu were both educated in those schools, and both of their families were members of the Arya Samaj. Swami Achhutanand, who was educated in an army school, joined the Arya Samaj in 1905 and worked with it until 1918. He established and taught in an Arya Samaj school in Manipuri District and was an active participant in its activities. Jatav organizations in Agra and other parts of western UP advocated vegetarianism and Vedic style rituals. The ideals of the Arya Samaj had a particular appeal to Chamars because they strengthened Chamar claims to superior status.

By recognizing the embeddedness of Chamar Hindi-language histories and their political activism in the northern Indian cultural and political milieu, we can move beyond the stereotypical representations of Chamars as a marginal and isolated group. The Hindi-language Chamar histories, as well as the cultural and political meetings reported by the police reports, inform us about a Chamar elite that was well informed and participated in debates that concerned other groups of Indians. Chamars were not passive recipients but active agents of social and political change.

Conclusion

The notion of a unified colonial archive rests primarily on the sources of colonial sociology, the census and caste and tribe surveys, which inform much of the debate on the subject, including the study of caste. A reconsideration of archival sources for writing Dalit histories by emphasizing the role of local-level revenue records turned out to be a major unintended methodological innovation. Land revenue records have rarely, if ever, been used to write Chamar histories. In addition, the ethnographic approach of engaging with Dalit activists during archival research in different parts of UP illuminated new connections and linkages with the themes embedded in the revenue reports. A focus on the district-level settlement reports of the 1880s, with their detailed revenue and rent information, allowed me to grasp Chamars' locations in the different regions of UP. My focus on this strategy was motivated and inspired by the kinds of questions and discussions I had with Dalit activists in different towns of northern India. My second strategy of engaging with Dalit activists proved most beneficial in assisting me with getting documents (the local caste histories) from their personal collections that are not usually available at metropolitan archives. It also connected well with my third priority, creating connections with the accounts available in police intelligence reports, the only source of Dalit activism for the early twentieth century. The police accounts provided detailed information that resonated with the claims of Kshatriya status made in Chamar Hindi-language histories. These nontraditional sources, like settlement reports or police reports, are rarely emphasized in the writing of Dalit histories, in contrast to a solely ethnographic live-in methodology to search for authentic voices.

The postcolonial notion of the colonial archive, although useful in many ways, relies far too much on the sources of colonial sociology. There is a real danger of ignoring land revenue records of localities, which we must recognize as new sources for writing Dalit histories. We must register a substantive distinction between the notion of the colonial archive and colonial sociology to avoid merging the two into one. Instead, we may want to think of colonial archives as a form that is informed by the "genres of documentation" that were generated by diverse motives. We may want to underscore the heterogeneity of the colonial archive, informed by the local-level motivations that shape land revenue documents but markedly absent in the sources of colonial sociology. Recognizing these motivations encouraged me write a new history of untouchability in northern India.

NOTES

1. *Census of India, 1911*, vol. 15, part 2: *Tables*, 756–62. See also, *Census of India, 1961*, vol. 15, part 5, 4–7.

2. Interview with J. R. Kaniria, resident of Gawalior, Madhya Pradesh, March 3, 2009.

3. Cohn, *An Anthropologist among the Historians and Other Essays*, 230 and 250.

4. Dirks, *Castes of Mind*, 44–45. See also Gyanendra Pandey, *The Construction of Communalism in Colonial North India*, chapter 3; Pant, "The Cognitive Status of Caste in Colonial Ethnography."

5. Dirks, *Castes of Mind*, 94.

6. This is the main point of difference between parts 2 and 3 in ibid.

7. Ibid, 118.

8. Amin, introduction, xxxix.

9. *Collection of Papers Connected with an Inquiry into the Conditions of the Lower Classes of the Population*, 8.

10. Stoler, *Along the Archival Grain*, 20.

11. Ibid., 11.

12. Steedman, *Dust*, 12–13.

13. Burns, *Into the Archive*, 11–12.

14. Moon, *Growing Up Untouchable in India*, 175; Namishray, *Apne-Apne Pinjare*, 17.

15. Rawat, "Occupation, Dignity, and Space."

16. P. Deshpande, "Caste as Maratha," 32.

17. Hooper, *Report of the Settlement of the Basti District*, 28; see also 18–22.

18. Crosthwaite and Neale, *Report of the Settlement of the Etawah District*, 20. See also Clark, *Report on the Revision of Settlement of the Bharaich District, Oudh*, 66; Currie, *Report on the Settlement of the Shahjehanpore District*, 61; Reid, *Report on the Settlement Operations in the District of Azamgarh*, 31; T. Smith, *Report on the Revision of Settlement in the District of Aligarh*, 130; Wright, *Report of the Settlement of the Cawnpore District*, 46.

19. *Further Papers Relating to Under-Proprietary Rights and Rights of Cultivators in Oude; Collection of Papers Connected with an Inquiry into the Conditions of the Lower Classes of the Population; Collection of Papers Relating to the Conditions of the Tenancy and the Working of Present Rent Law in Oudh.*

20. Boas, *Report on the Eleventh Settlement of the Moradabad*, 10.

21. Drake-Brockman, *Report on the Settlement Operations of the Saharanpur District, 1921*, 25–26.

22. Fremantle, *Report on the Settlement of the District Bareilly, 1903*, 4–5.

23. Evans, *Report on the Settlement of the Agra District, 1880*, 28–29; Mudie, *Report on the Settlement and Record Operations in District Agra, 1930*, 20.

24. Stoker, *Report on the Settlement of Land Revenue in the Bulandshahr District, 1891*, 16–21.

25. Impey, *Report on the Settlement of the Jhansi District, 1893*, 91.

26. Drake-Brockman, *Report on the Settlement Operations of the Saharanpur District, 1921*, 12.

27. Evans, *Report on the Settlement of the Agra District, 1880*, 57.

28. Atkinson, *Statistical, Descriptive and Historical Account of the North-Western Provinces of India*, 3:560–61.

29. Fremantle, *Report on the Second Settlement of the Rae Bareli*, 19.

30. *Further Papers Relating to Under-Proprietary Rights and Rights of Cultivators in Oude*, reports by Maconochie, Settlement Officer, Oonao [or Unnao], March 16, 1865, 386 and 407, Harrington, Settlement Officer, [block] Durriabad, Lucknow District, April 4, 1865, p. 518, Settlement Officer, Hurdui [or Hardoi], April 30, 1865, p. 154.

31. Siddiqi, *Agrarian Unrest in Northern India*, 10–15.

32. "Report on the Awadh Peasant Movement," 687–93, F. No.50/1921/B. No. 133–4 General Administration Department, Uttar Pradesh State Archives, Lucknow (hereafter UPSA).

33. "Papers Relating to Peasant Movement of 1921," 21, File No. 1, Baba Ramachandra Papers, Nehru Memorial Museum and Library, Delhi.

34. Ibid.

35. Yadvendu, *Yaduvansh ka Aitihas*, 133.

36. Interview with Puttulal Jatav, September 12, 2002. Born in 1927, he has been involved since the mid-1940s with Jatav politics in Agra, where he now lives as a retired district judge.

37. See chapters 4 and 5 in Rawat, *Reconsidering Untouchability*.

38. Ibid. And, Jatav, *Shree 108 Swami Achhutanand ji ka Jeevan Parichay*, 14; R. Singh, *Achhutanand Harihar*, 41.

39. Yadvendu, *Yaduvansh ka Aitihas*, 206–31. Yadvendu was an important member of the Jatav Mahasabha and a founder of the All India Jatav Youth League in 1932.

40. Briggs, *The Chamars*; Wiser and Wiser, *Behind the Mud Walls*.

41. Stoker, *Assessment Report of Tahsil Khurja of the Bulandshahr District*, 27.

42. "Rasad and Begari Agitation in UP, 1920," 1 and 3, file no. 694, box no. 153/1920, GAD, UPSA.

43. *Statistical, Descriptive and Historical Account of the North-Western Provinces of India* 9:88.

44. Currie, *Report on the Settlement of the Shahjehanpore District*, 61.

45. Raghuvanshi, *Shree Chanvar Purana*; Sagar, *Yadav Jivan*; *Suryavansh Kshatriya Jaiswar Sabha*; Yadvendu, *Yaduvansh ka Aitihas*.

46. Satnam Singh, *Chamar Jati ka Gauravshaali Aitihas*, chapters 8–15. The book's publisher, Samyak Prakashan, is a prominent Dalit publishing house in Delhi, and it has published books on Dalit leaders and Buddhism, and posters and calendars.

47. Thapar, *Cultural Pasts*, 135.

48. Dalmia, "Vernacular Histories in Late Nineteenth-Century Banaras," 60.

49. Ibid.

50. Ibid., 78.

51. Harischandra, "Khatriyon ki Utpatti," 247–50.

52. Ibid., 251–53.

53. Harischandra, "Aggarwaloin ki Utpatti," 5–12.

54. Pollock, "The Ramayana," 3:38.

55. Quoted in Sagar, *Yadav Jivan*, 21.

56. I make this statement on the basis of a detailed study of the reports of the weekly police reports from 1922–32. Officially known as the Police Abstracts of Weekly Intelligence, they are available in the Criminal Investigation Department office in Lucknow, UP and are cited hereafter as PAI. The evidence for such protests is available from 1922, when the PAI series starts. The activities mentioned in PAI were not reported in the nationalist press, particularly *Pratap*, *Abhyudhuya*, and *Aj*, which began to report such activities only in 1924 with the beginning of the Arya Samaj's shuddhi activism, or the practice of purifying untouchables.

57. Rawat, *Reconsidering Untouchability*, 120–54.

58. PAI, November 4, 1922.

59. PAI, May 24, 1924.

60. Hardiman, *The Coming of the Devi*, 163.

61. Ibid.

62. PAI, November 3 and 10, 1923.

63. *Pratap*, March 3, 1924; *Abhyudaya*, May 17 and June 21, 1924; PAI, March 1, 1924.

64. PAI, January 20, April 14, May 5, May 26, June 2, June 9, June 16, June 26, June 30, October 20, and October 27, 1923; February 9, March 1, April 5, April 19, May 3, May 10, May 17, August 26, September 9, and September 13, 1924; May 23, August 1, August 15, October 17, and December 19, 1925; February 13, May 15, May 29, June 26, July 24, October 9, and November 16, 1926; April 23 and October 1, 1927; July 21, August 18, and October 13, 1928. The records indicate the peak of Arya Samaj activities and a decline from 1926 onward.

65. Rawat, *Reconsidering Untouchability*, 136–44.

66. *Pratap*, April 10 and June 1, 1925; *Chand*, May 1927.

67. *Pratap*, March 24 and August 11, 1924; *Abhyudaya*, August 16, 1924, and March 31, 1928; PAI, March 10 and November 3, 1923; April 5, October 18, and October 25, 1924; April 2 and October 8, 1927.

3

Social Space, Civil Society, and Dalit Agency in Twentieth-Century Kerala

P. SANAL MOHAN

The modern social space in Kerala was created through mobilizations in which Dalit movements played a crucial role. However, this story is unknown outside Kerala. The anonymity of Dalit movements is directly linked to an elitist historiography that emphasized the roles of the Ezhava movement, the Sree Narayana Dharma Paripalana (SNDP) movement, the movements of other upper castes such as the Nairs or Namboodiri Brahmans, and later the communist movement as the harbingers of modernity in Kerala society. Such elitist histories and historiographies have dominated the intellectual and political sphere, circulating several myths about contemporary Kerala. Yet no Dalit intellectual endeavors have emerged to challenge these ideas. This essay attempts to analyze some of the crucial issues problematized by the Dalit movements of the early twentieth century that made Dalit engagements with modern social space and civil society in Kerala possible. Modern civil society could emerge in Kerala only because of the relentless struggles waged against caste domination and oppression. It is necessary to identify here the most significant moments in the struggles that are crucial to the formation of modern civil society in Kerala.

From the perspective of Dalit history it is difficult to think of civil society without referring to the mobilization against caste slavery in the mid-nineteenth century. The social space and civil society in Kerala was caste determined. The modern middle class that became decisive in the formation of civil society was almost exclusively constituted of the upper castes— including the Ezhavas, although they are referred to as a backward caste. A close examination of the mid-nineteenth-century developments in various regions of Kerala shows that in spite of regional differences there were certain visible trends that vouchsafed a colonial transformation. We may identify several aspects of colonial modernity that began to evolve during this phase. The ideas of missionary Christianity, such as the notions of salvation and improvement or the agenda of social transformation were beginning to reach the Dalit communities in the native states of Kerala.[1] As the Anglican missionaries were trying to work among the slave castes from the late 1840s on, the possibility of an alternative public also began to evolve. This alternative public was exemplified in what the missionaries termed slave schools and chapels, where slave-caste men, women, and children were taught the word of the Lord. In addition to this, basic literacy was imparted to them.

A close reading of missionary writings of the mid-nineteenth century in the Travancore region of Kerala shows how much missionaries were concerned with the changes in the habits of Dalits who joined the missions. Following John Comaroff and Jean Comaroff, one may call it a "revolution in habits."[2] Changes in habits were important for the evolution of Dalits as modern citizens. Moreover, in the prevailing situation of distance pollution and untouchability, slave-caste men and women had to evolve as socially presentable bodies by adopting new social practices. This would be possible only if they abandoned habits that the upper castes abhorred. It appears that such a change of habits had been considered as fundamental for claiming social space and becoming part of the evolving civil society that was always inimical to them. Sometimes the missionaries asked their congregations to refrain from eating carcasses. This, they said, would raise the Dalits in the eyes of the upper castes as well as of the Syrian Christians in the Anglican congregation. This disciplining assumes significance when combined with the fact that even as late as the early decades of the twentieth century the Syrian Christians would invoke health sciences and notions of hygiene to support the segregation of Dalit Christians in the churches.[3]

Beginning with the example of the liberation of the slaves of the Munroe island whom the missionaries purchased along with the land and later liberated as free individuals ascribing them the new status of laborers to be hired, we witness the coming of the notion of wage labor instead of slave labor which was a significant matter considering the fact that such a notion was alien to the native society.[4] As far as the slaves were concerned, this was an important moment as the new experiment offered them the possibility of evolving into free laborers, which would liberate their bodies and minds from the control of the masters. However, this evolution did not occur, as the abolition of slavery did not mean the abolition of its condition of existence— that is, the caste system that determined the social power relations in which the slaves had to live even after their formal liberation in 1885. As a result, the social hierarchy continued to exist largely unchallenged even after the abolition of slavery. Abolition was an integral part of Dalit political agency in the late nineteenth century. In the first half of the twentieth century, with the coming of the anticaste movements, the political agency of Dalits underwent significant changes. It may be pointed out here that modern civil society emerged in Kerala in the first half of the twentieth century through the struggles against the caste-determined social and public sphere.

In spite of the histories of social movements such as the Sadhu Jana Paripalana Sangham (SJPS, Society for the Protection of the Poor), led by Ayyankali; the Prathyaksha Raksha Daiva Sabha (PRDS, Church of God of Revealed Salvation) of Poyikayil Yohannan (known after his death as Sree Kumara Guru Devan); and Pampady John Joseph's Cheramar Mahajana Sabha (Association of Cheramar Dalits), the reigning paradigms of historiography remain unchallenged.[5] It is pertinent at this point to analyze how Dalits figured in historiographical discourses. Prominent events of the nationalist movement have been the staple of historians of modern Kerala. Many of these narratives highlighted the events of the anticolonial mobilization in the Malabar region, which was under the Madras presidency. Although most histories of the Indian National Congress from the nationalist perspective emphasized its anticolonial character, it was in effect an elite movement based on the initiatives of the middle-class legal professionals in Calicut.[6] The native states of Cochin and Travancore, constituting the southern part of Kerala, were under the indirect rule of the British. The policy of the Indian National Congress was to work in the native states through its political affiliates. In both native states there developed nationalist politics, with distinct organizations such as the Travancore State Congress and Cochin Praja Mandalam (Cochin State Congress).[7]

Marxist historiography has emphasized the history of working-class mobilization under the communists in various parts of Kerala that was instrumental in the development of radical politics and the subsequent policy interventions of the postcolonial phase, such as the land reforms of the 1970s.[8] The Dalit movements in the early twentieth century had problematized the oppressive conditions that caste domination had produced. Dalit movements had used all available means to press for Dalit demands such as access to public space, cultural and symbolic capital, human dignity, and civil rights. These issues never figured in the historiographical debates as they did not directly challenge the colonial powers; sometimes the colonial powers reacted favorably to the demands of Dalits and other "lower castes." Most historiographies failed to reconsider colonialism from the multiple locations of the colonized as they had a one-dimensional view of colonialism. This refers to their understanding of colonialism as uniformly incapacitating the colonized, without taking into account forms of exploitation and oppression that preceded colonialism and that continued to exist even as colonialism succeeded in establishing its domination. In the case of Kerala, caste formation qualifies as such a form since the types of oppression that it created continued under colonialism. This obliges us to see how caste oppression was dealt with in historiography.

The most eloquent representation of caste oppression is available in the nineteenth-century accounts of missionaries that were printed and circulated in publications that had an international reach.[9] It is in the course of such writings that the missionaries problematized the historical caste slavery of Dalits in nineteenth-century Kerala. This should be considered as the moment of Dalits' entry into historical records in a spectacular manner. We shall consider the missionary writings as a distinct historiographic genre. Most studies on slavery in Kerala had referred to the existence of slave castes, and there is a historiography of slavery that refers to the origins of caste slavery in the precolonial social formations, sometimes stretching back to ancient times.[10] The latter-day historians of the European Christian missions in Kerala depended a great deal on the historical information available on the slave-caste communities in missionary writings. Many of these scholars are dismissive of the spiritual dimensions of Dalit engagement with missionary Christianity.[11] However, the source materials of various Dalit religious movements contradict those views.[12]

Religious Conversion to Modernity

Historically there have been two visible trends in Dalit mobilization from the mid-nineteenth century. The first and most important trend was the acceptance of missionary Christianity by Dalits from the 1850s onward. This experience was decisive in transforming their individual and social selves. The abolition of caste slavery in 1855 took place a couple of years after the first Dalit "joined the way of Christ" in the Travancore region of Kerala as part of a movement. By the early decades of the twentieth century, thousands of Dalits, mostly from the Pulayar and Parayar communities, had joined the church. Contrary to an instrumentalist understanding of the Dalit interface with the missionaries, one could reconfigure these interactions as a "contact zone" that made it possible for different trends to flourish simultaneously. The notion of a "contact zone," according to Mary Louise Pratt, "is an attempt to invoke the spatial and temporal copresence of subjects previously separated by geographic and historical disjunctures, and whose trajectories now intersect." She also uses the term "contact" to "foreground the interactive, improvisational dimensions of colonial encounters so easily ignored or suppressed by diffusionist accounts of conquest and domination."[13] This perspective allows us to map the contested spaces that missionaries and Dalits occupied simultaneously. By the first decade of the twentieth century, more than half of the Church Missionary Society (CMS) members in the Travancore region of Kerala was drawn from Dalit communities, in spite of the fact that they were discriminated against in the church.

The second trend, which had obvious connections with the first, was the genesis of powerful social and religious movements of Dalits from the first decade of the twentieth century onward. These movements fall into two broad categories that are similar to movements in other parts of India. First, some of the movements were sociopolitical and political in character—they addressed mostly political, economic, and social problems of Dalit communities. These problems included the continuing manifestations of caste slavery, access to social and public spaces, access to modern education, ownership of land, access to modern institutions such as the judiciary, and rejection of demeaning social practices imposed on the community by the upper castes. The second category of the movements was religious: through intervention in the religious sphere, they opened up another front of social praxis and created an alternative public that simultaneously engaged with the spiritual and material realms.

In the context of Kerala, religious movements evolved because of the dominance of caste within the churches, which forced Dalits to create their own churches and religious movements. This involved a problematization of the sacred realm of the church and a critique of the Bible, as accomplished by Poikayil Yohannan.[14] While the SJPS falls in the first category of movements, Yohannan's movement, the PRDS, falls in the second. There were many other exclusively Dalit churches or congregations in the early twentieth century that were radical responses to the prevalence of caste discrimination within the mainstream churches due to the hegemony of upper-caste Syrian Christians. In addition, there were individual Dalits who had established small groups of followers through their new religious ideas derived from the Bible, which the European missionaries critiqued as heresies.[15] For the present purpose, such movements can be thought of as another form of anticaste mobilization, although they functioned in the realm of religion. All these mobilizations were determined by the agency of Dalits, which reached a turning point in the early decades of the twentieth century.

One of the significant results of Dalit interaction with European missionary Christianity had been the articulation of a new and different consciousness by Dalits that was very complex. This consciousness is not adequately encompassed within the instrumentalist analysis of scholarship on missions, which interprets Dalits' attraction to missionary Christianity as merely an effort to improve their socioeconomic position. Dalit consciousness found expression in social movements that problematized all aspects of their subordination. There was another closely related opinion held by some of the missionaries as well as the later scholars of missions: that Dalits did not understand the high moral principles of religion.[16] Some scholars went so far as to argue that even Dalits' prayers were purely instrumentalist, meant only to get something from God.[17] In the first half of the twentieth century there were several powerful movements in various Dalit communities, such as the SJPS of the foremost Dalit leader of Kerala, Ayyankali, which had members not just from the Pulayas; the PRDS of Yohannan; Cheramar Mahajana Sabha of Pampady John Joseph; and a host of other organizations that occupied almost the same social space although within different communities. It may be observed that theoretically Ayyankali's and Yohannan's movements were open to all Dalits, irrespective of their caste background. There were other organizations such as Brahma Prathyaksha Raksha Dharma Paripalana (Organization of Parayars to Protect the Revealed Salvation of Social Order of Brahma), Parayar Mahajana Sangham of Kantan Kumaran and movements led by other popular leaders such as Paradi Abraham Issac and Vellikkara Chothi, who were named to the Popular Legislature of Travancore. There existed spaces in which these movements could interact socially and politically. Of them, the SJPS was the most widespread in the Travancore region of Kerala, having a thousand branches at the peak of its prominence.[18] Similarly, in 1926 the PRDS had 10,000 followers in sixty-three parishes.[19]

Modern civil society emerged in Kerala in the first half of the twentieth century through the struggles against the caste-determined social and public sphere. The social movement of Ezhavas under the leadership of Sree Narayana Guru is generally considered to be a paradigmatic reformist movement in Kerala. However, it would be wrong to reduce Dalit movements to offshoots of this movement. Because of the economic development of the Ezhava community in the second half of the nineteenth century, a powerful upwardly mobile middle class evolved in the community that spearheaded the movement. Although the Ezhavas also suffered from caste disabilities such as untouchability, their situation was not as severe as those of the Dalit communities whose members were not allowed to use public roads and institutions. Even by traditional standards of distance pollution, Ezhavas remained in a better position than Dalits, who had historically been agrarian slaves. In spite of the caste disabilities that the Ezhavas had experienced, by the late nineteenth century they were able to use the avenues opened up in the context of colonial modernity to come to the public domain along with the so-called Malayalis, or Nairs, and to submit a petition known as Malayali Memorial in 1891 to the native ruler of Travancore. The petition was signed by ten thousand people—mostly Nairs, with a smattering of Syrian Christians and Ezhavas—who voiced their concern over the monopolizing of the jobs under the Travancore government by what they referred to as foreigners, meaning not the British, but non-Malayali Brahmans.[20]

The memorial did not help the Ezhavas in any way, and the educated members of the community had to leave their native state of Travancore and seek employment elsewhere in British India. It was in this context that they submitted their own memorial, the Ezhava Memorial, raising their demands for employment in 1896. The memorial was signed by 13,176 Ezhavas.[21] But in the last decade of the nineteenth century the new middle-class Ezhavas formed the reformist movement SNDP and started their forays into the evolving civil society by establishing modern institutions. The first institution was a temple in 1887 at Aruvippuram near Neyyattinkara, south of Trivandrum, in which Sree Narayana Guru consecrated the image of Siva, thus challenging the ritual privilege of Brahmans in consecrating a deity. In the traditional reading of the modernization of Kerala, this is considered the epitome of the anticaste moment, which led to social revolution in Kerala. In subsequent years, under the leadership of Sree Narayana Guru, there were several other temple consecrations. After a while, he suggested that what the people required most were temples of learning—modern educational institutions. His radical thinking was at its best when he consecrated in one of the temples a mirror as the presiding deity. Sree Narayana Guru's interventions in the social and religious realm of Kerala created an environment in which anticaste progressive thinking and action could thrive. From the Adviata Vedanta tradition represented by him to the atheistic thinking and practice of Sahodaran Ayyappan, multiple ideological positions flourished within the SNDP. Another important aspect of the movement is the critical use of the resources of the Sanskritic tradition, which Ezhavas could access. What is notable here is the innovative use of the tradition by Sree Narayana Guru to establish a modern religious movement.

In contrast, the Dalit movements in Kerala in the early twentieth century could not draw on a high traditional culture as a resource for engagement with modernity. They therefore completely adapted to modernity, since it was the only resource open to them. However, they had to wage relentless struggles to access some of the resources that modernity offered to them. The major developments in Kerala in the nineteenth and twentieth centuries that could be considered as markers of modernity had a distinct impact on Dalits in general and certain communities in particular. Christianity had been in Kerala from the early Christian centuries, prior to or simultaneous with its taking root in European society. However, we do not find any Dalits becoming Christian in traditional Kerala society. Dalits' conversion to Christianity as a social phenomenon occurred only from the 1850s onward, although Anglican missionaries had been in Kerala since the early nineteenth century.[22] Anglican missionaries initially worked with traditional Christians to help them acquire modern practices and encourage them to accept Anglican methods. This led to differences between the traditional Christians and the Anglican missionaries and to the final severing of connections between the two groups in 1836.

It was after this break with the traditional Jacobite Church that Anglican missionaries of the CMS discovered Dalit communities. The Dalits' interaction with Anglican missionaries was entirely different. It was the first time that anybody had approached them with a purpose different from that of their masters. The missionaries who went to the slave castes of Kerala were subjects of modernity, which enabled them to see the denial of freedom and justice to the slave castes and their inalienable rights as human beings that their creator had bestowed on them. Unlike many other colonial Christian missionaries who worked in agreement with slave traders and the system of slavery, the Anglican missionaries in Kerala in the mid-nineteenth century were abolitionists. They were able to rouse the imagination of the untouchable slave castes with their antislavery posture and mobilization, thus bringing modernity to them. I shall call this a crucial moment of Dalit engagement with modernity, which transformed them into "conscripts of modernity." From this perspective I shall argue that the Dalits' conversion in Kerala in the mid-nineteenth century was a double conversion: not only a religious conversion, but also a conversion to modernity.[23]

No community in Kerala had adapted to modern ideas and institutions to the extent that the Dalits did, though the road to transformation was new, uncertain, and tortuous. This is largely because of their slave status, from which they had to evolve into modern subjects. I shall make a comparison here with the Ezhava community, which was charting another course on the journey into modernity. In certain regions of Travancore such as Mavelikkara, Ezhavas had joined the CMS. Missionary accounts of the late nineteenth and early twentieth centuries provide explicit information on the Ezhava background of some congregations.[24] But the missionaries' work among the Ezhavas never achieved the visible success as it did among the Pulayar and Parayar communities. The peculiar position of the Ezhavas in the caste hierarchy would explain why they did not convert en masse, as happened in Dalit communities. In the caste hierarchy, Ezhavas were above Dalit communities such as Pulayas and Parayas but below Nairs and Namboodiris, who regarded them as polluting untouchables. In the British Malabar region of Kerala, the German missionaries of the Basel Evangelical Mission had the majority of their converts coming from the Tiyya community, which occupied the same social position as that of the Ezhavas in the south of Kerala.[25] In the early decades of the twentieth century, members of the Ezhava community were campaigning for the removal of caste disabilities that prevented them from entering Hindu temples for worship, and one section of the Ezhava movement was in favor of conversion to Christianity or Sikhism, or remaining atheists.[26] It is interesting to see that Sree Narayan Guru did not have any objection to such proposals being discussed by the people of the community. Throughout the 1920s, the Ezhavas held out the threat of mass conversion, and this threat was the major reason why temple entry was permitted in 1936.[27] This permission has been hailed as a crucial moment in the formation of the Hindu community in Kerala. The Ezhavas became Hindus even as they were threatening to leave Hinduism. Such a move would have discredited the native state of Travancore, which was supposed to be a Hindu state ruled by a sovereign on behalf of a Hindu deity, although the raja and the kingdom had already come under British paramountcy.

Another crucial moment of modernity for Dalits was their introduction to socialist and communist ideas. The communist movement had a decisive impact on the Dalit communities in Kerala. Communist ideas of equality found ready acceptance among Dalit communities, and communist parties continue to have substantial influence among Dalits in spite of the inroads made among Dalits in Kerala by other political parties, including the Congress Party, the Bharatiya Janata Party, and regional political parties. As has happened in the case of many oppressed social groups, ideologies and movements that seek an egalitarian and just future society were readily accepted by Dalits. Quite often such movements spread in these groups through kinship ties and social relations.

The movement of Ayyankali, the SJPS, was founded in 1907 and thus preceded the caste reform movements among the Nairs and Namboodiris.[28] It was second only to the movement of the Ezhavas in order of appearance. This chronology is important, as it refers to the coming of new ideas of modernity and modern forms of political mobilization among Dalits. The most significant political act of Ayyankali was his forced entry into public space that was specifically closed to Dalits. In 1898 he broke the ban on entering the public road imposed upon the Pulayas and other Dalit communities by riding in a decorated bullock cart, a mode of travel reserved for upper-caste people. Entry into the public space was to become a major feature of the movement in the years to come. Ayyankali's followers in other parts of southern Kerala mobilized locally, which led to several open confrontations between Dalits and members of upper castes in various parts of Travancore.[29] One major mobilization in Quilon in 1915 erupted in a riot in which both Dalit and Nair houses were set on fire. When Ayyankali was consulted for guidance by the local leaders, he advised them to retaliate, stating that they had nobody to support them except God, and that the only course open to them was to carry the movement forward. Immediately following the riots, the local leaders, in consultation with Ayyankali, made arrangements for a public meeting in Quilon that was also attended by some upper-caste reformist leaders. In the course of his speech there, Ayyankali exhorted his people to continue to mobilize and asked the upper castes not to oppose anticaste mobilizations.[30]

This movement had repercussions in various parts of Travancore, as Dalits under the leadership of Ayyankali were ready to violate the code of spatial control and discipline that had been in existence for centuries. Ayyankali had organized a small group of men that by then had become famous as Ayyankali Pada (Ayyankali's army). In 1898 he led another expedition on the public road from his village, Venganoor, to Aralummood, defying the prohibition on the Pulayas.[31] These rebellious acts, as I noted above, had a domino effect in mobilizing Dalits to claim public space, and the acts resulted in violence in many parts of Travancore as Dalits clashed with upper-caste opponents.

In the first decade of the twentieth century, a new politics began to emerge with the coming of Dalit movements. Movements like the SJPS were very radical in their mobilizations and programs. Ayyankali led the movement to claim access to public spaces such as roads and markets that were essential for securing the civil rights of Dalit communities. Similarly, he led struggles to secure school admission for Pulaya children, which led to violent clashes between Pulayas and members of upper castes. In 1913, in the face of opposition from upper-caste Nairs, Ayyankali led the first Pulaya agricultural workers' strike for school admission for Pulaya children.[32] The strike lasted for a year, and the Pulayas of South Travancore region endured in spite of being without wages and experiencing severe threats to their livelihood.[33] In this situation they sought the help of the fishing community of Vizhinjam, which is in close proximity to Ayyankali's village, Venganoor. The strike was remarkable in that the fundamental issue at stake was not economic demands such as increased wages. On the contrary, the strike raised a strongly contested cultural issue, that of school admission for Pulaya children. Ayyankali demanded that the government order of 1907 granting admission to everyone irrespective of caste be implemented without any changes. This was followed by mobilization in various parts of the Travancore region on the question of school admission for Dalit children. In 1914 the attempt of Pulayas to have their children admitted to a school at Pullad, in central Travancore, led to clashes with Nairs and Syrian Christians. Similarly, in the village of Ooroottamblam, near Trivandrum, the efforts of Ayyankali to have a girl named Punchami admitted to the local school led to riots by Nairs, who subsequently set fire to the school.[34]

What infuriated the upper castes was the Dalit emphasis on education above all other things in the changing social context. Dalit social movements of the early twentieth century carried on the program of social change, which in many ways was reminiscent of the project that the missionaries had envisaged. Anglican missionaries had initiated educational projects among Dalits from the very beginning of their work with the community, although those projects were confined to the elementary skills of reading and writing. Similarly, the missionaries had taken up the question of access to public space when they found that the Dalit members of their congregation, including teachers, were not allowed to use the public roads.[35] By the late nineteenth century, the rulers of Travancore had laid down rules to enforce Pulayas' access to public spaces, but the local bureaucracy and the upper castes effectively kept such rules from being implemented. Opposition to the Pulaya use of public roads was so intense that some of the missionaries in the early 1890s observed that such restrictions would end only if powerful movements emerged from within Dalit communities.[36]

As there were oppositions to admitting Dalit children to existing schools, Ayyankali started a school in his village in 1904. In the words of the historian T. H. P. Chentharassery, "the first school started by him was demolished and burnt by the upper castes on the very first day of its establishment."[37] With regard to education, the opposition from the upper castes was reminiscent of the nineteenth-century burning of slave schools and chapels in many parts of Travancore, as the upper castes—both Christian and Hindu—feared that the liberation of slaves would jeopardize their agricultural interests.

It would be instructive to think of the manner in which the Dalit movements tried to address the challenges they were facing. They adopted modern forms of associations and mobilization. Such associations necessitated organizational work and training people in methods that were new to them. The Dalits might have used the prevailing practices of missionaries as a model, as some in the leadership of the Dalit movement, like V. J. Thomas Vadhyar and Haris Vadhyar, were teachers in the mission schools.[38] The struggles of Ayyankali and his organization to establish the right to education would enhance their belief in the significance of education. In traditional society the slave castes were not allowed any access to learning. Ayyankali realized the urgency of the need to educate the new generation even though it was beyond the Dalits' means, and financial support from the government was not forthcoming. Ayyankali's statement that he wished to see ten graduates in his community is often recalled to show the importance that he attributed to the educational development of Dalit communities. It is also important to reiterate that Pulayas and other Dalit communities were never allowed to learn or participate in intellectual life and knowledge production. Ayyankali and other representatives of various Dalit communities raised the issue of education in the legislative assembly of Travancore. Without going into further details of the history of the movement, I shall argue that the task ahead for the Dalits in the first half of the twentieth century was very formidable. One of the major differences between the movement of Ayyankali and the movement of Sree Narayana Guru was that the former was not explicitly concerned with religion. It may be recalled here that in the beginning of his public activism, Ayyankali was influenced by some of the reformists. During the initial stages of his movement he had interactions with a reformist sannyasi, Sadananda Swami, and his reformist organization, Brahma Nishta Matam.[39]

Swami feared that the Dalits would convert to Christianity and tried to impress on the upper castes the consequences of not giving civil rights to Dalits. The upper castes were not ready to listen to his counsel. A Hindu reformist constituency developed that wanted to establish some influence in Dalit communities, and the Hindus were able to do so at a later stage, although it was not a big success. However, Ayyankali was not impressed with the religious reformist ideas of Swami, and he continued his mobilization projects.[40] Similarly, we do not find Ayyankali or his movement investing in establishing temples or making temple entry their major issue. Instead, Ayyankali's concerns were to fight for entry into the modern social space, mobilize people to acquire cultural capital through modern education, fight for the dignity of the community, and fight against all forms of humiliation that were heaped on them. Cultural capital, following Pierre Bourdieu, could be considered as a form of knowledge, an internalized code or a cognitive acquisition that equips social agents with empathy toward their subjects and appreciation of, or competence in deciphering cultural relations and cultural artifacts. Cultural capital also concerns forms of cultural knowledge, competences, and dispositions.[41] It may be reiterated that to establish their right to walk on the public roads, Ayyankali led agitations and faced his enemies head on, leading to pitched battles. None of the upper-caste reformers of his time had to face the threat of physical violence.

Another significant aspect of the SJPS was its organizational activities, especially the formation of the community courts.[42] These courts were necessary since Dalits were not allowed to go near the official courts and so could not get legal redress for their problems. They were allowed only to yell out their problems from the required distance (to avoid pollution), which middlemen would repeat loudly for the magistrates and advocates to hear.[43] This would take place after usual office hours. Ayyankali felt that this was an insulting practice, and instead of approaching such a court for the redress of Dalits' problems, he set up community courts. These courts followed the procedures of official courts, and Ayyankali sought the help of advocates who were sympathetic to the Dalits' cause. Ayyankali was the high power judge of the chief court, which had subcourts functioning under the direction of the SJPS.[44] This particular institution had the necessary support staff, such as court messengers to pass on the decisions of the chief court to the subcourts and warrant sepoys to summon offenders. It has been observed that this system of a parallel judiciary functioned in an efficient manner.[45] But it is not clear how effective the community courts could have been if an offender belonged to the upper castes. Perhaps the courts could have succeeded only if both the parties involved in a case belonged to Dalit communities.

With the support of the Diwans, Ayyankali was able to convene the annual meetings of his organization, the SJPS, after the concluding session of the Popular Legislature. The activists of the SJPS would come to Trivandrum from various parts of the state, and women formed a majority of the participants. As they were not allowed to use public roads, they had to take the alleys specially meant for their use. In spite of the fact that they were denied use of public roads, they were allowed to use the Victoria Jubilee Hall, which was also the venue of the Popular Legislature meetings. One interesting aspect of the annual meetings of the SJPS is the support the movement had from the Diwan and bureaucrats at the higher levels, which included the presence of important officials who took note of the deliberations.[46] It was the most important occasion Ayyankali had to present the problems of Dalits in front of government officials and an occasion to draw the attention of the ruler to their problems. The government officials were often asked to find ways of resolving the problems listed by Ayyankali, with the concurrence of the ruler.[47]

The experience of the SJPS showed a qualitatively different politics emerging from Dalit communities. On the one hand, they adopted radical mobilization to claim their rights; on the other hand, they also used the available legislative avenue to articulate their problems and press the native government to resolve their problems. This particular politics was effectively used by the SJPS, as it resorted to radical mobilization under the leadership of Ayyankali.

In 1913, the princely state of Cochin witnessed the emergence of a powerful movement of Pulayas named the Pulaya Maha Sabha (The great association of Pulayas). It was led by Krishnadi Asan, who subsequently converted to Christianity as he became disheartened by the slow pace of progress the movement was making. This left the movement without leadership, though later, with the coming of leaders like P. C. Chanjan and K. P. Vallon, it received a new lease on life. The two men were named to the Cochin Legislative Assembly in 1926 and 1931, respectively. Their mobilization was instrumental in opening up the public space to Dalit communities. Similar to the SJPS, their movement used the legislative space to argue for the cause of the Dalit communities. As we have seen in the case of Travancore, through the Pulaya Maha Sabha, the members of Dalit communities demanded educational facilities, cultivable land, and other civic amenities in addition to the removal of all restrictions imposed on their free movement.

The experience of the PRDS shows another form of radicalism emerging, which was more religious in nature and more typical of religious movements. The PRDS was founded in 1910 in the central Travancore region of Kerala by Poyikayil Yohannan and his colleagues, who belonged to Dalit communities. This movement originated as a radical response to the continued existence of caste inequalities between upper-caste Syrian Christians and Dalit Christians within the CMS and other denominations.[48]

From its beginning, the PRDS created alternative institutional structures for its followers together with a radically different reading of the Bible. Within a few years there was a phenomenal increase in the membership of the movement as it gradually spread to other villages in Travancore.[49] Yohannan encouraged his followers to acquire wealth in the form of land as their meager resources permitted and to attain modern education by establishing schools. In addition, there were mass mobilizations for claiming access to public space. Following the death of Poyikayil Yohannan in 1939, the movement was briefly led by his second in command, Njaliyakuzhi Simon Yohannan. In the power struggles that followed, Poyikayil Yohannan's second wife, Janamma, came to control the affairs of the movement.[50] In 1950 one group of the movement's followers proclaimed themselves Hindus under her leadership, leading to the reversal of many of their practices that had been construed as Christian. It was during this phase in the movement's history that Poikayil Yohannan's posthumous identity as Kumara Guru Devan developed.[51] He began to be thought of as God who had taken birth as an untouchable slave to redeem the descendents of slaves from the inhuman slave sufferings.[52] There were substantial changes in the foundational canons of the PRDS with the coming of this new notion of Poikayil Yohannan as Sree Kumara Guru Devan. The Guru Devan cult emerged as a consequence of the process of deification of the religious reformers of the late nineteenth and twentieth century in Kerala. This could be the larger context in which new discourses evolved within the movement. The ideas of Dalit history introduced by Yohannan were carried forward by his followers in the subsequent decades and made into a living tradition.[53]

However, I wish here to foreground certain aspects of the movement that were significant for the formation of civil society in twentieth-century Kerala. As in the case of the SJPS, radical mobilization and interventions to claim social space were central to the PRDS. The major difference was that the latter was a religious movement that had emerged out of Christianity, and the people who followed it came from different denominations. The PRDS had problematized sacred space, as its members' struggle was to claim a sacred space outside the mainstream worship places of Hinduism and Christianity. This alternative space was constituted by reinterpreting the twin notions of revelation and salvation of the Bible.[54] This critique of caste within the church was part of the wider critique of caste and slavery that they had developed in Kerala. Their critique of caste led to the construction of the historical experience of slavery that Yohannan theorized as a foundational aspect of his narrative of history. Along with this, he developed another notion of the experiential aspect of slavery that did not reduce it to a mere socioeconomic category.[55] In other words, he attempted to invert the experience of slavery and make it a resource around which to unify the community. It seems that Yohannan's project was to create a new, liberating religion by radically stretching the meaning of the Bible through a critique of existing interpretations. For example, he famously argued that the Bible was "not meant for this generation" and that its message was not meant for the Pulayas and Parayas of Travancore as the Bible does not contain anything on them.[56] Yohannan is alleged to have burned copies of the Bible.[57] He asserted that there was no revelation in it for them, and he argued instead that liberation for Pulayas and Parayas could only come through him. The oppressed Dalits who joined his movement considered him to be a prophet; sometimes they even considered him a god who had come to the earth to bring revelation and salvation. Gradually, Yohannan came to be considered the god who took on the garb of a slave to redeem orphaned slave children from inhuman sufferings.[58] He combined the biblical notions of salvation with the ideas drawn from Dalit life world to develop an emancipatory discourse. It was this discourse of emancipation that made it possible for his movement to stake claims on civil society. Yohannan constructed an alternative public for contesting religious and secular ideas and practices.

As in Dalit movements in other parts of India, an engagement with religion became fundamental to their struggles for representation in the civil society in Kerala. This situation was created more by the hegemonic power that Hinduism had over Dalits than by any other aspect of religion. In that sense, a critique of religion was fundamental to their liberation. In the case of Yohannan, this critique was not limited to only one religion, but it included a religion that was supposed to be based on the principle of salvation of the despised. Yohannan was named a member of the Popular Assembly of Travancore, where he represented the members of his caste. His speeches in the assembly, however, show that he was articulating the general problems of Dalits as well as the problems that the PRDS members were facing. It may be recalled that Yohannan's movement tried to develop institutional structures that were much more durable than the institutional structures that the SJPS was able to develop. The PRDS made efforts at self-representation that were crucial in the early twentieth century, particularly in light of the emerging political trends in which community-based politics were solidified under the guise of caste reform movements. It is in this broader context of reform-driven community formation in Kerala that the movements such as the PRDS, the SJPS, and several others developed. In spite of the facts that powerful social and religious movements had developed from Dalit communities and that they were able to articulate their critique of the traditional order, they failed to become major players in the evolving political society. As a result, the gains made through interventions in civil society and through social and religious activities were relegated to a place of secondary significance when new civil society initiatives came up in the postcolonial phase.

Another movement that is important in the analysis of Dalit interventions in civil and political society in Kerala in the early twentieth century was Cheramar Mahajana Sabha, founded in 1921 by Pampady John Joseph.[59] First, this movement's members did not consider the religious divisions among Dalits to be a serious problem in forging a unified organization and argued that they needed to focus on the shared historical experiences that formed their collective identity.[60] Second, while engaging with the social and economic issues of Dalit communities, the movement focused especially on the problems of Dalit Christians and took up the question of the discrimination and inequality that they experienced within the church. As part of its organizational efforts, the movement acquired property in many parts of Travancore to set up its offices and coordinate its activities. John Joseph represented the movement to the native rulers as part of an effort to change the caste name from Pulayas to Cheramars. This name identified the indigenous Pulayas with the ancient kingdom of the Cheras, and the proposition was acceptable to many Pulayas in Travancore irrespective of religion. It may not be out of place to suggest that John Joseph not only tried to constitute a different identity for the Pulayas, but that he also initiated a discourse of ethnicity in the 1920s in Kerala as an antidote to the oppressive caste system.[61] Moreover, he took up the question of the oppression and discrimination that Dalits had been facing in church and submitted a memorandum to the British Parliament detailing the social conditions of Dalit Christians and the need for the intervention of the British Parliament in resolving it.[62] Like his other contemporaries, he was also named to the Popular Legislature of Travancore, and he used that forum to articulate Dalits' problems.

The examples discussed so far show the manner in which Dalit communities expressed themselves in the first half of the twentieth century. This raises certain questions about the experience of Dalits in the missionary churches that existed alongside the PRDS and other such movements. The Anglican missionaries of the CMS were the first to live with and interact closely with the slave castes in Kerala—which was contrary to the practice of the Hindu upper castes, who considered "lower-caste" slaves polluting, and of traditional Christians of Kerala, who regarded them in much the same manner. However, Dalits who joined the missions had to face severe caste oppression and discrimination from traditional Syrian Christians. This led to the emergence of exclusively Dalit congregations within churches and sometimes to the departure from churches of Dalits, who subsequently formed exclusively Dalit churches. Interestingly, traditional churches also began to work among Dalit communities by the last decade of the nineteenth century, an effort which some in the CMS hoped would counteract their divisive effects on the church. The work of traditional churches among Dalits, however, led to the formation of denominational differences among Dalit Christians.

In the early twentieth century, the religious radicalism of Dalits was expressed in the formation of movements such as the PRDS that led to the imagination of a new divine power for Dalit communities. Organizations such as the Cheramar Daiva Sabha (God's Church of Cheramar),[63] the Thennindian Suvishesha Sangham (the South Indian Gospel Association),[64] and smaller churches were all expressions of this desire for a different religious and social vision. In the 1920s, Pentecostalism began to emerge as a distinct movement as it drew large numbers of Dalits from other denominations. I have argued elsewhere that religion could be considered as an alternative public for the Dalit communities. It is important to emphasize that this experience would have been more of a reality for those who joined the churches than for those who remained Hindu. In spite of the caste segregation prevailing within the churches, perhaps biblical theology provided the necessary ideological resource for the flourishing of such movements and sects. This possibility did not apply to those who did not become Christian. The Dalits joining the CMS Anglican Church in the mid-nineteenth century should be understood as their first social movement, although the missionaries were instrumental in initiating it. However, this trend had real subversive potential when one considers struggles for equality within the churches.

Historically in Kerala, the CMS Anglican Church had the largest Dalit membership, and the discontent that Dalit communities felt within the church took a decisive turn in the early decades of the twentieth century. This culminated in the formation, with the support of the church, of an organization of Dalit Christians known as Sadhu Jana Christiya Sangham (The Poor Christian's Assembly) in 1912.[65] Yet there were no policy initiatives to resolve this crisis. Another moment of articulation of Dalit rights within the CMS took place with the demand for separate administration of churches, which was raised by a vocal group of Dalits within the church. The Dalit groups moved a resolution in 1941 for separate churches that was supported by English Bishop B. C. Corfield of the Anglican Church. Since he supported the move, the Syrian Christians were forced to do so, too, but surprisingly nothing substantial came out of the decision. After the formation of Church of South India in 1931, the ongoing discontent of Dalit Christians with the domination by Syrian Christians of the church reached a critical stage, leading to open agitation in 1961–66 that was known as the Separate Administration Movement.[66] As there was no resolution of the conflict, a group of Dalit Christians broke away from the church and formed the CMS Anglican Church in 1966, under the leadership of one of the prominent Dalit priests, Stephan Vattappara.[67] This exclusively Dalit church continues to function today, with 160 small congregations that have their own clergy. However, one group of Dalits remained in the Church of South India. To assuage their feelings, in 1967 another senior Dalit priest, the Rev. T. S. Joseph, was consecrated as a bishop.[68]

Anti-Caste Struggles, Nationalism, and Communism

The 1940s saw the gradual decline of the Dalit movements of the first half of the twentieth century that were instrumental in securing many of the democratic civil rights of Dalit communities in Kerala. The Dalits still faced many issues that had not been adequately addressed in spite of the powerful presence of these movements. One could note here economic deprivation, landlessness, educational backwardness, and a host of other problems that were addressed by the earlier social movements but remained unresolved. In the 1930s and 1940s we see the growth of the Communist Party of India (CPI) as well as the nationalist movement under the Congress Party in the Malabar region of Kerala, and the State Congress in Travancore.[69] The state of Cochin also had a nationalist organization, the Cochin Praja Manadalam (Cochin State Congress). The three geographical regions of Kerala subsequently had nationalist and leftist political mobilization dominating the political sphere. The political movements of the first half of the twentieth century had anticolonial struggles as their major program and were not concerned with the anticaste struggles in the way the SJPS was. The Malabar region of Kerala, which was under direct British rule, had the Indian National Congress, which was organized by members of the educated upper castes, mostly in the legal profession.[70] Their activities were not ideologically different from the activities of the Congress elsewhere in India. The Indian National Congress did not take the caste question seriously until the Kakinada Congress of 1923, in which T. K. Madhavan, who was a close follower of Sree Narayana Guru, moved a resolution stating that temple entry was the birthright of all Hindus.[71] One of the major political events in Kerala during this period was the mobilization known as the Vaikom Satyagraha. Although it was begun with the goal of temple entry, it was ultimately limited to the question of opening up to the "lower castes" the roads that passed through the temple area. Because Gandhi played a crucial role in the Vaikom Satyagraha, his leadership brought together all the upper-caste community organizations since it was widely perceived as a question of the Hindu community. The Indian National Congress leaders from the Malabar region were the organizers of the movement, joined by local people and volunteers from Nayar, Ezhava, and Pulaya communities. The outcome of the struggle was that a resolution introduced in the Legislative Council, to allow Ezhavas to use the roads near the temple, was defeated by one vote.[72] Subsequently the Travancore government constructed diversionary lanes and managed to defuse the situation.[73] The Vaikom Satyagraha is celebrated in the nationalist accounts of anticaste struggles, whereas in the Dalit accounts it does not figure prominently.

Another important moment in the anticaste mobilization was the Guruvayur Satyagraha in 1931, which claimed entry into the famous Sri Krishana temple at Guruvayur, in the Ponnani *taluk* (block) of Malabar, for all Hindus.[74] Here again the mobilization was led by elite Congress leaders who came from Nayar landlord backgrounds. It seems that it was not just a question of the entry of "lower castes" into temples; on the contrary, discontents within caste society became the prime concern of such a mobilization. For example, the contradictions within the caste hierarchy between Nairs and Namboodiri Brahmans came into the open as Nairs sought to abolish the exclusive privileges of Namboodiri Brahmans in the temple. At the same time, the mobilization had the goal of bringing the "lower castes" into the nationalist program. The language of dominance employed in nationalist discourses is evident in the argument that the inherent uncleanliness of Pulayas and Cherumans made their temple entry necessary.[75] In the leadership of the Guruvayur Satyagraha we find veteran Communists such as P. Krishna Pillai and A. K. Gopalan, who played leading roles in the movement along with other Congress leaders such as K. Kelappan and K. Madhavanar. One of the results of the mobilization was the beginning of the construction of a hegemonic Hindu community that was established through the movement for temple entry. Without going into the details of the movements seeking temple entry, I wish to underline the fact that such mobilizations failed to enlist the support of the Dalit masses, unlike their own autonomous movements in the first half of the twentieth century. I wish to emphasize the fact that, while Dalit movements of the early twentieth century recognized the religious dimension of their subordination, their mobilization was more con-cerned with gaining education; access to public spaces; and the acquisition of symbolic resources as well as land and other material resources, if we go by the example of the sJPS. Dalits' participation in movements based on religious grievances, it seems, remained elusive in spite of the efforts of dominant reli-gious and political groups.

Dalits who were mobilized first by the missionaries and subsequently by the autonomous Dalit movements were influenced by other forms of politics that began to grow with the start of the CPI's work among the agricultural laborers and marginal peasantry.[76] With respect to the long-term dynam-ics of Dalit movements, the Communists' work among the Dalit agricultural laborers in the wetland tracts of Kerala has been significant.[77] It seems to me that even if one talks about mobilization in class terms, it is difficult not to be caught in the net of caste. For example, if one talks about the organization of toddy tappers (producers of coconut palm wine), as toddy tappers came exclusively from the Ezhava community, some aspects of the social relations rooted in the culture of the community must have informed their work and the political solidarity of the union that made use of the resources of that particular community. Similarly, the organization of Dalits in agricultural workers' unions must have also had the same dimension of solidarity fos-tered on the basis of caste. This would mean that the class characteristics of agricultural workers, including the conditions of their mobilization, are determined by their caste and solidarities that caste was able to generate. This argument is strengthened by the fact that in the wetland tracts of Kerala where agricultural workers' organizations were very strong, a large majority of the laborers came from the Dalit communities. The mobilizations of the communist parties in the agrarian sector had substantial support from Dalit communities, especially from the late 1930s onward. This situation continued well into the 1970s, and even today a majority of Dalits in Kerala continue to support communist parties. However, in the view of these parties, the caste question was relegated to a place of secondary importance and declared to be an issue that could be resolved by economic development. It will be ap-propriate here to mention the difficult dialogue that Communists had with caste, which did not take into account the complexities of caste but used an extremely rigid class-based interpretation. As a result, in spite of the support that Dalit communities offered to the leftist movement, the movement failed to live up to the Dalits' expectations. I have argued earlier that Dalits were eager to embrace modernity in whatever guise it came to them: at first, it was salvation that the missionary churches offered, and next was the secular salvation that the Communist movement offered with its liberation agenda. It seems that there has been disillusionment with both of these movements in spite of the fact that large numbers of Dalits remain in both the churches and the communist parties.

There was a generation of Dalit activists who were attracted to the Gandhian nationalist idea of Harijan (children of god) uplift and who continued to support the Congress in the postindependence phase, entering parliamentary politics, becoming members of the legislature and even government ministers. In the Malabar region before independence, volunteers and activists informed by Gandhian vision, such as Swami Ananda Teertha, carried on activities against untouchability and caste with dedication.[78] Teertha was legendary in his social activism. In spite of being a Brahman belonging to Gouda Saraswata caste, Teertha took *sanyasam* (ascetic) from Sri Narayana Guru and dedicated himself to the cause of Harijan uplift. He led public marches with nationalist volunteers and Dalits, especially young people, breaking the barriers to access to public space for Dalits in Malabar. But he soon realized the limits of the Gandhian programs on caste and untouchability. There were several occasions when he was assaulted by members of upper castes, as many of those protectors of caste did not know his caste. This situation continued well into his old age, when he was severely beaten in the Guruvayoor temple in the early 1980s for violating the caste rules by entering the temple dining hall which was reserved for the Brahmans. Since he did not wear the so-called sacred thread, the protectors of caste did not know that he was Brahman. This became another important event as people rose up in protest against this incident, and one Dalit leader, Kallara Sukumaran, led other activists in another temple entry *jatha* (agitators) beginning on February 1, 1983, from Sree Padmanabha Swami Temple in Trivandrum to Guruvayoor, where they entered the temple dining hall that was meant for Brahmans on February 13.[79] But they were received there by the chief minister of Kerala, K. Karunakaran (who was notorious for his craftiness), and dined there with him. Karunakaran, who was not a Brahman, was able to enter the dining hall for the first time, although he was a great devotee of Guruvayoorappan (Krishna).

Dalit Movement: New Directions

After independence there was a considerable decline in the Dalit movement in Kerala. We shall identify here some of the major reasons for this, which extend back to the early days of the movements. There was an absolute lack of a second generation of visionary leaders to carry on the struggles led by the stalwarts of the SJPS, the PRDS, and the Cheramar Mahajana Sabha. Another important development in the political domain of Kerala was also a decisive factor: the new political configuration that unfolded sidelined Dalit movements and Dalit communities. The Joint Political Congress that brought together Ezhavas, Muslims, and Syrians and other Christians in their opposition to legislative reforms did not have any representation from the Dalit communities.[80] The Joint Political Congress, which was primarily an elite political formation, subsequently became the Travancore State Congress.[81] It appears that the 1930s were decisive, as the decade witnessed several developments that ultimately helped consolidate a hegemonic political culture in which Dalits were marginalized in the Travancore region of Kerala.

There were several internal factors that were responsible for the eventual decline of the early Dalit movements. Even during the lives of the first-generation leaders, subcaste rivalries emerged within the movements, leading to the coming of caste-based movements that did not have a social vision to hold the diverse communities together. For example, after Ayyankali left active politics, the new generation that took over was led by Kesavan Sastri, who dismantled the SJPS and started a new organization of his community in which, naturally, Pulayas alone were members. By that time, however, the SJPS had already experienced a decline in its membership. Sastri was also a worker in the Hindu Mission, thus playing into the hands of the upper-caste Hindus. According to Chentharassery, the biographer of Ayyankali, a truce was worked out by Sir C. P. Ramaswai Iyer, then the Brahman divan of Travancore, which culminated in the marriage of Ayyankali's daughter to a Brahman, Kesavan Sastri, which affected his leadership in the movement. The biographer provides information about Sastri's resentment against Ayyankali because Pampady John Joseph, instead of Sastri, was nominated to the Popular Legislature at Ayyankali's recommendation.[82] These developments show the extent of mediations by dominant external forces that determined the course of Dalit mobilization.

With the adoption of the new Indian constitution in 1950 and the new constitutional provisions of reservation and the implementation of development and welfare measures by the state and central governments, there was a false expectation that Dalit issues would finally be resolved. The expectations raised by the coming to power of the CPI in 1957 and the support the party had among the Dalit masses made the latter believe that, unlike initiatives of the Congress, the programs the Communists proposed (such as land reforms) would resolve their historical landlessness and other problems. The policy of land reforms was expected to have a substantial impact because it would create peasants out of a social group that had been slaves in the agrarian society for several centuries, and later in the twentieth century semislaves and attached laborers. But when the land reforms were implemented, the Dalits were not tenants and therefore did not get agricultural lands. This situation created discontent that has now come into the open, creating the current phase of land struggles led by Dalit organizations in Kerala such as the Chengara in the Pathanamthitta district.[83] The Adivasis and Dalits are now preparing for a long struggle for land. The relatively unimportant position of a large majority of Dalits, who remained as cadres of the CPI's agricultural laborers' unions, however, led to the erosion of the political agency of Dalits that had been created by the movements of the early twentieth century.

The vacuum created by the decline of the early Dalit movements was filled by community-based movements of Dalits. There was a revival of community organizations in the 1960s and 1970s, and many of them claimed that their roots were in movements of the early twentieth century such as Ayyankali's SJPS. The community organization of Pulayas, the Kerala Pulayar Maha Sabha, is a classic example of this, since it tries to link itself to the tradition of the SJPS. However, it was actually organized by some Dalit leaders who were members of the CPI. In their structure and functioning, these organizations resemble the community organizations of the dominant castes. Their resource base and influence are poor compared to the clout of the upper-caste community organizations. Nonetheless, they play important roles in coordinating the social life of the members of the organization, especially on the occasions of marriage, death, and so on. A host of other organizations such as the Sambavar Sangham (Sambavar association), Cheramar Sangham (Cheramar association), and Sidhanar Service Society focus more on social networking than political mobilization. In addition, some carry on development activities with the help of government departments. Ideologically most of these movements remain within the reformist paradigm that was set up in the early twentieth century.

The 1980s were very crucial for Dalit movements in Kerala as Ambedkarite ideas began to influence the new generation of Dalits. Leaders like the late Kallara Sukumaran, who had organized the Kerala Harijan Federation and its student wing, began to be influenced by the new currents of thought. The federation subsequently changed its name to the Indian Dalit Federation with the coming of the notion of "Dalit." Intellectuals like Paul Chirakkarod became very active and assumed leadership in the movement. In the same period, some of the Dalit youths who were part of radical leftist movements disassociated themselves from those movements and began to concentrate exclusively on Dalit issues, forming organizations such as Adh- asthitha Navodhana Munnani (the Political Front for the Renaissance of the Downtrodden) in the late 1980s and early 1990s. They were highly critical of the growing Hindu right in Kerala and its cultural politics. One important mobilization was against the canonical text, Manusmriti, copies of which were burned as a symbolic protest at Vaikom, which in the popular imagina- tion is the site of anticaste struggles. The youths also campaigned against the revival of Vedic rituals by the upper castes and the Hindu right.

In the 1990s, Dalit Christians' demands for reservations became more strident, with organizations such as Dalit Christian Leaders' Forum coming to the fore.[84] The major demand of Dalit Christians has been the extension of scheduled caste reservation benefits to them, as in the case of Dalits who are Sikhs or Buddhists. The church leadership also began to throw its weight behind the demands of Dalit Christians. Some Dalit Christians now work with international solidarity networks created in the new global context. All these organizations were formed to mobilize Dalit Christians to get the ben- efits of protective discrimination extended to them. However, they had to get the support of political parties to raise their issues in Parliament, and most often they failed to do that as Dalit Christians have not been a major political force. It is worth mentioning that even during the 1980s there was not as much resistance to the demand of the Dalit Christians for inclusion in the scheduled caste category from other Dalit communities as there is today. Other Dalits fear that they would lose some of their benefits if reservation benefits were extended to Dalit Christians. Some of the other Dalits are ready to join the Bharatiya Janata Party because of its anti-Christian stance, while others are not. Of late, Dalit Christians in Kerala have formed a new organ- ization named the Council of Dalit Christians and are actively engaged in mobilizing support for the implementation of the recommendations of the Ranganath Mishra Commission that had recommended extending sched- uled caste status to Dalit Christians.[85]

Conclusion

I have attempted to analyze Dalit agency in twentieth-century Kerala by opening up certain crucial issues for further research, since academic stud- ies on such issues do not yet exist. The primary goal of Dalit movements has been to intervene in civil society. The movements of the first half of the twen- tieth century were effective in leading struggles and negotiating social space by successfully creating social space for Dalits through religious and social interventions. They critiqued the existing practices and understandings of religion, creating an alternative public sphere that subsequently fostered much of their struggles. A host of movements such as the SJPS and the PRDS developed a different and new discourse centered on the Dalit lifeworld. They also wrested agency for Dalits by developing a radical critique of caste in the first half of the twentieth century. I have already shown the historical genesis of these movements and their critical engagement with slavery, borrowing from the missionary critiques of these practices in Kerala. They were fundamental to the formation of critical Dalit consciousness. The nationalist strategy of atonement for the sins of caste and untouchability failed to understand the critique of caste developed by Dalits using their own resources in the context of colonial modernity. The Communists also failed to understand the Dalit social world and the complexities of caste that determined power structure as they were fixated on a mechanical notion of class formation and applied a reductionist category of agricultural laborers to Dalit communities. As a result, nationalists, Communists, and reformist organizations in anticaste struggles failed to mobilize Dalits in the way that Dalit movements such as the SJPS or the PRDS did. Dalit movements are extremely concerned with the conditions of modernity that enable them as agents of protest. It appears from this discussion that they had to embrace modernity as their tradition, unlike the upper castes in Kerala who could rely on their tradition. Dalit struggles in civil and political societies became fractured as religious divisions developed and as movements vied for resources from the government. Subsequently, dominant social, political, and religious forces easily intervened to enforce their hegemonic agendas. As a result, it is difficult to visualize a different Dalit mobilization emerging. However, Dalit cultural interventions from the late 1990s onward may be capable of creating a new politics of culture in the long run. Such interventions in the cultural sphere are capable of interrogating the hegemony of the public sphere in Kerala. Moreover, contemporary mobilization focusing on the Adivasi-Dalit land question is a move in the right direction that will initiate a new critique of politics in Kerala.

NOTES

1. For details, see the journals of Rev. George Matthan from 1845 on, in the Church Missionary Society Archives, Special Collections, University of Birmingham, Birmingham, UK (hereafter CMS Archives).

2. Comaroff and Comaroff, *Of Revelation and Revolution*, 2:8. See also "Rev. Oomen Mammen's Journal for the Quarter ending June 30, 1856," CMS Archives.

3. For details, see *Deepika*, April 11, 1910, microfilm at the Deepika Library, Kottayam, Kerala.

4. "The First Part of Cottayam Report, Appendix No. XII and No. XVI," accession no. 91 01/2, CMS Archives.

5. It may be noted that most of these histories have been written by an amateur historian, T. H. P. Chentharassery, in the biographical mode but with significant information on the movements. We do not yet have serious academic studies of such movements. See Chentharassery, *Ayyankali, Ayyankali: The First Dalit Leader*, and *Sree Kumara Guru Devan*.

6. P. K. K. Menon, *The History of Freedom Movement in Kerala*, vol. 2.

7. Thulaseedharan, *Colonialism, Princely States and Struggle for Liberation*.

8. The debate about the Kerala model of development focuses on these notions. For an analysis of the phenomenon, see Tharakan, "History as Development Experience." For a critique of the Marxist interpretations, see Rammohan, "Material Processes and Developmentalism."

9. For example, see publications of the CMS such as the *Church Missionary Register* and the *Church Missionary Intelligencer* of the mid-nineteenth century for information on "lower-caste" slaves in the Travancore region of Kerala, in particular, "Slaves of Travancore, Interview of the Travancore Slaves," *Church Missionary Intelligencer* 6, 1855. Also see "Slaves of Mallappally," *Church Missionary Record* 3:183–84. Both items are available in the United Theological College Archives, Bangalore.

10. Kusuman, *Slavery in Travancore*; Saradamoni, *Emergence of a Slave Caste*.

11. Saradamoni, *Emergence of a Slave Caste*, 83.

12. For example, see the Bible study notes of Chathamputhur Yohannan, the founder of the Thennindia Suvisesha Sangham, one of the Dalit churches of the late nineteenth and early twentieth centuries near Kottayam, Kerala. Also see the Bible study notes of the early members of the PRDS movement and lay propagandists (Upadeshis) of the CMS. These notes were collected as part of the Endangered Archives Project sponsored by the British Library in the School of Social Sciences of Mahatma Gandhi University, Kottayam, Kerala.

13. Pratt, *Imperial Eyes*, 7.

14. Samithi, *Sree Kumara Devan*, 46–47.

15. One of the missionaries based in Thiruvalla in the Central Travancore region of Kerala referred to a Dalit elder named Venkotta Yohannan, who had radical ideas derived from the Bible. The missionary condemned them along with the ideas of Yohannan, comparing both to heresies in missions of the CMS in Uganda and Niger. For details, see *Travancore and Cochin Diocesan Record* 28, no. 1 (1919), 19–20, Archives Section, the CMS College Library, Kottyam, Kerala.

16. Jeffrey, *The Decline of Nayar Dominance in Society and Politics in Travancore 1847–1908*; Kooiman, *Conversion and Social Equality in India*, 54.

17. For such an absurd level of argument, see Deliege, *The World of the Untouchables*, 9.

18. Chentharassery, *Ayyankali: The First Dalit Leader*, 16–19.

19. According to a memorandum submitted to Morris Watts, divan of Travancore, quoted in Baby and Babu Rajan, *Thiruvithamkur Prathyaksha Raksha Daiva Sabha*, 29.

20. Ibid.

21. Gladstone, *Protestant Christianity and People's Movements in Kerala*, 258.

22. One of the missionaries of the Church Missionary Society in Travancore refers to the conversion of a slave girl named Kali, who was christened as Lucy in Cochin. She was the first person from the slave castes to accept Christianity about whose conversion there is documentary evidence. In fact, she demanded that the missionary baptize her, as she had escaped from the fate of being taken out of Kerala to Java as a slave by a European. For details, see W. S Hunt, *The Anglican Church in Travancore and Cochin 1816–1916*, 1:161.

23. In using this concept, I am following David Scott, *Conscripts of Modernity*. Van der Veer, *Conversion to Modernities*, 4–7.

24. Gladstone, *Protestant Christianity and People's Movements in Kerala 1850–1936*, 142–47.

25. For details, see Raghavaiah, *Basel Mission Industries in Malabar and South Canara 1834–1914*; Raina, "Basel Mission and Social Change in Malabar."

26. Jeffrey, *The Decline of Nayar Dominance in Society and Politics in Travancore 1847–1908*, 118.

27. Gladstone, *Protestant Christianity and People's Movements in Kerala 1850–1936*, 370; Ninan, *Sabhacharitra Vichinthanangal-Anglican Kalaghattam*, 117–28.

28. For details, see Chentharassery, *Ayyankali: The First Dalit Leader*, 4; Jeffrey, *The Decline of Nayar Dominance in Society and Politics in Travancore 1847–1908*, 232. The Namboodiri reform movement was started in 1908. On Namboodiri and Nair reform movements, see Arunima, *There Comes Papa*, 165.

29. Chentharassery, *Ayyankali: The First Dalit Leader*, 15–23.

30. Ibid.

31. Ibid., 15, 23.

32. Ibid., 20–21. See also "A Question of Caste: Travancore Disturbances," *Times of India*, December 10, 1914.

33. "A Question of Caste: Travancore Disturbances," *Times of India*, December 10, 1914.

34. Chentharassery, *Ayyankali: The First Dalit Leader*, 21.

35. A. F. Painter, letter to Rev. J. Gray, January 7, 1884, CMS Archives.

36. Ibid.

37. Chentharassery, *Ayyankali: The First Dalit Leader*, 17–18.

38. Ibid., 19.

39. Ibid., 18.

40. Ibid.

41. Bourdieu, *The Field of Cultural Production*, 7.

42. Chentharassery, *Ayyankali: The First Dalit Leader*, 28–30.

43. Ibid., 28.

44. Ibid.

45. Ibid.

46. Ibid., 32–33.

47. Ibid.

48. For an early history of the movement, Kangazha, *Sree Kumara Guru Devan*, 8.

49. The movement had 7,000 followers in the early phase. See *Census of India, 1941,* vol. 25: *Travancore,* part 1: *Report,* 141 and 229.

50. Mohan, "Religion, Social Space, and Identity," 44–63.

51. The argument of one group of the followers was that they were reclaiming the name of Yohannan before his conversion at the age of five, Komaran or Kumaran. With the ascription of divinity to him, his posthumous identity of Kumara Guru Devan was created.

52. Mohan, "Religion, Social Space, and Identity," 56–57.

53. Ibid., 55–57.

54. Ibid., 45.

55. Mohan, "Imagining Equality."

56. *Travancore and Cochin Diocesan Record* 24 (Feb. 1914), 15.

57. Samithi, *Sree Kumara Devan,* 47.

58. Ibid., 52–54.

59. Chentharassery, *Pampady John Joseph.*

60. Mohan, "Dalit Discourse and the Evolving New Self," 11–12.

61. Ibid., 11.

62. Chentharassery, *Pampady John Joseph,* 76–85. See also N. John Joseph et al., "Before the Government of Travancore the Humble Memorial of the Representatives of the Depressed Class Christians in Travancore," Enclosure 3, 4, and 5, India Office Records, British Library, London; Joseph, *Memorial Submitted to the Honourable Members of the British Parliament.*

63. Chentharassery, *Pampady John Joseph,* 94.

64. The movement in 1896 in a village called Manganam, not far from Kottayam, under the leadership of Chathamputhur C. M. Yohannan and Chemmarappally C. J. Joseph. For details, see *South Indian Gospel Association* booklet (Kottayam: V. E., n.d.).

65. Mohan, "Dalit Discourse and the Evolving New Self," 4.

66. For details, see K. Raj, *Chennaikkalude Idayil Kunjadukal,* 103–18.

67. Ibid., 130–51.

68. Koshy, *Caste in Kerala Churches,* 82–83.

69. For a more recent Marxist analysis of the nationalist movement in Malabar, see Gopalankutty, "The Task of Transforming the Congress"; Panikkar, *Against Lord and State.* For a Marxist perspective, see Namboodiripad, *Em Esinte Sampurnakrtikal.* For a study of the anticolonial movements in the Travancore region, the princely state in Kerala, see Thulaseedharan, *Colonialism, Princely States, and Struggle for Liberation.*

70. For an analysis of the imbrications of caste nationalism and communism in Kerala, see D. Menon, *Caste, Nationalism and Communism in South India Malabar,* 89–118.

71. Ibid., 81. See also Gladstone, *Protestant Christianity and People's Movements in Kerala 1850–1936,* 388–89.

72. D. Menon, *Caste, Nationalism and Communism in South India Malabar,* 82.

73. Ibid.

74. For details, see *The History of Freedom Movement in Kerala,* 2:316–31.

75. D. Menon, *Caste, Nationalism and Communism in South India Malabar*, 83–87.

76. Kamalasanan, *Kuttanadum karshakathozhilalhi Prasthanavum*.

77. Ibid.

78. Ayrookuzhiel, *Swami Anand Thirth: Untouchability*.

79. Saseendran, *Dalit Saradhikal Theeyathikalilude*.

80. Thulaseedharan, *Colonialism, Princely States and Struggle for Liberation*, 104–5.

81. Ibid., 106–10.

82. Chentharassery, *Ayyankali: The First Dalit Leader*, 36–37.

83. The Chengara land struggle began as a local movement led by Laha Gopalan, a retired government employee. Under his leadership landless Dalits and poor landless laborers from other communities occupied one of the rubber plantations owned by Harrison Malayalam Plantations whose lease had expired. The plantation was developed on the land leased to the private company by the former government of Travancore. Those who occupied the plantation argued that since the lease had expired, the land should be considered as excess land held by the company to which the landless poor had a natural claim. The struggle began in August 2007 and, in the mid-2010s, the agitating laborers and the government of Kerala reached an agreement. For details of the mobilization, see T. Jency, "Contemporary Dalit Mobilization for Land" (MPhil diss., Mahatma Gandhi University, 2009).

84. There is an absolute lack of English language academic writings on Dalit Christians in Kerala. For a recent study in Malayalam language on Dalit Christians in Kerala, see Chirakkarode, *Dalit Christhavar Keralathil*, 233–46.

85. *Report of the National Commission for Religious and Linguistic Minorities*.

4

Dilemmas of Dalit Agendas: Political Subjugation and Self-Emancipation in Telugu Country, 1910–50

CHINNAIAH JANGAM

The history of organized politics among the untouchables in India is usually studied and analyzed as a derivative phenomenon following the exposure and access to modern institutions and ideas during colonial rule. Undoubtedly, the fruits of modern education—along with modern means of communication like railways, roads, newspapers, and magazines and new employment opportunities—gave some of the untouchables economic independence from their traditional oppressors and instilled a spirit of self-respect and an aspiration for social equality. Access to Western education made them aware of liberal ideas new to them, like humanism, democracy, equality, and liberty. And access to public employment, even though at the lowest rungs of government, freed them from the clutches of caste-bound professions and their consequences, such as unpaid labor and a humiliating existence. On the one hand, access to Western liberal education under the aegis of colonial state, Christian missionaries, and secular educationalists (working under the nationalist reformist paradigm) provided untouchables with intellectual imagination for constructing the paths of liberation on the basis of Western liberal ideas of human equality and social dignity. On the other hand, economic independence in the form of a guaranteed monthly income enabled them to assert their basic rights and organize to achieve them through meetings, processions, gatherings, and traveling across the Indian subcontinent to conferences organized by their brethren and sympathizers to share and acquire new tools of articulation to be used against the practice of untouchability and socioeconomic exploitation by caste Hindus. Writings on western India focusing on anticaste histories and movements by Rosalind O'Hanlon, Eleanor Zelliot, Susan Bayly, and Anupama Rao have amply demonstrated the catalyst role of colonial education and employment opportunities in the military, on the railways, and in other institutions as enabling factors in anti-Brahman and anticaste articulations by Jotiba Phule and B. R. Ambedkar, the greatest untouchable leader in Indian history.[1] However, scholars such as Anupama Rao in particular point out the contradictions in the colonial state's principles and practices, especially the collaboration between colonialism and Brahmanism.[2] Despite multiple contradictions, historically colonialism may be regarded as an enabling factor in the composite and complex processes of articulation (and emancipation) of untouchable communities in different parts of India.

This essay is an attempt first to chart the history of untouchable organizations in southern India, specifically the Telugu-speaking areas within both the territory of the nizam of Hyderabad and the Madras presidency. While tracing the roots of political articulations of untouchables in this region, the essay will unravel an undocumented history of untouchable organizations, and politics that predates Ambedkar. Second, the essay explores the political and intellectual context of the formation of these organizations to examine the ways in which they transformed themselves both ideologically and structurally according to changes in the country's political and intellectual environment. In particular, the essay analyzes the continuities and differences between the origin, nature, and objectives of the Telugu untouchable organizations in the nizam's territory and those in the colonial Madras presidency (while also focusing on the unique public sphere of Hyderabad at the intersection of both). The essay also points out the major ambiguities and contradictions within these organizations—some of which, in fact, can be historically understood as the roots of a few persistent issues in untouchable politics in India, such as the subcaste differences and discontents within untouchable groups.

The Rise of Dalit Activism (1910s)

The nizam's territory was a late entrant into the field of social reforms and cultural and literary organizations. Due to the slow growth of Western education in this area, we see hardly any organizational activities in those areas in the nineteenth century. Only after 1900 was there even a slow growth of literary and cultural consciousness in Telugu, because the state language in the nizam's territory was Urdu and all regional languages there suffered due to the lack of official patronage. The emergence of nationalist politics and the rising awareness of the language and identity gave birth to new organizations and associations. In 1901, the Sri Krishna Devaraya Andhra Basha Nilayam (Sri Krishna Devaraya Andhra [Telugu] Library) was established in Hyderabad under the patronage of the rajah of Munagala.[3] The Sri Raja Raja Narendra Andhra Basha Nilayam (Sri Raja Raja Narendra Andhra [Telugu] Library) was established at Hanumakonda in 1904, and the Vigyana Chandrika Mandali (Society for the Seekers of Knowledge) was established in Hyderabad in 1906.[4] The Andhra Jana Sangh (Andhra People's Association), which was established in 1921 by Madapati Hanumantha Rao, still had to face innumerable difficulties and opposition from the government.[5] During this period, the atmosphere was inhospitable to political activities in the region. Most of the organizers confined themselves to social and religious reforms and literary activities to avoid persecution from the government. The government maintained its restrictions on modern ideas and activities irrespective of religious and caste boundaries. As a result, untouchables faced both discrimination from caste Hindus and opposition to organization from the government, and their activities were aimed at overcoming these dual impediments.

The earliest roots of untouchable consciousness in Telugu-speaking regions resulting in any organization can be traced to Hyderabad, the capital city of the nizam. Echoes of untouchables' political and social consciousness were heard in this city as early as 1906. Under the leadership of Maadari Bhagyayya, popularly known as Bhagya Reddy Varma, the untouchables were organized to speak for themselves. Bhagya Reddy was born in 1888 in Hyderabad. Controversy surrounded about his use of Reddy as a surname, as the title was exclusively used by the land-holding caste. According to P. R. Venkatswamy, Suravaram Pratapa Reddy asked, "If everyone called himself a Reddy what would happen to the original Reddys?"[6] Bhagya Reddy's son wrote in his biography of his father that in November 1888, their family guru visited them and named the child Bhagya Reddy instead of Bhagyayya, as the parents called him. He hailed from the prominent untouchable Mala caste, the second largest group of untouchables in the nizam's territory. Their prominence came from their early participation in modern education and occupations, in which they were much ahead of other Dalit groups in the region.

Bhagya Reddy's introduction to modern education and new ideas was the result of an interesting episode in his life: "He lost his father at an early age while he was still attending school. One day his mother chided him for his quarrelsome behavior, and as a result he left home and began working as a butler in the house of two 'Roman Catholic barrister brothers.' The elder of these two barristers, Francis Xavier Dos Santos, was very kind to him, and with his sponsorship Bhagya Reddy obtained his education and became acquainted with elite men of the legal profession. His employer bore all his expenditure on books and Telugu journals."[7]

During this period, Bhagya Reddy was exposed to contemporary events in India and the larger world, most importantly social reform movements and politics. While he was still working in the house of the Roman Catholic brothers, he became actively involved in the activities of the Jagan Mitra Mandali (Friends of Peoples Society).[8] The main activities of this organization were to organize Harikatha (stories from Hindu epics) performances and *Bhajans* (devotional songs) to encourage untouchables to rid themselves of social evils. The organization also published pamphlets and tracts on pre-Aryan culture written by Bhagya Reddy. It was renamed the Manya Sangham (Society for Self-Respect) at a general meeting held on January 1, 1911.[9] The Manya Sangham continued to work to ameliorate the social conditions of untouchables through its reformist activities. Its main objectives were to (i) to educate untouchable children, (ii) discourage child marriages, (iii) ban nonvegetarian food and intoxicants at marriages and other auspicious functions, (iv) abolish the *devadasi* system known as the custom of *parvatis* or *jogins*[10] that was prevalent in the community. As untouchable communities were plagued by illiteracy, addiction to alcohol, and other backward practices that were identified as the important reasons for the stigma of untouchability and poverty, the above-mentioned objectives attempted to address those issues. Moreover, with the intention of involving the prominent educated men from untouchable community in spreading the message of reform and working for the uplift of their brethren, the following executive committee was elected: Walthati Seshaiah, president; H. S. Venkat Ram, vice president; J. S. Muthaiah, secretary; H. S. Shivaram, treasurer; and Bhagya Reddy, organizing secretary.[11] As part of his effort to provide education to untouchable children, Bhagya Reddy set up primary schools at the following neighborhoods in Hyderabad city, the Manya Sangham's office, Easamiah Bazaar, Lingampally, and Boggulakunta in 1910. Later four more schools were opened at Chenchalguda, Sultan Shashi, Dhoolpet, and Gunfoundry in Hyderabad. Funds for these schools were collected from public donations. Gradually the

Manya Sangham spread its influence to different localities in the Hyderabad and Secunderabad areas through its new schools and organized meetings to remove practices considered marks of untouchability.

Bhagya Reddy Varma and Dalit Organizations (1920s)

Bhagya Reddy became increasingly recognized as a social reformer and activist through his extensive travel and work in organizing various forums where untouchable voices could be heard. He founded the Adi-Hindu (The Original Inhabitants of India [Untouchables]) Movement in Hyderabad and organized the first All-India Adi-Hindu Conference, held in Hyderabad on March 29–31, 1922. Delegates from Bombay, Poona, Karachi, Nagpur, Yavatmal, Raipur, Bezwada, Machilipatnam, Rajahmundry, Eluru, and many other places attended the conference. Most importantly during this conference, the Manya Sangham was renamed the Central Adi-Hindu Social Service League to work for the uplift of Adi-Hindus,[12] also known by different regional names such as Adi-Andhras, Adi-Karnatakas, Adi-Dravidas, and Adi-Maharashtrians. The renaming of the organization reflects the growing assertion among the untouchables of their social identity in caste Hindu society and their increasing efforts to reclaim their status as original inhabitants of the nation. At this conference Kusuma Dharmanna of coastal Andhra recited his famous poem, "Maakodhu ee Nalladhorathanamoo" (We do not want this black landlordism"), denouncing the caste Hindus' domination and oppression of untouchables. The involvement of Coastal Andhra untouchable leaders in the conference demonstrates that untouchable leaders of the two regions collaborated for the emancipation of their brethren. Significantly, Bhagya Reddy did not confine his organizational activities to untouchables but attempted to bridge the gap between caste Hindus and untouchables. On the last day of the conference, therefore, speeches were made by prominent social reformers of Hyderabad who were also part of the Adi-Hindu movement: Justice Rai Balmukund, Pandit Keshav Rao, Seth Lalji Meghji Jain, N. G. Wellinker, Pandit Raghavender Rao Sharma, R. E. Reporter, and T. Dhanakoti Varma.

The conference touched on the issues of social practices and religious rites and ceremonies and urged the necessity of education for untouchable children. It adopted an agenda for change and reform in the form of the following resolutions: (1) The demeaning names thrust on the so-called untouchables by the Aryan Hindus should be replaced by the collective term "Adi-Hindu" (meaning original pre-Aryan Hindus) and region-specific terms such as "Adi-Andhra," "Adi-Dravida," "Adi-Karnataka," and "Adi-Maharashtra." (2) Adi-Hindus' duty would be to give education to their children and take full advantage of the facilities given to them by the British government and by their native states. (3) The states and the British government should open special primary schools for Adi-Hindu children, and penalties should be imposed on authorities at other private and public middle and high schools if Adi-Hindu students were not admitted to these institutions. (4) Marriages at very early age should be prevented; brides should not be younger than fourteen, and grooms should not be younger than nineteen. (5) The dedication of girls to deities as devadasis, also known as jogins, *murlis*, and other names in different parts of India, should be declared immoral and the custom abolished. (6) In marriages and other auspicious functions, liquor and meat (non-vegetarian food) should not be served, and extravagant expenditures should be avoided. (7) Adi-Hindu Jangams and Acharyas should work for the moral uplift of the Adi-Hindus and dissuade them from superstitious beliefs.[13]

In these resolutions, the conference again identified the broader issues faced by untouchable communities and attempted to create solutions. It was also the beginning of the use of the Adi-Hindu identity to do away with the stigma of untouchability. By employing this inclusive category as an overarching identity for untouchables, the conference tried to unify untouchables. The idea was to reclaim their historical heritage as the original inhabitants of the nation and thus restore their sense of self-respect. Therefore the new name of the Central Adi-Hindu Social Service League represents the growing aspirations of untouchables, their consciousness about their social position, and their claims to self-respect and a rightful position in history and society. For this reason, delegates in their resolutions once again emphasized the education of untouchables as an important vehicle of social and moral uplift. The refutation of demeaning attributions and the assertion of a self-respecting identity as Adi-Hindus were new developments in the context of emerging identity politics, where different caste groups were fighting for space in the emerging public sphere.

Bhagya Reddy Varma:
Public Intellectual and Untouchable Activist

After renaming the Manya Sangham, Bhagya Reddy's activism among untouchables and also in the larger civil society of Hyderabad took concrete shape, and he devoted all his time to social, religious, and political activities. He did not confine his activities exclusively to the emancipation of the untouchables. He also involved himself with reform activities among caste Hindus. The reformist trend among caste Hindus, particularly in regard to the social and religious practices, was an all-India phenomenon, and Bhagya Reddy was swept away by this current. He was one of the founders of the Hindu religious reform organization, the Brahmo Samaj in Hyderabad, along with Aghorinath Chattopadhyaya and N. G. Wellinker.[14] Moreover, his involvement with caste Hindu reformist organizations proved crucial for his organizational activities among untouchables. It helped him to emerge as a public intellectual and activist in Hyderabad civil society. He offered important positions to Hindu reformers who had supported his activities financially or politically. He made Balmukund, a retired high court judge and influential Hindu reformer, president of the Central Adi-Hindu Social Service League. Balmukund offered large financial resources for running the organization. Wellinker, Pandit Keshav Rao, and Waman Ramachandra Naik, prominent citizens in Hyderabad, were made vice presidents. As an astute organizer, Bhagya Reddy tried to present his organization as representative of all sections of society. The executive committee consisted of twelve Adi-Hindus; prominent among them were Walthati Seshaiah, M. L. Audaiah, Arigay Ramaswamy, and K. Rajalingam. There was also an advisory board, which consisted of thirty-four prominent Hindus, one Muslim, one Christian, one Parsee, and two Jains. Included were leading figures of Hyderabad like Aravamudu Aiyangar, a high court judge and the chairman of the reforms committee established by the nizam in 1938; Rajah Bahadur Venkata Rama Reddy, the city police commissioner and a prominent Reddy reformer;[15] Baji Kishan Rao; and Shama Rao.[16] This grand plan of including every prominent person in Hyderabad may seem ambitious for an organization representing untouchables, but by involving a cross-section of society, Bhagya Reddy wanted to combine the cause of untouchables with general social and religious concerns. Most importantly, it helped him generate needed financial resources for his activities.

Despite the involvement of caste Hindus in the league, its main focus was always on the issues of untouchables. Its aims and objectives were to (1) generate mutual sympathy and fellow feeling among the Adi-Hindus, discourage the use of some ignoble appellations given to them by other classes of people, to make them known as Adi-Hindus, and to persuade other provinces to adopt, according to their language, such names as Adi-Dravidas and Adi-Andhras already recognized by the Madras government; (2) remove the existing social evils of the Adi-Hindus; educate them in a manner that would ultimately lead to their social, moral, religious, economic, and literary uplift; and adopt adequate measures for them to attain their birthright and privileges and noble character; (3) undertake research work in the ancient history of the Adi-Hindus and spread knowledge among them by publishing books and leaflets in an Ancient Indian Historical Literature Series" and having them start their own newspapers; (4) establish societies, schools, reading rooms, *bhajan mandalis* (devotional song associations), and boy scout associations, chiefly for the benefit of the Adi-Hindus in the nizam's territory; help existing institutions; and convene meetings and arrange for lectures on such subjects as come within the purview of the second aim; and (5) strive for and achieve due recognition with the help and cooperation of all classes of people.[17]

Among the activities of the league, the establishment of schools for Adi-Hindu children can be seen as most significant. As a part of this work, Audaiah founded an Adi-Hindu primary school at Secunderabad, William Barton Boys School. The school was named after the British Resident of Hyderabad, Sir William Barton (1926–30) who was also its chief patron. The number of schools started by the league in and around Hyderabad and Secunderabad grew to twenty-six, which collectively could educate about 2,500 students at any one time. Resources to run these schools came mostly from the Jeeva Raksha Jnana Pracharak Mandali (Society for the Knowledge and Protection of Human Lives) and also from caste Hindu sympathizers. However, maintenance of this elaborate network of schools became a difficult task financially because it relied too heavily on the contributions from caste Hindus and other sympathizers. In 1933, Bhagya Reddy pleaded with the nizam's government for adequate grants, and in response the government came up with a proposal to take over these schools. The league had agreed to hand over the schools on certain conditions—that is, the medium of instruction should be the mother tongue of the pupils (Telugu) and not Urdu,[18] and handicrafts must be introduced, for the benefit of the pupils. The government agreed to these demands, and the schools were handed over in November 1934. Scholarships were also introduced for students who were pursuing higher studies.

Apart from organizing social and religious reform activities for the emancipation of untouchables and endeavoring to reform caste Hindu society, Bhagya Reddy played a pioneering, but unrecognized, role in the field of journalism and publication in Hyderabad. He established the first untouchable-owned publishing house, the Adi-Hindu Press and a Telugu fortnightly newspaper called the *Bhagyanagar Patrika* in 1925, which was published for two years and then discontinued because of his ill health and absence from Hyderabad (he was in Mysore for medical treatment). After his return in January 1930,

Bhagya Reddy revived the *Bhagyanagar Patrika*.[19] He also wrote and published many books and pamphlets on themes related to history, culture, and contemporary social and political movements. In historical accounts Bhagya Reddy tried to build historic antecedents for untouchables. He strived to build pre-Aryan roots for untouchables to claim their rights to the Indian nation as its original inhabitants, and he concentrated on writing the ancient history of untouchables. For example, he wrote *Purana Charitramu: Bharatha Kanda Pracheena Jathulu* (History of the ancient tribes of India) and *Veera Suratha Manjari, Mala Pillanu Raakumarudu Pendliyaduta* (A royal prince marries an untouchable [Mala] girl). In his first work, he traced the history of untouchables to pre-Aryan times, and in his second work he built a royal lineage for untouchables. His primary goal was to reform untouchables' social, religious, and personal habits that destroyed their personality and economic resources; another goal was to urge caste Hindus to get rid of the practice of untouchability. He therefore wrote pamphlets such as *Antudhoshamu Manarela* (Why cannot they do away with the practice of untouchability) and *Madhyapana Nishedha Keertanaloo* (Songs against alcohol consumption). Interestingly, he also wrote pamphlets in Hindi intended for Jains of Hyderabad who supported his activities with financial aid, urging them to allow Adi-Hindus into Jain temples; one such pamphlet was *Jaino! Achuthonko Jaina Mandirome berok anedho* (Oh Jains! Let the untouchables freely enter Jain temples).[20] Bhagya Reddy combined his activism with writing and publishing to spread his message to all sections of society.

Historically and intellectually, the publication of the *Bhagyanagar Patrika* was Bhagya Reddy's most significant contribution to the public life of Hyderabad and to the cause of the untouchables. The *Bhagyanagar Patrika* was one of the few Telugu-language newspapers published in Hyderabad, since the official language of the state was Urdu and most people were interested in learning it to avail themselves of public employment opportunities. His launching of a Telugu-language newspaper was not only an adventurous step, but it also reflected the emerging political consciousness among the Telugu-speaking people about their language and regional identity. Therefore, he was one of the architects of Telugu nationalism in Hyderabad. The *Bhagyanagar Patrika* was also the first successful newspaper run by an untouchable, and it was circulated widely across the country. Interestingly, Bhagya Reddy mobilized resources for his publications from the well-to-do sections of society. Even in terms of symbolic representation, the *Bhagyanagar Patrika* combined symbols of cultural and historical significance to represent the growing sense of regional and nationalist consciousness by publishing illustrations of historical sites such Charminar (a unique sixteenth-century mosque in Hyderabad), Ajanta and Ellora (Buddhist cave monuments), and Golconda Fort on its cover.

An analysis of the contents and thematic focus of the *Bhagyanagar Patrika* reveals the contradictions in Bhagya Reddy's cultural and ideological articulations, especially the way in which he oscillated between the construction of a separate identity and history for untouchables and attempts to integrate untouchables into the Hindu social and cultural processes within the reformist framework. Even though he never diluted his focus on untouchables, and though all issues of the *Bhagyanagar Patrika* had a column on the conditions and sufferings of Adi-Hindus in Telugu-speaking areas, he also published and encouraged caste Hindus to write on the conditions of untouchables and requested them to write on means of uplift for untouchables.[21] But major sections of the newspaper were devoted to preaching to untouchables about social and religious reform; abstaining from intoxicants; and discontinuing the practice of animal sacrifice at marriages, festivals, and funerals. The *Bhagyanagar Patrika* published stories taken from the Hindu Puranas like the Mahabharat and Ramayan and short stories on reformed untouchables as great devotees of Hindu gods and pure vegetarians who abstained from all temptations, including women and alcohol.[22] Bhagya Reddy also urged untouchables to perform bhajans in the temples and recite Hindu mantras. In other words, he emulated Hindu Brahmanical rituals and practices and also preached them to untouchables, which contradicted his own refutation of Aryan Hinduism and exaltation of pre-Aryan roots of untouchables. He saw the addiction to alcohol as a cause of the social and moral degradation among untouchables and published articles written about these themes. For example, Gorantla Rangaiah from Anantpur wrote an article on the bad effects of the consumption of alcohol, not just from the economic point of view but also from the standpoint of moral and physical health. He also highlighted how liquor had been used to sway voters and win elections.[23]

Another important aspect of the *Bhagyanagar Patrika* reveals Bhagya Reddy's political ambiguities. He published a witty satirical column called Chanakyudu Vinodha Vallari (Chanakya's comical stories), about contemporary happenings and political leaders. Bhagya Reddy agreed with the Congress nationalist politics and mocked Ambedkar and other non-Congress leaders.[24] As a reformist nationalist, he serialized popular books on the issue of untouchability such as *Helavathi* and *Neerudhabharatham*.[25] The *Bhagyanagar Patrika* became very popular, and its circulation had spread beyond the boundaries of the Telugu language as non-Telugu readers requested Bhagya Reddy to bring out an English-language version. As we have said, Bhagya Reddy was negotiating between his radical rejection of oppressive Hinduism and his desire for untouchables to have a separate identity and history. He published and popularized new iconic symbols for the Adi-Hindus such as an Adi-Hindu national flag, which consisted of two colors and a swastika on top, with a bow and arrow and a wheel in the middle of the flag.[26] The Adi-Hindu national flag represented his notions of untouchables' pre-Aryan roots and reclaimed non-Brahmanical Hinduism as the untouchables' religion. He also published cartoons highlighting the wretched conditions of untouchables. One cartoon, for example, depicted untouchability, poverty, and alcoholism dancing on the head of an Adi-Hindu.[27]

As the Census of India probed the issue of the identity of communities and their social status and strengthened the marker of difference between communities on the basis of precolonial caste identities, it forced communities to vie with one another for higher social status. Caste associations were formed to petition the census commissioner to use different nomenclature for caste names or to enter them as higher in relation to other castes.[28] In this context, Bhagya Reddy's organization and his activities reflected untouchables' growing aspiration for self-respect and assertion of identity and the outright rejection of a degraded social status as Malas, Madigas, and Panchamas. Achieving self-respect and equal status for untouchables with other communities became an important enterprise for Bhagya Reddy. Expressions of these aspirations of untouchables were articulated through the Central Adi-Hindu Social Service League. Emerging educated untouchables' searches for a respectable identity for themselves in relation to the other communities like caste Hindus made them want to get rid of their old degraded identities. Sometimes they even tried to construct their identity with roots in ancient history and culture. However, in this respect Bhagya Reddy as an intellectual and a leader of untouchable communities was in the forefront in carving a respectable identity for all untouchable communities as Adi-Hindus in opposition to the demeaning names like Panchamas, Asprushyas, Malas, and Madigas. Before the commencement of the 1931 census operation in Hyderabad, on behalf of the league Bhagya Reddy petitioned the nizam to consolidate all untouchable communities into one group as Adi-Hindus, different from other Hindus.[29] The nizam's government responded positively to his request and agreed to record untouchables as Adi-Hindus. According to the census commissioner, "the agitation of the depressed classes for separate treatment had been in progress when the census started. The objective of the

Adi-Hindu Social Service League of Hyderabad was to consolidate the several castes into Adi-Hindus."[30] Bhagya Reddy had also campaigned among the untouchable communities in both rural and urban areas to regard themselves as Adi-Hindus when census enumerators visited to record their castes. It was remarkable to note that his campaign yielded successful results, and untouchables responded and recorded themselves as Adi-Hindus instead of Malas and Madigas. Even the census report for Hyderabad in 1931 included an elaborate discussion about Bhagya Reddy's movement. Due to the success of his campaign, the untouchable population in Hyderabad was entered as 2,473,230 Adi-Hindus, representing 16 percent of the total population of Hyderabad.[31]

Dalits and Constitutional Reforms in Hyderabad State (1930s)

Even though the nizam's government was quite slow in implementing representative politics and democratic institutions, it finally announced the formation of a Constitutional Reforms Committee under the chairmanship of Aravamudu Aiyangar on September 22, 1937. The committee, popularly known as the Aiyangar Committee, was to recommend constitutional reforms. Its members were mostly caste Hindus and Muslims; there was no representation for untouchables. In response to this announcement, the untouchable organizations, such as the Central Adi-Hindu Social Service League and the Youth League of Ambedkarites, expressed their disagreement with this decision. Bhagya Reddy organized a meeting on December 19, 1937, under the chairmanship of B. S. Venkat Rao of the Youth League of Ambedkarites, to discuss the political demands of Adi-Hindus as a whole (including all the subcastes of untouchables) to be submitted to the Constitutional Reforms Committee. There was a strong objection from the Arundatiyas (Madigas) against Bhagya Reddy's representation of all the Adi-Hindus.[32] Despite the acrimony, Bhagya Reddy put forward the following demands on behalf of Adi-Hindus. He stated:

> As the depressed classes of the state have certain specific economic and social problems they should be provided with adequate special representation in the council. Till the majority community [Hindus] create full confidence in them, they should be provided with 10 seats in the council. These seats should be reserved for the depressed classes for a period of 15 years, the number increasing proportionately with the strength of the council. These seats should be distributed over the

16 districts of the state . . . but any depressed classes' candidate of any one constituency may stand for any other constituency. The above-mentioned seats should be contested in elections on the basis of separate electorates. The suffrage of the depressed classes should be so wide as to enfranchise a major portion of their population. In addition to the reserved seats, the depressed classes' candidates must be eligible to [sic] other general seats in any other general seats in any constituency from any part of the state.[33]

Nevertheless, the Youth League of Ambedkarites also submitted a memorandum on behalf of depressed classes of the state, demanding the statutory confirmation of their fundamental rights of citizenship by the legislature and special protection of the rights of depressed classes and minorities. The league also requested 18 percent representation for depressed classes, since they constituted 18 percent of the state's population. And it argued that if the elections to various bodies were held on joint electorates or general elections, reservation of seats should be proportionate to the classes' numerical strength. In the event of adopting a framework of separate electorates for elections (which would allow Dalits to vote and elect candidates from their community in the reserved constituencies and caste Hindus could only elect candidates from their community), there should be separate electorates for the depressed classes.[34] They further demanded special representation in the muncipal council, on district and *taluqa* (administrative unit) boards, and in other organs of the government. Even though only a fraction of their demands were accepted and supported by the Aiyangar Committee, it did take note of their existence and activities. Finally, as a result of this, though the Aiyangar Committee refused to recommend separate electorates on the ground that such an arrangement would foster communal sentiment, it accepted the special needs of Adi-Hindus, saying: "A demand has been made on behalf of *Harijans* that seats should be reserved and separate electorates formed for them. We cannot endorse the principle, which generally underlies communal representation. But in the social, educational and economic interests of the *Harijans*, we nevertheless consider it necessary that they should be granted representation in the Legislature."[35]

The committee also recommended that one untouchable be elected as a representative for municipal committees and town committees, one to serve on the district board, and two as representatives in the legislature.[36] In this way, Bhagya Reddy's Central Adi-Hindu Social Service League, along with other depressed classes' organizations, articulated the political rights of untouchables. He was also recognized as the credible representative of the Adi-Hindus or untouchables.

Hindu Reform Activities

Given Bhagya Reddy's activism that embraced the untouchables and the caste Hindus, he actively participated in events organized by the Brahmo Samaj and the Arya Samaj movements, the two Hindu social and religious reform organizations spearheading the campaign for the abolition of untouchability. With his charismatic leadership, Bhagya Reddy was able to attract many untouchables into the Brahmo Samaj fold. Even the untouchables themselves felt that this was an important means of escaping the stigma of untouchability and other social prejudices. But that did not really bring any positive social and moral elevation of untouchables, nor did it bring any change in caste Hindu attitudes. In contrast, over time, Brahmos were identified with untouchables, according to Venkatswamy: "If a Hindu was asked his caste the questioner would not feel satisfied with the simple answer Hindu. He would be anxious to know his sub-caste also. Under such circumstances an untouchable should say either a *Mala* or *Madiga* or some other sub-caste. If a member of Brahmo Samaj was asked his caste, he would straight away say, without the fear of stigma, that his caste was Brahmo. As the movement developed the word Brahmo had lost its significance and whoever said that he was a Brahmo was suspected either to be *Mala* or a *Madiga*."[37]

Bhagya Reddy had also taken an active interest in the Arya Samaj movement. In recognition of his services, Arya Samaj wanted to honor him with the title of *sharma* (a title exclusively used by Brahmans and synonymous with pandit), but he preferred the title of *varma*, as he considered himself a practical man of action.[38] After this title was conferred on him, he was popularly known as Bhagya Reddy Varma.

Bhagya Reddy was the organizing secretary of the Jeeva Raksha Jnana Pracharak Mandali (Society for the knowledge and protection of human lives), which was founded by Rai Balmukund in 1913.[39] Balmukund worked as a full time organizer. This association proved crucial for his reformist activities among the untouchables, especially for the schools he had established, which were financially supported by its members. Balmukund's commitment to the uplift of untouchables was quite commendable; in his will, he instructed his family to hand over his dead body to Adi-Hindus to perform his last rites. In fulfillment of his wish, Bhagya Reddy along with activists in the Central

Adi-Hindu Social Service League performed Balmukund's last rites.[40] Primarily due to the campaigns of Bhagya Reddy, in a special *firman* (order) on February 5, 1920, the nizam banned cow slaughter in his dominions on Bakri-Id day (a Muslim festival celebrated with a goat sacrifice). Bhangya Reddy continued working in this organization until 1927, leaving it when his programs there were not implemented due to the oganization's heavy financial burden.[41]

Bhagya Reddy and Telugu Nationalism

As noted above, Bhagya Reddy was one of the earliest public intellectuals to insist that the nizam's government teach Telugu in schools, and he also launched a Telugu-language fortnightly newspaper in Hyderabad. Even though it is difficult to gauge the exact cultural and ideological influences responsible for his attachment for the Telugu language and identity, his extensive travels and engagements outside Hyderabad, especially his contacts with the early nationalist leaders and social reformers in coastal Andhra districts, were certainly an important influence on him. Most importantly, Bhagya Reddy was elected president of the first untouchables organization, the Andhra Rashtra Adi-Andhra Mahajana Sabha (The Andhra association of untouchables) held at Vijayawada in 1917, and he was supported by caste Hindu reformers, indicating the close links among and influence between Andhra leaders and intellectuals. Even though consciousness about Telugu language and identity in Hyderabad was the result of more significant political and cultural encounters, Bhagya Reddy inherited Telugu consciousness as part of his larger political and social engagements. His close association with Madapati Hanumantha Rao naturally made him part of the Nizam Andhra movement led by Telugu language caste Hindus. Bhagya Reddy used the platform provided by the movement to further the cause of the untouchables. He participated in the annual conferences of the Andhra Maha Sabha, an organization set up by caste Hindus to create Telugu linguistic identity. However, it is pertinent to note that the caste prejudices and discrimination against untouchables continued even at the political conferences in which caste Hindus were advocating political rights. Bhagya Reddy attended the first Andhra Maha Sabha conference, held on March 3–5, 1930, at Jogipet town in Medak District to promote the Telugu language in the nizam's dominions. At this meeting, Bhagya Reddy had a very humiliating experience. By then he was a very well recognized social activist and a leader of stature. He went to the dais to read out the resolutions he was proposing. While making his way to the dais through the crowd, he touched many people. The moment he went up to the dais many people started protesting and began to leave the hall because he was an untouchable. The organizers were at a loss, and in the end, Waman Naik, a prominent social reformer from Hyderabad, had to convince the audience to come back and take their seats.[42] This humiliating incident gives us an idea of the discrimination practiced by the politically conscious caste Hindus even against a leader and public intellectual. Indeed, it also reflects the nature of hardships faced by the untouchable leaders and activists in general.

As a representative of the untouchables, Bhagya Reddy proposed two important resolutions at this conference. In the first one, he requested the nizam's government to take proper steps to meet the educational needs of the untouchables; in the second, he condemned the government officials who were forcing untouchables to perform *vettichakiri* (forced labor without compensation) and requested the government to take the necessary action to stop this practice.[43] Bhagya Reddy also participated in the second Andhra Maha Sabha conference held on March 3–5, 1931, at Devarakonda, in Nalgonda District, along with other members of the Central Adi-Hindu Social Service League, Ch. Chitharaiah, Gurakula Mallesha Rao, and Matari Balaramaiah. They urged all caste Hindus to disavow the practice of untouchability, allow untouchables access to temples and community wells, and treat untouchables as human beings with equal rights. Resolutions pertaining to the uplifting of untouchables were proposed and discussed by Rao, and the conference accepted them unanimously.[44] Simultaneously, Bhagya Reddy and his colleagues organized untouchables from Devarakonda and neighboring villages. Balaramaiah performed *Sati Sulochana Harikatha* (story of Sulochana from Ramayana), and Chitharaiah and Bhagya Reddy spoke and requested the untouchables to give up drinking alcohol and eating meat. Bhagya Reddy could not attend the third Andhra Maha Sabha conference, held at Khammamumettu in 1934, but he sent a message to the conference, which was read as a prominent person's statement.[45]

In this way Bhagya Reddy contributed enormously to the Telugu language and journalism, and by participating in the Andhra Maha Sabha conferences along with his followers, he strengthened the cause of Telugu nationalism in Hyderabad. Simultaneously he used the platform and the opportunity provided by the conferences to expose the oppression and exploitation of untouchables and espouse their rights. Through his participation and leadership, he made the Andhra Maha Sabha move beyond its exclusive focus on Telugu linguistic identity to take up untouchables' issues. Significantly, the historic pamphlet published by Andhra Maha Sabha on *vettichakiri* (forced labor)[46] was the best indication of how he was able to influence the agenda of the Andhra Maha Sabha for the cause of the untouchables. However, it is important to note that the agenda of untouchables disappeared from the Andhra Maha Sabha movement when it was transferred into the hands of communists under the leadership of Ravi Narayan Reddy.

Bhagya Reddy and Gandhian Nationalism

There were numerous contradictions in Bhagya Reddy's ideas and actions, which significantly limited untouchables articulation of a radical agenda. Especially as an ideologue and activist he oscillated between two contradictory ideological paradigms—the pre-Aryan roots he tried to construct for the untouchables through his idea of Adi-Hindu identity, and the rigorous self-critique he used to situate them within the Hindu framework. For him, Adi-Hindu identity meant the pre-Aryan and non-Brahmanical roots of untouchables. But he did not argue for the separation of untouchable communities from the broader Hindu social and religious life. Instead, he was critical of untouchable communities and argued that "the degeneration leading to social ostracism was due to their own apathy and ignorance."[47] He also thought that the social evils among untouchables, especially alcoholism, the dedication of girls to goddesses, the sacrifice of animals, and the eating of meat, were the main reasons for their degraded social position. In a way, through his overly critical attitude toward untouchable communities he diminished his own community and glorified Brahmanical Hinduism and its ideology and practices. All through his writings, including *Bhagyanagar Patrika,* we notice these assertions. Ideologically he had imbibed reformist Hindus ideas and conceived himself that his community was part of the broader Hindu society. He never argued for the conversion of untouchables to other religions such as Islam and Christianity or even Buddhism, which he admired (every year he celebrated Buddha's birthday). Even during the 1932 dispute between Gandhi and Ambedkar over separate electorates for caste Hindus and untouchables in elections, Bhagya Reddy sent a message through Baji Kishna Rao, a well-known social reformer, requesting Ambedkar to withdraw the demand for separate electorates.[48] But it was this ideological commitment that made him better suited to the sensibilities of the reformist Hindus, Jains, and Marwaris. They not only sympathized with his reformist activities but also contributed enormously to them, both by supporting him financially and by providing a public platform for his social service activities.

Politically and ideologically, Bhagya Reddy can be located within the reformist Gandhian nationalist paradigm. Even though he started his social and religious reform activities among untouchables before Gandhi's appearance in the Indian public sphere, his intellectual and political ideology exactly suited the nationalist paradigm led by caste Hindus. Bhagya Reddy's political and ideological inclinations were clarified when Gandhi visited Adi-Hindu Bhavan as part of his Andhra tour. On this occasion special functions and meetings were organized all over Hyderabad and Secunderabad. Prominent Congress leaders such as Waman Naik and Madapati Rao apprised Gandhi of developments in Hyderabad. On April 7, 1929, the Adi-Hindu bands led Gandhi to a big meeting organized at the Vivekavardhini High School. After the meeting he paid a visit to the Adi-Hindu Bhavan, the office of the Central Adi-Hindu Social Service League. Four hundred students from nine Adi-Hindu schools welcomed him. Waman Naik explained the Adi-Hindu schools and the activities of the league to Gandhi. The headmaster of the schools, Sevakadasu, presented a certificate of appreciation to Gandhi on behalf of the league, praising Gandhi's efforts to uplift the Adi-Hindu community by speaking against the practice of untouchability.[49] Maybe it was for this reason that caste Hindu Gandhian nationalist leaders idealized Bhagya Reddy and wanted him to be emulated by all untouchable castes. He was made the hero of a famous novel, *Maalapalli*, written by Unnava Laxminarayana in 1922.[50]

On the issue of uniting disparate untouchable communities into one Adi-Hindu community, Bhagya Reddy had a problematic position. He and Arigay Ramaswamy, another untouchable leader and his rival, had a major disagreement about the issue of caste differences among untouchables. Both of them stood for the reformist Hindu ideas within the Gandhian nationalist paradigm and emulated Hindu Brahmanical ideas and practices, urging their brethren to follow them. However, they had fundamental differences on the issue of resolving subcaste differences among untouchable communities. Though Bhagya Reddy coined the identity of Adi-Hindus for untouchables of all castes, his views in relation to the subcaste differences remained conservative. He argued for the preservation of those differences and did not even encourage Malas and Madigas to eat together, let alone intercaste marriages. In contrast, Ramaswamy argued for the abolition of subcaste differences and unifying untouchables into one community as Adi-Hindus. He personally conducted many intercaste marriages between Malas and Madigas and got his adopted daughter married to a Madiga boy.[51] Bhagya Reddy and Ramaswamy fell apart on this important issue of unifying untouchables, and over time the gulf between them widened as they competed with each other for the leadership of the untouchables. Starting with this ideological difference and competition for leadership, the untouchable movement in Hyderabad state suffered rifts in both ideology and organizations.

Gandhian and Other Alternatives

In the Madras presidency, caste Hindu reformers, especially Brahmans such as Guduru Ramachandra Rao, Vemuri Ramji Rao, and Nallapati Hanumantha Rao, worked for the uplift of untouchables to counter the campaigns of the Christian missionaries against the Hindu religion. Through reformist activities, they made inroads into the untouchable communities and organized untouchables in the fields of social, religious, and political activities. It was due to their efforts that an untouchable leadership with pro-Hindu leanings emerged across the Telugu-speaking areas of Madras presidency. Prominent among them were Rayudu Gangaiah, Naralasetti Devendrudu, Sundru Venkaiah, Kusuma Venkatramaiah, Undru Subba Rao, Vemula Kurmaiah, Jala Rangaswamy, Kusuma Dharmanna, and many others. These new untouchable leaders organized untouchables at various levels through conferences and reformist activities to facilitate their assimilation into the broader Hindu fold. Their activities were quite similar to those of Bhagya Reddy in Hyderabad, and they also strived to introduce social and religious reforms among the untouchables such as the celebration of Hindu festivals and the discontinuation of eating nonvegetarian food and consumption of alcohol and other practices that did not conform to the reformist caste Hindu sensibilities. At this time two political trends were prevalent in coastal Andhra. One trend was represented by the reformist Adi-Andhra leaders who were associated with the caste Hindu reformers and who were trying to organize untouchables in the Hindu fold through caste conferences and other moderate means, like performing bhajans in Hindu temples and organizing temple entry movements. Christian converts represented the other trend. Though they did not organize politically as a parallel group, they were appointed by the government to represent Panchamas in the representative bodies, which evoked serious objections from the non-Christian Panchamas. The tension between these two trends heightened in the course of the nationalist movement, which was imbued with the Hindu consciousness. Moreover, even though the reformist Adi-Andhra leaders enjoyed considerable sympathy and support from reformist Hindus, their efforts to integrate untouchables with the rest of Hindu society through temple entry and other social and religious practices resulted in serious tensions between caste Hindus and untouchable communities.

By the 1920s Gandhi's appearance in nationalist politics brought mass mobilization politics to center stage. As part of this strategy, the Congress Party, under the leadership of Gandhi, sought to unite all sections of Indian society against British colonial rule. As part of these efforts and with the goal of drawing untouchables into the nationalist movement, Congress addressed the issue of untouchability. As a result, Gandhian nationalist activists in the Andhra region focused on the needs of untouchables and started working among them. Pre-1920 reformers, mostly Brahmans, sided with Congress and its activists and became part of the nationalist mainstream under Congress. Added to the old reformers were new activists and reformers such as Unnava Laxminarayana and N. G. Ranga, who organized untouchables in Andhra districts and also wrote on the issue of untouchability. Their novels *Maalapalli* and *Harijananayakudu*, respectively, were celebrated as depicting the best Gandhian solutions for the emancipation of untouchable communities. Gandhi's visits to Andhra from 1921 on not only strengthened the vigor and commitment of Gandhian activists but also had a considerable impact on the nature of untouchable assertions and associations. These efforts made the untouchables cognizant of their strength and the necessity of their inclusion into the nationalist politics; subsequently, they made demands for more representation in representative bodies, social equality, and a greater share in economic resources. Another effect of the leadership of Gandhi and the all-encompassing nationalism was the shrinking of space between the untouchables and nationalist politics under Congress. Yet untouchables remained subjugated within the nationalist movement. Their independent initiatives to build a parallel politics evaporated.

Under the shadow of Gandhian nationalism, the prominent untouchables organization, the Andhra Rashtra Adi-Andhra Mahajana Sabha (Untouchable's association), held its fifth conference at Hindu High School in the Guntur district on July 29, 1928. Prominent participants in this conference were the Congress nationalist leaders Nallapati Hanumantha Rao, Guduru Ramachandra Rao, Vellanki Krishna Murthi, Ranganatha Mudaliar, and the Adi-Andhra leaders Naralasetti Devendrudu, Rayudu Gangaiah, Kusuma Veeraswamy, Chunduru Krishnaiah, Thiruvakolluri Venkata Subbaiah, P. Venkatswamy, and Prathipati Audinarayana. There were more than three hundred participants. Baddela Ramakrishnaiah was the secretary of this conference, and Sundru Venkaiah delivered the presidential address.[52] Eighteen resolutions were passed at this conference. Some important ones were a request to the government to allot wastelands, grant revenue concessions, and establish cooperative societies; to help the Adi-Andhras financially to cultivate lands; to amend the local board act so that untouchables would have representation on local boards and in municipalities and legislatures on the basis of their numerical strength, or at least a minimum 5 percent; and to prevent caste Hindus from preventing untouchables' access to the village tanks, wells, and travelers rest house. The conference also requested the government to establish special schools to train Adi-Andhras and additional hostel facilities for their children in all the districts.[53]

These resolutions reflect the growing confidence among untouchable representatives in the expanding public sphere in the context of nationalist politics. Every community was claiming its social, economic and political rights, and untouchables also wanted their share. They therefore urged the government to grant them wastelands and requested the establishment of cooperative societies to ensure their financial security and independence from the caste Hindus. This indicates their aspirations to lead independent lives and to lay claim to the country's economic resources. Untouchables then took another step forward and demanded 5 percent reservation in local bodies. This bold request for the right to represent themselves was another significant move in the context of their increased political organization. Their demands for public utilities, civil societal rights, and educational opportunities demonstrate their aspirations for equality in terms not only of political representation but also of daily affairs that directly affected their existence vis-à-vis caste Hindu society at large. The conference resolutions represented an independent outlook and aspiration, but in reality they were articulated within the Gandhian nationalist framework.

Gandhian Assimilation

As noted above, the influence of Gandhian nationalist politics on the untouchables became a dominant phenomenon in the late 1920s. By 1929, untouchable articulations had lost their tone of independence and aspiration for separatist alternatives. The Andhra Rashtra Adi-Andhra Mahajana Sabha was taken over by Gandhian nationalist untouchable ideologues, who equated untouchable agendas with Gandhian programs. In this context, the sixth Andhra Rashtra Adi-Andhra Mahajana Sabha conference was organized on November 5, 1929, at Bezawada. The well-known Gandhian nationalist Vemula Kurmaiah was the reception committee chairman, and another Gandhian, Prathipati Audinarayana, delivered the presidential address.

Mangalagiri Chenchudasu acted as secretary. The agenda of the conference was borrowed from the Gandhian nationalist paradigm, and the main issues put forward related to temple entry satyagraha and impending administrative changes.[54] In his presidential address, Audinarayana spoke rhetorically about the degraded conditions of untouchables: "We lost our past glory and education, we have no influence, money we have none, and even our health is ruined. We are left with poverty and slavery."[55] But essentially, he was guided by the Gandhian nationalist ideology. On the economic upliftment of untouchables, he declared:

> Agriculture is the only source of income for us. Countries which have alternative industries provide better economic opportunities. We rely only on agriculture for our betterment and have no alternative. Because of this restriction most of us become bonded laborers. Many changes are happening around the world but we remain the same. To come out of these clutches our people have to look for alternative professions such as spinning and carpentry to earn their livelihood. We should request the government to give us industrial training along with education. Unless we explore alternative sources of income there is no way of developing.[56]

The conference also passed resolutions again about representation for Adi-Andhras on local boards and in legislative councils. They requested the government to select their representatives by election instead of nomination. The conference also registered a protest against the banning of untouchables from entering the Janardhanaswamy temple in Eluru. The conference condemned the attitude of the temple authorities and appointed a subcommittee—consisting of Atmakuri Govindacharyulu, Athili Suryanarayana, Guduru Ramachandra Rao, Mangalagiri Chenchudasu, Ayyadevara Kaleshwara Rao, and Naralasetti Devendrudu—to organize a temple entry satyagraha in Eluru.[57]

Another local-level conference was organized by the Krishna District Andhra Rashtra Adi-Andhra Mahajana Sabha at Batlapenumarru Village in Diwi taluq on June 12, 1931, under the leadership of Mangalagiri Bujangadasu. This conference also put forward the Gandhian reformist agenda as the untouchables' liberation. The main issues dealt with were the abolition of liquor and eating animal flesh on all occasions, keeping Adi-Andhra hamlets clean, and compulsory education for all Adi-Andhra children under eighteen.[58]

Gandhi's rise as an undisputed leader in nationalist politics and his powers of persuasion led to a major dispute between him and Ambedkar over the leadership of untouchables. Even though Ambedkar was to make his mark as the champion of untouchables' rights and was recognized as their leader, the limitations of his organizational and ideological appeal across India created a wide gap between him and many untouchables. The regional specificities and historical and social factors also worked against Ambedkar. Due to the Congress's organizational structure and caste Hindus backing, Gandhi was able to win over untouchables, and his followers among the untouchables emerged as their leaders and activists. The fast undertaken by Gandhi to protest against the separate electorates for untouchables because it would allow them exclusive right to elect candidates from their community in the reserved constituencies, whereas the caste Hindus could only elect candidates from their community. Gandhi argued that separate electorates would lead to the division of Hindu society and therefore he fasted against its annulment. Gandhi's fast gave significant momentum to the leadership of untouchables. The issue was not only the individual leadership of Gandhi or Ambedkar over the untouchables but also the legitimacy of nationalism led by caste Hindus and its appeal to untouchables. This was apparent at the seventh Andhra Rashtra Adi-Andhra Mahajana Sabha conference, organized at Bezawada in August 1932, with Vemula Kurmaiah as the president. Conference deliberations centered on Gandhi's fast. Again at this conference Gandhi's followers held sway. Kurmaiah's presidential address was mostly devoted to the issue of Gandhi's fast; he praised Gandhi for sensitizing caste Hindu society to the deplorable conditions of untouchables and making the abolition of untouchability part of the Congress program. He spoke about the disabilities of untouchables and their social and economic exploitation, quoting a British official David Claude Kempu who said, "A subjected nation can have no politics." Since "untouchables are subjugated to subjected people, their plight is indescribable."[59] But as a Gandhian nationalist, Kurmaiah differed with Ambedkar on the issue of separate electorates for untouchables. He supported joint electorates with reserved seats and urged untouchables to fight for the liberation of the country along with Congress. He justified his position on the basis of earlier conferences beginning in 1917, in which untouchables conceived themselves to be part of Hindu society.[60] The conference participants unanimously decided to support the joint electorate system and declared Gandhi their leader, instead of Ambedkar.[61] By accepting Gandhi as the leader of the untouchables, the 1932 conference ended years of oscillation between different means of liberation by untouchable organizations. It chose the Gandhian assimilation program rather than the separatist independent alternatives.

Conclusion

In the politics of articulations of the marginalized in southern India, the Telugu untouchables were one of the earliest communities to realize their deplorable conditions and organize themselves into a political community. Even though Hyderabad, due to its unique historical situation as a princely state headed by a Muslim ruler and controlled by Hindu feudal lords of the landholding caste, including Brahmans, created multiple types of caste-based oppression and servitude for untouchables and other marginalized people in rural areas, it was also historically one of the most fertile grounds for radical articulations among the marginalized. In the context of untouchables, Hyderabad had a unique trajectory. Modernization of the capital city, especially in terms of education and employment opportunities, gave untouchables access to those opportunities and enabled them to form themselves into a political community. Under the leadership of Bhagya Reddy, this culminated in the first organized leadership among untouchables, long before Ambedkar and definitely preceding similar leadership in other parts of the nizam's territory as well as the coastal Andhra and Rayalaseema regions of present-day Andhra Pradesh. The Hyderabad public sphere witnessed multiple articulations and diverse ideological streams among untouchables. It can be argued that, contrary to popular perceptions that depict Hyderabad (under Muslim rule) as backward in terms of colonial modernization (compared to coastal Andhra and Rayalaseema), the politics of untouchables in Telugu regions actually originated in Hyderabad, and leaders like Bhagya Reddy travelled to different regions (including coastal Andhra and Rayalaseema) in an effort to galvanize the Telugu untouchables. However, as noted above, in spite of being a pioneer in articulating the aspirations of untouchables, Bhagya Reddy faced challenges that often ensued from his own ambiguous or contradictory positions—at one level, he wanted to unite the untouchables under the Adi-Hindu banner, but at another, he refused to accept intercaste marriages and dining among diverse communities of untouchables. This conservatism proved costly for his leadership and also split the organization vertically by alienating the numerically strong Madiga community. Historically this split marks the beginning of the political and organizational rift between Malas and Madigas, who split into rival communities. Arigay Ramaswamy spent his life trying to bridge this gap.

However, Bhagya Reddy's success and acceptance within the nationalist reformist paradigm can be best contextualized in terms of the intricacies of regional caste politics. Untouchables in coastal Andhra and Rayalaseema, despite their early access to missionary education and colonial institutions, faced enormous oppression from landed non-Brahman castes who questioned Brahman domination yet kept untouchables and other marginal communities under their feet for economic benefits and as a means of articulating domination. Therefore, in these regions Brahman reformers entered untouchable huts not only to drum up support for nationalist politics but also to counter the rising waves of non-Brahman politics. Hence Brahman reformers considered Bhagya Reddy, who accepted the reformist Hindu agenda, to be the most suitable leader and provided needed logistical support for his activities in the region.

The untouchables' organizational activities also aimed to counter the influence of Christian missionaries, and this resulted in the alienation of the Christian untouchables from its organizational structures. Therefore the Madiga community, whose members had embraced the American Baptist missionaries' efforts at conversion in this region as early as the nineteenth century,[62] were consciously kept out of the Adi-Andhra Mahasabha; they were also branded as traitors and did not reap the benefits of nationalist politics. This too fed into the historical trajectory of the evolution of untouchable politics in Andhra Pradesh, and the contemporary Mala-Madiga political conflict may be traced back to it.

NOTES

1. O'Hanlon, *Caste, Conflict, Ideology*; Zelliot, *Doctor Bahasaheb Ambedkar*; Rao, *The Caste Question*.

2. "Introduction," in Rao, *The Caste Question*.

3. K. Srinivas, "Rendu Prapancha Yudhala Madhya Telugu Sahityam: Telanganalo Sahitya Punarvikasam 1919–1939," 143.

4. Sarojini, "The Movement for the Social and Cultural Revival of Telangana in the Hyderabad State," 218.

5. For a detailed discussion on the Andhra Jana Sangham, see M. Rao, *Telangana Andhrodhyamamu*, parts 1 and 2.

6. Quoted in Venkatswamy, *Our Struggle for Emancipation*, 1:3.

7. Gautam, *Bhagyodayam, Maadari Bhagya Reddy Varma*, 2.

8. Bhagya Reddy's son Gautam claims that his father was the founder of the Jagan Mitra Mandali (ibid.). According to P. R. Venkatswamy, Bhagya Reddy was involved with this organization from the beginning (*Our Struggle for Emancipation*). It is quite difficult to identify the founders of this organization, which was involved in the reform movement among the untouchables of Hyderabad.

9. Gautam, *Bhagyodayam, Maadari Bhagya Reddy Varma*, 2.

10. Jogins are "large number of small girls traditionally or superstitiously dedicated to the village gods, but eventually abandoned to the woods—to the caprice and avarice of mere mortals" (Mowli, *Theirs Is the Kingdom of God*, 3).

11. Gautam, *Bhagyodayam, Maadari Bhagya Reddy Varma*, 3.

12. Vadlakonda Narasimha Rao, "Nizam Rashtra Andhrodhyamamu," *Andhra Patrika*, November 14, 1923, 170.

13. Gautam, *Bhagyodayam, Maadari Bhagya Reddy Varma*, 51.

14. Apparao, *Akhila Bharatha Brahma Samajamu*, 542.

15. He was also the founder of hostels and schools meant to uplift the Reddy community from which he came. He had assisted Central Adi-Hindu Social Service League financially. See S. Reddy, *Rajah Bahadur Venkata Rami Reddy Jeevitha Chartra*.

16. Venkatswamy, *Our Struggle for Emancipation*, 1:39.

17. Ibid., 40.

18. Bhagya Reddy was also actively involved in the Andhra Jana Sangham, which was led by Madapati Hanumantha Rao. The organization worked for the development of the Telugu language and culture in the nizam's dominions, and this demand emanates from his involvement in that movement.

19. Ramesan, *The Freedom Struggle in Hyderabad*, 4:79.

20. All the titles of the pamphlets and books listed here were published in the back page of most issues of the *Bhagyanagar Patrika*.

21. Untitled article, *Bhagyanagar Patrika*, July 15, 1932.

22. Puthalapattu Sriramulu, "Adimandhra Bhakthuni Jeevithamu" (Life of an Adi-Andhra devotee), *Bhagyanagar Patrika*, July 1, 1932.

23. Gorantla Rangaiah, "Matthupadharthamulu" (Intoxicants), *Bhagyanagar Patrika*, June 15, 1932.

24. Ibid.

25. Thallapragada Suryanarayana Rao wrote *Helavathi*, and Mangipudi Venkata Sharma wrote *Nirudhabharatham*. These two novels are known as the earliest reformist reactions against the practice of untouchability.

26. "Adi-Hindu National Flag," *Bhagyanagar Patrika*, November 1, 1932, 41.

27. "Adi-Hinduvuni Paristhithi," *Bhagyanagar Patrika*, March 1, 1933, 3.

28. *Census of India, 1933, Vol. 23, Part I: H.E.H. the Nizam's Dominions (Hyderabad State)*, 246.

29. Ibid., 255.

30. Ibid., 234.

31. Ibid., 248.

32. Venkatswamy, *Our Struggle for Emancipation*, 1:128.

33. Quoted in ibid., 108–9.

34. *Report of the Reforms Committee-1938*, 130.

35. Ibid., 59.

36. Ibid., 116.

37. Venkatswamy, *Our Struggle for Emancipation*, 1:9.

38. Abbasayulu, *Scheduled Caste Elite*, 33.

39. Ramesan, *The Freedom Struggle in Hyderabad*, 4:235.

40. Mudiraj, *Pictorial Hyderabad*, 2:516F.

41. Gautam, *Bhagyodhayam, Maadari Bhagya Reddy Varma*, 10.

42. M. Rao, *Telangana Andhrodhyamamu*, 2:77–78.

43. Nizam Rastra Prathamandhra Maha Sabha (Jogipet), *Presidential Address of Suravaram Prathapa Reddy and the Resolutions* (Hyderabad-Deccan: Shyama Sundara Mudrakshara Shala, 1930), 47 and 49.

44. M. Rao, *Telangana Andhrodhyamamu*, 2:86–87.

45. Ibid., 2:100.

46. The pamphlet, which was mainly concerned with the untouchable communities, became quite popular. Christian missionaries used to carry it to each and every untouchable hamlet they visited in Telangana to expose the caste Hindu oppression and convince untouchables to convert to Christianity. Madapati Rao said it became almost a second Bible for them, giving them access to untouchables (*Telangana Andhrodhyamamu*, 2:141).

47. Quoted in Mudiraj, *Pictorial Hyderabad*, 2:516D.

48. *Bhagyanagar Patrika*, October 1, 1933.

49. Anjaneyulu, *Andhrapradesh lo Gandhiji*, 417–18.

50. K. Srinivas, "Rendu Prapancha Yudhala Madhya Telugu Sahityam," 197.

51. Venkatswamy, *Our Struggle for Emancipation*, 1:26.

52. "Fifth Andhra Rashtra Adi-Andhra Mahajana Sabha, July 29, 1928 (Fifth Andhra Untouchables Conference)," *Krishna Patrika*, August 4, 1928, 13.

53. Ibid., 15.

54. "Sixth Andhra Rashtra Adi-Andhra Mahajana Sabha," *Krishna Patrika*, October 26, 1929, 16; *Krishna Patrika*, November 2, 1929, 17.

55. Quoted in "Sixth Andhra Rashtra Adi-Andhra Mahajana Sabha Proceedings," *Krishna Patrika*, November 2, 1929, 17.

56. Quoted in "Sixth Andhra Rashtra Adi-Andhra Mahajana Sabha Proceedings," *Krishna Patrika*, November 16, 1929, 16.

57. Ibid., 17.

58. "Krishna District Andhra Rashtra Adi-Andhra Mahajana Sabha," *Krishna Patrika*, June 6, 1931, 19.

59. Quoted in "Seventh Andhra Rashtra Adi-Andhra Mahajana Sabha," *Krishna Patrika*, August 23, 1932, 17.

60. Ibid.

61. "Special Meeting of the Andhra Rashtra Adi-Andhra Mahajana Sabha," *Krishna Patrika*, September 24, 1932, 16.

62. Clough, *While Sewing Sandals*.

5

Making Sense of Dalit Sikh History

RAJ KUMAR HANS

Growing out of the powerful, anticaste *sant* tradition of the fourteenth and fifteenth centuries in northern India, the Sikh variant of Guru Nanak (1469–1539) and his successors evolved into an organized religious movement in the Punjab in the sixteenth and seventeenth centuries.[1] It became a rallying cry for the untouchables and members of "lower castes" that they be allowed a respectable social existence. As a young, vibrant religion of the subcontinent, the Sikh religion has witnessed high and low points in its journey of five hundred years. So have the Dalits of Punjab, who joined it in great numbers in the seventeenth century and found dignity and equality within its egalitarian fold. But in the process of its growth and expansion in the last quarter of the eighteenth century and the first half of the nineteenth, its body politic came to be afflicted by casteism and untouchability from which the great gurus had tried to extricate its followers.

Being a religion of the book from within the Indian tradition, Sikhism has received worldwide scholarly attention in the last hundred years. A strong and respectable body of literature about Sikh religion, history, polity, and society has appeared in the last fifty years. Besides academic historians, social scientists, and litterateurs, a large number of activists, professionals, and officers have entered the field and enriched the body of Sikh scholarship. Yet another factor that has contributed to the vast body of literature on various facets of Punjabi life and Sikh religion is the large Punjabi and Sikh diaspora, especially in the West.[2]

Whether due to the strong doctrinal position of egalitarian Sikhism or the hegemony of the dominant Jatt Sikh caste, whose members have also been the focus of academic work, the issues of caste and untouchability within Sikhism's history have received scant attention. The remarkable contribution of Dalits to the Sikh tradition has been missing from mainstream Sikh discourse. Naranjan Arifi, a nonprofessional Dalit Sikh historian writing in the Punjabi vernacular, laments the discriminatory attitude of Sikh historians. "If the Sikh historians had honestly and impartially recorded history from the point of view of history writing," he writes, "today's general readers would not have been confused on several issues."[3] On the basis of his reading and analysis of the body of historical and hagiographical works on the Sikhs and Sikh gurus, Arifi is convinced that "Sikh history needs to be rewritten from the start without bringing in miracles and magic so as to give a scientific and analytical orientation to history."[4] While researching the Dalit heroes of the Sikh past and completing the first part of his history of Rang-hretas or Mazhabis (untouchables) in 1993, Arifi was made acutely aware of these problems in Sikh history. This chapter first deals with the great attraction of Sikhism for Dalits—that is, its egalitarianism. Second, it covers the forgotten facets of Dalits—their glorious moments, their heroes, and their achievements—within the Sikh tradition. Last, it discusses the emergence of the Hindu caste system, particularly the practice of untouchability, within the Sikh tradition after the mid-eighteenth century and the setbacks and resultant sufferings of Dalit Sikhs. This section also deals with the efforts of Sikh reformers to eradicate the revived untouchability within Sikhism.

Egalitarianism and Caste Hierarchy in Sikhism

The conversion of large numbers of Dalits to Buddhism, Islam, Christianity, and Sikhism amounts to a search for equality and human dignity that had been an anathema to Hinduism. B. R. Ambedkar believed that bourgeois nationalism, republicanism, and traditional Marxism did not provide any satisfactory solution to the problem of caste and untouchability. He therefore turned to religion for sustained relief. Before Ambedkar turned to Buddhism, he had considered the option of embracing Sikhism along with his followers, thereby opening the same path for Dalits of the subcontinent. Being a notable intellectual of twentieth-century India, he carefully weighed the implications of such a move in contrast to turning to other non-Hindu religions. He was aware of the strong anti-Brahmanical principles and practices of Sikh religion.

Guru Granth Sahib, the sacred text of the Sikhs, consists of the compositions of six of the ten Sikh gurus and contributions of fifteen Sikh bards and fifteen non-Sikh sant poets of various social, ethnic, and religious backgrounds, including the eminent Muslim Sufi, Sheikh Farid. This makes the sacred text an inclusive expression of spirituality in the history of world religions. Spread over 1,450 pages, *Guru Granth Sahib* seeks to build spiritual awareness and searching through a lifelong process of living and learning for the most liberating, empowered condition of human life. One possible way to reach out to the essence, or the core, of the text's message is to see it as a part of the "philosophy of liberation" propounded by the Latin American philosopher Enrique Dussel. He asserts:

> Philosophy of liberation is a pedagogical activity stemming from a praxis that roots itself in proximity of teacher-pupil, thinker-people. Although pedagogical, it is a praxis conditioned by political (and erotic) praxis. Nevertheless, as pedagogical, its essence is theoretical and speculative. Theoretical action, the poetic intellectual illuminative activity of the philosopher, sets out to discover and expose (in the exposition and risk of the life of the philosopher), in the presence of an entrenched system, all moments of negation and all exteriority lacking justice. For this reason it is an analectical pedagogy of liberation. That is, it is the magisterium that functions in the name of the poor, the oppressed, the other, the one who like a hostage within the system testifies to the fetishism of its totalization and predicts its death in the liberating action of the dominated.[5]

Following this "pedagogical" device for Sikhism, the very word "Sikh" denotes the relationship between the guru (teacher) and the Sikh (pupil). And the whole Sikh movement was a proximity of thinker-people, an organic relationship between the gurus and their followers. At the pinnacle of Sikh thought, the merger of the two (*aape gur chela*) achieves a radical position within the Indian tradition. J. P. S. Uberoi puts it aptly in the case of the last guru, Gobind Singh (1666–1708): 'The tenth guru of the Sikhs . . . became in effect the disciple of his disciples at the new revolutionary moment of reversal, inversion and reflection of the leader/follower relation."[6] The pedagogy of liberation epitomized in *Guru Granth Sahib* also turns out to be "magisterial"[7] in the sense that it resists all systems of oppression and injustice, especially perpetrated on the poor. As it speaks in the name of the low, the poor, the oppressed, the text envelops the philosophy of liberation. It does this so completely that Guru Nanak, coming from the upper caste of Khatris, identifies completely with the lowest of the Indian social order, Dalits:

> I am the lowest of the low castes; low, absolutely low;
> I am with the lowest in companionship, not with the so-called high.
> Blessing of god is where the lowly are cared for.[8]

The Sikh guru embraced untouchables by distinctly aligning himself with them to challenge the Hindu caste system. He destroyed the Hindu hierarchical systems—social as well as political. The subversion of the system reached its climax in the creation of Khalsa by the tenth guru, Gobind Singh, in 1699. The real historical force emerged out of the long gestation of the liberation praxis and philosophy that not only fully integrated the untouchables into the struggle for liberation but also succeeded in abolishing the inhuman practice of untouchability in the Sikh practice. It is another thing that untouchability was to re-enter the body politic of the Sikh religion in the mid-eighteenth century and fully corrupt it in the nineteenth century.

By and large, the literature on Punjab and Sikh studies ignored the aspect of caste prejudice in Sikhism. But as sociological and other empirical studies have highlighted the prevalence of caste and untouchability among Sikhs,[9] it is no longer possible to avoid or hide this embarrassing question in historical discourses as was the case in the last fifty years. W. H. McLeod, who studied the religion for half a century, recently admitted to such a tendency:

> To understand Sikh history and religion adequately, one must first grasp the true nature of Sikh society. It is here that caste becomes significant. To understand Sikh society, one must comprehend the nature of caste as it affects the Panth. An understanding of the future development of the Sikh religion makes an understanding of caste as practised by Sikhs absolutely imperative. Social scientists already recognize this, although some of their books or articles may skate round it or omit all mention completely. For those of us who are historians, it is likewise imperative. Without it our understanding of both the Panth and its religion must inevitably be flawed.[10]

By practicing what they preached, the gurus became the exemplars of their message. Guru Nanak felt that the real cause of the misery of the people was the disunity born of caste prejudices. To do away with caste differences and discords, he laid the foundation of *sangat* (congregation) and *pangat* (collective dining).[11] Thus, all ten of the gurus took necessary steps to eliminate the differences of varna and caste. No special places were reserved for people of high rank or caste. The pangat institution in particular was encouraged and strengthened by Guru Amar Das. He insisted that everyone partake of simple food when coming for *sat sangat* (holy congregation). The orthodox Brahmans and Khatris were so alarmed by these revolutionary practices that they complained to Emperor Akbar: "Guru Amar Das [1479–1574] of Goindwal hath abandoned the religious and social customs of the Hindus, and abolished the distinction of the four castes. . . . He seateth all his followers in a line, and causeth them to eat together from his kitchen, irrespective of caste—whether [they] are Jats, strolling minstrels, Muhammadans, Brahmans, Khatris, shopkeepers, sweepers, barbers, washermen, fishermen, or carpenters."[12]

After a careful reading of the gurus' compositions, McLeod argues that the gurus "accepted the notion of *varan*, but never as a system of high and low status. All were equal when it came to access to liberation and to this extent it can certainly be claimed that Guru Nanak and his successors preached the end of the Hindu caste system, at least for those who were their Sikhs."[13] But to explain the prevalence and persistence of caste and untouchability among Sikhs, McLeod introduces the "Sikh concept of caste," which he says "is certainly hierarchical, but it structures hierarchy in terms of economic power and (to a lesser extent) the size of the individual jatis. This renders it very different from the traditional concept of caste. The one exception to this (admittedly a large one) is . . . the general treatment by caste Sikhs of those Sikhs who are Dalits."[14] We get direct testimony from Bhai Jaita (c.1657–1704), a legendary Dalit Sikh, in his epic poem *Sri Gur Katha*, which was composed after the Khalsa formation and before his death in 1704. Bhai Jaita was rechristened as Jiwan Singh, after the creation of "Khalsa," a new identity of Sikhs conferred by Guru Gobind Singh in 1699 (but I will continue to use his Dalit name). He says that Guru Gobind Singh's Sikh do not recognise *baran* (varna) and *jaat* (caste) distinctions but considers only good deeds as good baran.[15] Quite contrary to McLeod's contention that Sikh *Rahit-Namas* (manuals of code of conduct) do not refer much to *jati* (caste), the *rahit* (code) by Bhai Jaita in *Sri Gur Katha* begins with a strong denunciation of caste:

Now listen to the *rahit* of the Singhs,
The Singh should pray to God keeping the war in mind.
When a victim and a needy person beseeches help;
Forgetting his own, a Singh should remove others' suffering.
Not keeping in mind differences of high and low caste,

The Singh should consider all humans as children of God.
Abandoning the Brahmanical rituals and customs,
The Singh should seek liberation by following the gurus' ideas.[16]

Dalit Initiatives in Sikhism

As most literature on Sikh history and religion has failed to take account of the Dalits, John Webster's pioneering formulation on the "Dalit history approach" is quite instructive. Ever since he published the first edition of *The Dalit Christians: A History*[17] in 1992, he has been deepening his thought on the concept of "Dalit" for a non-Hindu religion, and in an important recent article he discusses its implications for Sikh history.[18] According to him, "the Dalit history approach is based on two assumptions. The first is that of Dalit agency. In this case, Dalit Sikhs move to centre-stage to become the chief actors and shapers of their own history; the historian will therefore focus upon them, their views, their struggles, their actions. The second is that a conflict model of society, with caste as not the only but the most important contradiction in Indian society, provides the most appropriate paradigm for understanding their history."[19]

There is no work on Sikh history and tradition in English that has been produced from the Dalit history perspective. Major historical works reflect what Webster calls the "Sikh history approach."[20] Only a few books available in Punjabi (Gurumukhi) language—not all of which are by professional historians—can be seen as written from the "Dalit Sikh approach."[21] While denouncing the established histories as nothing but high-caste histories, S. L. Virdi stresses the need for a Dalit history: "India needs such a history that germinates revolutionary consciousness for social change because history plays a very significant role in this respect. Society assumes a character and shape as molded by its history. From this perspective Dalit history has a very important role. 'Dalit history' is another name for 'revolution' in Indian society."[22]

While Shamsher Singh Ashok wrote his history of the Mazhabis—commissioned by K. S. Neiyyer, a Dalit Sikh settled in London[23]—Naranjan Arifi, a Dalit officer in the revenue department of the Punjab government, wrote a bulky volume on the history of Dalit Sikhs after a great deal of research. He gives us a comprehensive account of Ranghretas or Mazhabis joining the Sikh fold as early as the period of the fifth guru, Arjun (1563–1606). Arifi very diligently extracts Dalit information from the Sikh writings available since the early eighteenth century. In this volume he provides fascinating details about Ranghretas up till the mid-nineteenth century, giving them the names and voices and highlighting their individual and collective participation in the growth of the Khalsa.

The fact that a large number of Dalits, seeking liberation from discrimination and degradation, had joined and secured respectable status within the Sikh order was exemplified by the gurus' special relations with some of the Dalit families. One notable Dalit family was that of Bhai Jaita. His great-grandfather, Bhai Kaliana of Kathunangal Village, near Amritsar, is said to have converted to Sikhism during Akbar's time. He had served the fifth and sixth gurus well. His son, Sukhbhan, migrated to Delhi and became a great musician and established a music school, named Kalyan Ashram after his father, in Raiseena, a nearby village. Kalyan Ashram later came to be known as Kalayane di Dharamshala, and Sikh visitors to Delhi used to lodge there. Sukhbhan's son, Jasbhan, was an equally accomplished musician and a notable Sikh of Delhi, close to the seventh and eighth gurus. Jasbhan's two sons, Agya Ram and Sadanand, continued to render *Gurubani* (Sikh Guru's compositions) in musical notes for the Delhi Sikh congregations. Sadanand emerged as an accomplished musician and became a close companion of the ninth guru, Guru Tegh Bahadur (1621–75).[24] Such intimate ties of his family to the gurus motivated Jaita, the elder son of Sadanand, to carry the severed head of Guru Tegh Bahadar under the most violent circumstances from Delhi to Anandpur in 1675. Overwhelmed with emotions, the young Gobind Singh, the tenth guru (1666–1708), had embraced Bhai Jaita with this blessing: "Ranghrete guru ke bete" (The untouchables are the Guru's own sons). Jaita emerged as a fearless Sikh warrior who so endeared himself to the tenth guru that he was proclaimed by the guru as the *panjwan sahibjada* (fifth son), in addition to the guru's own four sons.[25] It is at the time of the creation of the Khalsa in 1699 that Bhai Jaita was rechristened as Jeevan Singh. He was killed in a fierce battle with Mughal armies in 1704 at Chamkaur.

Even though the Sikhs have been particular about preserving objects and sites related to the Sikh gurus, heroes, and martyrs, they have ignored iconic figures like Bhai Jaita even though many sites he is associated with have been adorned with *gurdwaras* (Sikh temples).[26] Moreover, there are reports that Dalit families who have been taking care of such places have been harassed by workers of the Shiromani Gurudwara Prabandhak Committee (SGPC), the highest statutory body managing Sikh affairs, especially the gurdwaras.[27] Bhai Jaita remained neglected to such an extent that it was hardly known let alone acknowledged that he was also a scholar poet. He had composed a long poem, *Sri Gur Katha*, mentioned above, that provides an eyewitness account of important events surrounding Guru Gobind Singh. It is worth noting that this composition had escaped the notice of Sikh scholars, whose efforts to unearth literature and materials pertaining to the Sikh tradition are otherwise remarkable.[28] It is only with the recent emergence of Dalit Sikh scholarship that a body of literature has begun to be built up around Bhai Jaita in attempts to recover Dalit Sikh pasts. The way Bhai Jaita had been integrated not only into Sikh religion but also into the family of Guru Gobind Singh makes it understandable that any other identity would have been meaningless to him. His identity as a Ranghreta had been subsumed by his identity as a Sikh, as he says: "O Jaita, the savior guru has saved the Ranghretas. The pure guru has adopted Ranghretas as his sons."[29]

The numbers of Dalits who became Sikhs can be gauged from their presence in Guru Gobind Singh's army. Arifi gives interesting details about some leading Dalit warriors, and some of them were also among Guru Gobind Singh's fifty-two court poets. The notable among them were Kavi Dhanna Singh Ghai, Aalam Singh, Dhakkar Singh, Dharam Singh, Garja Singh, Man Singh, and Nigahi Singh.[30] By the mid-eighteenth century, when—amid sustained persecutions by the Mughals—the Sikhs organized themselves into five *dals* (warrior bands), one of these was composed entirely of Mazhabis or Ranghretas under the command of Bir Singh Ranghreta, who had raised a force of 1,300 troopers. The Dalit reinterpretation of the eighteenth century argues in detail that the rising power of Bir Singh Ranghreta, who had become an influential commander, was put a stop to by the treachery of the Jatt commanders. According to Arifi, the Sikhs had succeeded in establishing their independence by the early 1760s, and some of their commanders aspired to have individual chiefdoms in different parts, which Bir Singh Ranghreta opposed. He insisted on following the guru's injunction and the democratic principle that power should lie in the Guru Panth, the Khalsa collective. Charat Singh—grandfather of Ranjit Singh and Baba Aala Singh, founder of Patiala State—hatched a conspiracy to invite Bir Singh Ranghreta from Peshawar to Amritsar and treacherously disarmed his soldiers (using as a reason that they should not enter the Golden Temple with weapons), then slaughtered them inside the sacred precinct in the batches of five in which they were told to move.[31] Thereafter, Mazhabis were not allowed to hold any command position, but their military prowess was used by several *misals* (Sikh kingdoms).[32] Mazhabis were present in the Nishania misal in great numbers, even though its leadership was in the hands of Hindu Khatri community. Yet in another group, called the Dallewalia misal, one Mazhabi, Tara Singh Gheba, assumed the leadership of the misal after the death of its founder,

Gulab Singh, and ruled its territories from its headquarters at Rahon, near Sirhand, until his death in 1807.[33]

Evidence of Dalits' participation in the Sikh movement coming from the Persian sources, quite hostile to Sikhs in tone and tenor for political reasons, is quite instructive. After the death of Guru Gobind Singh, Banda Bahadur (1670–1716), whom the guru had sent from Maharashtra to save the Sikhs from the Mughal oppression in Punjab, succeeded in mobilizing Sikhs to fight against Mughal governors.[34] Muhammad Shafi Warid bitterly underlines the leveling effects of Banda Bahadur's policies after the victory of Sirhind:

> After the slaying of Wazir Khan, he [Banda] laid down that of Hindus and Muslims, whoever enrolled among his Sikhs, should be one body and take their meal together so that the distinction in honour between the lowly and the well-born was entirely removed and all achieved mutual unison, acting together. A sweeper of spittle sat with a *raja* of great status, and they felt no hostility to each other. . . .
>
> Strange it was how through God-decreed fate, the courage and bravery of the inhabitants of those places had departed. If a lowly sweeper or cobbler (chamar), more impure than whom there is no caste (*qaum*) in Hindustan, went to attend on that rebel [Banda], he would be appointed to govern his own town and would return with an order (*sanad*) of office of government in his hand. . . . He [the official sent by Banda] would demand whatever precious goods were in anyone's house and deposit it in the ill-destined treasury of the Guru.[35]

The trend continued throughout the eighteenth century, as noted above. The strength of Dalits in the Sikh Panth and Ranjit Singh's army was considerable. We have an account of the Sikhs in Ghulam Ali Khan's history of the eighteenth-century north Indian state of Awadh, written in 1808. He says:

> Finally, now [1808 AD] the whole country of the Punjab up to the Attock River [Indus], and this side up to Multan, and from the banks of Sutlej to Karnal . . . is in the possession of this sect. Their leaders of high dignity are mostly from the lower classes, such as carpenters, shoemakers and Jats. . . .
>
> In addition to the army, which they call DAL, the number of Sikhs in the Punjab has reached millions (lit. "thousands of thousands"), since yogurt-sellers, confectioners, fodder-vendors, grain-sellers, barbers, washermen, all [fully] keep their hair and, saying *Wahi Guru di*

fateh, interdine with each other. They are not confined to the Punjab only. In the whole of Hindustan from Shahjahanabad [Delhi] to Calcutta, Haidarabad and Chennapatan [Chennai], groups after groups are found to belong to this sect; but most of them are market people (*bazarian*), and only a few are well-born.[36]

Though substantially diminished in their power, the Dalit Sikhs continued as soldiers and fighters. They continued to be influential during Ranjit Singh's rule, which enabled them to construct the Mazhabi Singhan da Bunga (the lodging of Mazhabis) in the Golden Temple complex in 1826. The Mazhabi Bunga was later demolished and the premise was incorporated into the Guru Ramdas Langar building. Mazhabis had their *Bunga* (lodging) at the holy Sikh temple in the city of Tarn Taran.[37] After the British takeover of Punjab in 1849, the control of the Golden Temple and other gurdwaras was given over to the Hindu *mahants* (priests) by removing Mazhabis from all their positions.[38] Thereafter, Hindu Sikhs had complete control over Sikh religious institutions, which will be discussed in the next section.

Creativity, especially literary creativity, is another area in which the Sikh religion seems to have played a significantly positive role in the life of Dalits. Reference has already been made to Bhai Jaita's *Sri Gur Katha* (Story of Sikh gurus), an epic composed at the beginning of the eighteenth century. The second Dalit poet, sant Wazir Singh (c. 1790–1859), prolifically composed metaphysical and social poetry, both in Punjabi and Braj Bhasha. He attracted a number of people as his followers, including five poet disciples hailing from high castes. One of the five poets was Nurang Devi, who was the first female Punjabi poet groomed under sant Wazir Singh's tutorship.[39] The next Dalit intellectual writer Giani Ditt Singh (1852–1901) emerged as a poet, teacher, polemicist, journalist, orator, and ardent Sikh missionary, who turned out to be the pillar of the Singh Sabha movement.[40] Sadhu Daya Singh Arif (1894–1946), who came to master the Gurmukhi, Urdu, Persian, Arabic, and Sanskrit languages, was the most popular intellectual poet of his time in Punjab. His first poetical work, *Fanah-dar-Makan* (Doorstep to dissolution), was published when he had just turned twenty. The work which made him a household name throughout Punjab was *Zindagi Bilas* (Discourse on life), which was completed in 1916. Overall, it was didactic poetry that caught the masses' imagination, and *Zindagi Bilas* became the most frequently published, read, or heard poetic creation after Waris Shah's *Heer*. All of them have remained neglected in the histories of Punjabi literature. From the early twentieth century a series of Dalit writers are writing with a clear Dalit consciousness.[41]

Caste and untouchability came to afflict the Sikhs, particularly in the past two centuries. There was a gradual rise of Sanatan Sikhism,[42] a fine admixture of Hindu caste-centric practices and Sikhism, in the second half of the eighteenth century. By the close of the nineteenth century, it had assumed a vicious form. Features of Sanatan Sikhism were first outlined in a genealogical history of Sikh gurus by Kesar Singh Chhibber in *Bansavalinama Dasan Patshahian ka*, completed in 1769.[43] Chhibber belonged to a Brahman family of Jammu. He attributes the Guru Gobind Singh's power and success to the worship of a Hindu goddess and gives considerable importance to the role of Brahmans in his account of the Sikh gurus. Arifi devotes more than a hundred pages of his book to a close examination of Chhibber's work and lashes out at him, saying that the work is "a complete conspiracy against the gurus' philosophy as its purpose is to introduce Brahmanical ideas. . . . Even if it is a bundle of lies in which 80–90 percent of the dates are wrong, imaginary characters are introduced, and the principles and traditions of the gurus are colored with Brahmanism."[44] Historian J. S. Grewal is also highly critical of Chhibber's work and calls it "Brahmanizing the tradition": "Whether consciously or unconsciously, Kesar Singh Chhibber makes a consistent and an earnest attempt at Brahmanizing the Khalsa tradition."[45]

It is ironic that the Hindu caste-centric practices entered Sikhism during the reign of Ranjit Singh (1780–1839), who founded the first Sikh empire in India. Even in the first decade of the nineteenth century the egalitarian spirit of the Khalsa had remained intact, as observed by John Malcolm: "Wherever the religion of Guru Govind [Gobind] prevails, the institutions of Brahma must fall. The admission of proselytes, the abolition of the distinctions of caste, the eating of all kinds of flesh, except that of cows, the form of religious worship, and the general devotion of all Singhs to arms, are ordinances altogether irreconcilable with the Hindu mythology, and have rendered the religion of the Sikhs as obnoxious to the Brahmans, and higher tribes of the Hindus, as it is popular with the lower orders of that numerous class of mankind."[46]

Henry Steinbach, a European soldier in Ranjit Singh's army, made an astute observation about a definite change that had taken place since Malcolm's statement: "The assumption of irresponsible power by Ranjeet Singh destroyed, in some degree, the potency of the Khalsa."[47] That the Hindu practices were fast creeping into Sikh culture during Ranjit Singh's time was also observed by another European traveler in 1836, Baron Charles Hugel, who noted that "like every other religion grounded in deism, the faith of the Sikhs is already deteriorated; image worship and distinction of castes are gradually taking place of the precepts enjoined by their original institutions."[48]

The Golden Temple at Amritsar has been the sanctum sanctorum for Sikhs, as Mecca is for Muslims, and many lives were lost defending the temple's sanctity during the eighteenth century. It had assumed such an importance in the religious and political life of Punjab that Ranjit Singh abolished the system of collective management and assumed the right to appoint a temple manager. This precedent was used by a subsequent ruler of Punjab, Lieutenant-Governor Sir Robert Egerton, in 1881 to appoint his own temple manager.[49] By that time, the Mahants had already introduced non-Sikh practices in the precincts of the temple, and the commissioner of the Amritsar Division, Robert Needham Cust, could foresee in 1858 what was in store for the faith. He observed that "unsupported by the State, plundered by its own guardians, in due course of time the temple will fall to ruins; the sect which was founded by Baba Nanak will cease to exist; the nucleus of nationality which was created by Guru Gobind Singh will be dispersed, and [the] proselytising and fanatic Sikh will fall back into the ranks of the lethargic and uninspiring Hindu."[50]

Idols were placed in the Golden Temple, and Dalits were prevented from bathing in the *sarovar* (holy tank). In 1877, there was consternation among the temple authorities as some Mazhabi soldiers and their families attempted to bathe there.[51] The deterioration in the Sikh religion was observed at the beginning of the twentieth century by John Campbell Oman, a keen student of Indian epics, mysticism, cults, customs, and related issues. During his extensive visits to the Golden Temple Oman noticed quite a few Hindu practices within the complex. In front of the Akal Bunga, goats were slaughtered on the Dussera festival. He found that along the northern side of the pool, a Brahman was worshipping tiny images of Ganesh and Krishna. At the northeast corner of the tank, there was a Shiva temple with a lingam, and along the eastern side there was another temple of *devi* (goddess). At the devi temple Oman "encountered Brahmans engaged in worship, *separately*, of course. One had before him a saligram and a picture of the temple of Badrinath; while the other adored a saligram and a *tulasi* (holy basil) plant. The latter worshipper appeared quite at home in the precincts of the Sikh temple, for he blew sundry loud blasts by means of a *conch*, from which he managed to produce some three or four distinct notes."[52] In the concluding paragraph of his chapter on the Golden Temple, he observes that the "advanced" party—alluding to the radical members of the Singh Sabha—succeeded in removing the Hindu idols from the complex in 1905, but he added: "Nonetheless, only last year (1907), an apparently well-informed writer in the *Civil and Military Gazette* of Lahore lamented the fact that the distinctive differences between Sikhism and Hinduism were melting away, a conclusion at which I had myself arrived some years ago."[53]

Caste prejudice and the practice of untouchability being central to Hinduism, any individual, organization, or ideology questioning it was always seen as an enemy, and no effort was spared to eliminate the challenge. In the context of the Sikh religion, A. E. Barstow observed in the 1920s that "Hinduism, [due] to its wonderfully assimilative character, had thus reabsorbed a good part of Sikhism, as it had absorbed Buddhism before it, notwithstanding that much of these religions is opposed to caste and the supremacy of the Brahmans."[54] Bhagat Lakshman Singh (1863–1944), a scholar and intellectual who was a new convert to Sikhism, believed that the Sikh creed had been Hinduized after the establishment of Sikh rule. The high-caste Hindus had made advances toward the new power in an attempt at reconciliation, and a compromise was affected through which the Sikhs abandoned their revolutionary program.[55] Sikhism began to lose its distinct identity. Khushwant Singh is straightforward in admitting that "Sikhism did not succeed in breaking the caste system. . . . and Sikhs of higher castes refused to eat with untouchable Sikhs and in villages separate wells were provided for them."[56]

We have some accounts from Sikh newspapers in the first quarter of the twentieth century that already give evidence of the problems caused by the Hinduization of Sikhism. Dalit Sikhs had started either following the Hindu vedic religion, supposedly casteless, advocated by Arya Samaj or converting to Christianity, which forced the Sikh reformers to address the issue of caste inequality and stem the tide. Singh Sabhas had initiated the process, but caste attitudes were too deep-seated to make much difference. The Sikh press started pushing the cause forcefully. In an editorial titled "Isaai hon de Karan" (Reasons for becoming Christian) in the *Punjab Darpan* of October 10, 1917, the Sikhs were warned to mend their ways:

> In the last eight months 1,600 Hindus have become Christians. . . . For this mission, the pastors have relinquished professorships in the mission colleges as they have also abandoned the comforts of churches. Compare this with the Sikh community: there are thousands of those baptized Sikhs rendering Gurbani with musical instruments that are called Mazhabis, Ramdasias, or Bishth. But high-caste Sikhs always oppress those who simply labor for their sustenance. . . . Because these

illiterate Sikhs hate them more than they hate Muslims, it is necessary to inspire the Sikh Sardars, Numberdars, and Zaildars in the villages to embrace their brethren in faith rather than making them the enemies of their religion by rebuking them all the time.[57]

The growing anxiety about the virus of untouchability among educated Sikhs is reflected in most of the community-oriented newspapers and magazines. One reader signing himself "Sewa Singh BA" wrote a letter to *Khalsa* (community) newspaper in 1923 (a translation of the title would be "One's most necessary duty: for the attention of Chief Khalsa Diwan"), in which he drew attention to the problem of untouchability.[58] Referring to Arya Samaj, the writer urged the diwan to shoulder "the improvement of untouchable castes." On June 24, 1923, *Khalsa* published a report on a *divan* (assembly) about a *shudhi* (purification) at Amritsar's Jallianwala Bagh that had been held on June 21. The divan was devoted solely to the removal of untouchability. The report said:

> Sardar Dalip Singh, the secretary of the divan, while introducing the purpose of the divan said that even now Guru Gobind Singh's baptized Sikhs, who are called Ramdasia, Mazhbis, and Chuhras, are thrown out of *langars* [community kitchens] and their Prasad is not accepted in the gurdwaras. That's why today's divan is organized, to find out remedy for this malaise. . . .
>
> Later on Bhai Mehtab Singh 'Bir' lamented how due to our indifference hundreds of our so-called untouchable brothers are being swallowed up by other religions. He reported that twenty-five Rahitiyas became Aryas in 1903 and after that 10,000 Rahitiyas joined the Arya Samaj.[59]

The Sikh leadership by that time had gotten so lost in the struggle to liberate gurdwaras from the clutches of Brahmanized Mahants that the agenda to liberate Sikh minds from casteism was set aside. The helpless situation drove Bhai Pratap Singh, the head *granthi* (priest) of the Golden Temple, to write a treatise on the issue.[60] Besides looking into the theological and practical high points against untouchability in the Sikh tradition, he summarized the efforts of the SGPC for the removal of untouchability between 1921 and 1933.

Ambedkar's engagement with Sikhism was another factor contributing to the introspection on the part of a small group of Sikh reformers seeking to remove untouchability. It started with Ambedkar's powerful move in 1936 to envisage a dignified life for the Dalits in the Sikh religion. Sardar Amar

Singh, secretary of Shri Guru Singh Sabha Shillong (in Assam), wrote two articles in *Khalsa Sewak* on March 17 and 22, 1936 (in English, the title of the articles is "The need of the Sikhs' preaching among the untouchables and some suggestions for that").[61] An editorial in *Khalsa Sewak* on March 7, 1936, reports that Ambedkar had written letters to the SGPC but laments that the committee's response was unsatisfactory. The editorial notes with sarcasm that with all this "the Sikhs are so indifferent that they would not stop bragging of their reforms on paper, which is just a show, but in practice not a single step forward has been taken."[62]

It is the Dalit voices that are most vociferous about caste and untouchability in Sikhism. Pandit Bakshi Ram, who was born in a Balmiki family toward the close of the nineteenth century, recalls in his memoirs the condition of untouchability. He narrates two incidents from his village to show how Dalit Sikhs were treated by the dominant Jatt Sikhs. Once, a Rahitia (a Dalit who observed the Sikh code of conduct) boy was beaten up by Jatt boys while drawing water from the school well. Another time, when a Rahitia wedding-party used the village pond for cleaning their backs in the morning, they were thoroughly beaten up by Jatts.[63] "Untouchability has become deep-rooted in the Jatt-dominated villages," Ram says, and asks "Isn't practicing caste and untouchability against *gurmat* (Guru's teachings)?"[64] Observing how after independence the Jatts came to completely control the politics and economy of Punjab as they opposed the Dalits' economic demands, Ram asks: "If the Jatt Sikhs demand higher prices for their agricultural produce don't the labourers have right to demand higher wages? And if the latter struggle for their right the former boycott them. Isn't it the height of injustice? If Akalis have their pickets for their demands why can't Dalits exercise their right to make their demands?"[65]

Prem Gorkhi, an eminent Punjabi short-story writer who graduated from a daily worker to a full-time employee as a library peon (office-boy), and then becoming a respectable journalist, recalls with bitterness:

> I have seen that if Punjabi writers are intimate friends they also carry deep casteist ideas within. . . . I have close relations from the high to the low . . . they respect [me] as well. . . . I go to everyone's house, eat and sleep there . . . but over taking sides on any vital issue, the cobra within spreads its fangs. . . . There is no drastic change in the caste situation from what it was a hundred years ago . . . only the ways of untouchability have changed. Today if you eat from the same plate, you also kill the same person—and who you call Dalit today is not a century-old

thoughtless, egoless person without identity. He has reached the stage of deciding for himself what is good for him.[66]

Gurnam Aqida, a Punjabi writer and journalist, is forthright about the hegemony of Jatts: "Jatts control all the organizations and institutions that decide the fate of society. They dominate the bureaucracy. They have replaced the traditional minstrels, the Mirasis, in the field of singing, and the traditional thieves, the Sansis; the Jatts have replaced even the famous woman brigand Phoolan Devi in pillages. The Jatts are responsible for Dalitism in villages; they are the police officers, professors, and principals and even the ruling politicians. So much so, that a crime committed by them becomes an entertainment."[67]

For a fairly long time in the history of Sikh growth, especially during the phase of Sikh struggles against political powers, Dalits and Jatts had served as two arms of the Sikh religion, transcending caste differences in keeping with the spirit of the new religion. During this period between the sixteenth and eighteenth centuries, caste was not completely eliminated and the caste differences that continued to persist did not constitute any kind of caste discrimination. Without religious sanction, untouchability had been reduced considerably within the Sikh fold. But if in the past hundred years Dalit articulations clearly identify the major source of their oppression and misery as the emergence of Jatts as a dominant caste, this requires an explanation. Is it that Sikhism as an ideological and social force was failing and falling? Is it that the liberating religious ideology that had survived political attacks was succumbing to economic ones?

There is no denying the fact that Jatts as ordinary peasants historically shared an oppressed life with other lower segments of Punjab under successive revenue-centric state systems. Their joining the Sikh movement en masse immensely helped them raise their status in the caste hierarchy during the long period of political resistance of Sikhs in the seventeenth and eighteenth centuries. Their carving out of independent political fiefdoms in the last quarter of the eighteenth century—with the eventual formation of the Sikh regional state under Ranjit Singh, who happened to be a Jatt by caste—instilled them with immense pride. Being landholders, they succeeded in establishing their supremacy and hegemony over other castes, including Brahmans and Khatris in the Punjab countryside. The end of the Sikh political power in Punjab at the hands of British colonialism by the mid-nineteenth century did not necessarily mean the end of Sikh social and economic power. By and large Sikhs' loyalty to the British Raj in the 1857 uprising helped them further consolidate their hold over other castes in the villages, as they came to form the backbone of the Anglo-Indian army.[68] The Punjab Land Alienation Act of 1901,[69] though largely an official effort to protect agriculturists—especially distraught Muslim peasants of western Punjab—from rapacious moneylenders, proved to be a grand colonial gift to the Sikh Jatts. The act prevented nonagricultural communities from buying and occupying lands. The Dalits of Punjab proved to suffer the most from this act as they had been declared as nonagricultural menials in official enumerations, despite the fact that within the Sikh fold they had become soldiers, artisans, or peasants. As agriculturists at several places they tilled lands as owners or tenants.[70] But after passage of the act, even the houses in which their families had been living for generations did not belong to them; all land in villages now belonged to peasant proprietors, predominantly Jatts. Dalits had been completely thrown to the mercy of Jatts and rendered extremely vulnerable by the colonial law. From once honorable warriors of the Sikh religion the Dalits had been reduced to untouchable Sikhs without land or homes of their own. In such circumstances, caste came to be used by Jatts as a convenient way to obtain a virtually free supply of agrarian labor from Dalits for their class interests, in service of their land operations. The Jatt domination of the Sikh religion and in the Punjab countryside in the twentieth century created problems for other dependent caste communities in general (and for Dalits in particular), which resulted in the building of caste-oriented gurdwaras.

Conclusion

Sikhism emerged as a vital religious force and movement with ideas of equality and liberation for the downtrodden. It succeeded in empowering those groups of Punjabi Dalits who joined it. They excelled in several fields, including religion, warfare, and literary creativity. If Sikhism as a social force was failing in its mission, what alternatives were left open to the Dalits of Punjab? Some Dalits succeeded in finding social-religious solutions, such as the Ad-Dharam movement in the 1920s. The movement aimed at securing a respectable place for Dalits through cultural transformation, spiritual regeneration, and political assertion rather than seeking patronage from above. The argument of its founder, Mangoo Ram Mugowalia, that Dalits were the original inhabitants of India had an enormous psychological impact on the untouchables of Punjab, inspiring them to fight for their liberation. Within a short time, the movement became a mass Dalit struggle for a separate identity. Though after independence it petered out, its success lies in the fact that those who continued to identify themselves as Ad Dharmis have made far greater progress in all fields when compared to those Dalits who continued to follow established religions, including Sikhism.

The nonreligious path to emancipation was a socialist revolution. The Communists have had a few successful movements in Punjab since the 1920s but only once addressed the Dalit question explicitly. The exception was the young revolutionary Bhagat Singh, who wrote a lengthy article titled "Achhut da Sawal" (The question of untouchability) in 1928. Pointing at the competition between different religions to win the untouchables to their respective folds out of sheer political greed and vested interests, he issued a clarion call to Dalits to unite and fight their own battles, as no one else would fight for them.[71] But after Bhagat Singh was martyred in 1931, no Communists followed his approach. Assuming that the end of class rule would automatically resolve cultural issues, the Communists failed to see the significance of caste and untouchability in the Indian cultural context. Even the best Dalit poets and activists in the extreme left Naxalite movement—namely, Lal Singh Dil and sant Ram Udasi—experienced casteist insults and died in difficult circumstances if not altogether in ignominy.

Dalits in general and Dalit Sikhs in particular find themselves at a crossroad as far as the question of religion is concerned. A group of Dalit Sikhs whose families have retained memories of the glorious past are unable to understand what has happened to the religion, and they still entertain hopes that Sikhism will restore what has been lost. Yet a majority of Dalits have experienced the tensions of conflicting attitudes and feel frustrated as they turn away from Sikh religion. Education, political awareness, and Dalit assertion pose the challenge to older religious identities as Dalits find alternative ways to seek dignity and pride.

NOTES

1. For a discussion of a broad range of bhakti sant movements and issues, see Schomer and McLeod, *The Sants*.

2. Grewal, "Contesting Interpretations of the Sikh Tradition"; Juergensmeyer, *Sikh Studies*.

3. Arifi, *Ranghrehtian da Itihas*, part 1, 13. All translations from Punjabi are mine.

4. Ibid., 35.

5. Dussel, *Philosophy of Liberation*, 178.

6. Uberoi, *Religion, Civil Society and the State*, 74.

7. Mann, *The Making of Sikh Scripture*, 133.

8. "Neechan andar neech jati, Neechi hun ati neech / Nanak tin ke sang sath, Vadian siyon kya rees / Jithe neech sanmalian, Tithe nadr teri bakhshish" (quoted in Puri, "The Scheduled Castes in the Sikh Community," 2694).

9. Jodhka, "Dissociation, Distancing and Autonomy" and "Sikhism and the Caste Question"; Judge, "Religion, Caste, and Communalism in Punjab"; Juergensmeyer, *Religion as Social Vision*; Marenco, *The Transformation of Sikh Society*; Puri, "The Scheduled Castes in Sikh Community"; Indera Singh, "Caste in a Sikh Village"; Walia, "The Problem of Untouchability among Sikhs in Punjab with Special Reference to Mazhabi Sikhs."

10. McLeod, "Sikhs and Castes," 106.

11. "Sangat" in Gurmukhi means to accompany or to sit with others. Thus, praising God through the words of the guru in the company of the learned is known as keeping sangat in the Sikh tradition. "Pangat" in Gurmukhi is derived from the Sanskrit *pankti*, which means a line or row. Thus, eating food sitting in a row without any differentiation or discrimination is called pangat in the Sikh tradition.

12. Quoted in Macauliffe, *The Sikh Religion*, 105.

13. McLeod, "The Sikh Concept of Caste," 173.

14. Ibid., 186.

15. Gandiwind, *Shaheed Baba Jiwan Singh*, 174. This important writing by Bhai Jaita (also known as Jiwan Singh) came to light only in the second half of the twentieth century. *Sri Gur Katha* (the full title is *Sri Gur Katha krit kavi Baba Jeevan Singh [Bhai Jaita]*) was first published in Arifi, *Ranghrehtian da Itihas*, part 1, 396–424. Other books in which *Sri Gur Katha* was published are Baldev Singh *Panjwan Sahibjada*, 465–501; Gurmukh Singh, *Bhai Jaita Ji*, 49–82.

16. "Ab rahit sunuh gur singhan ki, hari dhian dhare ur judh chitare / jab arit aye pukar karenh, nij sookh taje tin dookh nivare / nahi jaat sujaat bichar kareh, ar poot khudaye janahen sabare / rahu reet geh nahin bipran ki, ar gurmat prapat mokh duare" (quoted in Gandiwind, *Shaheed Baba Jiwan Singh*, 181).

17. Webster, *The Dalit Christians*.

18. Webster, "The Dalit Sikhs: A History?"

19. Ibid., 138.

20. Ibid., 133.

21. Some of these are Arifi, *Ranghrehtian da Itihas*; Ashok, *Mazhabi Sikhan da Itihas*; Nirbhay, *Mazhabi Sikhan di Jaddo-jaihad*; and Giani Singh, *Guru ka Beta*. For general histories of the Dalits of Punjab, see Ishar Singh, *Sikh Ithas de Visre Panne*; Virdi, *Punjab da Dalit Itihas*.

22. Virdi, *Punjab da Dalit Itihas*, xxxi–xxxii.

23. Ashok, *Mazhabi Sikhan da Itihas*.

24. For details, see Arifi, *Ranghrehtian da Itihas*, 224–26.

25. See the novel by Baldev Singh, *Panjwan Sahibjada*.

26. Murphy, "Materializing Sikh Pasts."

27. Gurnam Aqida, "Baba Jeevan Singhji di mahan kurbani nu vi nahin samjhia," 10–11.

28. The researchers of Punjabi literary texts, especially those pertaining to the Sikh tradition—including Shamsher Ashok, Gurinder Maan, Pritam Singh, and Piara

Padam—and historians including J. S. Grewal, W. H. McLeod, Ganda Singh, and Pashaura Singh do not mention Bhai Jaita's *Sri Gur Katha*. It is just possible that it was not easily available. Naranjan Arifi discovered a copy with Kultar Singh, the oldest son of Daya Singh Arif, which had been given to him by some of the Assamese Dalit Sikhs in 1950s. See Arifi, *Ranghrehtian da Itihas*, 394–95.

29. "Jayayte taranhar gur, taar diye ranghretde / Gur paras ne kar diye, ranghretde gur betde" (quoted in Arifi, *Ranghrehtian da Itihas*, 409); see also Baldev Singh, *Panjwan Sahibjada*, 481.

30. Arifi, *Ranghrehtian da Itihas*, 465–514.

31. Ibid., 432–58.

32. This term seems to have been derived from the Arabic word *misal*, meaning equal.

33. Arifi, *Ranghrehtian da Itihas*, 517–24.

34. Ganda Singh, *Life of Banda Singh Bahadur*; Sohan Singh, *Banda the Brave*.

35. Warid, "Banda Bahadur and his Followers from Muhammad Shafi 'Warid,'" 161–62.

36. Irfan Habib, "An account of the Sikhs, 1808 from Ghulam Ali Khan, Imadus Saadat," 214–15.

37. Arifi, *Ranghrehtian da Itihas*, 429–65; Ashok, *Mazhbi Sikhan da Itihas*, 171.

38. Arifi, *Ranghrehtian da Itihas*, 570.

39. Hans, "Sant Poet Wazir Singh."

40. Malhotra, "Living and Defining Caste."

41. Hans, "Rich Heritage of Punjabi Dalit Literature and Its Exclusion from Histories."

42. According to Harjot Oberoi, "the social universe of Sanatan Sikhism can best be summed up under the Brahmanical paradigm of varnasrama dharma" (*The Construction of Religious Boundaries*, 105–6).

43. Chhibber, *Bansavalinama Dasan Patshahian Ka*.

44. Arifi, *Ranghrehtian da Itihas*, 145. His examination of Chhibber's work spans pages 37–145 of his book.

45. Grewal, "Brahmanizing the Tradition," 85–86.

46. Malcolm, *Sketch of the Sikhs*, 151.

47. Steinbach, *The Punjaub*, 159.

48. Jervis, *Travels in Kashmir and Panjab*, 283.

49. Kerr, "British Relationships with the Golden Temple, 1849–90," 140.

50. Quoted in ibid., 142.

51. Ibid., 145. See also Grewal, "Contest over the Sacred Space."

52. Oman, *Cults, Customs and Superstitions of India*, 98.

53. Ibid., 102–3.

54. Barstow, *The Sikhs*, 19.

55. Grewal, *Contesting Interpretations of the Sikh Tradition*, 71.

56. Khushwant Singh, *The Sikhs*, 45–46.

57. Editorial, "Isaai hon de Karan," *Punjab Darpan*, October 10, 1917.

58. Sewa Singh, "Ik Atti Jaruri Sewa: Chief Khalsa Divan de Dhian yog," *Khalsa*, February 21, 1923.

59. Untitled article, *Khalsa*, June 24, 1923.

60. Bhai Singh, *Jaat Paat te Chhut-Chhaat sambandhi Gurmat Sidhant*.

61. Sardar Amar Singh, "Achhutaan vich Sikhi Parchar di lor ate kujh Sujaho," *Khalsa Sewak*, March 17 and 22, 1936.

62. Editorial, *Khalsa Sewak*, March 7, 1936.

63. Pandit Ram, *Mera Jeevan Sangharash*, 4.

64. Ibid., 96.

65. Ibid., 99.

66. Gorkhi, "Dhukhdi Dhooni Pharolani Payee."

67. Aqida, *Kakh Kande*, 55–56.

68. Fox, *Lions of Punjab*.

69. For a detailed account and discussion of the act, see Sri Sharma, *Punjab in Ferment*. On the caste angle of the act, see Cassan, "British Law and Caste Identity Manipulation in Colonial India."

70. For an example, Chet Singh, the Ranghreta general of the Bhangi misal's cavalry in the last quarter of the eighteenth century, owned a large amount of agricultural land, plowed by seven plows, in Bhaike Dialpur village in the present Barnala District. He was killed in a battle with Ranjit Singh's army. Committed to Guru Gobind Singh's idea of the Sikh Panth (collective) and seeing its erosion in the personal rule of Chet Singh, Ranjit's younger brother Kahla Singh had preferred to give up agricultural land and moved to another village of Raisar. These details are recorded by Gurdas Singh Gharu, Dalit writer and activist, in his autobiography, *Pagdandian taun Jeevan Marg Tak*, 29–30.

71. This article was published in the June 1928 issue of *Kirti* under the pen name Vidrohi. See J. Singh, *Shahid Bhagat Singh ate uhna de Sathian dian Likhtan*, 221.

PART II. Probing the Present

6

The Dalit Reconfiguration of Modernity:
Citizens and Castes in the Telugu Public Sphere

K. SATYANARAYANA

Sahu, who was a Naxalite leader, coauthor of the famous novel *Komaram Bheem*, and a member of the A. P. Viplava Rachayitala Sangham, popularly known as Virasam,[1] is said to have criticized the organization for its failure to publicize his illegal detention by the police as a violation of the democratic rights of a writer belonging to an oppressed caste. This led to an open debate. Virasam responded by saying that Sahu was a well-known Naxalite leader and that he enjoyed the support of the large segments of the public, particularly Adivasis. This view implies that there is no need to publicize Sahu as a writer in the domain of the middle-class public. K. Srinivas, a literary critic, intervened in this debate to suggest that the crucial issue is that Dalits, other minorities, and women are demanding recognition in the middle-class world, not just in the popular domain of the people. The middle-class domain, in this context, is the domain of the authorized public sphere—"key spaces where public opinion is molded."[2]

Dalit writers and critics argued in the 1980s and the 1990s that they were denied recognition in the Telugu public sphere on the basis of caste identities. Yet now they seek recognition in the public sphere on the very basis of those identities. The shaping of a distinct Dalit public and Dalit identity are crucial to understanding the question of recognition and the emergence of Dalit discourses such as Dalitvadam (Dalit sociopolitical debates) and Dalit literature in the Telugu public sphere. It was in the context of Dalit mobilizations against caste atrocities and the struggles over caste-based reservations in the 1980s and the 1990s that the Dalit public emerged as a subaltern public, challenging the exclusionary norms of the Telugu public sphere represented by both the liberal and the revolutionary leftist writers and critics.

I have argued that we can conceptualize the shift toward the new notion and function of Dalit writing through mapping the larger structural changes in Telugu public sphere (such as the emergence of the new social groups and the rise of Dalit writing) and through a reading of Dalit discourses in the form of debates, literary controversies, and Dalit poetry. Through the category of Dalit writing, Dalit writers advance a critique of the human citizen (read: Hindu, upper caste, and male), a figure of the modernist project of Telugu modern literatures, and posit the not-quite-citizen figure of the Dalit to reconfigure the Telugu public sphere. Dalit claims to self-representation in the Telugu public sphere cannot be read just as claims of producing authentic literature. These are claims specifically made for recognition in the public domain as poets, writers, scholars, and critics. Reading discourses such as Dalitvadam and Dalit literature as pure literature or culture and justifying this body of writing on the ground of authenticity will obscure the new politics of caste or recognition and the refiguring of the Telugu public sphere.

Telugu Publics

In this section, I map the contours of the Telugu public sphere by reading the critical discourses of the liberal and the revolutionary leftist critics. Velcheru Narayana Rao, a prominent Telugu literary critic and a professor of languages and cultures of Asia at the University of Wisconsin–Madison made a major intervention in 2002. In a Telugu-language journal article, he attempted to assess the literary value of new claimants to literary recognition in the Telugu public sphere.[3] His criticism of Dalit poetry is also applicable to the newly emerging Dalit literary movement as a whole in Telugu. It is important to note that Narayana Rao is popularly known as a Marxist critic in Telugu literary circles. His *Telugulo Kavita Viplavala Swaroopam* (Poetic revolutions in Telugu) is a widely acclaimed study of Telugu poetry. Narayana Rao says: "Whatever may be the views or theories that literature proposes and propagates—first, it should be literature. In fact, those who are in the literary field will not judge its literary merit based on the views and proposed aims in literature. There is no one in [the] Telugu [world] today who would assert—you propose whatever politics and social values you want to propose only if your work has literary merit, then we recognizse it as literature and respect it."[4]

He believes that the institution of literature should be autonomous and independent. He insists that "literature" is a special kind of knowledge that only specialists can judge. "What is good poetry," Narayana Rao argues, "should be decided only by poets."[5] He bemoans the fact that "there is no one in [the] Telugu [world]" to perform the function of judging what is good literature.[6] He offers an explanation for the decline of "literature" as an institution in Telugu society. In the 1970s Virasam came on to the stage, making literary commitment a key issue in the discussions of Telugu poetry. Narayana Rao believes that Virasam propagated ideas like "social consciousness," "writing for the people," "the poet as someone who stands for the armed people," and so on.[7] Even after the weakening of Virasam, these ideas continue to prevail in the evaluation of poetry. "The feminist and Dalit poets," Narayana Rao argues, "rejected Virasam but followed the path of Virasam in literary discussions and controversies" and believed that "literature is a vehicle to propagate their views."[8] As a result, *sahityam* (literature) as an institution "got weakened." Criticizing Virasam writers and literary critics as "middle-class opportunists," Narayana Rao says that they have no special training or qualifications to be called literary people. He attributes the destruction of the boundaries of literature to the entrance into the literary domain of ineligible people and notes that "many of these people are not poets, writers, or critics and not at all pundits."[9] Arguing that no standards are followed in publishing literary works in Telugu, Narayana Rao points out that Telugu poets "publish whatever they write as it is. Those who write books themselves are publishers. Because of this, we do not have traditions established separately by the publishing houses."[10] These practices in Telugu literature, he says, contributed to the blurring of distinctions between literature and society and between the language of addressing problems in society and the language of literary criticism. Therefore, literature lost its special status.[11]

Narayana Rao's argument that literature is a special kind of domain is not a new one. His conception of "pure" literature is closely linked to his endorsement of an elite domain in the public sphere. What is relevant in Narayana Rao's argument for our purposes is his elaboration on the nature of the Telugu literary public sphere. He idealizes the Telugu literary public sphere of the Bavakavitvam (Romantic poetry) days (the 1930s), when poets discussed poetry, its rhythm, language, structure, and so on. Poets used to judge what a good poem was and who wrote well.[12] Narayana Rao marks the 1970s as a point when there was a significant break from the past, and nonpoets (read:

revolutionary writers) began to occupy this public sphere. Narayana Rao's description is useful in pointing out the significant change in the Telugu public sphere. The elite public sphere was broadened and the notion of "literature" redefined. "Literature" is no longer a domain of special knowledge. The notion of the "poet or critic" as a privileged person, gifted with powers of imagination and trained in the skills of analysis, was thoroughly discredited. Narayana Rao is responding to these transformations.

The other complaint Narayana Rao makes is that there are no institutions to protect literary standards. He points out that there are no reputed publishing houses or well-edited and peer-reviewed journals to select and publish good literature. Telugu writers, operating as small political forums, publish their poetry with their personal funds or donations. Very often printing of the books is paid for by donations collected from individuals and social groups. Recently, books have been published with the support of funding agencies. State support is nearly unavailable for publishing literature. This scenario of self-publishing, Narayana Rao feels, is a serious problem as he sums up his view elsewhere: "it does not allow for dispassionate literary evaluation by competent reviewers but encourages self-promotion and sycophancy."[13] What is at stake here is Narayana Rao's vision of a democratic society and his Eurocentric view of Telugu literary culture. Telugu poets function outside the domains of the state and the official public sphere, but Narayana Rao is insisting on disciplining this literary culture. As Narayana Rao puts it, "in those countries where there is a strong democratic culture, publishing houses and educational institutions create a stable autonomy . . . publishing houses are cautious about what books to publish and what not to publish as they have to protect standards. To ensure standards, they take the help of poets, writers, critics, and editors. The publishers and the award-giving institutions, whatever be their political perspectives or ideology, are committed to insist on one literary standard and one taste."[14]

Narayana Rao's criticism of the Telugu literary public sphere is from the point of view of American or European society. He is invoking a kind of Habermasian liberal public sphere with civil-societal institutions, publishing houses, and award-giving institutions. The public that shapes literature, in this view, is the bourgeois elite (that is, the upper caste in India)—poets, writers, critics, and editors. Narayana Rao's complaint is that Telugu society is not yet democratic, as it has not produced a bourgeois class. Locating himself on the high discursive ground of Western or global modernity, Narayana Rao invokes this normative liberal public sphere, which is informed by a singular notion of the "public," and categorizes the Telugu public sphere as backward and chaotic.

To explain the backward and the chaotic character of the Telugu literary public sphere and make sense of Telugu public life, the Habermasian concept of a liberal public sphere is quite useful.[15] The liberal public sphere, according to Habermas, is an institutional arena in which citizens discuss common issues. This site is separate from the state and produces discourses that are in principle critical of the state.[16] Nancy Fraser critiques and reworks the Habermasian concept of the public sphere. She argues that Habermas idealizes the liberal public sphere as the only public arena in which "inequities of status [of citizens] were to be bracketed."[17] She describes the public sphere as "an institutional arena of discursive interaction" that thematizes inequalities. She emphasizes the conflictual relations between the bourgeois public and other publics and proposes the concept of "multiple publics." She further suggests that "subaltern counter publics" are "parallel discursive arenas where members of subordinated social groups invent and circulate counter discourses to formulate oppositional interpretations of their identities, interests and needs."[18] She adds that these subaltern publics function as "spaces of withdrawal and regroupment" as well as "bases and training groups for agitational activities directed toward wider publics."[19] Fraser's redefinition of public sphere allows us to recognize the split in the unitary domain of the liberal public sphere and also to stage the active negotiations of subaltern social groups to enter this domain. In the 1990s, Dalit writers broke the invisible and transparent boundaries of the secular space of the Telugu revolutionary public sphere and publicly articulated their caste identities.

I have outlined Narayana Rao's Eurocentric view of the Telugu public sphere to highlight the shift in conceptualizing the public sphere by Virasam writers, feminist writers, and later Dalit writers. Instead of lamenting the disruption of the normative public sphere, one should attempt to explain the changing character of the Telugu public sphere and counterdiscourses. The concept of subaltern counterpublics may help us capture the reconfiguration of the Telugu public sphere.

Narayana Rao conceives the poets of revolutionary, Dalit, and feminist movements as a group of nonpoets who cannot be part of his idea of the public sphere. In fact, the Dalit argument takes an interesting turn. The Dalit critics argue that the counterpublic of the revolutionary Left is indeed the dominant public of the 1990s. What Narayana Rao refers to as "the path of Virasam" is the paradigm that Dalit critics engaged with in the 1990s. As the focus of this essay is to understand the Dalit reconfiguration of modernity, let us look at the constitution of the Telugu public in the 1990s. The story of the rise of Virasam is crucial here.

Virasam consciously and actively undermined the pure literary character of the Telugu public sphere in the 1970s and the 1980s. The divide between literary and other social spheres was broken completely, and the dialectical relationship of different social domains was emphasized. The literary public sphere has not been seen as a separate, distinct arena of a small section of elite experts and scholars, but as one of the many domains of social life. To put it succinctly, the literary sphere is an arena of continuous struggle among competing social groups.[20]

To understand Virasam's claims about the democratization of the institutional domain of literature, it is worth elaborating the distinctive character of the new writers, readers, and kinds of writing. Virasam argued that "every individual is capable of becoming a writer and it is important to create a social environment and opportunities to bring out the creativity in the human intellect."[21] This idea helped produce a new group of writers from different class and caste backgrounds. Virasam's official journal, *Arunatara*, publishes the poetry of the armed Naxalite activists, some of whom are only semiliterate. Similarly, writing that focused on the agrarian poor and tribal people was written in Telangana and other tribal dialects. The new cultural movement, represented by Jananatya Mandali and its popular balladeer Gaddar, reworked folk art forms and songs and addressed vast masses of illiterate people in the villages and towns.[22] Many artists who joined the cultural organizations such as Jananatya Mandali, Virasam, and others were illiterates and poor laborers.[23]

Though Virasam reorganized the Telugu public sphere by including people (workers, women, Adivasis, and other poorer groups) into its project of a new democratic culture, the framework of literature proposed and practiced by Virasam remained elite and upper caste in character. The contribution of Dalit critics is to point out this limitation in Virasam's framework.[24] While the new public includes poorer groups, it also reproduces a hierarchical relationship between the vanguard and the proletariat. T. Madhusudanarao, known as a commentator on Virasam and a Marxist critic, puts it this way: "The writers are not able to learn people's language as they are living far away from the people. . . . The writers should respond to the thoughts, experiences, and the hearts of the workers and the peasants. They should learn the language from people with commitment. . . . In fact, the only way a poet can acquire proletariat culture and character is by living with that class."[25]

The middle-class or upper-caste writer has to declassify himself (a popular phrase in leftist circles) in the process of writing about the proletariat. The new democratic culture is in principle open to all, including the workers and the peasants, but it is the middle-class or upper-caste writers who dominate it. While it is the people who are the agents in the new democratic culture, the poets (read: middle-class or upper-caste individuals) must be committed to the unity and class consciousness of the proletariat.

While Narayana Rao's conception of the Telugu public sphere is narrow and elite as it privileges the pundits, the revolutionary Left aims to include people in its new democratic culture as subjects. Yet this project fails because it is committed to a teleological model of modernization in which the goal is apparently known. The vanguard remains educated, upper-caste, middle-class males. The class-based citizen and the unified project of democratic culture gets trapped in a statist modernist project. Therefore, I argue that Viplava Sahityam (revolutionary literature) attains the status of the dominant modern literature, and its subject remains the middle-class or upper-caste Hindu (the vanguard). The entry of Dalits into the domain of the Left literary public has several consequences.

Dalit Publics

The social struggles and the public debates on Dalit massacres, the issue of reservations, the upsurge by oppressed castes in the electoral arena, and the renewed interest in B. R. Ambedkar and Jotirao Phule point to two important developments. First, new social groups—Dalits and "Backward Classes"—appeared on the stage of the Telugu public sphere. Second, a new Dalit critique was established—often referred to as Dalitvadam (Dalitism) in Telugu.[26]

In this section, I will discuss the rise of new social groups in the 1990s. An important factor in this development is the phenomenon of mass killings of Dalits in Andhra Pradesh. Dalits raised their voices when their people were massacred in the 1980s and 1990s.[27] The central issue that Dalits raised in their protests against atrocities is self-respect. Dalit intellectuals often described Dalit struggles of the 1990s as struggles for Dalit self-respect.

The Karamchedu massacre in 1985 marks a turning point in the history of Dalit assertions in Andhra Pradesh.[28] The Dalit Mahasabha was formed in response to the massacre. Bojja Tharakam, a lawyer and leader of the Dalit civil rights movement, and Katti Padmarao, leader of the rationalist movement, were elected president and secretary, respectively. Incidentally, both are poets and writers. As K. Srinivasulu, a social scientist, points out, "what the *dalit* movement, especially in the context of AP, brought forth with clarity was the need to address the question of caste in its specificity, since the unfolding social conflict involved caste-specificity: it could not therefore, simply be seen as a class question, although the class dimension was closely related to it."[29]

The Dalit Mahasabha addressed "the question of caste in its specificity." It organized Dalit youth and intelligentsia as a distinct social group, cutting across political affiliations and foregrounding caste as a critical category of social analysis and Ambedkarism as a philosophical outlook of the Dalits. Several Ambedkarist associations were formed throughout the state of Andhra Pradesh, and issues of caste violence and discrimination were raised in the public sphere.[30]

The struggles for and against reservations also contributed to the rise of new social groups in the 1990s.[31] The constitutional provisions for providing reservations in education and employment for "Other Backward Classes" (OBCs) have become a site for caste conflict in postindependence India. The 1986 decision of the Telugu Desam government in Andhra Pradesh to increase the quantum of OBC reservations in education and employment sparked stiff resistance from upper-caste students. Commenting on the antireservation offensive, K. Balagopal, the noted human rights activist, says "there is little difference between anti-reservation agitations and 'atrocities on harijans.'"[32] One revelation of the reservation controversy is the centrality of caste in upper-caste arrogance and violence and the role of caste as an indicator of the social backwardness of the BCs. In the 1990s, the politics of caste was split into two parts: the politics of caste of members of the upper castes and that of the oppressed (Dalits and BCs).[33] The understanding of caste as a premodern identity has been ruled a myth. Caste has resurfaced and is now a new entity in public discourse.

With the implementation of the Mandal Commission Report, which provided 27 percent reservations for OBCs in 1990, the struggle over reservations moved to center stage in national politics.[34] The intelligentsia, students, and political parties were virtually divided into two camps: the upper castes and the oppressed castes. The modernization of Indian society and the erasing of caste identities from the body politic of the nation turned out to be a failed project. The dominant Indian sociology and its modernist framework failed to explain new forms of caste violence and untouchability and faced a crisis when caste identities resurfaced in the modern domain.[35] In the Mandal moment, caste was debated as a systemic issue at the national level in the media, academia, judiciary, and Parliament. The significance of this debate is that the question of caste was seen as not just a social evil to be rooted out but also as a question of power and identity at the national level.

Yet another significant development was the rediscovery of Ambedkar, "a totally forgotten figure"[36] and Phule as Indian national icons in the 1990s. The suppressed Ambedkarite perspective was now available to the public, and this perspective opened up new ways of thinking about Indian society. The "upsurge" in the electoral arena expressed through the victory of Bahujan Samaj Party and Samajwadi Party in the 1993 Uttar Pradesh elections is seen as an assertion of the oppressed castes—Dalits and OBCs—in the electoral arena.[37]

In the context of Andhra Pradesh, the public intellectuals, writers, poets, activists, and students belonging to the Dalit community formed themselves into a distinct group under the broad category of Dalit. Srinivasulu rightly points out that Dalit as a category represents "a community of oppressed castes with specific experience of being treated as untouchables and being humiliated through the conscious denial of self-respect and honour by the caste Hindus."[38] It was the Malas and Madigas, two numerically and socially dominant subcastes in the untouchable social groups (classified as scheduled castes [SCs] by the government), who occupied the category of Dalits in the early 1990s. The concept of Dalit was available in the 1970s. Masterjee, a Dalit singer and activist, established the Dalit Kala Mandali in 1978. Scheduled Caste Employees' Welfare Associations and Ambedkarist organizations were established in the Telangana and Andhra regions and were active in the 1970s, propagating Ambedkar's ideology and responding to issues of caste discrimination.[39]

Though Dalit cultural and social organizations were working in the 1970s, they were not a visible public force. In the 1990s, the Dalit intelligentsia acquired a new visibility through its social and cultural organizations and its powerful Dalit literary movement. The formation of Dalita Rachayitala, Kalakarula, Medhavula Ikya Vedika (known as Darakame, a united forum of Dalit writers, intellectuals, and artists) in 1993;[40] the rise of small journals like *Godavari Keratalu, Nalapu, Edureeta, Ekalavya,* and *Gabbilam*; and the formation of *Satya Sodhak*, a research centre of Dalit-Bahujan (Scheduled and Backward Caste) intellectuals are some of the significant events that shaped the emergence of the Dalit public in Andhra Pradesh. The distinctive aspect of these Dalit initiatives is that the existing forums and spaces were critiqued, and new forums and spaces were invented so the Dalits could speak in new voices about new politics.

The Dalit movement foregrounded the category of caste to analyze and understand the denial of civic status to Dalits. It was the Dalit movement that made it clear that the antireservation offensive is an anti-Dalit protest and a display of upper-caste arrogance and power. The notion of civic status and the category of caste are two important concepts to use in analyzing power relations and the Dalits' situation in India. What is relevant here are the views that Dalits have not been proper citizens and that caste is a mode of power in India.[41] To illustrate the impact of the new theoretical understanding informed by Dalit critique, I will cite the discussions in the Andhra Pradesh Civil Liberties Committee (APCLC), a Marxist organization established in 1973 that has spearheaded the civil rights movement in the past four decades in Andhra Pradesh. Balagopal, then general secretary of the APCLC, reflecting on his experience of civil liberties activity in 1996, admits that the APCLC did not take up caste as a basic civil rights issue until 1991.[42] The APCLC viewed Dalit massacres such as the one at Karamchedu as issues of state violence against poor *harijans* (Scheduled Castes). It intervened in the cases of Dalit killings to force the state to act and deliver justice to the Dalits. This state-centric perspective reduces Dalit killings to an issue of atrocity. Balagopal suggests that this inadequate understanding had to do with the Marxist origins of the civil liberties movement in Andhra Pradesh. The APCLC's initial agenda was to take up issues regarding the suppression of workers and peasants by landlords and capitalists. Karamchedu, Balagopal tells us, forced the APCLC to rethink the categories of class and other economic categories and to accept caste as a basic civil rights issue. The APCLC had to rethink the presumed status of Dalits as citizens in a liberal democracy. Balagopal draws on Ambedkar's work to suggest that Dalits are not considered citizens. The denial of civic status to Dalits, Balagopal points out, cannot be addressed within the liberal or Marxist conceptions of democracy.

The status of Dalits as not proper citizens in the 1990s is an important observation. One approach to solving this problem is to demand the status of citizenship for the untouchable castes. As Balagopal points out, members of these castes are not considered human beings and, therefore, are not autonomous individuals who are eligible for the status of citizens. The untouchables are certainly part of the abstract category of the people. Dalits are included as the people in the Left's project. As the normative subject of the Left's discourse is the secular individual with no markers of caste, Dalits have to be educated to become the people, so they can attain civic status. In this context, the untouchable castes have to fashion new forms of subjectivity to reject the not-yet-citizen status in the Left's pedagogical project of modernity and enter the domain of the authorized public.

What we have seen in the struggles and conflicts of the 1990s points to the reality that Dalits continue to be brutally murdered and marginalized in postindependence modern India. The state-led programs of modernization such as the Green Revolution[43] and reservations have indeed sharpened caste divisions and identities.[44] It has certainly been proven that the modernization project will not resolve the contradictions. I wish to suggest here that the Dalit movement and its discourses articulated and elaborated the failure of the modernization of the Indian nation-state and proposed new ways to conceptualize democracy.

The concept of subaltern publics allowed us to conceptualize the Dalit public as a distinct domain. But this characterization does not help us conceptualize the nature of Dalit political activity. It is in this context that Partha Chatterjee's distinction between civil society and political society is useful to analyze the democratic visions of Dalits in the 1990s and to account for the not-quite-citizen status of Dalits and other oppressed castes.[45] Redefining the framework of state-society relations to analyze political developments in India since independence, Chatterjee, a distinguished political theorist, proposed a split in the domain of society. One half is civil society, which refers to "those characteristic institutions of modern associational life originating in western societies that are based on equality, autonomy, freedom of entry and exit, contract, deliberative procedures of decision-making, recognized rights and duties of members, and such other principles."[46] The other half is political society, which is the domain of the population represented by parties, movements, nonparty forums, and so on.[47] According to Chatterjee, civil society is restricted to a small section of proper citizens, while political society includes different groups of people who are not quite citizens.[48] The contradiction between the project of modernization and the aspirations of democracy were embedded in the Indian nation-state from its inception, becoming visible in the 1970s. It is in the domain of mobilizations of the populations,[49]—that is, political society—that the contradiction between modernization and democracy is mediated through the language of social policy.[50] Following Chatterjee, I suggest that the domain of the Dalit public is a domain of political society.

To put it simply, the untouchables are not bourgeois citizens, they are populations. I invoke the category of political society as it captures the location of the untouchable castes outside the domain of the authorized public of the secular middle-class or upper-caste Hindus. It is these secular middle-class citizens who are the agents of the modern Telugu literary discourses. At the level of conceptualization, the untouchables are included as poor people in the abstract category of the people. The caste-specific identity of the untouchables is denied in this inclusion. The nebulous zone of the political society is useful to analyze the Dalit critique of the Left's modernist project and to delineate new forms of subjectivity and conceptions of caste and democracy.

My argument here is that the 1990s represent a new phase of politics, a Dalit politics of caste. Dalit critics posited Dalit, caste, and minority religious identities. Telugu critics described the new politics as *asthitva rajakeeyalu* (politics of identity) or *gurtinpu rajakkeyalu* (politics of recognition). But neither of these terms, coined by Left critics, captures the transformative thrust of the new caste politics.

I want to emphasize here that the formation of identity based on social origins is at the core of Dalit literature in Telugu.[51] The new literatures based on identities of castes or subcastes problematize the humanist conception of literature as a domain of universalism. The literary domain is reconfigured as a site of contestation of caste and other identities and ideologies. In other words, Dalits constitute, to use Chatterjee's concept, a political society, the domain of populations. Dalit writings have created a space in which to critique the domain of modern literature. It is through their own mobilizations that Dalits and other marginalized social groups struggle for a share of power, which Chatterjee describes as a desire for democracy. Self-representation is one of the central features of the new mobilizations of Dalits and other social groups.

New Subjects and Caste Collectives

Reading the new Dalit poetry in conventional literary frameworks would restrict its political and theoretical thrust.[52] One of the significant functions of Dalit poetry in the 1990s was to constitute a new Dalit subject. While marking the normative subject of revolutionary literature as the middle-class and upper-caste Hindu, Dalit poets invoked untouchable caste identity as a new entity that is at the core of the Dalit subject. Untouchable caste groups (Madigas, Malas, and others) imagined caste as a new form of community in the 1990s.

The well-known Dalit poet and critic Sikhamani voices the concern of many Dalit writers when he says: "Birth, life and experience are the prerequisites to express the anguish of your community. If you are not a born Dalit, then the authenticity and the punch essential to express angst will be missing."[53] Dalit writers created a new public (their "community") through a new set of organizational and political initiatives. These writers posited caste identity ("a born Dalit") as a positive identity and used it to demand equal space in the public sphere. They narrated the experiences of humiliation, discrimination, and exclusion based on caste identity. Simultaneously, they redeployed the category of caste to invoke caste ties and imagine a new community. It is imperative to pay close attention to the self-fashioning of the untouchable castes before we call caste ties primordial, parochial, or casteist.

Sikhamani critiques Telugu modern poetry in his poem "An Apology" ("Kshamapana"). In this poem, he apologizes for his failure to depict Dalit life and problems:

I apologise, dalit!
I am a poet, a rare poet
Why my name,
My background?
I'm a Brahmin
With a glorious lineage
Oh, please accept my apologies, dalit!
Never had the time to write
a line about you
the past thousand years,
so engrossed I was in
amorous and ascetic literary pursuits.

Our old poet
Calls Sudra's poetry
the sweet pudding
maligned by crow.
You are not even a Sudra!
How can I write poetry about you?
My apologies, dalit,
I'm a poet, a modern poet
and a post-modern poet

How can I write poetry about you?
I can write about the
great Vietnam
Tiananmen Square,

the fall of [the] Berlin wall
and hunger in Somalia
but not
about the wound of Chundur
the pestles of Karamchedu and
the flame of Neerukonda
I am an International poet,
I certainly cannot write
Poetry about mala colonies

I sang, to my heart's content, the heroic
deaths of martyrs of revolution
but the swollen, stubbed corpses of
butchered dalits
didn't move me.
I cried about alienation
alas, I cannot be
moved by dehumanisation.
I have lamented about curfew
in evocative poetry
but cannot expend a drop of ink
to condemn caste killings.[54]

The poem is a critique of the secular self of the revolutionary poet. Sikhamani highlights the failure of the revolutionary poet, who is marked as a Brahman, to not condemn "caste killings." Karamchedu, Chundur, and Neerukonda are the contexts of caste killings that show up the limitations of revolutionary poetry. The international outlook of the revolutionary poet is so limited that it could only depict the American war against Vietnam, the student struggle at Tiananmen Square in China, and hunger in Somalia—not Dalit life, "mala colonies," or the massacres of Dalits. What is at issue here is not just themes of poetry but a critical perspective on the life and struggles of the Dalits. The revolutionary poet views the world through his concepts of imperialism and revisionism. The Vietnam War becomes an important theme in revolutionary poetry as it is seen as a historic anti-imperialist struggle against America. Similarly, hunger in Somalia is a product of imperialist exploitation. In addition, the Chinese students' struggle is viewed as a struggle against revisionist Marxism. The centrality of the state, Sikhamani indicates, is implied in the themes of "alienation" and "curfew" in revolutionary poetry. Sikhamani contrasts "alienation," one of the key themes in revolutionary poetry, with the "dehumanisation" of Dalits in life and death ("the swollen, stubbed corpses of butchered dalits"). Sikhamani's poem effectively sums up the Dalit critique of the revolutionary poets' modern Telugu poetry. It highlights the failure of a certain Marxist understanding and its categories to represent Dalit life and caste violence in poetry.

Sikhamani does not single out the revolutionary poets for their failure to represent Dalit life. He subjects himself to self-criticism in the same poem and says, "I can write about / flower-vendors and blind beggars / in words tender like flower petals / but [have] none to describe the insults of Padiri-kuppam."[55] Sikhamani had written about flower vendors and blind beggars in his early collections of poetry. He did not bother to write about atrocities like the one at Padirikuppam (a village in Chittor District where Dalits were attacked).

Sikhamani, also known as a modern poet, reinvents himself as a Dalit poet in the 1990s. He posits "authentic" Dalit subjectivity based on "the birth, life and experience" in the context of the consolidation of the untouchable castes as Dalit community in the 1990s.[56] It is the "authentic" Dalit subject that acts as the nucleus of the new Dalit and caste communities.

Dalit poets announced their arrival in the 1980s and the 1990s through the thematization of caste violence and Dalit resistance movements. It is rare to find a Dalit poet who did not write a poem on atrocities against Dalits. Let us look at another poem about the Chunduru Dalit massacre. Satish Chandar, a Dalit poet, invokes the image of Christ on the cross in his poem "A Child Is Born (Sishuvu Nedu Lechenu)." He starts the poem with a reference to Chunduru, where Dalits were massacred by Reddy upper castes in 1991:

Why only boulders across the graves?
Let them line up whole mountains
Surely, a Jesus will rise
in an explosion of light
like the morning sun.
A cemetery in the middle of the village
casts out the whole population![57]

When the Reddy upper castes killed eight Dalits in Chunduru, other Dalits ran away to Tenali, a nearby town, and took shelter in a church. They returned to Chunduru among large-scale protests by members of Dalit and other social groups. The bodies of the Dalit dead were buried in the center of the village as a mark of protest. Drawing on the Christian belief that Christ returned to life on the third day after his burial, Satish Chandar visualizes the rising of Dalit heroes from the grave. He evokes the story of Christ to convey the brutality of caste oppression and atrocities against Dalits:

> It is against the law to have two feet
> They drive nails so he shall not walk.
> It is against the law to have two hands.
> They drive holes so he shall not ask for work
>
> It is against the law to have a brain.
> They stick a crown of thorns on his head
> So he shall not write a constitution again
> It is against the law to have a lovely face.
> They spit on him so no mother can kiss him.
>
> The child is killed on the cross
> in the open rice fields.
>
> Mothers, heavy with grief for the loss of your children,
> welcome him in white clothes.
> A child is born
> Hallelujah.[58]

The poem depicts how Dalits are crippled, dehumanized, and finally killed. It is "the law" of Manu Dharma (ancient legal text of Hinduism which pre-scribes the duties of the four varnas) that dehumanized and mutilated the Dalits. The violated body, the poet emphasizes, is a human body that lives even after death. "The child," "Christ," and the "Dalit" are born again. The symbol of Christ simultaneously represents the Dalit, Ambedkar, and the Chunduru Dalit martyrs. By evoking the myths of death and resurrection, the poet pow-erfully communicates the caste-based killings of Dalits and the simultaneous rise of Dalits in the 1990s. The poem also highlights the centrality of Chris-tianity and its mythology in Dalit imagination in coastal Andhra.

The imagining of the human figure as the Dalit subject is one of the re-curring themes of Dalit poetry. In his well-known poem "Fifth Note" ("Pan-chama Vedam"), Satish Chandar writes about a talented Dalit student who was abused and humiliated in the classroom by a Brahman teacher. He failed an examination and, therefore, in life. Here is the section that raises the issue of casteism:

> No, it isn't kerosene that burned me,
> I burned from pride.
> Tell that to the press.

I could not suffer the stink of my own corpse
When it burned
It was the same odour your living body emitted.
Then I knew the difference between you and me:
Caste stinks alive.[59]

Sociologists conceive of caste as "a stink" in the framework of "purity and pollution." Satish Chandar's notion of "stink" is a powerful critique of sociological notions of caste and a redefinition of caste. In this poem, the Brahman teacher's body is a caste body that "stinks" alive. The Dalit student commits suicide, asserting his self-respect ("pride"). Like the stinking Brahman body of life, it is the student's corpse that stinks.

Dalit poets demonstrate that caste is not just a form of brutal violence on a mass scale. Caste structures our everyday life. Recollecting his childhood and early life as a poet in his poem, "The Steel Nibs Are Sprouting!," Sikhamani narrates a series of incidents of a new form of caste discrimination.[60] The Dalit boy in the poem faces caste discrimination in daily life. He is insulted and humiliated because of his "lower caste" status (with terms such as Mala bastard, Madiga food, reservation fellow, and sc).[61] The purity-pollution framework cannot explain the immediacy of discrimination in everyday situations of modern life.

The special feature of contemporary Dalit poetry and other Dalit writing is to speak from Dalit vadas (Dalit colonies) and Madiga vadas (Madiga colonies). The Dalit poet does not posit a tradition-modernity dichotomy and dismiss village life as static. When the upper castes push the Dalits out of Chunduru, the Dalits come back en masse and occupy the center of the village to build a cemetery for the murdered Dalits. They make these experiences of caste a public issue. They debate it and put the upper castes on the defensive. While making their claims through their literary practice, I suggest, they transform the structures of the village and occupy center stage in the village.

While early Dalit poetry posits Dalit identity as a common identity of all the untouchable castes, in the late 1990s the new poetry of Madigas and other untouchable castes appeared in the Telugu public sphere, keeping in mind the tension that arises between the categories of Dalit and Madiga identities. Madiga critics interrogate the abstract category of Dalit and attempt to give it a new meaning. This new logic of specific caste identities acquires a new political thrust and focuses on new kinds of tensions within Dalit politics in particular and in the politics of society in general.

Yendluri Sudhakar, a modern poet, reimagines himself as a Dalit poet in the 1980s. He declares: "An ostracized man am I / my breath is still untouchable."[62] The poem "Ostracized" ("Nettuti Prasna"), written in the context of mass killings of Dalits, analyzes new forms of caste violence and brutality ("The present hacks all five fingers"). In this poem, he is speaking as an untouchable, and he is arguing for a new voice.

Sudhakar also speaks as a Madiga in his long poem "Drumbeat" ("Dandora"; literally, announcement).[63] The Telugu title of the poem refers to the contemporary mobilizations of Madigas as a community by establishing the Madiga Reservation Porata Samiti (MRPS) movement in 1994.[64] Madigas acted as village servants who had the job of making public announcements in the village, preceded by the drumbeats of their *dappu* (a traditional drum used by Madigas and other "lower caste" groups to make public announcements in the villages). The MRPS redefined the term *dandora* as an announcement of struggle for their rights. The poem is both an announcement of the struggle and an elaboration of the Madiga identity. It highlights the social inequality between the untouchable castes:

Today I am speaking as myself
as a low caste, as a beggar,
as a cobbler stitching shoes,
as a gravedigger in the burial ground
as a sweeper
I am all of them
My people
I am talking about caste

Now I am arguing about my share
I am bringing up rights that belong to me
I am not good at deception or insults
Telling the truth, fearlessly, is in my nature.
Now I am talking about you
I lay bare hidden knots of suffering
I ask who built the bridge of untouchability
between your street and our cluster of slums.
But what I see and write is
that the ladder of inequality, of insults
does not come only from the high caste
we have it amidst us

we have those who quickly turn away
from our traditions and customs

Why do you talk ill of us
you throw up if you eat our lentils
you hold your breath
when you come to our cluster of slums
your feet cannot step onto our threshold
your thirst disappears
when you see our tumblers
I ask you
Whose delusion is this?
Forget about marriages
You cannot bear our proximity.[65]

The poet is addressing the Malas, one of the numerically large subcastes of
SCs in Andhra Pradesh. It has been mentioned that Dalit poetry is generally
addressed to different sections of the upper castes. In this poem, the poet is
directly speaking to the Malas, declaring, "There is a bamboo screen / between
the two of us / revolt is not on the streets / but against domination."[66] The poet
points out that the Malas live in the *vada* (the streets) and the Madigas in the
geri (the slums). What is to be noted here is the physical distance between
the two living places. The poet's declaration of the struggle for rights, therefore, is not against the Malas but against domination. While pointing out the
physical distance between the two castes and "the bridge of untouchability,"
Sudhakar is inviting the Malas to help resolve the conflict when he says, "Let
us make the two steps between us into one."[67]

What is relevant for our discussion is the construction of Madiga identity
as a separate identity. The most interesting development in the second half
of the 1990s is the mobilization of the Madigas and other castes as a pressure
group. The poem powerfully represents the MRPS viewpoint for the subdivision of SC reservations into four groups. As Sudhakar points out, the internal
social inequality among the SCs is the key issue in this debate. The response
of the established Dalit leaders (with some exceptions) and the Mala leaders
is that any discussion of these internal social inequalities would destroy the
unity of the Dalits. Drawing on social and cultural backwardness and oppression and the numerical strength of the population, the MRPS constructed a
Madiga identity that was distinct from the Dalit identity despite some broad
similarities.

Sudhakar declares, "Today I am speaking as myself." He wrote poetry as a secular modern poet as well as a Dalit poet. He was one of the key figures of the Dalit literary movement in the 1980s and the early 1990s. He is clearly marking his distance from those subject positions. When he announces "No language can come in the way of my cries / Today I toss my art onto the dung heap / I toss my fame up into the sky / I stump underfoot the worldly rhythm of alphabets / I push aside my beautiful sounds,"[68] he is speaking as a Madiga. Who is a Madiga? He is constructing a Madiga as a member of a "lower caste," a beggar, a cobbler, a gravedigger, and a sweeper. He presents himself as the representative self of the Madiga community: "I am all of them / My people." The identity of Madiga is an identity of a group of SCs. The Madigas and the Malas are the two untouchable castes that are numerically and socially dominant in Andhra Pradesh. They were led by Manda Krishna and Krupakar, who renamed themselves Krishna Madiga and Krupakar Madiga, mobilized Madiga subcastes and other socially oppressed castes in the SCs, and forged the new identity of Madiga. The Madiga identity that Sudhakar is evoking is a collective identity of a community ("My people") constituted within the context of the MRPS.

Sudhakar's poem is part of the Madiga discourse on sharing the rights of reservations. Representing himself as the angry Veerabahu, the gravedigger, who was known as the forefather of the Madigas in the caste puranas, Sudhakar says: "gratitude marks my blood / equality is my caste principle / the tradition of my forefathers / Is to share the meat of our kill amongst us all."[69] The notion of a share of the meat is taken from Madiga community life. The Madigas propose the idea of sharing rights (reservations in the sectors of education, employment, and welfare). The poet suggests that the values of "gratitude" and "equality" should be the basis for forging a new community and that there is a need to destroy "the bridge of untouchability" and "the ladder of inequality" between the Madigas and the Malas. While the "I" in the poem refers both to the Madiga poet and to his caste community, "we" refers to the collective community of Madigas and Malas. When the poet refers to the issue of internal inequality, he says "we have it amidst us." Therefore, he concludes the poem with a call to the Malas: "Let us make the two steps between us into one / We will destroy the rungs of the ladder / We will create a new Dalit world."[70] It is interesting to note that the category of Dalit is still invoked as a collective imaginary of the new community.

Conclusion

Dalit critics have pointed out that the Left's national modern project makes caste invisible, transparent, and, therefore, unspeakable in the public. Dalit and Madiga poets broke this silence and made caste identities opaque in the Telugu public sphere. The new Dalit and caste collectives have undergone internal transformation and emerged as new political communities. In their transactions in the intellectual and institutional domain of modernity, these groups own their caste-based occupations and take pride in their caste cultures, caste names, and labor practices. They cite all these caste solidarities as evidence for their status claims in the modern political domains. Combining social oppression with population data and sociocultural status, the new caste collectives demand their share of the power and resources of society. Describing these new caste collectives as premodern and casteist is an attempt to undo the resurfacing of caste in the 1990s and to suppress desires for democracy. The modernist assertions of our liberal nationalist and leftist intelligentsia endorse caste privilege and, more importantly, suppress the fashioning of alternative modernities and subjectivities.[71]

NOTES

I thank Devesh Kapur and Ramnarayan Rawat for inviting me to the Dalit Studies Conference in 2008. I thank members of the audience at the conference for their comments. Ram has gone through this essay carefully and offered very concrete suggestions to improve it. Short versions of it were presented at Anveshi Research Centre in Hyderabad, and South Asian studies at the University of Minnesota. The discussions at these places helped me to revise the essay. Susie Tharu read initial versions of it and offered valuable suggestions. R. Srivatsan, a senior fellow at Anveshi, helped me in reformulating some arguments in the essay. However, I am responsible for the views expressed here.

1. The A. P. Viplava Rachayitala Sangham (the Andhra Pradesh Revolutionary Writers' Association) is an organization of Marxist-Leninist writers of Andhra Pradesh. It emerged as a new organization after the decline of the mainstream leftist literary organization, the Progressive Writers' Association. Virasam (an acronym for the Andhra Pradesh Revolutionary Writers' Association) was formed in response to a pamphlet published by the students of Andhra University, in Visakhapatnam, on the occasion of the eminent modern Telugu poet Sri Sri's sixtieth birthday (*sashti poorti* in Telugu). The pamphlet asked writers "Whose side are you on?" The students posed this question in the context of severe repression of the Srikakulam tribal revolt led by the Naxalite parties. The birthday celebration was canceled, and Virasam was formed on July 4, 1970, to voice support for the struggling people. The terms "Virasam

writers," "revolutionary writers," and "leftist writers" are used interchangeably in this essay.

2. K. Srinivas, "Virasam Sampradayalu Silasashanala?" *Andhra Jyothi Dinapatrika,* July 11, 1993.

3. See Narayana Rao, "Sahityanni Sahityanga Choose Vallu Kavali," 19–26. All the quotations from this article are my translations.

4. Ibid., 23.

5. Ibid., 29.

6. In response to Narayana Rao's criticisms, Sarathi, a Marxist critic, argued that in evaluating literature Narayana Rao failed to recognize the role of social practice and to appreciate the fact that literature and arts belong to the people. The intentions of an individual writer, Sarathi says, may be commendable, but if the work of literature is not popular and well received among the people, it cannot be recognized as great literature. In judging a work of literature, Sarathi argues that literary critics, observers, writers, and people must participate in the process of evaluation. Sarathi highlights the central role of social groups in defining good literature. Narayana Rao, in contrast, sees no role for social groups in the determination of what is good literature. See Sarathi, "Roopavadaniki Tirogaminchina Velcheru," *Andhra Jyothi Dinapatrika,* May 19, 2003, and "Sahityam Sahityam kosam kadu, Prajala Kosam," *Andhra Jyothi Dinapatrika,* July 14, 2003.

7. Narayana Rao, "Sahityanni Sahityanga Choose Vallu Kavali," 20.

8. Narayana Rao, "Sahityanni Sahityanga Choose Vallu Kavali," 20–21.

9. Ibid., 21.

10. Ibid., 25.

11. Ibid., 21.

12. Ibid., 19.

13. Narayana Rao, *Twentieth Century Telugu Poetry,* 320.

14. Narayana Rao, "Sahityanni Sahityanga Choose Vallu Kavali," 23.

15. I have greatly benefited from the essays on this subject in Craig Calhoun, *Habermas and Public Sphere,* particularly those by Nancy Fraser and Geoff Eley.

16. Fraser, "Rethinking the Public Sphere: A Contribution to the Critique of Actually Existing Democracy," 110–11.

17. Ibid., 115–16.

18. Ibid., 123.

19. Ibid., 124.

20. One must note the contribution of Virasam in redefining the literary sphere as one of the social spheres of political negotiation for a new democracy. Virasam actively undermined the elite composition (in the case of both writers and readers) of the literary sphere and worked for the democratization of literary and artistic fields. It was noted in a critical assessment of the revolutionary literary movement that "democratization in literature is expressed in three stages. First, emergence of more and more writers, development of literary creativity, and overall interest in literary taste; second, production of literature by groups of people who had no introduction to literary activity; third, the birth of new modes of expression, expansion

in diverse direction, literature in dialects and new languages" (*Viplava Shityodya-mam*, 4).

21. Ibid., 5.

22. Venugopal, "Avisranta Janahrudaya Spandana: Jananatya Mandali."

23. Dalit critics identified the revolutionary literature of Virasam as the dominant and authentic modern Telugu literature. The Dalit critic Kalekuri Prasad (*Dalit Udya-mam*, 24) mentions that the dominant trend in literature at the time of the Karam-chedu massacre was the literature of Virasam and *Jananatya Mandali* of Gaddar.

24. When feminist and Dalit writers appeared on the scene, Virasam claims that it provided the base for the emergence of Dalit and feminist movements through its practice of rebellion in Telugu literature. While extending critical support to Dalit and feminist literary movements, Virasam argues that caste issues will be resolved as a part of the class struggle (*Viplava Shityodyamam*, 17). Virasam framed the Dalit question in terms of a problem to be addressed and solved in the struggle for democratic revolution, one more issue on its agenda of class struggle.

25. Madhusudanarao, *Kavitvam-Chaitanyam*, 10.

26. S.V. Satyanarayana, *Dalitavada Vivadalu*.

27. Sambasivarao, *Dalitarananninadam*; Srinivasulu, "Caste, Class and Social Articulation in Andhra Pradesh," 169–74.

28. In 1985, six Dalits were killed and three Dalit girls were raped by caste Hundu Kamma landlords in a village called Karamchedu, in Andhra Pradesh.

29. Srinivasulu, "Caste, Class and Social Articulation in Andhra Pradesh," 46.

30. Dalits continued to register their public protests and agitations against a series of massacres of Dalits at Neerukonda (1987), Timmasamudram (1990), Chunduru (1991), and so on. For a detailed list of atrocities against Dalits, see Andhra Pradesh Civil Liberties Committee, *The Chunduru Carnage*.

31. Balagopal, *Probings in the Political Economy of Agrarian Classes and Conflicts*, 175–85; Chalam, "Caste Reservations and Equality of Opportunity in Education"; Dirks, *Castes of Mind*, 275–96; Omvedt, "'Twice-Born' Riot against Democracy."

32. Balagopal, *Probings in the Political Economy of Agrarian Classes and Conflicts*, 185.

33. Kothari, "Rise of Dalits and the Renewed Debate on Caste," 439–58.

34. Dirks, *Castes of Mind*, 275–96.

35. S. Deshpande, *Contemporary India*, 98–124; Ilaiah, "Caste in a New Mould."

36. Baxi, "Emancipation as Justice: Babasaheb Ambedkar's Legacy and Vision," 13.

37. Ilaiah, "Uttar Pradesh Prajaswamika Viplavam."

38. Srinivasulu, "Caste, Class, and Social Articulation in Andhra Pradesh," 30.

39. Ramulu, *Sahitya Charitrani Kottachooputo Tiragarayali*, 97–104.

40. Ramulu, "Introduction," 55–56.

41. On the question of Dalit engagement with modernity, see Guru, "Dalits in Pursuit of Modernity"; Nigam, "Secularism, Modernity, Nation." Satyasodhak social scientists, a group of Dalit and bahujan scholars, articulated the view, for the first time publicly, that caste is a mode of power in a seminar on caste and power in March 1994 in Warangal, Andhra Pradesh.

42. These arguments are a summary of Balagopal's lecture, "Caste and Civil Rights' Movement in Andhra Pradesh."

43. This is a process of modernizing agriculture that involves the introduction of technology, high-yielding varieties of seeds, and fertilizers. The Indian state introduced this process in selected districts of the country with the aim of increasing the supply of food grains. This led to new conflicts in India, as the process created new imbalances and tensions.

44. Srinivasulu, "Caste, Class and Social Articulation in Andhra Pradesh."

45. Chatterjee, *The Politics of the Governed*.

46. Chatterjee, "Introduction," 10.

47. Ibid., 15.

48. See Chatterjee, *The Politics of the Governed*, for this argument.

49. Michel Foucault invokes the concept of population groups identified and deployed in the administrative and developmental project of the state ("Governmentality," 87–104). In Chatterjee's analysis, it is the marginalised social groups of OBCs, SC, ST, communities and religious minorities such as Muslims. These marginalised populations, Chatterjee argues, articulate their interests, make political innovations, and shape democracy.

50. Chatterjee, "Introduction," 16.

51. Sambhasivarao, "Yadhatadha saampradaya Dhrukpatham to Dalita Sahityodyama viplava Dhrukpaathaniki pottu kudaradu," 13. A commentator on Dalit-Bahujan politics and an activist, suggests that the normative perspective of modern Telugu literature is that of the upper middle class or the middle class and that the Dalit and feminist literary movements represent the new subjects of contemporary Telugu literature, such as women, subordinated castes, and Dalits. Similarly, G. Lakshminarasaiah, the editor of the first published anthology of Dalit poetry, *Chikkanavutunna Pata*, defines Dalit poetry as poetry of the marginalized caste groups and religious minorities. In this view, "Dalit" acquires a new definition as a broad category Scheduled caste, Scheduled Tribe communities and Muslim minorities. The social origin of the poets is foregrounded in this construction of the category. The liberal and leftist critics dubbed this formulation casteist and reiterated the view that modern Telugu literature is a domain of universal values.

52. Sikhamani, a Dalit poet and critic, analyzes Telugu Dalit poetry in terms of its new mythological imagery, its new language, its artistic qualities, and its use of alternative symbols such as bat, crow, and hen. See *Dalitasahityatatvam*. Similarly, Jaaware ("Eating and Eating with the Dalit") and Dharwadkar ("Dalit Poetry in Marathi") have discussed Marathi Dalit poetry as modernist poetry. These studies are completely formalistic in approach and take the conception of literature as given.

53. Sikhamani, "Portraying People's Plight: An Interview," *Hindu*, November 1, 1999.

54. Sikhamani, "An Apology," in *The Black Rainbow*, 15–17. "An Apology" was translated from Telugu by M. Sridhar and Alladi Uma. For the original Telugu version, see Sikhamani, "Kshamapana" in *Chikkanavutunna Pata*, 95–97.

55. Ibid., 16.

56. Sikhamani, "Portraying People's Plight: An Interview," *Hindu*, November 1, 1999.

57. Chandar, "A Child Is Born," 232–34. This poem was translated into English by Narayana Rao. For the original Telugu version, see Chandar, "Sishuvu nedu Lechenu," 144–46.

58. Satischandar, "A Child Is Born," 232–34.

59. Chandar, "Fifth Note," 234–37. This poem was translated into English by Narayana Rao. For the original Telugu version, see Chandar, "Panchama Vedam," 136–39.

60. Sikhamani, "The Steel Nibs Are Sprouting" in *The Black Rainbow*, 25–27. This poem was translated into English by Indraganti Kiranmayi. For the original Telugu version, see Sikhamani, "Inupa paleelu Moluchukostunnayi, 149–51.

61. Sikhamani, "The Steel Nibs Are Sprouting" in *The Black Rainbow*, 25–26.

62. See Sudhakar, *Nalladraksha Pandiri*, 112–15, for both Telugu and English versions of the poem "Ostracized" ("Nettuti Prasna"). This poem was translated by C. L. Jayaprada.

63. Sudhakar, "Drumbeat," 495. This poem was translated by the editorial team of *The Little Magazine*. For the Telugu version, see Sudhakar, "Dandora," 306–8.

64. See Balagopal, "A Tangled Web," for a detailed discussion on this issue.

65. Sudhakar, "Drumbeat," 495.

66. Ibid.

67. Ibid.

68. Ibid.

69. Ibid.

70. Ibid.

71. Rajeev Bhargava says: "An alternative modernity, though radically different from indigenous traditions and mainstream Western modernity, is still a version of modernity" ("Introduction," 29).

7

Questions of Representation in Dalit Critical Discourse:
Premchand and Dalit Feminism

LAURA BRUECK

On July 31, 2004, members of the Bharatiya Dalit Sahitya Akademi (the Indian
Dalit Literary Academy; BDSA, whose name constitutes an obvious riposte to
the Bharatiya Sahitya Akademi, India's premier national literary institution),
burned multiple copies of a book in New Delhi's Jantar Mantar, a popular site
of social and political protest actions in India's government center. The book
was the celebrated novel *Rangbhūmi*, by the iconic nationalist-era Hindi author Munshi Premchand. The raucous gathering of around a hundred people
shouted, cheered, and snapped grinning photos of one another as a small pile
of copies of *Rangbhūmi* went up in flames. The members of the BDSA saw
themselves as a righteous group making a powerful case for the need to fight
upper-caste (*savarn*) prejudice in literature and education. The provocation
for the group to burn *Rangbhūmi*, they said, came from a recent decision by
the National Council of Educational Research and Training (NCERT) to replace Premchand's novel *Nirmala* with *Rangbhūmi* on the syllabus of twelfth-
grade[1] students in Delhi government–funded public schools. According to
the BDSA and its supporters at the book burning, *Rangbhūmi* is offensive
to Dalits and dangerous to the "soft minds"[2] of young students, who could
become biased against Dalits because of the novel's constant repetition of
caste-specific terminology—specifically, the repeated references to the main
character of the novel, Surdas, as "Sūrdas *Chamār*." According to the BDSA's

president, Sohanpal Sumanakshar, the BDSA first petitioned the NCERT to drop the book from the syllabus, or at least to delete the word "*Chamār*" from copies of the novel distributed to students. Then the BDSA filed suit in the Delhi High Court, arguing that the novel violated the Scheduled Caste and Scheduled Tribe (Prevention of Atrocities) Act, passed in 1989, that is meant to protect Dalits from violence and public shaming on the basis of their caste.[3] According to Sumanakshar, a lack of response to both of these pleas resulted in the book burning as a protest.

The burning of *Rangbhūmi* should be seen as more than a zealous, reactionary response to a lack of administrative attention to the BDSA's campaign to have the book replaced on a school syllabus, or a minor dispute over the use of a single word taken to extremes. Rather, what we might call the *Rangbhūmi* incident has a much deeper significance when seen in the context of a historical debate among Dalit writers and critics over whether or not Premchand's literature can be considered Dalit literature, or whether non-Dalit writers can ever genuinely represent Dalit experience. It brings to the fore the fundamental dilemma of applying authentic standards to Dalit identity and experience as well as contested standards of legitimacy for representations of a Dalit perspective in literature. Such a determined and violent banishment of Premchand from the fold of Dalit literature demands a closer look at the political and social character of the contemporary Hindi Dalit literary sphere. Where are its boundaries? Who is included, and who is excluded? Who has the authority to make these decisions, and how are they contested? How do gender and class interact with caste in negotiating these boundaries? What is perhaps most fascinating about this incident (and others that followed, which are discussed below) are the strong reactions and condemnations it attracted from other Dalit writers, publishers, editors, and critics, and the vigorous debate about it within the alternative discursive space of the Hindi Dalit literary sphere. Important to consider as well is how this incident makes clear the ramifications of the discussions, debates, and performances in the Hindi Dalit literary sphere in more mainstream public sphere discourse. Almost a year and a half after the book burning it appeared that the BDSA's protest had been successful. In January 2006, the NCERT agreed to replace the word "*Chamār*" with "Dalit" and also decided to include the works of Dalit writers in the curriculum for the ninth and eleventh grades.

Recently, historians of caste in modern India have increasingly focused on the multiple political and cultural processes that have contributed to the profound transformation of Dalits from stigmatized subjects into modern political agents.[4] Central to this modern project of identity construction is the oft-cited critical reclamation and rewriting by the Ambedkarite movement of the very term "Dalit" from its use as a term of subjugation and humiliation to a radical assertion of political awareness and agency. These studies have been exemplary in their employment of local-level historical, legal, and media archives to seek out the rhetorical processes of identity construction. This essay seeks to extend this project of understanding the processes through which the Dalit identity continues to be, as Anupama Rao puts it, "vibrantly contested" by turning to literature, in this case the Dalit critique of non-Dalit literature, as the principal site of contemporary culture wherein Dalits are engaging in fundamental debates about caste, class, and gender.[5] In the following discussions of the Hindi Dalit literary sphere's various critical engagements in recent years with the literature of Premchand, it becomes clear that Dalit critical discourse is a central site for the shaping of the contours of a vital Dalit public sphere.[6]

There has been substantial and important work on Dalit literature in various Indian languages in the past decade that has made important progress in improving our understanding of the role of literature. Dalits have embraced literature as a way to imagine new versions of social reality and reconstruct their communal identity and cultural projects that are intimately paired with the real-world political mobilization.[7] Yet few scholars of Dalit literature have paid attention to the flip side of Dalit literature, the Dalit critical engagement with an already existing mainstream modern Indian literary sphere in which Dalits have been the objects of representation by non-Dalits for at least the past century. The Hindi Dalit literary sphere is a vibrant site of not only Dalit creative writing—autobiographies, short and long fiction, poetry, and drama—but it is also full of a specific brand of literary criticism, one that evaluates modern Indian literature, by both Dalits and non-Dalits, from a Dalit perspective. But what the following discussions—of the ways in which this critical gaze has reevaluated, critiqued, and, in one very powerful example, literally rewritten Premchand's nationalist-era realist prose of social consciousness—will attest to is the diversity of perspectives and concerns in the Dalit literary sphere. It is in the friction between these subject positions where the work of constituting Dalit identities is achieved. The productive work of Dalit literary criticism is in revealing those social ideologies that have become normalized in, among other places, literary representation and against which a Dalit counterpublic must push. Dalit literature and literary criticism therefore function as a corrective space where the intimate connection between fiction and the construction of reality is laid bare.

The burning of *Rangbhūmi* in 2004 and the discussions about identity and authenticity it has engendered in the Hindi Dalit literary sphere warrant significant attention as a cultural performance, one that can provide insights into the ways in which this alternative public sphere engages, opposes, and redefines the limits of traditionally elite Hindi literary discourse and sociopolitical rhetoric. The public burning of *Rangbhūmi* in India's capital city, pointedly enacted on the 125th anniversary of Premchand's birth, was an attack by the BDSA on one of India's most revered literary heroes. For the BDSA to take on the monumental figure of Premchand in such public and literally incendiary fashion is a powerful testament to the identification of the group's members with a sense of self-definition and purpose that has been constructed at variance with the normative northern Indian public imagination.

A towering figure in the modern Hindi literary mainstream, Premchand has also come to inhabit special, and more contested, terrain in the Hindi Dalit literary sphere in the years since the BDSA's burning of *Rangbhūmi* and the subsequent acquiescence of the NCERT to the demands of the BDSA. A close analysis of the various debates that have sprung from this radical symbolic act allows us to understand the nature of the Hindi Dalit literary sphere as a space for the complex negotiations of various Dalit identities. I assert that these debates raise important questions about the politics of collective identity formation among marginalized communities whose members are intent on making critical interventions in mainstream public discourse.

Rather than characterize all of Dalit writing—be it poetry, fiction, autobiography, criticism, or journalism—as a singular mode of oppositional discourse, it is far more accurate and productive to consider the Hindi Dalit literary sphere to be a space where different discourses can encounter each other and exchange ideas—discourses that are all relevant to the contemporary Dalit experience in Indian society and that do not find a place in the discursive contours of the dominant public. The Hindi Dalit literary sphere is constituted by the existence of debates and discussions about Dalit experiences, aesthetics, politics, and so on. It is a space for discourse that is unlike that in wider and more dominant public spheres for the very reason that it privileges above all others the voices of Dalits and entertains topics of discourse that are ignored in more mainstream discursive spaces. Specifically—and this is most exemplified by the final example of the Dalit reevaluation of Premchand examined in this essay—the Hindi Dalit literary sphere engages literature itself as a corrective space, ever conscious of the perilously close connection between literary representation and the constitution of social reality.

The debates about Premchand provide a context in which to negotiate disparate subidentities and agendas within the Dalit public sphere that fracture particularly along lines of class and gender. It is through this framework, then, that I approach the discussion about Premchand's writing in Dalit literary counterdiscourse of the past decade from a variety of angles. First, tracing public debates among Dalit critics in the months following the *Rangbhūmi* incident in 2004, I will consider the employment of the critical concept of "Dalit consciousness" as it applies to a particular reading of Premchand's "The Shroud" ("*Kafan*," 1936) a story that is broadly criticized in Dalit counterdiscourse, while widely appreciated in the Indian literary mainstream as a sensitive portrayal of the societal degradation of untouchables. Next I will consider a growing articulation of a Dalit feminist rhetorical identity as it is refracted through continued debates over "The Shroud," debates that emerged after the publication of a particularly controversial book by the Dalit critic Dharamveer in 2005, and I will weigh the responsibilities of Dalit writers in the twinned projects of representing the reality of Dalit life and imagining the utopian possibilities of a transformed social order. Finally, I will proffer the example of a short story by the Dalit author Ajay Navaria, first published in 2009 and included in his 2012 short story collection, *Yes Sir*, that boldly engages with the "problem" with Premchand and offers readers a completely new version, not just of his major works, but also of the author himself.

Premchand and the Dalit Hindi Sphere

The interventions of the Hindi Dalit literary sphere in the analysis of mainstream literature and literary figures, in moves both literary and nonliterary, are key to constituting that sphere as a provocative and powerful alternative public in its own right. Thus, by choosing such a potent cultural icon as Premchand as the center for debates about issues of inclusion and exclusion and authority and identity, Dalit writers are defining the very boundaries of the Dalit public sphere. Key issues that arise in the renewed debate over the significance of the BDSA's action that erupted in the Hindi Dalit literary sphere after the book burning in 2004 include the charge that Premchand's literature lacks realism; that he privileges class over caste in his social critique (a perspective at odds with Ambedkarite politics); and finally that as a non-Dalit and a follower of Mahatma Gandhi, he is incapable of Dalit authorial authenticity. In between the printed lines of debate and polemic and in the shadows of reasoned discussion, personal attacks, and sometimes outlandish claims lies the negotiation of the boundaries of the Dalit public sphere, along with answers to questions of inclusion and exclusion that are fundamental to its construction.

The discourse of cultural symbols, both celebratory and critical, is a practice that intimately engages the representative symbol and its constitutive public in a reflexive process of construction and reconstruction. There are high stakes for members of the Hindi Dalit literary sphere in defining a relationship with Premchand, in embracing him or rejecting him as a Dalit author, a member of that same counterdiscursive sphere, because the whole of the Hindi Dalit literary sphere will then in some sense be known, understood, and assessed by its members' stance toward his texts within the more dominant mainstream. There is some danger in uncritically embracing him in the hope that his name and status will confer respectability on the lineage of Dalit literature, if, as we will see, the mode of his representation of Dalit characters does not fit the nascent ideology of the Hindi Dalit literary aesthetic, one that is still finding its feet in the first decades of an organized Hindi Dalit literary sphere. Yet there is also danger in rejecting Premchand, in asserting that only authors who can claim a Dalit identity from birth can have authority over and access to Dalit representation. In this case, Dalit writers may be charged with isolating and radicalizing their literary sphere, limiting others' access to it and thereby reducing its integrative and transformative possibilities.

Premchand's prose has long been celebrated among mainstream audiences as the vanguard of socially conscious realism in Indian literature.[8] And in Premchand's realism, sometimes a corrupt system breeds corrupt victims, as in his story "The Shroud." The story is about two Dalits, Ghisu and Madhav, a father and son, both from the Chamār caste. When the story opens, Ghisu and Madhav are sitting outside their small hut eating roasted potatoes and trying to ignore the screams of Madhav's wife inside, who is dying in childbirth. Neither will go inside to see her out of a certain amount of shame, and also because each man fears that the other will guzzle more than his fair share of potatoes if left alone. Finally, their bellies full, they lie down to sleep in front of the dying fire. Premchand explains that the two are known as the laziest people in the village, and that in their pursuit of doing as little work as possible, they constantly live on the edge of starvation. He writes, "in a society where the circumstances of people who labored night and day was not much better than [Ghisu and Madhav's], that such a consciousness should be born among those who, compared to the farmers, knew how to profit from their own impotence, and who were at times almost prosperous, should come as no surprise."[9] When Madhav's wife and unborn child are found dead in the morning, Ghisu and Madhav set out begging for the money to pay for the wood and shroud required for the cremation. They manage to collect five rupees and arrange the wood, but they balk at spending the rest of their money on a shroud that will only be burned up with the bodies. Instead, they spend the money on liquor and fried snacks, and as they become more and more drunk, they alternately praise Madhav's wife for her gift of abundance after death and fall into spells of grief at her difficult and joyless life. The story ends with father and son drinking themselves into oblivion, and showing no final respect to the corpse of Madhav's wife.

The pages of Dalit literary journals in the months after the burning of *Rangbhūmi* subjected Premchand to the critical gaze of the Dalit public sphere, and many Dalit writers severely criticized Premchand's depiction of these two Chamār characters as heartless and lazy drunks, paying little attention— unlike other critics—to the critique of the system of institutionalized inequality that produces such characters.[10] Writing in the prominent Dalit literary journal *Apeksha*, Sumanakshar asserted that "in six-lakh [six hundred thousand] villages in the country today you can go into any Dalit settlement and not find a single man with such a lack of sympathy."[11] He accused Premchand of creating negative Dalit characters only to win the praise of elite readers who would exult in finding confirmation of their opinion of Dalits as slovenly, inhuman creatures. Such characters are not realistic, according to Sumanakshar, whose notion of realism is inextricable from the exigencies of honor and forthrightness outlined in the concept of "Dalit consciousness."[12] His notion of realism is also tightly intertwined with an idealistic view of Dalit society as ultimately humane and compassionate, and Sumanakshar believes that any "realistic" Dalit character would be representative of that ideal. He regards Premchand's depiction of Ghisu and Madhav as devious and selfish, therefore—showing not individual characters but false representatives of a Dalit community under vicious attack by a non-Dalit writer interested in catering to the casteist ideology of the dominant public.[13]

The assessment of authentic realism is made in Dalit readings of Premchand by using the critical lens of Dalit consciousness. The first line of Sharankumar Limbale's *Towards an Aesthetic of Dalit Literature* reads, "by Dalit literature I mean writing about Dalits by Dalit writers with a Dalit consciousness." He goes on to define Dalit consciousness: "The Dalit consciousness in Dalit literature is the revolutionary mentality connected with struggle. Ambedkarite thought is the inspiration for this consciousness. Dalit consciousness makes slaves conscious of their slavery. Dalit consciousness is an important seed for Dalit literature, it is separate and distinct from the consciousness of other writers. Dalit literature is demarcated as unique because of this consciousness."[14] Omprakash Valmiki writes of Dalit consciousness in *Dalit Sahitya ka Soundarya Shastra* (Aesthetics of Dalit literature): "Dalit consciousness (*chetnā*) is deeply concerned with the question, 'Who am I? What is my identity?' The strength of character of Dalit authors comes from these questions."[15] "Dalit consciousness" is an idea based on the liberation ideology of B. R. Ambedkar expressed in a text in which a Dalit character is fully cognizant of the religious and political origins of his exploited social status and, rather than accepting that status, is enlivened by a desire to struggle for freedom—not just for himself, but for his whole community. It is an expression of loyalty to the Ambedkarite message of the human dignity of Dalits. It is Dalit experience rendered realistically. But for many Dalit writers, then, the question of whether the Dalit experience has been depicted realistically also depends on how honorably the Dalit character is portrayed.[16]

According to some, a lack of Dalit consciousness can come from confusion between caste and class-related oppression. Omprakash Valmiki—one of the most celebrated Hindi Dalit writers, whose autobiography was recently translated into English by the Canadian academic Arun Prabha Mukherjee—also finds fault with Premchand's characterization of the Dalit men in "The Shroud." Valmiki suggests that Premchand wrongly conflates Dalits with farmers and peasants who face economic exploitation but who do not suffer from the specific problems born of the system of caste inequality:

> On one hand in his works he writes about the goal of changing one's heart, on the other hand he also reprimands Dalits for drinking alcohol and eating the meat of dead animals. The characters of Ghisu and Madhav in his story "Kafan" are Chamārs, but the story does not raise any issue that is related to the problems of Chamārs or Dalits. There is only a detailed depiction of their idleness and heartlessness. Even leftist critics believe this story of Premchand's to be his best and most artistic. Many critics say that Ghisu and Madhav are representative of the agricultural class which is known as the lumpen proletariat.[17]

The charge here that Premchand ignores the caste-related abuses faced by Dalits in a Marxist-leftist outlook on Indian society is not uncommon among Dalit writers and critics. Valmiki argues further that "not just Premchand, but several Hindi writers, thinkers, and critics put all farmers, laborers, and Dalits in the same box when they think about them. But all these people do not have the same problems—caste is purely a religious and social issue, one that influences every other aspect of life. In Premchand's works, this is a point of confusion. He sees this from a stance of idealism and reformism."[18] The reformism that Valmiki denigrates here is the process of Sanskritization, suggested by Premchand's exhortations (as read by Valmiki) to Dalits to stop drinking alcohol and eating meat. This idea of social reform, common in nationalist-era Hindu reform movements but strongly rejected by Ambedkar, places the responsibility of the abjectness of Dalits squarely on their own shoulders as a result of their dirty habits and suggests that by emulating Brahmanical caste practices regarding food and other such things, they may raise themselves out of destitution. Like Sumanakshar of the BDSA, Valmiki sees an unfair attack on all of Dalit society in Premchand's representation of the characters of Ghisu and Madhav. Unlike Sumanakshar, however, Valmiki suggests this is due to Premchand's misguided belief in the primacy of poverty over untouchability as the reason for Ghisu and Madhav's depravity. Caste and its attendant problems, according to Dalit critics, are entirely separate from economic inequality, which is a symptom of social oppression rather than its cause. Premchand is relegated to the margins of authentic Dalit discourse by figures such as Valmiki for failing to recognize the primacy of caste over class in the Dalit worldview.

Similarly, the point comes up again and again in discourse in the Dalit public sphere that, in matters of social reform, Premchand was a follower of Gandhi, not of Ambedkar. This is a significant matter for Dalit writers who feel that Dalit consciousness was inspired solely by Ambedkar and who believe that Gandhi betrayed the Dalits in the name of national unity. The disagreement between Ambedkar and Gandhi over a separate electoral system for Dalits (a system in which the voting population of a country or region is divided into different electorates based on certain factors like caste, and members of each electorate vote only to elect representatives for their electorate), Gandhi's fast in opposition to a separate electoral system, and the ultimate resolution in the form of the Poona Pact arise regularly as examples of Premchand's infidelity to Dalits, since he wrote vociferously at the time in support of Gandhi.[19] Valmiki writes: "When Gandhi did his fast unto the death over the question of separate electorates in Yarvada Jail, Premchand wrote continuously on this subject. But he too saw these problems with exactly the same perspective as Gandhiji, he too shared the opinion of every Hindu author, politician, and thinker. He too exhorted Dalits to put faith in nationalism (*rāshtriya-dharm*), despite the hellish lives they lived, attacks they suffered, and inferior lives full of insult they were forced to face."[20]

Mohan Dass Naimishray, another of Hindi Dalit literature's widely respected and translated authors, who has been helping shape the Hindi Dalit literary sphere with his literary, historical, and critical contributions since its inception in the early 1980s, adds: "Was Premchand a storyteller with a Dalit consciousness? The concept of Dalit consciousness is so well-defined that it is not possible to attribute it to Premchand. He was a *Kāyasth* (a caste group of Hindus who traditionally acted as keepers of records and administrators of the state) by birth and Dalits cannot be blind to this fact. . . . During Ambedkar's Mahar movement when the *Manusmriti* was burned, Premchand kept silent and this is sufficient basis to say that he was not a Dalit writer."[21] For Valmiki and Naimishray, Premchand's political affiliations and public expressions outside of literature are intrinsic to his ability to understand and convey a sense of Dalit consciousness. For Valmiki, it is Premchand's vociferous support of Gandhi in nationalist politics that makes it impossible to consider Premchand a representative of Dalit interests in literature, and for Naimishray it is Premchand's own caste identity and lack of affiliation with Ambedkar's infamous public sphere performance of burning the *Manusmriti*—the obvious inspiration for the more recent performance of the BDSA—that makes him incapable of expressing Dalit consciousness in any of his works.

True to the form of public sphere discourse, however, there is another side to the literary and ideological debate about Premchand, one that suggests Hindi Dalit writers need to rethink the ways in which they judge and categorize literature. The writer and critic Anita Bharti, critiquing the reactionary responses of members of the Dalit community, such as the BDSA's members, who categorically refuse to view Premchand as a contributor to Dalit literature, writes in defense of Premchand: "So then what is this opposition of Dalit writers toward Premchand? On the one hand, they believe that besides 'Kafan' his stories 'Thākur kā Kuān,' 'Pus ki Rāt,' 'Sadgati,' and 'Ghāsvali' to be great Dalit stories, but on the other hand, taking up the subject-matter of 'Kafan' they label him with epithets like 'anti-Dalit' and 'non-Dalit.' If we were to make a comparison between Premchand's Dalit characters and other Hindi writers' Dalit characters, then we would decidedly conclude that Premchand's characters are everywhere more prominent, argumentative, fearless, rebellious, and willing to clash with Brahmanism."[22]

Bharti further suggests that some Dalit writers have also depicted Dalit characters who are less than sympathetic, but that these writers have not faced the same kind of criticism as Premchand for the very reason that they themselves are Dalit. She censures Dalit writers who reserve their criticism only for non-Dalit writers: "Doubtless it is because Dalit writers are also casteist, they all sit in their own circles and consider themselves to be better than anyone else."[23] Her chief claim is that Dalit women have regularly been defamed by Dalit male writers in public discourse in much the same way as these two Chamār characters were by Premchand, yet no one considers this to be hypocritical. Bharti's comments suggest here the existence of voices of feminist critique in this literary and political community, adding yet another layer to the growing complexity of the discourse in the shared public sphere. This critique will be made even more explicit in the following section of this chapter.

Other writers, some non-Dalit but writing from the platform of the various publications of the Dalit public sphere, have warned of the danger posed by defining Dalit literary reception along caste lines to the mission of promoting Dalit literature in the broader public sphere. The literary critic Mohammad Dherivala suggested that an expansion of the definition of Dalit consciousness could in fact uncover sympathetic representations of Dalits in Indian literature going back long before Ambedkar.[24] He urged Dalit writers to rethink ascribing the authority to represent Dalit consciousness only to those who are Dalit by birth. Rather, Dherivala urged writers to also include a more liberal, inclusive side of an ongoing, deep-seated debate in Dalit counterdiscourses. Can only Dalits' experience epitomize Dalit consciousness? Should a specific caste identity be required to embody a subject position that is authorized to voice the narrative of caste-related suffering? These are fundamental questions about who constitutes the Hindi Dalit public sphere, about who has the ultimate authority to speak not as an individual, but as a representative of the community.

Several Dalit writers recognize this need for constant public debating and restating these questions and the contemporaneous rereading of texts to continuously reconstruct the critical space so carefully carved out by Hindi Dalit writers and readers. Jaiprakash Kardam—the eminent Hindi Dalit literary critic and author, and editor for many years of an annual collection of the best of Hindi Dalit literature—writes: "To raise questions or to record differences of opinion is not only a man's democratic right but is also a signifier of intellectual progressivism. No man or opinion is immune to questioning. Even if someone is to raise questions about Premchand then this should be viewed as a productive thing. Raising questions about something is not the same as insulting it."[25] And Bharti—though a staunch opponent of the burning of *Rangbhūmi* as a careless, reactionary, media-grabbing event and a critic who has written many times in defense of Premchand as a Dalit writer—also resolutely defends the right to criticize Premchand and other mainstream writers in Dalit critical discourse, though she maintains that these criticisms should be thoughtful rather than reactionary: "Today there are politics surrounding Premchand. If some Dalit writer wants to discuss issues surrounding Premchand's perspective on Dalits (*dalit paksh*) then what is wrong with that? Can't a non-Dalit writer raise questions about Dalit literature, its subject matter, its philosophy, the standard of its aesthetics? How is this a different thing—the thought is still mine and the paper is mine too? Several non-Dalit writers who are blindly reverential (*andhabhakt*) to Premchand are committed to decrying 'anti-Premchandism' ('Premchand *virodhi*'). It seems to them that being against Premchand is somehow Dalits' first priority."[26]

The purpose of the above discussion is to show that the problem of Premchand has had longevity and a larger context as a subject of discussion in the Hindi Dalit literary public sphere. When members of the BDSA burned Premchand's *Rangbhūmi* in 2004 in an open square in the heart of New Delhi it brought these issues into clearer focus in the print media of the Hindi Dalit public sphere. An event that the mainstream media briefly seized on and quickly rejected as reactionary protest by a radical, marginal community retained an overwhelming presence in Dalit critical conversations for more than a year after the event. In an article published in the March 2005 special issue of *Apeksha* that was entirely devoted to Premchand and the debate over *Rangbhūmi*, the critic Ish Ganganiya deftly summarizes the different interests implicated in this debate.[27] He characterizes the debates about Premchand and other mainstream, non-Dalit figures of Indian literature and history who have voiced the experiences of Dalits as a kind of subaltern project of rereading and rewriting literature and history from below. Perhaps part of the struggle of those who are charged with the rhetorical call to shape the ideological identity of the Hindi Dalit literary sphere has to do with the fact that they are faced with an author whose inclusion in the Dalit literary canon could be beneficial to the mainstream acceptance of Dalit literature, yet whose depictions of Dalit characters, based on the exigencies of the genre of Dalit literature as social justice literature, may at times not support the requirements of the politics of the movement. What emerges, therefore, is a struggle between Dalit writers as Hindi authors and Dalit writers as social activists, or even between Dalit writers as individual artists and Dalit writers as mouthpieces of a communal movement. The struggle between individual expression and community representation is becoming increasingly endemic to the discursive constitution of the Dalit public sphere.

"The Shroud" once again came to the fore of debates in the Dalit public sphere in 2006 with the publication of a controversial book by the well-known Hindi Dalit writer Dharamveer, *"Premchand: Samant ka Munshi"* (Premchand: Master of feudalism). At the book's release party, several Dalit women in the audience rose in protest while Dharamveer was speaking and threw their shoes at him from the audience, in a galvanizing display of gendered critique.[28] It was an event that shook the Hindi Dalit literary world in Delhi and contributed to reorganizations, in recent years, of Dalit literary groups there. In the ensuing discussions, published principally in Dalit literary journals, about both this event and the substance of Dharamveer's analysis in the book, the debate about "The Shroud" shifted to take on a decidedly gendered dimension that highlighted a second set of discourses in the Hindi Dalit literary sphere surrounding sexual violence and the constitution of Dalit women's literary identities. These discussions principally critiqued the gendered limits of Dalit consciousness as a rhetorical construction of collective identity formation, while also complicating a Dalit feminist standpoint that hinges on the understanding of gendered violence as primarily constitutive of the experience of Dalit womanhood. The Dalit feminist reaction to Dharamveer's interpretation of "The Shroud" makes clear that neither discursive construct is wholly representative of caste or gendered identity and experience, and, when taken together, they have the potential to reduce Dalit women to a hypersymbolic state of victimhood.

The uproar among Dalit feminists revolves around Dharamveer's following imaginative reinterpretation of Premchand's story:

> The whole story would become newly clear if Premchand would have written in the final line of the story this reality of Dalit life that Budhiya [Madhav's wife] was pregnant with the zamindar's child. That he had raped Budhiya in the field. Then, those words would shed light on the story like a lamp and we would understand everything. That even while Ghisu and Madhav wished to be able to do more, in fact they could only resist by refusing to call the child their own. That this is the real pain of Dalits—who will say this?—a Dalit or a non-Dalit? This is the reality of Dalit exploitation and oppression—that so often their offspring are not actually their own. Compared to this kind of exploitation, the economic exploitation of Dalits seems so inconsequential![29]

The intervention of such an interpretative claim on Premchand's story, whose meaning is widely understood to reflect a widespread culture of corruption and dehumanization engendered by the practice of casteism, has an ominous tone. Dharamveer seems to suggest here that if Budhiya were in fact raped by an upper-caste zamindar, the callous act of allowing her to die without attempting to help her would actually have been an understandable and perhaps even laudable act of sociopolitical resistance by Ghisu and Madhav. Following this line of reasoning, Dharamveer coolly asks, "What would be better—allowing Budhiya and her child to die, or raising another's child while calling it your own?"[30]

In an insightful article about the revision of history in Dalit literature, Toral Gajarawala has asserted that Dharamveer's reading of "The Shroud"— in particular, his reworking of underlying assumptions and narrative chronology—constitutes a political practice of "unreading" from a peculiarly Dalit perspective that "challenges the structure of typicality, and the ensuing allusive chain, on which an upper-caste reading is premised."[31] Gajarawala's astute analysis of the mechanics of Dharamveer's interpretation, however, obscures the ethical consequences of his argument, and in naming his reading an uncontested Dalit one, she may accept the patriarchal overtones of much of what has come to be constituted as Dalit consciousness in the work of the Hindi Dalit literary sphere. It is critical therefore to contextualize Dharamveer's reading in the firestorm of criticism from Dalit feminists that exploded in its wake for the purpose of complicating the notion of a singularly Dalit perspective and restoring the voices of Dalit women to the ongoing construction of a Hindi Dalit literary sphere. To do this it is necessary to lay bare the gendered dimensions of such a perspective.

Charu Gupta, in her work on Dalit masculinities, has pointed to the colonial representation of Dalits, and Chamars in particular, as docile agricultural laborers whose bodies are continuous with other forms of agricultural machinery.[32] Premchand critiques this very mode of colonial representation by making Ghisu and Madhav essentially opt out of their predicated role as cogs in the wheel of colonial agricultural machinery, suggesting instead that they cannily work the system and eke out a living with the minimal amount of labor. Yet he also provides a strident critique, as has been pointed out already, of the animalizing consequences of casteist and colonialist exploitations of human labor by portraying Ghisu and Madhav as almost entirely devoid of human compassion for Budhiya. As I discussed in the first section of this essay, Dalit critics responded angrily to this lack of humanity, arguing that it was against Dalit consciousness, but Dharamveer's interpretation presents Ghisu and Madhav's callousness as a positive choice that effectively restores their power and agency by restoring their masculinity. Historians and anthropologists such as Gupta and S. Anandhi have made clear the logic by which Dalit men, who are robbed of their masculinity through economic and caste-based hierarchies, often reassert it by enforcing patriarchal structures and asserting excessive control over the movements and sexuality of women—both of their own and higher castes.[33] And as feminist scholars and activists such as Gabriele Dietrich has pointed out, the inability of Dalit men to "protect their women" against the collective threat of sexual violence by the upper castes is seen as "a collective weakness and vulnerability" or a kind of emasculation.[34] In his patriarchal reading of Premchand's story, then, Dharamveer clearly imagines himself to be reasserting the masculine, not merely the Dalit, agency of Ghisu and Madhav by arguing that in allowing Budhiya and her child to die, they are actively denying the attack on their masculinity by an imagined (because it is nowhere suggested in the text of the short story) assault and the colonization, as it were, of Budhiya's body and womb by an upper-caste zamindar.

Dharamveer's interpretation of the story, and his extension of that interpretation into a commentary on the intersection of caste and gender in the construction of oppressive social hierarchies, does in some ways echo the claim made by many feminists that the key difference in Dalit women's experience and identity from both those of Dalit men and those of other women is the constant threat of sexual violence.[35] Collective violence against, customary access to, and expropriation of women's bodies are what undergird the logic of what I have referred to elsewhere as the "Dalit rape script." In this analysis, it was argued that sexualized violence employed against Dalit women is a critical tool in maintaining caste hierarchies.[36] It is around the societally enforced logic of this rape script that the Dalit feminist standpoint as predicated by scholars like Sharmila Rege and Vasanth Kannabiran and Kalpana Kannabiran, as well as activist organizations like the National Federation of Dalit Women (NFDW), is constructed. Yet while the understanding of sexual violence as constitutive of Dalit women's subjectivities has emerged as common currency and been used strategically and effectively in many scholarly and activist agendas, the appropriation of such an argument by a masculinist Dalit critic like Dharamveer and his reading of "The Shroud" through such an interpretive lens promotes a more ominous agenda for a restoration of Dalit masculinity that reinforces a patriarchal ideology that thoroughly subjugates Dalit women.

The angry and organized reaction of Dalit feminist critics to Dharamveer's reading of "The Shroud" demonstrates the operation of an internal gendered critique of the easy reinforcement of patriarchy that such an interpretive application of Dalit consciousness supplies. This is a critique that is mirrored in the short fiction of Dalit feminist writers like Kusum Meghwal, whose "rape revenge narratives" directly contradict the literary determinism of sexual violence evident in much Dalit literature.[37] Dalit feminist authors and critics who contributed to a special issue of the Delhi-based Dalit and Adivasi literary magazine *Yuddhrat Aam Aadmi* (The struggling common man) in the summer of 2007 devoted to a Dalit literary response to Dharamveer's argument advocated that a feminist Dalit consciousness in literature requires a reconsideration of the idea that the primary differentiating experience of Dalit women's lives is sexual violence, or the threat of it. What come to the fore in these discussions are the consequences of transference of this foundation of a collective construction of both feminine and masculine Dalit identities from the realm of political activism (such as that of the NFDW) to the imaginative realm of literature, a realm Dalits have celebrated as constitutive of new modes of discourse of Dalit dignity and political and cultural assertion. The critique of Dharamveer's proposed rescripting of Premchand's story and its ramifications for the identity formation of women in Dalit society demonstrates the ways in which a new wave of Dalit feminist discourse is working to alter the terms of the social script of the gendered violence of caste.

The fundamental argument of the feminist contributors to this special issue is that despite the reality of Dalit women's victimization by the social scripts of caste, gender, and sexual violence, literature—as a corrective space—needs to serve as a medium in which the dignity of Dalit women is restored. Therefore Dalit women writers such as Bharti, Meghwal, and Pushpa Vivek critique what they refer to as the "obsession" of many Dalit writers with narratives of the rape and sexual exploitation of Dalit women. Such a critique demonstrates how, as in the case of Dharamveer, the discursive constructions of Dalit consciousness and what is sometimes imagined and asserted as the singular difference of Dalit women can collude to rob Dalit women of any kind of agency outside of that of allegorical victim of caste oppression. Bharti asks: "How many Dalit writers do we have in front of us now who provide dignity to Dalit women and give importance to their lives? There are certainly exceptions, but we can count them with our fingers. Usually, in trying to pointlessly become an 'icon' of Dalit literature, they just call [Dalit women] names like budhiya [old woman], devdasi [temple prostitute], rakhail [mistress]. Those who graciously don't do this, slap those who do on their backs."[38]

The narratives Dalit women write about their own lives, these critics argue, are "much more expansive. It's about their education, labor, organization of community rights etc. . . . sexual exploitation is not the only problem facing Dalit women."[39] In particular, Dalit feminists like Bharti look to the genre of Dalit women's autobiography as a necessary corrective to this myopia because they pay attention to the nexus of *ghar-parivar-samaj*, or both the domestic and public spheres, rather than emphasizing one over the other. In a recent essay about the growing number of Dalit women's autobiographies in several Indian languages in the last few years, Bharti writes: "There is no doubt that Dalit women's autobiographies are both individual and societal. The use of 'we' in place of 'I' expresses the desire for the liberation of the whole of the 'woman caste.'" That's why their autobiographical voice is overflowing not just with Dalit consciousness, but with feminist consciousness as well."[40]

Many Dalit women writers also express their frustration over their isolation and a general patriarchal condescension toward their perspectives and literary aspirations. In an open letter to Dharamveer in the special journal issue mentioned above, Vivek asserts: "Today's woman is educated and has come to understand her rights. Whenever she tries to exercise her own authority over those rights, then our own male Dalit authors ridicule her and throw stumbling blocks in her path, because they cannot stomach the idea of advancing women to the equal status of men."[41] She cites in particular Dharamveer's vitriolic condemnation of Bharti, whose defense of Premchand's literary treatment of Dalits was addressed in the first section of this essay. In his book, Dharamveer writes: "I find it even worse when some Dalit woman protects a non-Dalit man, whether it's Anita Bharti or someone else. Anita Bharti praises an adulterous man like Premchand. . . . Does Anita Bharti want to end up like Budhiya? I don't think the poor woman was at fault but there is a major problem with Bharti's thinking. When the Dalit woman was sexually assaulted, then the home was robbed. Then the zamindar's seed took hold in the belly of the Chamar." According to Dharamveer, the Dalit problem is not tied to poverty or inequality, but to the sexual misappropriation of Dalit women: "The issue is not limited to poverty—the issue is not poverty at all—it's the enslavement of the sexuality of Dalit women."[42]

Vimal Thorat, whose editorial opens the special issue, argues that the "new version" of "The Shroud" that Dharamveer constructs to recuperate the masculine honor of Ghisu and Madhav (in giving them a righteous reason for letting young Budhiya languish and finally die) does so only at the expense of Budhiya herself.[43] Thorat argues that this kind of automatic reliance on the abuse and stigmatization of women results from a *Manuvadi* perspective (literally, views of the upper castes, which are said to be codified as law in the infamous classical text *Manusmriti*, that condemns both Dalits and women to abject existences). In a highly sarcastic piece (she regularly refers to Dharamveer as "Dharmguru" [teacher of dharma]) in which she condemns Dharamveer and other male writers who support him for ironically adopting a Brahmanical attitude toward Dalit women, she suggests that the bigotry toward sexually abused women that results in this kind of interpretation of the story is no different than the bigotry manifested toward both women and Dalits in Manu's 3,000-year-old treatise. While Thorat's critique of Dharamveer is astute in that she makes a connection to a long history of misogyny in Indian literature, by referring to Dharamveer's attitude as Brahmanical, she may be sidestepping the trickier problem of recognizing a duplication of patriarchy within Dalit society itself. Indeed, activist-scholars such as Kancha Ilaiah[44] and Dietrich[45] have illuminated in their work the fact that one way Dalit men attempt to restore their masculine agency is to enact the kind of patriarchal control over Dalit women's sexuality and honor that upper-caste men have traditionally exerted over upper-caste women.

Bharti similarly does not shy away from recognizing both the real-life experience of gendered violence that marks Dalit womanhood: "Even today Dalit women are pronounced witches or demonesses and killed with stones and *lathis* [a long, heavy stick used as a weapon, especially by police]. They have sticks thrust in their vaginas as punishment."[46] But she and others also read Dharamveer's analysis as enacting a similar kind of virtual violence against women, fetishizing and exploiting this violence to aggrandize themselves and limit the imaginative possibilities of Dalit women's literary roles. The rancor of their various critiques aside, these feminist critics charge that Dharamveer's manipulation of the rape script in his attempt to critique and rescript Premchand's story from the critical position of a Dalit consciousness reifies Dalit women's bodies as merely marginal, hypersymbolic sites where allegories of caste oppression are performed. Dalit feminist critics in the Hindi Dalit literary sphere thus demonstrate the inability of either of these discursive constructions of community to fully represent their identities and life experiences and advocate the wresting back of their subjectivities from their passive use as transactional objects in power struggles between men.

Conclusion

Over the course of the past decade, then, through book burning and shoe throwing and vitriolic public debates, and through reinterpretation and rewriting, Premchand has emerged as a singularly powerful cultural symbol in which various counterdiscourses of the Dalit public sphere can productively intervene to advance various social and political agendas that support the construction of Dalit literary and political identities. A critique of Premchand is at the core of both a reconstitution of the contemporary Dalit public sphere and the development of power to make effective interventions into the mainstream literary sphere.

The specific example of these debates over Premchand's "The Shroud" demonstrates in a broader context the ongoing processes of renegotiation of identity and representation in the literary spheres of the Dalit public. This brief analysis of the rhetoric of critical counterdiscourses in the Hindi Dalit literary sphere reminds us that caste, class, and gendered identities are regularly repositioned by advocates for the competing interests of diverse social collectivities. It is these very debates that sustain the health and viability—indeed, the vibrancy—of the Dalit public sphere as a discursive space at the forefront of the growth of ever-changing conceptions of belonging and unbelonging.

The discussion of Premchand in the Hindi Dalit literary public sphere was appropriated by Dalit women writers to challenge the gendered construction of Dalit collective identity. Dalit women writers have criticized Dharamveer's rereading of "The Shroud" for promoting a Dalit masculinity that reinforces patriarchal ideology by thoroughly subjugating Dalit women. Many of them were critical of their male counterparts' obsession with narratives of the rape and sexual exploitation of women. In contrast, Dalit feminist writers emphasized discussions of issues relating to their struggles for education, work, and rights.

Finally, the above discussions demonstrate that in recent years literature specifically has emerged as a vibrant and important corrective space for contemporary Dalit identity construction. The power of Dalit public discourse is in the creative impulse of Dalit literature and literary criticism to establish a Dalit public identity from a Dalit perspective, to resist the various identities—those of exploited victim, reviled criminal, silenced majority, and illiterate innocent—that have been forced on them by the long tradition of hierarchical caste society. Members of the Hindi Dalit literary sphere may differ in their perspectives on the most effective way to establish a self-invented, affiliative public identity, but they are unified in their resistance to being silenced. Dalit writers and activists are here engaging in a struggle for power and authority over their own representation.

NOTES

1. In the Indian education system, students matriculate from high school after the tenth grade, and twelfth grade is equivalent to a second year of junior college.

2. This was a term used by president of the Bharatiya Dalit Sahitya Akademi, S. P. Sumanakshar, in an interview with the author of this paper after the book-burning.

3. For the full text of the act, see appendixes A to C in *Broken People: Caste Violence against India's "Untouchables"* at http://www.hrw.org/legacy/reports/1999/India /India994–16.htm, Human Rights Watch, New York, March 1999.

4. A. Rao, *The Caste Question*; Rawat, *Reconsidering Untouchability*.

5. A. Rao, *The Caste Question*.

6. It is important to point out at the start that I do not necessarily agree with or endorse any of the critical readings presented here, but also that my endorsement or not of them is inconsequential in the face of what they reveal about the currents of dissension and disagreement that persist in the Dalit literary sphere, as well as the nature of a critical Dalit engagement with modern literature.

7. Ganguly, *Caste and Dalit Lifeworlds*; Rege, *Writing Caste/Writing Gender*.

8. According to the Indian literary historian Sisir Kumar Das, "Premchand is the greatest artist of the suffering of untouchables, not only because of his great anxiety for the century-long oppression of the Harijans, but for his uncanny sense of realism with which he presents the characters belonging to the oppressed group, free from all sentimentality and pious idealism" ("The Narratives of Suffering," 174). Francesca Orsini suggests that Premchand's "strong social conscience and radical politics, which brought him closer and closer to socialism, were rooted in an utterly secular and inclusive view of the Indian nation, which makes him a particularly valuable and rare role model these days" (*The Hindi Public Sphere*, xxvi).

9. Premchand, "Kafan," 219–20.

10. For example, Geetanjali Pandey writes: "'Kafan' has Premchand at his realistic and tragic best. He brings out with sure and subtle touches the alienation and dehumanization that institutionalized injustice and poverty can produce" (*Between Two Worlds*, 123).

11. Sumanakshar, "Rangbhoomi ko Jangbhoomi banane ke liye zimmedar kaun?" 18. This and all other translations in this chapter are my own, unless otherwise attributed.

12. For further discussion of Dalit consciousness, see Brueck, *Writing Resistance*.

13. Barbara Harlow has highlighted such aggrandizement of the benevolent nature of oppressed communities by their leaders in *Resistance Literature*. For example, she quotes Maxime Rodinson's *People without a Country*: "Ideology always goes for the simplest solutions. It does not argue that an oppressed people is to be defended

because it is oppressed and to the exact extent to which it is oppressed. On the contrary, the oppressed are sanctified and every aspect of their actions, their culture, their past, present and future behavior is presented as admirable. Direct or indirect narcissism takes over and the fact that the oppressed are oppressed becomes less important than the admirable way they are themselves. The slightest criticism is seen as criminal sacrilege. In particular, it becomes quite inconceivable that the oppressed might themselves be oppressing others. In an ideological conception, such an admission would simply imply that the object of admiration was flawed and hence in some sense deserving of past or present oppression" (quoted in *Resistance Literature*, 29).

14. Limbale, *Towards an Aesthetic of Dalit Literature*, 1 and 32.

15. Valmiki, *Dalit Sahitya ka Soundaryshastra*, 28–29.

16. Toral Gajarawala has written insightfully about the Dalit reception of Ghisu and Madhav, in particular noting that "Ghisu and Madhav are the most salient examples of what Dalit critics read as Premchand's irrevocable kayastha (effectively, 'upper caste') perspective; despite his attempts at a benevolent social realism that would incorporate the world of the peasant into the literary sphere, his upper caste status permitted him to see the Dalit only as objects of pity and disdain. . . . Ghisu and Madhav, in other words, are not realistic representations of Dalits, rather, literary Dalits are most easily read as Ghisu and Madhavs" ("Some Time between Revisionist and Revolutionary," 579).

17. Valmiki, "Premchand," 28.

18. Ibid.

19. Passed on September 24, 1932, the Poona Pact set into place reserved seats for untouchables within the general electorate. This is still widely regarded in the Dalit community as a significant defeat for Ambedkar, who had advocated for separate electorates for untouchables, at the hands of Gandhi and the casteist interests of the Congress Party.

20. Valmiki, "Premchand," 28.

21. Quoted in Ibid.

22. Bharti, "'Kafan' aur 'Dalit Stree-Vimarsh,'" 210.

23. Ibid.

24. Dherivala, "'Thakur ka Kua' Dalit Chetna ka Dastavej," 16.

25. Kardam, "Sahitya men Dogalaapan nahi chalega," 88.

26. Bharti, "'Rangbhoomi-dahan' aur Dalit-asmita ka prashan," 63.

27. Ganganiya, "'Rangbhoomi,' Gandhi, aur Ambedkarvadi-Vimarsh," 25.

28. I have discussed this event, and the basic contours of a feminist critique of Dharamveer, elsewhere (Brueck, "At the Intersection of Gender and Caste"). My discussion here takes on a new dimension, however, when paired with the other examples of Dalit critical engagement with Premchand's prose in this essay, and my thoughts on what is at stake in these discussions continue to evolve.

29. Dharamveer, *Premchand*, 17.

30. Ibid., 29.

31. Gajarawala, "Some Time between Revisionist and Revolutionary," 580.

32. C. Gupta, "Feminine, Criminal, or Manly?"

33. Ibid. See also S. Anandhi, "Work, Caste, and Competing Masculinities."

34. Dietrich, "Dalit Movements and Women's Movements," 58.

35. In these discussions, violence has emerged above all else as the axis around which both the experience and the enforcement of gendered and caste identities revolve. For example, Vasanth Kannabiran and Kalpana Kannabiran argue that the logic of sexual violence is central to both caste and gender as twin mediators of oppression ("Caste and Gender"). Citing numerous high-profile cases of sexual assault against Dalit women by upper-caste men, they point to the "mediation of inter-caste relations through a redefinition of gendered spaces" (254)—in other words, the ways in which upper-caste men appropriate Dalit women's bodies as a way to emasculate and control Dalit men. If the "'manhood' of a caste is defined both by the degree of control men exercise over women and the degree of passivity of women in the caste," then, logically, "the structure of relations in caste society castrates [the Dalit man] through the expropriation of his women" (ibid.). An attack on a Dalit woman is an attack on her entire community, "an assertion of power over all women [and men] in her caste" (ibid.). According to Ruth Manorama, founder and president of the National Federation of Dalit Women, "certain kinds of violence are traditionally reserved for Dalit women: extreme filthy verbal abuse and sexual epithets, naked parading, dismemberment, pulling out of teeth, tongue, and nails, and violence including murder after proclaiming witchcraft, are only experienced by Dalit women. Dalit women are threatened by rape as part of a collective violence by the higher castes" (Ruth Manorama, "Background Information on Dalit Women in India," available at http://www.rightlivelihood.org/manorama_publications.html, accessed October 5, 2015).

36. Brueck, "At the Intersection of Gender and Caste."

37. Ibid.

38. Bharti, "Anyay ke Kilaaf Larna hai . . . ," 17.

39. Ibid.

40. Bharti, "Dalit Stree Atmakatha ke Sansar," *Jansatta*, July 2, 2011, 6.

41. Vivek, "Dalit striyan sabak sikhane ka hausla rakhti hain," 41.

42. Dharamveer, *Premchand*, 16.

43. Thorat, "'Manusmriti' ka Taalibaani vistaar."

44. Ilaiah, *Why I Am Not a Hindu.*

45. Dietrich, "Dalit Movement and Women's Movement."

46. Bharti, "Anyay ke Kilaaf Larna hai . . . ," 17.

8

Social Justice and the Question of
Categorization of Scheduled Caste Reservations:
The Dandora Debate in Andhra Pradesh

SAMBAIAH GUNDIMEDA

Since the 1990s the Dalit political activism in the south Indian state of Andhra Pradesh (AP) has paid particular attention to the question of affirmative action, or reservations. Certain Dalit castes such as the Malas and Adi-Andhras acquired social and political consciousness and social mobility through education and employment. They were able to do so because of their proximity to the Hindu upper castes, the reforms instituted by Christian missionaries in the form of schools, and the welfare programs for Dalits of the colonial and postcolonial governments.[1] It is this group of castes that has benefited most from the reservations for Dalits and that has become dominant within the Dalit community. In contrast, Dalit castes such as the Madigas and Rellis did not have the same opportunities and advantages as the Malas and Adi-Andhras and were too poorly equipped to take advantage even of facilities extended to them through the policy of reservation. This, in turn, has resulted in their continuous imprisonment in traditional, caste-based socioeconomic relations and occupations.

To counter this underrepresentation in education and employment by the state, which is evidently one of the primary reasons for their overall marginalization, the Madigas organized under the banner of the Madiga Reservation Porata Samithi (MRPS) movement in the 1990s. Through the MRPS they questioned the overrepresentation of the dominant Dalit castes in the quota for scheduled caste (SC) reservations and demanded caste-based redistribution or categorization of that quota. The categorization was to enable every caste within the Dalit category to access its due share. But the Malas and the Adi-Andhras rejected this demand on grounds that raised serious concerns: they argued that the Madigas lacked the merit to compete against the Malas and that the categorization would destroy the unity of the Dalit community. They even formed the Mala Mahanadu, a countercaste association, and organized a "no holds barred" campaign against the MRPS.[2]

Contrary to conventional understanding, "Dalit" is not a homogeneous category.[3] It is an outcome of British colonial legislation that grouped heterogeneous castes into a single category, first as Depressed Classes and later as SCs.[4] The categories in the domain of politics, as Gopal Guru argues, "are conscious constructions with either a positive or negative agenda as chalked out by their users."[5] The SC category, which was created "in the service of the colonial state,"[6] officially came into existence in 1936 when the government created one schedule to list all the untouchable castes. In the schedule Dalit castes were differentiated among themselves according to their standing in the caste hierarchy, levels of socioeconomic and educational progress, and levels of political consciousness. In other words, the existing description of the SCs is not based on the self-representation of the castes in question but derives from the worldview of native elites and colonial ethnographers.

The identity of untouchable castes as SCs has, as noted by Sudipta Kaviraj, given them power to resist. In other words, "the common identity has given rise to a trend which seeks to transfer its grievance from a caste language to class language, highlighting the idea of exploitation associated with social indignity."[7] However, the grouping of the disparate castes in the SC category has eroded the differences and diversities among them. For example, although both the Bhangis and Chamars in north India were untouchables, the former group is more deeply discriminated against by caste Hindu society than the latter. While the Bhangis were prohibited from engaging in any form of physical and social contact with both the upper castes and the untouchable castes, the Chamars appear to have social interaction with the other castes in many aspects of daily life.[8] In south India there is no direct indigenous equivalent of the Bhangis, and the Dheds of Gujarat are more akin to Mahars in Maharashtra than to the Bhangis. Such social realities of heterogeneity and inequalities were not only typically masked by homogeneity, but it also led to a fundamentally false perception that "there is no difference between them."[9] Nevertheless, the SC category had become the basis for the political representation of the untouchables in colonial India. And the makers of the Constitution of India, instead of addressing this fundamental question, blindly adopted the colonial category for the distribution of reservations in postindependence India.[10] But what grounds were used to justify the system of reservations for Dalits?

This essay interrogates the issue of social justice and the question of categorization of SC reservations and tries to reveal the paradoxes in the system of positive discrimination. I have divided the essay into two main sections. The first deals with the main principles according to which the system of quotas has been institutionalized, and what has happened to that system in postindependence India. The second section examines the acrimonious debate about social justice and the question of categorization between the Madigas and Malas in AP, a south Indian state. Finally, the second section identifies a major challenge to Dalit politics and activism raised by the question of categorization of marginalized castes.

The Indian Constitution and the Question of Minorities: The Dalits

By declaring the Indian state to be secular—a status that was justified because of three cardinal liberal principles, liberty, equality and neutrality—the Constitution of India prohibits the state from discriminating against any citizen. But against a historical background of entrenched social, economic, and political inequalities created and justified by the caste-based hierarchical social order, such principles would remain only paper principles. To overcome these inequalities there should be constitutionally guaranteed special provisions for the so-called backward classes. In a way, the makers of the Indian constitution were convinced that the transition from a rigid hierarchical Hindu order to an egalitarian Indian order required a deliberate departure from the formal principles of secularism.[11]

The Dalit question in the Constituent Assembly debates was considered to be a question of minorities.[12] But what was it that qualified a group for minority status? Part of the answer lies in B. R. Ambedkar's observations. In his draft provisions, which were submitted to the Minorities Sub-Committee of the Constituent Assembly, Ambedkar categorically stated that "social discrimination" constitutes the real test for determining whether a social group is or is not a minority.[13] And he justified his case for considering Dalits as minorities because of the tyranny of caste Hindus and their monopolization of the administration in free India. Indian nationalism, Ambedkar observed, had developed a doctrine called "the divine right of the majority to rule the minorities according to the wishes of the majority. Any claim for the sharing of power by the minority is called communalism while the monopolizing of the whole power by the majority is called nationalism."[14] Against such a background, what can swaraj mean to Dalits, who were "placed between [the] Hindu population and the Hindu-ridden administration, the one committing wrongs against them and the other protecting the wrongdoer?" "It can only mean one thing," Ambedkar emphasized, "that while today it is only the administration that is in the hands of the Hindus, under *swaraj* the Legislature and Executive will also be in the hands of the Hindus."[15] In this context it was therefore essential to enshrine safeguards in the form of reservations for minorities in the Constitution of India. In the remainder of this section, I shall look at the arguments that were put forward in the Constituent Assembly to justify political representation and reservations in employment for Dalits.

On the question of political representation for minorities, several minority groups such as Muslims and Dalits demanded separate electorates, which would enable minorities to elect representatives exclusively from their community in the reserved constituencies and the dominant caste Hindus who would elect their representatives separately, but this demand was summarily rejected by a majority of the Constituent Assembly's members. Instead, proportional representation was proposed as a mechanism that would facilitate the participation of minorities in legislative bodies. Proponents of proportional representation advanced their arguments mainly on two considerations: representation and democracy.

First, it was argued that the mechanism of what is commonly known as a "first past the post" electoral system, from the vantage point of democracy, violates the idea of individuals' political equality, for it disenfranchises the voters who did not vote for the winning candidate. Thus, it goes against the right of every individual to be represented by a person of his or her choice and to have a voice in the governance of the country. In contrast, proportional representation, its advocates forcefully argued, is more democratic, because it more adequately realizes the right to representation of every individual in a democratic framework.[16] In a way, proportional representation was seen as a mechanism for realizing the equal rights of individuals in a democracy. Furthermore, democracy was regarded as a system in which the legislature ought to mirror the diversity of interests in society.[17]

Second, the principle of proportional representation was also justified within the ideological framework of democracy. A parliamentary system with the "first past the post system" would lead to the concentration of power in one party, and such tendencies in a democracy are at best "undemocratic" and at worst the "tyranny of the majority." And in that respect, proportional representation gives the minority a voice in the parliamentary system and also effectively saves it from degenerating into fascism.

Justification of the provisions for educational and employment opportunities for Dalits in the debates of the Constituent Assembly came from different ideological grounds. For our purpose, those grounds could be divided into two broad categories: fairness and general welfare. Two types of fairness arguments were put forward by the supporters of the reservations. First, reservations were considered as reparation for a history of injustice against Dalits. The assumption here was that the state would compensate them for the historical oppression inflicted by upper-caste Hindu society on the "lower castes."[18] Second, it was argued that without some form of special provisions, it would be impossible for historically disadvantaged groups to access educational and employment opportunities. Without their participation in these opportunities, the constitutional provisions of equality of opportunities for all citizens would remain mere paper declarations. Here, a distinction was being drawn between formal and substantive equality of opportunity—or, as supporters of reservations put it, between "paper" and "real" equality. In a way, the idea behind this argument was that equality cannot be achieved between a group that was advantaged by its historical monopoly of access to opportunities and a group that was disadvantaged by a lack of that access. Reservations were essential not only to rectify the structural forms of discrimination but also to overcome persisting practices of discrimination, even after such practices had been outlawed and equality of opportunity had been formally instituted. Thus, reservations were being defended here as an extension of the norm of equal treatment of all individuals.[19]

Thus, in the above argument, justification for reservations as a matter of general welfare was made at two levels: first, the reservation measures were needed to reduce the vast socioeconomic disparities among groups; and second, although reducing inequalities among groups was in itself a necessity, the tackling of inequalities was an essential precondition both for national integration and for the country's general progress and development.[20] But what happened in practice to the system of reservations that were instituted with a "revolutionary gesture" by the Constituent Assembly?[21]

Affirmative Action and the
Conditions of Dalits in Modern India

The policies of positive discrimination have produced mixed results. First, one of the remarkable contributions of political representation for Dalits is that it did give them a "substantial quantitative presence"[22] that helped check the monopoly of the Hindu upper castes over legislative bodies. But what eventually matters is not simply the presence, but the quality of that presence. For a long time, Dalit representatives did not participate in debates in the legislative bodies even if the issues being debated concerned the Dalits and other marginalized groups. Such indifference on the part of the Dalit representatives was because a majority of them came from extremely privileged backgrounds. In fact, they were chosen by the mainstream political parties not because they spoke the language of common Dalits, but because they endorsed the upper-caste viewpoint. Furthermore, some of the Dalits who managed to get elected independently of the mainstream politicians were absorbed by mainstream parties "offering lucrative and prestigious posts in the establishment."[23] But even such members were eventually "ghettoized in the social welfare departments."[24] Such practical inconsistencies of Dalit representation led one Dalit to comment: "This system does the Scheduled Castes no good because the people in the reserved seats belong to the party in power and are often incapable persons. Although they are educated, they dare not speak out against the party in power. They do not represent their people to the party and the government, but represent the party in power to the people."[25]

Second, during the past six decades, if literacy levels among Dalits and their presence in institutions of higher education have risen dramatically, it is due solely to the reservations. Take, for instance, the literacy rate of Dalits in comparison to the rate of the general population. In 1961, while the literacy rate among the general population was around 24 percent, it was a mere 10 percent among Dalits. In 1991, the literacy rate among Dalits had increased to 37.14 percent, in comparison to 52.10 percent among the general population,[26] and enrollment of Dalits in undergraduate, postgraduate, technical, and professional courses had almost doubled within a span of fifteen years. While in the academic year 1978–79 only 7.08 percent of students enrolled in higher educational institutions were Dalit, their share had risen to 13.30 percent in 1995–96.[27] Yet one should not be too complacent about these figures. The seats earmarked for Dalit students often remained unfilled in universities in general and in medical and engineering schools in particular;[28] and of the 239 universities in the country (including the 12 central universities), only 2 percent of the reserved posts (for candidates belonging to SC and ST categories as their entitlement which make up for 23 percent of all the seats, if the shares for Dalits and Adivasis are combined) have been filled as of September 2005.[29] Furthermore, the Indian Institutes of Technology even today have not filled the Dalit quota but remain "modern day *agraharam[s]*"—Brahman enclaves.[30] A statement made by the chairman of National Commission for Scheduled Castes and Scheduled Tribes reflects this dismal condition: "These institutions are particularly resistant to Scheduled Caste reservations. Not one of them has filled the quota, including the Indian Institutes of Technology."[31]

Third, reservations in employment opportunities facilitated a steady increase in the number of jobholders among Dalits in all four categories of government employment. For instance, there were only 0.35 percent of Dalits in Class I jobs in 1953, but by 1994 that figure had risen to 10.25 percent. Similarly, during the same period, there was a rapid increase from 1.29 percent to 12.06 percent in Class II jobs, and from 4.52 percent to 15.73 percent in Class III jobs.[32] There are two remarkable consequences of this increase. First, it has secured the presence of Dalits in government institutions, and to that extent it has facilitated the breaking of upper-caste hegemony over government institutions. Second, the steady income and enhanced social status that goes along with holding a government job led to the emergence of a small but powerful middle class among Dalits, which has been acting as the gatekeeping agency to secure the interests of Dalits. However, as many studies have pointed out, it was only in Class III and IV jobs that the Dalit quotas were filled and in Class I and II jobs—the superior administrative and managerial occupations—Dalits were thinly represented. And such a condition, as rightly observed by Andre Beteille, is the result of the Hindu upper castes' prejudice against Dalits "even when they have the necessary qualifications."[33] Furthermore, social inclusion, the avowed goal of the reservations, remains a distant dream even for middle-class Dalits. The writings of Chandrabhan Prasad, a middle-class Dalit activist, reflect the social neglect suffered by this class in urban spaces. In one of his columns, for instance, Prasad mentions items of food and drinks consumed in a party: "seven bottles of fine whiskey, four bottles of vodka, four bottles of rum, 36 bottles of beer, eight kg of Bhetki fish, nine kg of Rohn fish, 10 kg of chicken legs, six kg of mutton, soda, mineral water and vegetables to serve a few hundred guests."[34] From this account, it is clear that members of the middle class can, like their counterparts among the Hindu upper castes, afford to spend huge amounts of money for a single-night party in an elegant hotel. Looked at in that light, it is an achievement on their part. But lack of recognition of that achievement, to my mind, led them to resort to such cheap tactics to attract attention.

Finally, the opportunities of the quotas have been cornered by the advanced castes within the Dalit category, a phenomenon that resulted in the emergence of both dominant Dalit castes as well as a middle class, most of whose members are from these dominant Dalit castes. Chamars in Uttar Pradesh (UP), Punjab, and Haryana; Mahars in Maharashtra; Holeyas in Karnataka; Parayars and Palars in Tamil Nadu; and Malas in AP "more or less monopolise the benefits given to the Dalit population."[35] This differential access to reservation opportunities by certain Dalit castes has been the focus of much scholarship, which, moreover, confirms the operation of caste patterns. For example, Suma Chitnis, in an empirical study on the distribution of post-matric scholarships (government scholarships for college students) among the Dalits in Maharashtra, shows how caste patterns operate in the use of this benefit. She notes that while the Mahars, who constitute 35.1 percent of the Dalit population in the state and which is one of the better-off groups within the Dalit category, received 85.8 percent of the scholarships. In contrast, the Mangs, who constitute 32.6 percent of the Dalit population and who are backward by any socioeconomic standard, account for only 2.2 percent of the scholarships.[36] Kusum K. Premi observes a similar pattern among the Dalits in Punjab.[37] The Ramadasis and Chamars, who together constituted 38.6 percent of the total Dalit population in the state, occupied 56.5 percent of the reserved seats in higher education, yet the Mazhabis, who accounted for 16.1 percent of Dalit population, obtained a mere 4.5 percent of the seats.[38] Not surprisingly, the Dalit castes that receive the most opportunities in education and employment also receive the most political opportunities. For instance, the overrepresentation of the Chamars of UP, Mahars of Maharashtra, and Malas of AP (we shall see this in detail below) in the seats reserved for SCs, both in Parliament and state legislative assemblies exemplifies this point. These investigations suggest that the use of the reservations by the better situated castes from generation to generation has not only facilitated their ascent on the socioeconomic ladder, which is of course a positive outcome, but, importantly, has also indirectly restricted the marginalized castes from accessing welfare benefits.

It may not be out of context to mention the B. N. Lokur Committee's report on the inequalities within the Dalit category. The inequalities as a result of reservations was one of the major concerns of the government in the 1960s, and in June 1965, the Government of India had appointed the committee. In its investigation the committee found that "a lion's share" of preferential benefits had been "appropriated by the numerically larger and politically well organized communities."[39] To correct the deleterious effects of the policy, the committee suggested descheduling some of the "relatively forward" castes and communities. In addition to fourteen tribal communities, this list included twenty-eight SCs, including the Chamars (in Bihar, UP, and Punjab), Mahars (Maharashtra and Madhya Pradesh), Malas (AP), and Namasudras and Rajbanshis (West Bengal). This suggestion held out the prospect of redistributing the benefits of the reservation policy to the marginalized castes within the Dalit group. However, politically such a step would have been a major catastrophe for the group as a whole. Although it would have left the southern SCs virtually intact (except in AP), it would have almost halved the SC population in north India, and that would have substantially reduced the number of reserved seats for Dalits at all levels in the political arena. Not surprisingly, Dalit leaders reacted angrily to the proposal and held huge demonstrations in front of Parliament, which led to the withdrawal of the government's support for the proposal. Apparently the Congress-led government was not serious about the committee's recommendations. The Congress Party had been the major beneficiary of the seats reserved for SCs—at the time of the report of Lokur Committee, the party held 72 out of a total of 114 SC seats—and was heavily dependent on the votes of the numerically sizable castes like the Chamars, Mahars, and Namasudras. Thus, according to B. P. Maurya, renowned Dalit leader and former Union minister, the purpose of the committee's report, issued just a year before the general election in 1967, was "to remind them [the advanced SCs] that there was such a possibility and how much they had to be grateful for."[40] But what was the context for the Madigas' demand for categorization of the SC reservations?

Since the early 1990s India has aggressively pursued a path of economic liberalization.[41] In what started as India's response to the crisis of the "balance of payments," the state has pursued a number of policies with "single-minded determination" in reforming trade, financial, and industrial investment sectors.[42] Conspicuously, no attempts have been made to revive and improve sectors such as the rural economy, agriculture, nonagricultural employment, and social security. While the policies of liberalization became a matter of grave concern for educated Dalits in general, for the Madigas in AP they have a different meaning. Until the early 1980s, a majority of the Madigas were eking out their livelihood as agricultural laborers. This livelihood was threatened by the slowdown in agricultural growth when the national and state governments began to neglect the agricultural sector and concentrate their energies on the industrial sector.[43] These developments have forced the Madigas to search for avenues of livelihood outside the agricultural sector. Correspondingly, since the early 1970s Madigas have become increasingly aware of the educational and employment opportunities available for Dalits. By the early 1990s this awareness had resulted in a sizable number of Madiga college graduates. They were threatened by the sudden retreat of state and an abrupt shrinking in employment opportunities in the public sector, and they worried that without the reservation quotas it would be almost impossible for them to gain entry into the private sector.[44] It was in this economic context that Madigas demanded the categorization.

The Categorization Debate: Malas and Madigas

In this section my main concern is to analyze the arguments and counterarguments concerning the categorization of SC reservations in the debate between the Madigas and Malas. The Madigas were represented by the MRPS movement, and the Malas by the Mala Maha Nadu (MMN). The main argument of the MRPS had been that Dalit reservations were not distributed equitably among all the castes within the Dalit group. A majority of the opportunities went to the already advanced castes, especially the Malas and Adi-Andhras. This injustice against marginalized Dalit castes should be rectified by dividing the Dalits in the state into four subgroups and apportioning the reservations to the subgroups in proportion to the population of each. The MMN opposed this demand, surprisingly relying on arguments similar to those that have been used by the Hindu upper castes to oppose reservations, and preferred the continuation of the existing pattern of group-based distribution of Dalit reservations. I have organized the debate into four key themes and analyzed each theme separately. In my analysis I shall situate myself between the two contending parties and try to argue their cases from their perspectives. Eventually, however, I shall take the stand of the MRPS and argue for categorization of the SC reservations as an effective means of distributing reservation opportunities among all castes within the Dalit category.

One of the key ideas on which the MRPS based its categorization demand was representation. It argued that although reservation opportunities have been provided for the Dalits as a matter of representation, the Madigas had been uniquely underrepresented. In pamphlets and political speeches, the leaders of the MRPS presented data about the opportunities in the sectors

TABLE 8.1. Distribution of Thirty-Nine Reserved Seats
Per Session of Andhra Pradesh's Legislative Assembly to Madigas
and Malas in the First Ten Sessions (1952–95)

| Seats | Number of seats reserved for scheduled castes | | | |
| | Madigas | | Malas | |
	Per session	For first 10 sessions	Per session	For first 10 sessions
Number per share of population	24	240	15	150
Number actually held	12	120	27	270

Source: Satyasodhana, *Reservationlu Madigalakem Chesindi*, 6–7.

of education, employment, and politics received by the Madigas and Malas. The data suggest that the Malas are overrepresented. Although the accuracy of the data in the field of education and employment is questionable, the data on political opportunities, especially on reserved seats in the AP Legislative Assembly as well as the Indian Parliament—which I verified—clearly establish the overrepresentation of the Malas. A pamphlet titled "Madiga Rights" was published by MRPS and distributed in several mass meetings such as the one in the town of Ongole on May 31, 1995. It presents statistics on political reservations for the Dalits in the state (see tables 8.1 and 8.2).

The statistics presented in Table 8.1 show the total number of Malas and Madigas elected to the first ten sessions of the Legislative Assembly. Of the thirty-nine reserved seats per session, the Malas held twenty-seven, while the Madigas held twelve. "If these seats were to be distributed between the Madigas and Malas on the basis of each caste's demographic weight," the pamphlet claimed, "the Malas would get 15 seats and the Madigas would obtain 24 seats. Injustice had been done to the Madigas in the last forty-five years to the tune of 120 assembly seats."

Table 8.2 shows the number of available reserved seats in Indian Parliament in Lok Sabha (the house of the people, consisting of popularly elected representatives) for the Dalits in the state and their distribution. Of the fifty-four seats in the first nine sessions, the Madigas held eighteen and the Malas thirty-six. But had these seats been distributed proportionally, the numbers of seats would have been reversed. "The underrepresentation of the Madigas," the pamphlet asserted, "is a gross injustice against the Madigas and

TABLE 8.2. Distribution of Six Reserved Seats
in the Lok Sabha in Indian Parliament for Madigas
and Malas in the First Nine Sessions (1951–95)

| | Number of seats reserved for scheduled castes | | | |
| | Madigas | | Malas | |
Seats	Per session	For first nine sessions	Per session	For first nine sessions
Number per share of population	4	36	2	18
Number actually held	2	18	4	36

Source: Satyasodhana, *Reservationlu Madigalakem Chesindi*, 6–7.

other similarly placed Dalit castes, an injustice that is against the equality principle of democracy."[45]

Two points are clear from this. First, injustice has been conceived of in terms of the Madigas' underrepresentation in the opportunities accorded to the Dalit group. Second, proportional representation of the underrepresented Madigas in these opportunities is associated with democratic equality, which in turn is envisioned as social justice. Before we discuss these ideas, let us examine the MMN's counterargument.

The MMN's response to the argument of under-representation was grounded on the notion of merit. Two claims made by members of this group are noteworthy. First, it was argued by the Mala youth that "the Madigas eat beef, drink and loaf around, whereas we work hard."[46] Second, C. R. Sekhar, a writer and an activist in the MMN, justifies the overrepresentation of the Malas in the following way: "The dominant presence of the Malas in the Scheduled Caste reservation is because of their self-respect and social conscience. . . . The Madigas were underrepresented in the reservations because they have neither self-respect nor social conscience. The self-respect and social conscience of the Malas helped them develop social consciousness, which in turn endowed them with not merely the intellectual ability and power to recognize social injustices but also the courage required to fight against those injustices. . . . We have developed merit and power as part of our ongoing struggle against social injustices."[47]

Two underlying elements in this argument are that self-respect and social conscience are equated with merit and that the overrepresentation of the

Malas and underrepresentation of the Madigas in the reservation opportunities were justified from the possession and nonpossession, respectively, of merit by the two castes.

The Malas' claim of merit is a moral claim on society. "It is simultaneously," as Satish Deshpande succinctly put it, "a claim in the sense of an assertion about myself (my capabilities, competence, and at the broadest level moral worth); and a claim in the sense of an expectation or demand addressed to the rest of the world."[48] As a moral claim, the merit argument of the MMN provides sufficient justification for their overrepresentation in the reserved opportunities. But how does one acquire merit, and how do we measure it? In other words, are there any indicators to measure merit? Deshpande, following Marc Galanter, points out three indicators of merit—(a) economic resources (for previous education, training, materials, freedom from work, and so on), (b) social and cultural resources (networks of contacts, confidence, guidance and advice, information, and so on), and (c) intrinsic ability and hard work—and it is the combination of these conditions that allows people to acquire merit.[49] When Malas justify their overrepresentation from the standpoint of merit, they are claiming that economic and cultural resources are not important, but differences in intrinsic ability alone account for the differences between the Madigas and Malas.

Interestingly, what Malas did not recognize is that their merit claim actually makes a strong case against them because it could exclude them from the purview of representation.[50] One of the considerations in the institutionalization of reservation opportunities for Dalits—in addition to compensating them for the historical inequalities heaped on them by the Hindu upper castes—is to eliminate socioeconomic inequalities between them and caste Hindus.[51] Whether or not the Malas have improved their socioeconomic conditions so as to be on par with caste Hindus, their very claim of merit implies that they already have improved themselves in comparison with the other members of the Dalit group. This means that the difference is not in merit, but in educational access, and this should take away the reverse discriminatory advantage that Malas receive. Otherwise, with their improved situation, they will continue to entrench themselves in the reservation opportunities and thus minimize the opportunities available for the marginalized castes.[52]

The issue of "under-representation of certain categories of people," according to Anne Phillips, "is often so stark that its injustice seems beyond question."[53] However, if one were to disaggregate injustice from underrepresentation and examine the latter on its own terms, the general claim that a lack of equal or proportionate caste presence in public employment constitutes an injustice could be disputed on three grounds.[54] First, it might be argued that a certain group of people is underrepresented in the government jobs in comparison with some other group of people because the first group's members lack the education and required skills for particular jobs. Second, it may be argued that the claim that a group's representation in the public employment must be proportional to its demographic weight is based on the assumption that the members of all groups have an equal desire for bureaucratic jobs. It is possible, however, that this assumption is false. In that case, "disproportionalities in group presence in the bureaucracy would reflect the diversity in preference between groups, rather than any injustice."[55] Third, it might be argued that since administrative jobs are mainly middle-class jobs, a group's underrepresentation in those jobs does not constitute injustice against that group. The bureaucracy would mirror the demographic profiles of the social groups, as David Rosenbloom observes, "only if all major social groups are distributed equally, in proportional terms, along the social stratification system."[56]

The above three arguments, however, could be contested from the points of view of social justice and of democracy. First, from the point of view of social justice, in any given society, if one group of people lacks the requisite education or skills for administrative jobs in comparison with other groups, that in itself constitutes structural injustice. To remedy such injustice, a structural solution that ensures the representation of the disadvantaged group in administrative jobs is necessary. Second, an individual's choice or preference in any given society is always formed both according to "what has been set as a norm"[57] and in consonance with the opportunities available to him or her. By restricting the "lower castes" to inferior occupations and viewing their culture as inferior, caste Hindus do not merely misrecognize the human agency of the "lower castes" but also reduce the self-confidence that they can acquire through their culture.[58] Furthermore, except for the reservations, the opportunities available to the "lower castes" are so meager that occupations beyond their traditional caste occupations are hard to imagine. It is the combination of structurally confined opportunities and a socially molded inferior personality that destroys the motivation and confidence needed for "lower castes" to aspire to prestigious positions in employment and education. Moreover, "to take preference as given would be to ignore the possibility that differences in preferences along group lines might be reflective of patterns of structural inequality, patterns that are themselves the product of the interaction of cultural and economic injustices, of injustice of recognition and injustices of distribution."[59]

The dominant presence of members of certain social groups and an absence of members of marginalized social groups in public employment, education, and other state sectors clearly provides evidence of injustice in a democracy.[60] In any case, what must be recognized here is that the system of reservation is a "representational mechanism" to mirror the proportion of Dalits and Adivasis in society in the domains of public educational and employment opportunities and legislative bodies and to ensure democracy.[61] And a categorization of that representation is simply extending this concept of mirror representation within the Dalit category.

Malas and Madigas: The Question of Fair Representation

The mass agitations of the MRPS triggered a new debate on questions of social justice and representation in the Telugu Public sphere. A key feature of this new debate was Madiga's contention that the Mala Dalit caste dominate all sectors of public employment, education, political institutions, and media. Dandora, "beating up of drums" in Telugu, now became a symbol of the struggle for social justice, categorization, and the public discussion was labeled as Dandora debate. The second key theme of the Dandora debate is what I call the unit of justice. While the MRPS demanded caste-based redistribution of reservation opportunities so that every caste in the Dalit category would have an opportunity to access its legitimate share, the MMN strongly objected and favored category-based justice (or the continuation of the existing pattern of distribution).

The MRPS has made two arguments in support of its demand. First, it has argued that although quotas were provided for Dalits as a group, the Malas have been monopolizing those opportunities. As a consequence, marginalized castes like the Madigas and the Rellis were deprived of their legitimate share in the common opportunities, and such deprivation, in turn, resulted in their further marginalization.[62] Second, "educationally [the] Madiga caste is far behind [the] Mala caste" and therefore the "first generation educated [Madiga] youth will find it difficult to make a mark in the competition for reserved posts." To support its argument about Mala dominance in the field of education, such as engineering, medicine, pharmacy, and management, the MRPS offered evidence (see table 8.3). As one activist of MRPS argued, "the quantum of reservation has been decided in proportion to the population of SCs against the monopoly of one or two castes. Similarly, no single subcaste should be allowed to corner reservation benefits disproportionate to their population. As such it is time that this issue is considered in all its aspects and

TABLE 8.3. Admission of Scheduled Castes Students in Educational Institutions of Andhra Pradesh in Academic Year 1996–97

Courses [in all educational institutions]	Group				
	Mala [C]	Madiga [B]	Adi-Andhra [D]	Relli [A]	Total
B.Tech	64%	26%	10%	—	100%
B.E	73%	23%	4%	—	100%
M.B.B.S	77%	20%	3%	—	100%
Law	56%	37%	7%	—	100%
B.Ed	71%	28%	1%	—	100%
Sciences [M.Tech, M.Sc.]	65%	33%	2%	—	100%
Arts [M.Com, M.A.]	71%	28%	1%	—	100%
Degree Courses [B.Sc, B.Com, B.A.]	68%	29%	2%	1	100%
Andhra Pradesh Welfare Residential Schools [class 5 to intermediate]	62%	35%	2%	1	100%
I.A.S. Coaching Admission	89%	10%	1%	—	100%

Source: Mehra, *Report: National Commission to Examine the Issue of Sub-Categorization*, 67.

entry of the less advanced among Scheduled Castes and Scheduled Tribes should be enabled through the method of sub-categorization" in the state.[63]

There are two crucial aspects of these arguments. First, caste is the crucial factor, both in the monopolization and deprivation of opportunities (for evidence, see table 8.4), and therefore caste should be the basis for any re-distributional measures. This would facilitate the marginalized castes' access to their legitimate share of benefits. And second, the MRPS also pointed out the gap between the abilities of the dominant and marginalized Dalit castes. While the former group, whose members have been benefiting from opportunities generation after generation, are equipped with the required skills for competition, the same is not true for the latter, whose members have just begun to enter the arenas of public education and government jobs. Thus, continuing the existing pattern of distribution would continue to deny the marginalized castes opportunities. Finally, it must be recognized here that the demand for categorization does not include a demand for compensation for

TABLE 8.4 Representation of the Scheduled Caste Employees,
specially Malas and Madigas, in the Total (State-Level) Opportunities
in Andhra Pradesh in the Reserved Category, 1991

	Groups				
Department	Mala (C)	Madiga (B)	Adi-Andhra (D)	Relli (D)	Total
Total scheduled caste employees	62,055	20,384	6,149	1,333	89,921
Central government and public sector undertakings	5,896	3,756	1,112	83	10,847
State public sector undertakings	735	369	33	3	1,140
Local bodies	1,675	1,431	383	348	3,837
Andhra Pradesh social welfare residential educational institutions	303	202	3	3	511
State government (15) district offices with sweepers and public health workers	10,703	7,282	2,402	577	20,964
State government (15) district offices without sweepers and public health workers	10,402	6,025	1,822	—	18,249
Secretariat (19 departments)	169	70	20	—	259
Head of the 66 university departments	2,101	1,216	149	43	3,509
Universities	534	423	110	150	1,217
Tirumala Tirupati Devastanam (temple trust)	951	357	115	126	1,549
Indian administrative service officers in the state	32	10	—	—	42
Indian administrative service officers in central and other states	85	15	—	—	100
Indian police service officers in the state	10	3	—	—	13
Indian police service officers in central and other states	25	4	—	—	29
Deputy collectors (civil service)	50	14	—	—	54

TABLE 8.4 (*continued*)

Department	Groups				Total
	Mala (C)	Madiga (B)	Adi-Andhra (D)	Relli (D)	
Magistrates	25	4	—	—	29
Government pleaders	15	3	—	—	18
Health department officers	17	5	—	—	22
Social welfare department officers	4	1	—	—	5
Andhra Pradesh state road transport corporation officers	20	4	—	—	24

Source: Mehra, *Report: National Commission to Examine the Issue of Sub-Categorization*, 69–70.

what the marginalized castes have been losing on account of the appropriation of opportunities by the dominant Dalit castes. The marginalized castes are seeking only justice in the present and future distribution of the Dalit quota.

The MMN has put forward two arguments in its opposition to caste-based reservations. First, Venkatarao Mallela has justified the MMN's position on the ground of the "distributional dynamics" of social justice.[64] In his theory of social justice, Mallela divides Indian society into three primary groups—exploiter, proletariat, and oppressed—and argues that the distribution of power and wealth among these three groups should be undertaken in a phased manner. In the first stage, the distribution of justice should be confined to the exploiter and the proletariat. Once that distribution has taken place, the second stage begins, during which the oppressed will be given their share of justice; this is also the stage at which the internal problems of the oppressed will be sorted out. I am sure that Mallela's theory of justice would be enthusiastically received by the Hindu upper castes, for he employs an argument that has been made by them since the inception of reservations.[65] It is clear that to ignore inequalities and differences within the Dalit group and to evade the MRPS's claim of caste-based justice, Mallela rather cleverly employs the idea of class groups and does not even acknowledge the existence of caste.

Second, P. V. Rao, president of the MMN, rejects the caste-based distribution or categorization demand as part of an erroneous and dangerous trend. He argues that it is inevitable that the more advanced group (the Malas) would benefit because of their high levels of education. He cautions that if "we begin the categorization process, we would have to continue this process until the end of human race."[66] There are two elements in this argument: categorization benefits the advanced sections within the marginalized castes; and categorization sets a dangerous precedent, for it creates space for further categorizations. Let us examine these arguments one after the other.

The argument that the benefits of categorization will be appropriated by the advanced groups within the marginalized castes applies equally to the Malas' own case.[67] It was the Malas' appropriation of common opportunities that forced the Madigas to demand categorization. And what must be clearly recognized here is that without categorization, even those advanced groups among the marginalized castes would not be able to avail themselves of the benefits of reservations. This means that as long as the castes that have been appropriating opportunities continue to do so, the marginalized castes will continue to be excluded.[68]

Arguably, the MMN's claim that categorization would result only in reproducing similar injustices is correct, since the immediate beneficiaries of categorization would almost certainly not be the most disadvantaged among the marginalized. This is, in fact, one of the main concerns of the Madigas. For instance, the Madigas of the Telangana region have been expressing concern over the disproportionate advantage likely to be taken by the Madigas from coastal Andhra in the event of categorization, since the latter group already enjoys better educational opportunities than the former.[69] Similar concerns are also expressed by the Madiga women: "Madiga women constitute half of the Madiga population. Of the total reservation benefits received by our men, we do not get even 1 percent of those benefits. As women we face triple discrimination against us, and that should be taken into consideration in the distribution of the reservations . . . we demand categorization of reservations on the basis of caste, and we also demand categorization on the basis of gender."[70]

The Madigas of the Telangana region feel disadvantaged on account of caste and regional backwardness, and Madiga women feel disadvantaged on account of gender, caste, and class. They demand that these three aspects should be taken into account in the distribution of opportunities. This is neither the first nor the last such demand from marginalized groups, for "we live in a society with deep group oppressions . . . [the] complete elimination of which is only a remote possibility."[71] It is incumbent on us to constantly seek ways to redress injustices and construct a just society. We must understand the MMN's argument for categorization and put in context the concerns expressed by Telangana Madigas and Madiga women.

Let me lay out my views of the present categorization demand.[72] If the SC reservations were categorized, the Madigas would, on the basis of their proportion of the Dalit group in AP, secure 7 percent of the opportunities reserved for Dalits. As AP is divided into three regions (coastal Andhra, Telangana, and Rayalaseema), to ensure that the Madigas in each of these regions get their share of opportunities, that 7 percent would be divided into three. While the Madigas in the coastal Andhra and Rayalaseema regions will be given 2 percent each, those in the Telangana region will have 3 percent simply because a majority of Madigas live there. Furthermore, each region's share should be divided equally between Madiga men and women. That distribution would take three aspects of backwardness into account: caste, region, and gender. In the future, if rural Madigas, disadvantaged by lack of opportunities in education and employment in comparison with their counterparts in urban areas, demand further categorization, then each region's share of opportunities would be divided into two equal shares. Thus, a further categorization of existing opportunities means dividing the share into four shares, where 1 percent of opportunities would be divided equally between Madiga men and women in urban areas and the remaining 1 percent would be distributed equally between Madiga men and women in rural areas. In the future, even after such distribution, if some Madigas were to demand categorization on another just basis, a further categorization should be made. If one were to add a fifth element of difference or backwardness to the already existing four elements (caste, region, gender, and rural versus urban), each 0.50 percent of opportunities would be divided into two shares of 0.25 percent, and any further addition to the existing list of differences would mean dividing each share of 0.25 percent again. Thus, each additional element would reduce the share of opportunities, and we would finally reach the point at which group differences would be replaced by individual differences, so that each person would avail him- or herself of opportunities. Thus, the argument that one categorization would open the door for other future categorizations is logically valid. But unlike the MMN, I would like to treat this as a way to solve inequalities among Dalits rather than as a barrier to solving them.[73]

The third key theme in the Dandora debate concerns opportunities for empowerment, while the MRPS grounded its demand for categorization on the idea of accessing modern opportunities. Vara Prasad, a MRPS campaigner, maintains that "just like the Malas or any other caste in the society, we also want to send our children to schools, colleges, and universities. . . . Unlike most of the Madigas, who toil throughout the year as agricultural laborers or sandal repairers, at least some of our children would have the opportunity to go to colleges, become educated, and get some jobs."[74]

Prasad's observation mirrors the genuine aspiration of the unfortunate Madigas to access modern opportunities and improve their lives. Although the MRPS's argument of deprivation is valid, discrimination against the Madigas justifies their demands more than their deprivation does. The response of the MMN is a typical one. "Since the Madigas had the leather-making occupation," it was argued, "the best way to empower them is to give them help so as to develop their traditional occupations, especially the leather work."[75] It is true that leatherworking was one of the traditional occupations of the Madigas. But such work—skinning dead cattle, tanning hides, and making and repairing sandals by hand—has never been an instrument in their socioeconomic advancement. In fact, besides being poorly rewarded, these occupations are stigmatized, and almost by definition they reduce the social status of the Madigas. It must be recognized here that the economic assistance argument is one of the most potent casteist arguments. K. Balagopal retorts: "Uplift them from their poverty and give them economic assistance to improve their traditional occupations . . . but do not breach our preserve of expanding knowledge and the status and opportunities it carries."[76] In other words, the premise of the Malas' arguments is that while Malas should work their way out of the structure of caste-determined occupations, the Madigas should continue to live inside them.

Malas and Madigas: Unity and Uniformity

Two major concerns in the Dandora debate are related to unity and uniformity. While the MMN rejected categorization on the basis of Dalit unity, the MRPS, in contrast, built its demand for categorization on the idea of the uniformity of the Dalit group. The MMN, in its rejection of categorization, made three arguments to emphasize Dalit unity:

> Malas and Madigas all are Dalits; all are oppressed and exploited in the Brahmanical caste system. The Manuvadis are jealous of our unity, and categorization is their political conspiracy to divide and rule the Ambedkar's family.[77]

> At present whenever there is any incident of atrocities against any caste among the Dalit community, all the castes together face the tyranny of the upper castes and agitate against such incidents united. However,

after the castes are divided into groups, members of other castes or groups will not come forward to protect the victims if the latter do not belong either to the caste or group of the former.[78]

After categorization people would give their vote to their caste candidates only . . . there will be unprecedented political competitions, which leads to social animosities among Dalits as every Dalit caste would field its own candidate in the reserved constituencies.[79]

Three points are clear from the above arguments. First, both the Malas and the Madigas are considered part of the Ambedkar family (that is, the Dalit category), and the Madigas have nothing to do with the demand for categorization, for that was a political conspiracy of the Hindu upper castes to destroy the unity of the family. Second, there are two negative consequences of Dalit disunity: (a) all the Dalits would not be obliged either to protect Dalit victims or protest against atrocities if the victims did not belong to their caste or subcaste (in other words, categorization would trick Dalits into thinking and acting to promote narrow, caste-based interests rather than the lofty goals of the larger group, and that would adversely affect the security of individual Dalit castes), and (b) disunity among Dalits would perpetuate the rule of the Hindu upper castes. This statement even suggests that the domination of the Hindu upper castes is necessary for the preservation of the brotherhood of Dalits. Finally, it is assumed here that categorization results in unwanted political competition and social animosities among Dalit castes (implying that such competition and animosities did not exist among Dalits prior to the categorization demand).

Now, let us examine the MRPS's argument of uniformity among the Dalits. Interestingly, the MRPS also used the language of family and Dalit unity. For the MRPS, however, unity could be achieved only when reservation opportunities were equally (that is, proportionately)[80] distributed among all the children of Ambedkar. Krishna Madiga maintains: "Ambedkar, the father to both Madigas and Malas, left them with the property of reservations but that property should be equally distributed between the two sons rather than appropriated by one son."[81] Arguing along similar lines, Krupakar Madiga insists that "distributive justice among all the castes is an indispensable step before we join other Dalit castes for political power."[82] He clearly recognizes the importance of Dalit unity in the fight against the forces of Hindutva, both in the social and political realms. But he believes that such a fight needs to be preceded by justice for all castes in the Dalit group. Thus, both the

Mala Mahanadu and the Madiga Dandora have sought Dalit unity on the similar grounds—to fight the common enemy and to promote common interests through political power. The one crucial difference between them is that while the latter asks that internal problems be sorted out before any common action is undertaken, the former sees that common action as a strategy of avoiding discussion on internal problems. For the former, the enormity of the threat posed by the enemy is a sufficient condition for seeking unity.

Is unity possible without equality? Before answering this question, let me bring in an argument made by Jupaka Subhadra, a Dalit writer and supporter of the Dandora. She argues: "How is it possible for a person on the floor to join hands with another person who is on the terrace for friendship, for unity, for working together, and for fighting against the Manu dharma? Is unity possible between two unequal individuals? . . . Unity is possible between equals and not between unequal[s]."[83]

Subhadra's argument has three elements. First, she points out the common enemy—the Manu dharma (ancient Hindu law)—of both the Madigas and Malas; second, she recognizes the need for a united front against that common enemy; and third, she emphasizes the conditions required for unity. Unity can only be achieved between two equal parties.

Now let us analyze the normative claims involved in concepts of "family" and "unity." First of all, we need to recognize that what is being claimed in the concepts of the "Ambedkar family" and "Dalit unity" is in the self-interest of both the Malas and the Madigas. This can be explained from two perspectives. First, both the Madigas and the Malas, as the castes at the bottom of caste hierarchy, are vulnerable to atrocities and discrimination on the part of the Hindu upper castes. No caste is strong enough to fight against the Hindu upper castes on its own. In fact, whenever the upper castes commit atrocities against Dalits, it is always strategically against an individual Dalit caste rather than Dalits as a group. For instance, in Karamchedu village, despite the presence of both Malas and Madigas, the Kammas organized a massacre against the Madigas alone; in Chunduru, they acted against the Malas alone. Thus, unity between the castes serves the interest of each one.

Second, on the political front unity is also in the interest of all Dalit castes. As Phillips points out, "partly this is no more than efficiency: to change the world we need the weight of numbers."[84] No Dalit caste alone has enough demographic weight to win elections. Phrases like "Dalit family" and "Dalit unity" are simply veils of social courtesy designed to hide the uglier face of self-interest. Of course, it is true that sometimes "members of families are bound by ties of sentiment and affection and willingly acknowledge duties in contradiction to self-interest."[85] But in the case of the Madiga Dandora and the Mala Mahanadu, it is not affection for an individual family, but their own caste group's sociopolitical interests, that motivated both the organizations to advance such arguments in the debate. Third, I do not agree with the MMN's argument that categorization would lead to intercaste competition, rivalry, and animosity among Dalits. In fact, the prevailing intercaste animosities are due to the domination of one caste or a few castes of the opportunities reserved for the group as a whole. And categorization, in my opinion, should lead to amity within the group, camaraderie rather than competition or animosity. In other words, competition among the Dalit castes is due to the disproportionate appropriation of opportunities by a few castes, and if that condition were eliminated, there would be no reason for intercaste rivalries and competition.[86]

Conclusion

Three major concerns of contemporary Dalit politics and activism are political power, reservations in the private sector, and the Dalits' share in the nation's resources.[87] The demand for the extension of reservations in the private sector has become very important in current Indian politics. This demand reflects the confidence of some Dalits that they can compete against the upper-caste groups in the job market. But a pertinent question that begs to be asked at this juncture is who among the Dalits, or which castes within the Dalit category, are actually equipped to compete against the upper castes? Above I noted that certain Dalit castes—namely, the Chamars, Mahars, Malas, Namasudras, Rajbanshis, Paraiyars, and Pallars—have availed themselves of a portion of the reservation opportunities that is disproportionate to their share of the Dalit population. Simply on account of their continuous domination of these opportunities, these dominant social groups are well equipped, materially and culturally, to compete against the upper castes in the private sector. Quite obviously, while claims of this sort and the demand for reservations in the private sector assumes the presence of advantaged Dalits on the one hand, the demand for categorization of the existing Dalit reservation by castes like the Madigas, Rellis, and Arundhatiyars assumes the presence of the disadvantaged Dalits on the other. If reservations for Dalits are extended to the private sector, indisputably the dominant groups among the Dalits would be the first to gain from that extension. Conversely, those Dalit castes that have already been disadvantaged in the public sector would not even dream of jobs in the private sector. This means that they will either be limited to caste-based occupations such as tanning, sandal-making, or—even worse—scavenging or be condemned to work as waged laborers in the urban areas forever.

In any case, what we have to recognize here is that neglecting the question of social justice for the marginalized Dalit castes would be counterproductive to the ongoing movement for reservations in the private sector. For, as we have already been warned, "unless a fair distribution of the reservation facilities through the method of categorization of reservations is guaranteed to the marginalized, we would go to the extent of launching a counter movement against the demand for reservations in the private sector."[88] Such warnings give us some indication of the future challenges posed to the Dalit movement from within the Dalit community. Whether or not the marginalized Dalit castes launch a countermovement against reservations in the private sector, the dominant Dalit castes will have to confront this opposition either before or after the realization of Dalit reservations in the private sector.

This essay is an attempt to interrogate the issue of social justice and the question of categorization of SC reservations. Through that interrogation it aimed to reveal paradoxes in the system of positive discrimination for the SCs in India. To understand and analyze the Dandora debate on the question of categorization in AP critically, I began this essay with an examination of the main principles behind the system of quotas. Following this, I briefly noted the mixed results that were produced among the Dalits by the quota system. At the root of these mixed results, I have argued, is the construction of the category called SCs. Disregarding the socioeconomic differences and advantages and disadvantages among the untouchable castes, the colonial state described them as SCs and instituted political reservations for them. This practice was diligently followed by the state in postindependence India. Although this might have given the divergent castes within the SC category a common identity, in fact it could not erase the socioeconomic and political differences among them. These differences inevitably played a crucial role in whether or not various Dalit castes could avail themselves of the reservations. Those castes that have historically been in an advantageous position, in comparison with the other castes in the Dalit category, have taken advantage of the reservations. The other castes could not do so, and their members continue to practice caste-based traditional occupations. Over time this has led to the emergence of dominant and disadvantaged castes within the Dalit category. The former are in a better position (both economically and culturally) to compete against the upper castes in the job market than the latter, whose members remain unequipped to do so. They are not even in a position to take advantage of opportunities in the public sector. Terrified by the withdrawal of the state from the welfare arena and market activities and the subsequent emergence of the market as the main source of employment, especially since the early 1990s, marginalized Dalit castes such as the Madigas demanded the categorization of the SC reservations. The dominant Dalit castes responded to this demand with impassioned protests. I have critically examined the categorization debate, or the Dandora debate, that took place between the MRPS of the Madigas and the MMN of the Malas in AP. What is interesting about this debate is that while the MRPS argued its case for categorization of the SC reservations based on the original principles behind the reservation system, the MMN argued against categorization by relying on ideas found in Brahmanism. In my analysis of the debate, I have situated myself between both sides and argued their cases from their perspectives. Eventually, however, I took the side of the MRPS and argued for categorization of the SC reservations as an effective method of distributing reservation opportunities among all the castes within the Dalit category. I have also noted the possible replication of the existing situation in the private sector, if the demand for SC reservations in that sector meets with success without the categorization of existing reservations.

NOTES

This essay is the result of my personal engagement with the categorization question for the past thirteen years, both as a Madiga who is yearning to see the realization of categorization not just for the empowerment of the Madigas but largely also for other marginalized castes in the Dalit category and as a scholar who is deeply interested in the project of broadening democracy and social justice for marginalized groups. Although I have penned this essay, the material and analysis come from Krishna Madiga, Krupakar Madiga, and millions of other Madigas who have been struggling for social justice for the past nineteen years—to them, my grateful thanks. I also would like to thank K. Balagopal, Prakash C. Sarangi, Sasheej Hegde, Chitra Panikkar, Sharmila Sreekumar, Sudipta Kaviraj, Rochana Bajpai, and Matthew Nelson for their ideas and comments on this essay. My thanks to the participants of the following conferences: the Forum for Cultural Studies, the University of Hyderabad in 2001; the Fourth Essex Conference on Political Theory, Rhetoric and Politics, the University of Essex, 2003; and the Princeton Institute for International and Regional Studies Graduate Student Conference, Princeton University, 2006. I thank Steven Wilkinson for commenting on the first draft of this essay and the two anonymous reviewers for their helpful suggestions on my essay submitted to this volume.
    1. On this point, see Ramaswamy, "Preference and Progress"; "Education and Inequality"; "Protection and Inequality among Backward Groups."
    2. Balagopal, "A Tangled Web," 1078.

3. For sociological and anthropological analyses and recent debates on the SC category, see Bharati, "Dalit"; Judge, "Hierarchical Differentiation among Dalits," 2990–91; Mariot, "Dalit or Harijan?," 3751–52; A. Shah, "The 'Dalit' Category and Its Differentiation."

4. Charsley, "'Untouchable'"; Cohn, *An Anthropologist among the Historians and Other Essays*; Deliege, *The Untouchables of India*.

5. Guru, "The Language of Dalit-Bahujan Political Discourse," 97.

6. Sharan, "From Caste to Category," 279.

7. Kaviraj, introduction, 9.

8. Mahar, "Agents of Dharma in a North Indian Village," 18.

9. Charsley, "'Untouchable,'" 1.

10. Galanter, *Competing Equalities*, 122–23.

11. Chatterjee, "Secularism and Toleration."

12. Galanter, *Competing Equalities*, 27.

13. Ambedkar, *States and Minorities*, 422–23.

14. Ambedkar, *States and Minorities*, 427.

15. Ambedkar, *States and Minorities*, 414–15.

16. Z. H. Lari, one of the most consistent supporters of the principle of proportional representation, has argued: "The twin principles of democracy are that everybody has a right of representation and that [the] majority has the right of govern[ing]. The electoral system must be such as to ensure representation to everybody. This is the significance of adult franchise. . . . It is better for us to adopt this principle [proportional representation] which is more progressive in instinct and which is really democratic" (*Constituent Assembly Debates: Official Report*, 7:299).

17. Perhaps it should be recognized here that proportional representation, as Anne Phillips argues, does not normally rest on a principle of individual equality that gives all citizens the same right to get their candidates elected. Instead, it is more commonly defended as a way of making the representative body more representative in terms of the opinions of citizens. Furthermore, the principle of proportional representation considers political equality in terms of some roughly proportionate representation of political preferences and opinions rather than that all preferences should have an equal chance of being adopted. Yet the adoption of this principle is desirable as it enhances the representativeness and, in turn, the democratic character of assemblies. See Phillips, *The Politics of Presence*, 107.

18. Galanter, *Competing Equalities*, 552.

19. Ibid.

20. For further analysis of the questions of political representation and reservations in employment for minorities in the debates of Constituent Assembly, see Bajpai, "The Conceptual Vocabularies of Secularism and Minority Rights in India," and "Constituent Assembly Debates and Minority Rights," 1837–45; Jha, "Representation and Its Epiphanies," 4357–60, and "Secularism in the Constituent Assembly Debates," 3175–80.

21. I borrow this expression from Kaviraj, "Democracy and Social Inequality," 99.

22. Galanter, *Competing Equalities*, 50.

23. Jaffrelot, "Reservations and the Dalits at the Crossroad," accessed September 20, 2015, https://casi.sas.upenn.edu/iit/cjaffrelot. See also Jaffrelot, *India's Silent Revolution.*

24. Guru, "A Subsidised Notion of Democracy," 40–41. See also Weiner, "The Political Consequences of Preferential Policies."

25. Quoted in Ghanshyam Shah, "Consequences of Reservations," 244.

26. Mendelsohn and Vicziany, *The Untouchables,* 141.

27. Government of India, *National Commission for Scheduled Castes and Scheduled Tribes.*

28. Chitnis, "Positive Discrimination in India with reference to Education," 36–37; P. Ghosh, "Positive Discrimination in India."

29. Jogdand, "Reservations in the Private Sector," 3345.

30. P. C. Vinoj Kumar, "Caste in Campus: Dalits Not Welcome in IIT Madras," *Tehelka,* June 16, 2007.

31. Quoted in Vidhya Subrahmaniam, "Reality of Dalit Power: Condemned Before," *Times of India,* August 9, 1997.

32. Galanter, *Competing Equalities*; P. Ghosh, "Positive Discrimination in India"; Mendelsohn and Vicziany, *The Untouchables.*

33. Beteille, *Society and Politics in India,* 203–4.

34. Chandrabhan Prasad, "Berwa at C-K-P-I Party," *Pioneer,* February 29, 2004.

35. P. Kumar, "Reservations within Reservations," 3507.

36. Chitnis, "Education for Equality"; V. Shah and Patel, *Who Goes to College? Scheduled Caste/Tribe Post-Matric Scholars in Gujarat*; Wankhade, "Educational Inequalities among Scheduled Castes in Maharashtra," 1553–58.

37. Premi, "Educational Opportunities for the Scheduled Castes."

38. Jodhka and Kumar, "Internal Classification of Scheduled Castes."

39. Quoted in Galanter, *Competing Equalities,* 136.

40. Ibid., 138.

41. Bhagwati, "The Design of Indian Development"; Corbridge and Harriss, *Reinventing India,* 143–72; J. Ghosh, "Liberalization Debates"; R. Jenkins, *Democratic Politics and Economic Reforms in India.*

42. Varshney, "Mass Politics or Elite Politics?," 249.

43. Bardhan, *The Political Economy of Development in India.*

44. Mallepalli Lakshmaiah, "Udyamam vargeekaranakea parimitam kaaraadu!," *Andhra Jyothi,* November 7, 2004.

45. Ibid.

46. Quoted in Balagopal, "A Tangled Web," 1076. From the point of view of sociology of caste, it may be interesting to note here while caste Hindus sometimes justified their discrimination against the Dalits on the basis of their practice of "beef eating," the same argument has been put forward by upwardly mobile Dalit castes to claim their superiority over marginalized Dalit castes.

47. Sekhar, *Dalita Shakthini Antamondinche Rajakeeya kutra Vargeekarana,* 22.

48. S. Deshpande, "Exclusive Inequalities," 2442.

49. Ibid., 2443; See also Galanter, *Competing Equalities.*

50. Khasim, a researcher from Osmania University, in Hyderabad, makes an interesting observation against the merit argument of the Malas: "While the upper castes have been chanting the merit mantra for the last fifty to sixty years, today the Malas have joined this congregation. . . . According to this, meritorious people [both the caste Hindus and the Malas], [who] have merit will have seat[s] and employment. Then what is the need for the reservations at all? Let's discontinue with the reservation system, and let's allow the meritorious [to] get the seat[s] and employment. Are the Malas ready for this?" (P. Srinivas, *Dandora Dagapadda Gunde Chappudu*). In my opinion this is a rather powerful argument.

51. For a detailed discussion of the reservation provision for the Dalits and other backward groups, see Bajpai, "Minority Rights in the Indian Constituent Assembly Debates, 1946."

52. I do not suggest blocking the Malas from availing themselves of reservation benefits. Most of the Malas are as poor as the Madigas.

53. Phillips, *The Politics of Presence*, 21. See also Kateb, "The Moral Distinctiveness of Representative Democracy"; Kymlicka, "Three Forms of Group-Differentiated Citizenship in Canada"; Phillips, *Engendering Democracy*; Pitkin, *The Concept of Representation*.

54. I have developed my argument on the issue of underrepresentation by drawing ideas from Bajpai, "The Conceptual Vocabularies of Secularism and Minority Rights in India," 179–98.

55. Ibid., 194–95.

56. Rosenbloom, *Federal Equal Employment Opportunity, Politics and Public Personnel Administration*, 38–39. See also Bajpai, "The Conceptual Vocabularies of Secularism and Minority Rights in India," 195.

57. Phillips, *The Politics of Presence*, 44. See also Sunstein, "Preferences and Politics."

58. For an excellent theoretical discussion of the politics of recognition and misrecognition, see Taylor, "The Politics of Recognition."

59. Bajpai, "Legitimacy Vocabulary of Group Rights in Contemporary India," 195. See also William, *Voice, Trust and Memory*, 16–17.

60. Incidentally, Amitabh Kundu, who chaired the second expert group to "examine and determine the structure of an Equal Opportunity Commission," argues that if a community (even a minority group) is already overrepresented in a given institution, it cannot claim any benefits (see "Report of the Expert Group on Diversity Index," accessed September 20, 2015, http://www.minorityaffairs.gov.in/sites/upload_files/moma/files/pdfs/di_expgrp.pdf).

61. Tharu et al., "Reservations and Return to Politics," 40.

62. Interview with Kakani Sudhakar in Hyderabad, March 26, 2001.

63. Ibid.

64. Venkatarao Mallela, "Vargeekaranato dakkeadi vatti-vistari," *Andhra Jyothi*, December 10, 2004.

65. Mallela's argument is akin to the grounds for objections made by the Brahmans and other Hindu upper castes both in colonial and postindependence India. A great

body of literature is available on these objections. For example, see Irschick, *Politics and Social Conflict in South India*, 218–74. For a compelling discussion of the upper-caste arguments opposing reservations for other backward classes proposed by the Mandal Commission Report, see Dirks, *Castes of Mind*, 275–302.

66. Interview with P. V. Rao, Hyderabad, May 2004.

67. Students familiar with the Mandal debate will immediately recognize the origin of the Malas' arguments. Rajni Kothari defended the caste-based reservations for the other backward classes ("Caste and Politics: The Great Secular Upsurge," *Times of India*, September 28, 1990). In response, M. N. Srinivas, A. M. Shah and B. S. Bavaskar (letter to the editor, *Times of India,* October 17, 1990) argued that caste-based quotas for those classes would provide new avenues of exploitation for the elites among them: "The ploy of caste-based reservations, encouraging caste-based politicization, is not the solution. . . . For all we know, this will benefit only the rich and the influential in all the castes and leave the poor and weak where they are" (quoted in Dirks, *Castes of Mind*, 287).

68. Conversation with Srinivas Gurram, a research scholar in the Department of Sociology, University of Hyderabad, Hyderabad, January 2004.

69. Interview with P. Srinivas, who produced a documentary in 2006 on the history of the Madiga movement titled *Dandora: Resonance of Deceived Hearts*.

70. Interview with Mary Madiga, president of the Madiga Mahila Samakhya, Hyderabad, May 2006.

71. Young, "Polity and Group Difference," 262.

72. I thank Matt Nelson for clarifying my thinking on this point.

73. A similar proposal has been made by the Justice Rajinder Sachar Committee (Sachar, *Report on the Social, Economic and Educational Status of the Muslim Community of India*). See also Khaitan, "Transcending Reservations."

74. Interview with D. M. Vara Prasad, an active MRPS campaigner, who later became a Congress (I) member of the legislative assembly (MLA) representing the Tadikonda constituency, Guntur district.

75. Sekhar, *Dalita Shakthini Antamondinche Rajakeeya kutra Vargeekarana*, 22.

76. Balagopal, "A Tangled Web," 1078.

77. Sekhar, *Dalita Shakthini Antamondinche Rajakeeya kutra Vargeekarana*, 22.

78. MMN memorandum to the National Commission for SCs & STs, 1998.

79. Suryarao Gollapalli, a Congress MLA of AP.

80. In the Dandora debate, the words "proportionality" and "equality" have been used interchangeably. Although conceptually they are two different terms, I too shall use them interchangeably.

81. Krishna Madiga made this point in an address to the Dandora activists in, at a meeting held at Ambedkar Bhavan Hall in Hyderabad on February 20, 1999, which I attended.

82. Krupakar Madiga, in P. Srinivas, *Dandora: Dagapadda Gunde Chappudu*.

83. Jupaka Subhadra, in P. Srinivas, *Dandora: Dagapadda Gunde Chappudu*.

84. Phillips, *The Politics of Presence*, 23.

85. Rawls, "Justice as Fairness," 187.

86. I am aware that the initiation of categorization at one level would solidify intercaste competitions, but it would open up intracaste competitions and rivalries. But this cannot be a good reason to reject categorization. In the future, if there is going to be intracaste competition as a result of categorization, we will need to find a way to resolve it.

87. Another issue that should have been a major concern of Dalit politics is Dalit human rights. But that concern has been monopolized by nongovernmental organizations. This does not mean that I underestimate the contributions made by nongovernmental organizations—both in India and elsewhere—in internationalizing the Dalit question. In any case, the question of what the organizations did to Dalit politics and movements is a serious one that merits careful analysis and examination.

88. Interview with Mallavarapu Nagaiah Madiga, President, MRPS, Guntur district in Mangalagiri, April 14, 2007.

9

Caste and Class among the Dalits

D. SHYAM BABU

Are the Dalits moving away from a tradition-sanctioned life of stigma, discrimination, and violence? One way of answering the question, according to many scholars, is to study how many Dalits are wriggling out of their caste identity and entering class. Caste is understood, for the purposes of this essay, as birth-based and primordial, immutable, and immobile, whereas class is more of an economic category associated with urban industrial society. Therefore, membership in a caste is preordained, while one can choose one's class. In fact, it is possible—though rare—for someone to move from the top class to the bottom one or vice versa during a lifetime. The way caste and class are defined in the preceding two sentences may be questioned or dismissed as lacking in clarity. However, the purpose of the exercise is to show the chief contrast between the two: one's caste as well as a caste's place within the system cannot be changed; but membership in a class is flexible in the sense that those seeking entry can gain it by fulfilling certain conditions, though class may also be rigid—an upper class can never become lower, and the underclass will be the same everywhere.[1]

There is widespread interest among scholars and policy makers in understanding the dynamics that engender better living conditions for the Dalits. There are about 201 million Dalits in India, according to the 2011 census. Officially known as the scheduled castes, the Dalits were known in the first half of the twentieth century as the depressed classes or Harijans. "Untouchables" is a more accurate appellation, as it transcends time and space: all over the world, the Dalits are known as the former untouchables. Moreover, they are untouchables due to custom and religion. But the law, enacted after India became independent in 1947, not only abolished the practice of untouchability but accorded full citizenship to the Dalits.

The history of the past six decades has been punctuated by several landmark laws and public policy initiatives, including an extensive program of affirmative action in the form of job and educational quotas. These efforts were meant to end the social and economic disabilities that the Dalits suffered due to their identity, and also to help them achieve parity with other groups. "In other words," write Loren Demerath, N. J. Demerath, and Surinder Jodhka—who call the idea behind the whole enterprise a "simplistic and evolutionist view"—"the 'closed' and 'hierarchical' structure of caste was to give way to an 'open' system of stratification based on individual achievement and merit."[2] This essay is meant to study exactly that.

Such a journey from caste to class must be seen as epoch making. But any attempt to understand that journey, or exodus, confronts hurdles that are more demanding than the original question. Even if one sets aside the question on how useful the caste-to-class approach will be, one suffers from the paucity of empirical studies that can have somewhat wider currency. A few area studies, undoubtedly useful, will give us at best a vague picture. The caste-to-class move of Dalits, being a relative issue, can be evaluated only in relation to other groups by a study of long-term social and economic trends.

This essay does not delve into the rich and extensive literature on caste, class, whether they are the same or different, and so on. Nor does it deal with the issue of ideology or culture-specific values. For example, Henri Stern warns us of the dangers of "Western ethnocentrism," which idealizes class "in terms of the 'objective' aggregate economic position of individuals" and of the tendency to "confuse the study of change with the study of structures" and declares his belief that "caste and class belong to two different universes"[3] and hence not fit to compare. In contrast, Andre Beteille takes a more nuanced view that caste and class "resemble each other in some respects and differ in others."[4] Irrespective of academic debates on whether caste and class are similar or they belong to different universes, the fact remains that the Indian state made its value choice when it sought to delegitimize caste in all its forms. For the "lower castes" whose backwardness is attributed to their caste, any betterment of their condition is treated as acquiring a new identity that either replaces their caste identity or becomes too predominant to ignore.

There are four points about caste and class among the Dalits that deserve our attention: we need to understand the links between caste and class; economic and social change reflecting change in social structures tends to vary across space and time, and that variation needs explanation; similarly, we should explore intra-Dalit variation in terms of change and mobility; and finally, we need to investigate how Dalits have fared relative to others. This essay will strive to explore these four points. The final section is devoted to highlighting the importance of how public perceptions and media imagery feed on each other to the detriment of the Dalits.

Is Class Relevant in a Caste-Ridden Society?

In a cartoon published in the *Indian Express* on April 1, 1978, the famous cartoonist Abu Abraham had one of his characters quip, "We shall need a commission to decide whether the atrocities are on Harijans or on peasants who happen to be Harijans."[5] Did it matter to the people who were subjected to violence which label had been used to trigger or justify the violence? It might as well be that Abraham was having a dig at his communist friends, who would reject caste as irrelevant to understanding India. However, more often the "class is irrelevant" school enjoyed popular support and academic respectability. Ironically, both viewpoints have rarely been advanced to benefit the Dalits or other victims of caste. In fact, most of the scholarly debate on caste falls, to borrow a medical analogy, into pathology and stops short of therapeutics. Can we use a cartoon published in 1978 to answer a contemporary question?

The Abraham cartoon serves as an appropriate metaphor in two respects even today. First, the reality on the ground still defies scholarship. Most viewpoints claim vindication by citing some recent official data or a research report. The ideological positions include only caste matters, only class matters, and caste is class. A stray incident is enough for people to debate whether caste— or class—is waning or reemerging. Two incidents that took place almost simultaneously in 2007 will, if considered in isolation from one another, lead one to arrive at two diametrically opposite conclusions on caste.

In assembly elections in Uttar Pradesh (UP) in that year, the Bahujan Samaj Party (BSP), a Dalit party, was voted into power as a result of the party's success in enlisting the support of the Brahman electorate, even though it was clear that Mayawati, leader of the BSP, would become the chief minister, which she did. The phenomenon, known as the Dalit-Brahman alliance, may have a narrow historical or political context or may even be transient, but it should never have happened in a caste-ridden society. What lessons, then, can one draw from the UP experience? Is caste no longer relevant? Is UP, of all places, an exception? No doubt the UP example is subject to a diametrically opposite interpretation: castes are too preoccupied in accumulating political power to be diligent about following the rules of caste. However, the fact that Brahman voters helped make a Dalit the chief minister is indicative of broader changes sweeping the country.

The other incident is that the Gujjars, a middle caste, unleashed a violent agitation in Rajasthan demanding they be given scheduled tribe status. If considered in isolation, this event would lead us to believe that caste and caste wars are all that happen in India.

Which of these two incidents, taking place during the same year in two northern states with a common border, is to be taken as representative of today's India? They cannot be brushed aside as isolated incidents and hence exceptions, because enough evidence can be found in the country to support either viewpoint.

On one hand, insistence on class is due to the concept's universality in the sense both scholars and policy makers will be comfortable with it. However, class formation has been a difficult historical phenomenon in predominantly peasant societies everywhere. Even the term "class" did not come into currency in Europe prior to the late eighteenth century.[6] It should not be a surprise, then, that India, still more than two-thirds rural, still contains identities that are local, variegated, and contradictory.

Second, as a result, scholarship on caste (or class) has been of little value to policy making in India, especially insofar as mitigating the condition of Dalits and other poor groups is concerned. An area study or a survey may be useful in academic terms, but it lacks wider applicability. This is not because scholarship on the subject is found wanting. In fact, seminal works on Indian society are legion. But public policy, being a blunt instrument, requires social categories that are applicable to larger geographical areas, if not to the whole nation.

Yet another aspect that puts in doubt the relevance of the study of the caste-to-class movement of Dalits is the question whether the movement is linear in the sense of being, at least, not easily reversible. I further explore below the ironical situations in which Dalits are identified in both caste and class terms. A Dalit officer, Dalit politician, and Dalit doctor are some of the day-to-day contradictions we confront. Having the first Dalit president, the first Dalit chief justice, and so on are undoubtedly moments of pride for the whole country as they symbolize certain progress. But can they be called part of a caste-to-class movement? The quibble is about identity. Michael Schumacher is a legendary Formula One champion. Nobody would even notice the etymology of his last name, which evolved from the profession of shoemakers. Maybe we are a couple of centuries too early to raise the issue of class among the Dalits. Even the target group thrives on the caste identity. M. N. Srinivas underscored what would be needed to eradicate the caste system (which must precede the emergence of class): "The moral to be drawn is that an ideological attack on caste which is not backed up or underpinned by a mode of social production ignoring or violating caste-based division of labour, is totally inadequate. A combination of wholly new technologies, institutions, based on new principles, and a new ideology which includes democracy, equality and the idea of human dignity and self-respect has to be in operation *for a considerable time* in order to uproot the caste system" (emphasis added).[7]

That being the case, what do scholars say about the links between caste and class? The majority opinion during the past five decades has been that there is a positive correlation between caste and class. In other words, members of upper castes tend to be found predominantly in upper-class positions, such as highly educated professionals, managers, and other leadership positions; members of the middle castes (Shudras) in middle-class positions, be they small and medium cultivators or other agriculturalists; and the Dalits are found in disproportionately high numbers in semiskilled and unskilled occupations. The so-called mobility or occupational shift usually takes place within a certain band, which cannot be called across-caste and across-class movement.

For example, one of the earliest studies on class-caste relation, by Edwin Driver, was based on interviews conducted among 1 percent of the male heads of households in Nagpur District to find out "the relation of caste to occupational structure in urban and rural Central India."[8] According to Driver, nearly 59.7 percent of Dalits (members of the scheduled castes) in rural areas and 78.3 percent in urban areas were found in the bottom two occupational categories, semiskilled and unskilled. He also found "a positive association between positions in the caste and occupational hierarchies. . . . The pattern in the urban area is more internally consistent. As one descends the caste hierarchy, the percentages of professionals and managerials decline, the combined percentages being: 39.4 for Brahmans . . . 4.1 for Scheduled Castes."[9]

Sanjay Kumar, Anthony Heath, and Oliver Heath[10] came to the same conclusions in 2002 as Driver did in 1962, in their study based on the National Election Study of 1996, conducted by the Centre for the Study of Developing Societies. The total number of respondents was 9,614, from 432 sampling points in 108 parliamentary constituencies. The study found that, in terms of mobility, 67 percent of the respondents remained stable, 19.4 percent experienced upward mobility, the condition of 6.6 percent of the respondents deteriorated, and 7 percent experienced horizontal movements.

Kumar and his coauthors acknowledge the past impact of caste in enabling members of upper castes to enter the privileged classes and assert that "upper caste membership still gives a statistically significant advantage." But in a curious U-turn, they write: "*Our suspicion* is that the class inequalities described in this paper are to be explained primarily by the resources—financial, educational, and social—that the members of different classes possess and should not be ascribed to caste" (emphasis added).[11]

Comparing sample data collected for the National Election Study in 1971 and 1996, the same authors in a subsequent study[12] sought to answer three questions: how mobile Indian society was; specifically, whether it became more mobile during the years between 1971 and 1996; and how much the relationship between caste and occupation had changed. Their conclusion was: "Another consistent pattern is for Dalits to be the group that is most highly concentrated in manual work. . . . Overall, both with father/son class mobility and caste-class mobility, the dominant picture is one of continuity rather than change."[13]

Anirudh Krishna has been able to deliver what is by far a definitive message based on a field survey about caste.[14] According to his fieldwork, conducted in the late 1990s in sixty-nine villages in the adjoining areas of Rajasthan and Madhya Pradesh, "caste continues to be a primary source of social identity in these villages, people live in caste-specific neighborhoods, and the clothes that they wear reveal their caste identity. Yet insofar as political organization is concerned, caste no longer has primary importance. Non-caste-based political entrepreneurs are more successful than others in delivering economic benefits and providing avenues for greater political participation, these findings show, and villagers associate with these entrepreneurs regardless of caste or religion."[15]

Krishna identifies three factors in the emergence of these new leaders (*naye neta*): the spread of education in rural areas, a vast expansion of public programs in the countryside, and intensified political competition among major parties. This is a new phenomenon that took shape during the 1980s and 1990s: "More villagers by far consult the *naye neta* for diverse tasks involving party politics, market brokerage, and interaction with government officials than any other type of leader."[16]

Krishna is justifiably cautious in not assuming that the phenomenon is generalizable beyond the surveyed areas. However, three inferences and a conundrum are inescapable. The first inference is that the newly emerged leaders truly fall into the category of class. They are not merely a new generation of educated leaders who replaced old, illiterate caste elders within their respective castes. They are also secular, in the sense that services are sought and rendered without reference to caste. Second, this ought to be celebrated as a peaceful revolution insofar as the Dalit emancipation is concerned. Having a 22 percent share in the population of surveyed villages, the Dalits accounted for 26 percent of the new leaders. This discrepancy can also be noted among Other Backward Classes, who constitute 41 percent of the population in the villages under survey and providing 49 percent of the new leaders. The over-representation of leaders belonging to Dalit and OBC groups in these villages came at the cost of upper castes and scheduled tribes. Third, if such a transformation could take place in Rajasthan and Madhya Pradesh, where society is more conservative, then surely caste must have become politically less relevant in other parts of India. As for the conundrum, Krishna makes it clear that this is a political phenomenon and that caste retains its salience in the social sphere. This only begs the question, what is happening to caste? This also reminds one of what Barbara Joshi wrote more than a quarter-century ago:

> Upper caste citizens often argue that while some of them may have retained old cultural forms once expressive of prejudice—such as exclusive food exchange patterns—most have changed the content of their attitudes about low status castes, so that prejudice is not really a problem in other social interactions such as those affecting employment. Many Scheduled Caste individuals have come to suspect that the reverse is more nearly true: that in many cases a few details of the cultural idiom of prejudice have changed, while the content of prejudiced attitudes has remained the same, and that many higher caste individuals who no longer complain about sharing a tea stall with Scheduled Caste customers will still consistently choose a non-Scheduled Caste job applicant over a Scheduled Caste applicant.[17]

Which of the two versions that Joshi mentions is true with regard to Rajasthan?

Is Caste Reasserting Itself?

The so-called reemergence or reasserting of caste cannot be overstated. The incidents warranting such a prognosis are dramatic (such as the Dalit-Brahman political alliance in UP), violent (for example, atrocities and Gujjar agitation in Rajasthan for scheduled tribe status), routine (such as the state assembly polls), and banal (such as the sprouting of new caste parties like the Praja Rajyam Party in Andhra Pradesh in 2008). But how does the persistence of caste help its chief victims? There are obvious reasons why even Dalits cling to caste identity.

Since 80 percent of the Dalits live in the countryside, they have no option but to be identified by their caste. The 20 percent who migrated to urban areas are theoretically free to be identified by class. Urban Dalits can be divided into two groups: one is the educated people working in the government, thanks to affirmative action; the other is the urban underclass living in the slums. And any statistical nuances will, being negligible exceptions, have little impact on the picture overall.

Ironically, affirmative action appears to have locked members of the community into an inferior status. A group of Dalits who, however small in numbers, are in a position to become a class are being induced by affirmative action not only to keep but to brandish their Dalit identity. This is ironical because affirmative action was designed in India to, first, compensate the Dalits (and the scheduled tribes) for the past injustices they suffered and, second, bring them to parity with other sections. As a policy instrument, it is too ineffective as it could benefit only a fraction of the community, and Ross Mallick rightly questions "the appropriateness of affirmative action for community betterment."[18] Moreover, given the way it operates, its beneficiaries find themselves in a contradictory status of economic independence and social inferiority.

Despite overwhelming statistical certainty that affirmative action will benefit a very few, the Dalits are conditioned to maintain their scheduled status in anticipation of its future utility. This tendency at times leads to situations in which the Dalits themselves demand retrograde policies. Such an incident took place a few years ago in Delhi. The Delhi State government decided to recognize those Dalits who had moved to the national capital from other parts of the country as members of scheduled castes if they fulfilled one of a few simple requirements. Given the local nature of caste, the government had been following a sound policy of not recognizing those Dalits who settled in states other than their own. This might be unfair to, for example, the children of Dalits migrated because of economic distress. But the Delhi decision was taken at the behest of Dalit employees. Yet another irony is that it goes against B. R. Ambedkar's advice to his people to migrate to urban areas for anonymity.

The reassertion of caste is, in fact, the assertion of "lower castes." This is old news, going back almost a century to backward class movements in the south. Dalits appear to have joined this trend in a more transformational way, with wider implications. It is difficult to answer the question of what triggered it. Probably the process Ambedkar set in motion reached a definitive stage, insofar as Dalits are concerned. First, it is no mere political phenomenon. Second, Dalits' awareness that being Dalit is nothing to be ashamed of is obvious across states. The two big Dalit subcastes in Andhra Pradesh, the Malas and Madigas, have started to add the caste name to their names. Ramaswami Mahalingam reports a similar story from neighboring Tamil Nadu: "[Dalits] are proud of their identity and demand social respect. For instance, middle class Dalits in Tamil Nadu proudly mention their caste in the marriage invitations (e.g., 'Narayana Pariah cordially invites you and your family to grace the occasion of his daughter's marriage')."[19] Such assertions of equality and self-respect do invite a backlash that draws its inspiration and legitimacy from the caste ideology. Prem Chowdhry explains succinctly how, in Haryana, the emerging Dalit middle class creates "a sense of insecurity and resentment" among the upper castes:

> Altogether, an entry into new professions, the availing of employment opportunities along with reservation of seats in the elected bodies like the gram panchayats, legislative assembly and the parliament has thrown up a considerable number of Dalits as a distinct middle class category, albeit a highly differentiated and layered one. Noticeable in public arena, this class . . . is primarily responsible for creating a sense of insecurity and resentment among the upper caste groups. Clearly, despite the emergence of a middle class among the Dalits, the caste ideology continues to play an important role in the reproduction of relationships and behavioral patterns.[20]

Therefore, the Dalits themselves appear increasingly not to care much about how they are perceived by others from an outlook frozen in the past.[21] The tricky part as always is whether exceptions are advanced as rules or rules are dismissed as exceptions.

The issue of job quotas for Dalits and tribal people in the private sector became a major national debate in 2004 when the United Progressive Alliance government included it in its common minimum program. The ensuing debate was acrimonious enough to attract the attention of even the Western media. The *Guardian* carried a story with a twist. The headline declared, "Untouchables in New Battle for Jobs," followed by a more illuminating deck: "India's lowest class raises its sights from the gutter"![22]—And the icing on the cake is a color photo of Arvind Vaghela that occupies almost a quarter of a page. A postgraduate student of Dalit economics who had no job and lost his father, Vaghela had no option but to take up his father's job—that of a municipal road sweeper in Ahmedabad, Gujarat.

Vaghela's is a story full of pathos, and most readers of the *Guardian* must have felt sorry for him: fate had been cruel to him. But the photo the paper chose to carry—along with a story essentially about Dalits' demand for jobs in the private sector—depicts Vaghela with a scarf covering the lower half of his face and holding his broom in the manner of a freedom fighter holding his national flag upright! It would not have been a very pleasant sight for the British corporate bosses with operations in India. Not known for lacking class consciousness, they might have dreaded the prospect of having to offer jobs to Vaghela and his fellow Dalits.

This is not a case of the Western media dishing out familiar negative stereotypes on India.[23] The correspondent who filed the story is a British-born Indian, without a whiff of prejudice. I have presented the episode as it epitomizes the problem of popular perception and media imagery, and how they feed on each other. For example, it is not just the international media that routinely qualify "Dalits" as "former untouchables" or "untouchables" make their stories accessible to their readers or viewers. Even the Indian media find it difficult to come up with imagery that does not perpetuate negative stereotypes. Moreover, for most media commentary on Dalits, which has to do with atrocities or poverty, the appropriate visual representations will be the community's abject poverty and squalor. One cannot blame the media for doing what they do, and therein lies the problem.

The image etched on most people's minds of a Dalit is either a shoemaker sitting on the roadside or a scavenger. Immaterial are the facts that only a fraction of even Chamars and Valmikis (whose respective caste-stipulated occupations are leatherworking and scavenging) stick to their ancestral callings and that these are only two of the hundreds of Dalit castes in India. A majority of Dalit castes have no supposedly polluting occupations attached to them and are, in tradition and lifestyle, essentially the touchable "lower castes." It is undeniable that Dalit identity carries with it the connotation of impurity, both in the ritual and the physical sense. Moreover, all Dalits may not be found in unclean occupations, but most people in unclean occupations are believed to be Dalits. Ashwini Deshpande captures the problem thus: "However, at a deeper level, to gain insight into the nature of change in the caste system, an investigation into ancient occupations that have survived changes in economic structure (i.e., priests in temples, scavengers, traditional money-lenders, and the whole spectrum of agricultural jobs) is required. Are these jobs still performed by castes to whom they were traditionally allocated, or is the reshuffling of the deck total, i.e. the modern occupational structure is randomly distributed across castes? *It is likely that we may find more continuity than change*" (emphasis added).[24]

Therefore, the caste-to-class movement of Dalits may not amount to much in the estimation of non-Dalits. This has been attested by many Dalits who made it into class: though they successfully overcame hurdles, they could never shake off their Dalit identity. Decades before the Government of India even attempted (and failed disgracefully) to abolish manual scavenging, a horrendous curse of untouchability and an oft-used image for Dalits, the writer E. M. Forster opined in 1956: "No god is needed to rescue the Untouchables, no vows of self-sacrifice and abnegation on the part of more fortunate Indians, but simply and solely—the flush system. Introduce water-closets [flush toilets] and main-drainage throughout India, and all this wicked rubbish about untouchability will disappear."[25]

Is it possible to eliminate the stigma and shame of being Dalit when society's perception of Dalits remains shaped by centuries-old history? Here Mahatma Gandhi was partly right in asserting that untouchability was a caste Hindu problem. It is caste Hindus' ideology and perceptions that need changing. In other words, Dalits' smooth journey from caste to class will be possible only on the day when caste Hindus are willing to treat, to use Ambedkar's expression, the individual as the unit and determine his or her merit and class status.

The Dalits followed on their own two routes to escape the stigma of their identity. One was through religious conversions, and the other was education. Conversions to non-Hindu religions might have met the spiritual needs of the converted but failed to raise their social standing. Take the case of Dalit Christians, the one group whose members allegedly escaped caste discrimination:

they have not been able to escape their caste identity even after a couple of centuries. While demanding affirmative action benefits for Dalit Christians, the National Coordination Committee for SC Christians distributed a pamphlet among members of Parliament, which highlighted the identity issue thus: "Except for the (wrong) records in the revenue offices he [the Dalit Christian] is a Dalit in every sense of the word; viz., ethnically, lineally, racially, socially, economically, culturally, vocationally, geographically, relationally, contextually, and emotionally. HE CONTINUES A FULL DALIT EVERYWHERE EXCEPT IN THE IGNORANT MIND OF THE EXECUTIVE."[26]

In contrast, education has enabled many Dalits to move up both in social and in economic terms. The state's failure, in general, to provide quality education to a large group of people meant that whatever education the Dalits received restricted their mobility. Thus, many Dalits for a couple of generations after independence moved away—thanks to affirmative action—from village life and traditional occupations but moved into petty government jobs not far from their villages. As long as someone's roots are firmly in the village, any newly acquired class status remains an appendage to his or her caste identity. That has been the broad change that has taken place in the country.

Class in the mere sense of an economic category mostly, but not entirely, based on one's profession will be effective in enhancing the status of Dalits, but the change will be commensurate with how many those Dalits are in higher or leadership positions within their class. The current class, the Dalit bourgeoisie, is still small in numbers and, even worse, it is ensnared in government service, effectively cutting itself off from providing leadership to the community. The next step in their liberation will have to be the emergence of an elite or intellectual class actively engaged with the others in a process of accommodation and acculturation. Naomi Hossain and Mike Moore have very effectively defined the intellectual class: "They are the people who make or shape the main political and economic decisions: ministers and legislators; owners and controllers of TV and radio stations and major business enterprises and activities; large property owners; upper-level public servants; senior members of the armed forces, police and intelligence services; editors of major newspapers; publicly prominent intellectuals, lawyers and doctors; and—more variably—influential socialites and heads of large trades unions, religious establishments and movements, universities and development NGOS."[27] Consider the above list. The Dalits enjoy adequate representation among ministers and legislators and a modest presence among upper-level public servants, lawyers, and doctors. They are completely absent from the other positions of influence. Their adequate representation among ministers and legislators—the lawmakers and rulers—has been rendered ineffective by virtue of their dependence everywhere on non-Dalits to get elected.[28] But the silver lining is that, among the categories that Hossain and Moore mention, many influential ones require for admission only quality education and some middle-class moorings. It is inconceivable that an elite class of Dalits will not emerge from among the third and fourth generations of urban Dalits who number, according to the 2011 census, more than forty-seven million.

Conclusion

Joshi cautioned against "generalizations about the Scheduled Castes, for the category covers a large number of diverse groups."[29] Since then, things got further complicated in unexpected places like UP (with the Dalit-Brahman entente) and Rajasthan (with its village transformation, according to Krishna). Politically, at the national level, the Dalits ceased to be a vote bank for a single political party when they realized that neither of the two national parties has any incentive to espouse their cause.

But field surveys, census data, and so on cannot be combined to provide a broader picture. This is not peculiar to the Dalits alone. Linguistic, subcaste, regional, and religious diversity renders India complex. However special the Dalits' case may appear to be, they share the ups and downs of the whole country. For example, since 1991 as the poverty rate started coming down for most groups, Dalits experienced the same trend.[30] India's long-term economic future depends on urbanization and industrialization, and these are the promising links in the Dalits' emancipation.

One coincidence, if it is one, is that large numbers of Dalits (and tribal people) are in the so-called laggard states, such as Bihar, Madhya Pradesh, Orissa, Rajasthan, and UP. Though there are significant differences among the Dalits across subcastes and region, those differences are not related to class. For example, the Mala-Madiga conflict in Andhra Pradesh is now being seen as a fight over splitting the job quotas, but this is only the latest phase of their decades-old antagonism.[31] A similar trend of conflict or estrangement can be found between Mahars and Mangs in Maharashtra and between Chamars and Valmikis as well as Chamars and Pasis in UP. Therefore, differences based on regions, subcaste, or religion are too varied to be amenable to comparison.

The story of Dalits vis-à-vis non-Dalits is no less complex. Debashis Chakraborty, Shyam Babu, and Manashi Chakravorty report that they tested "the hypothesis that atrocities are triggered in areas characterized by upward mobility among the Dalits, and not in the poorer areas,"[32] and found the hypothesis to be true. In simple terms, attempts by Dalits to migrate from caste to class are met with resistance and violence.

Thus, an attempt has been made in the preceding pages to figure out what is happening to the Dalits in terms of both caste and class: how far the caste-to-class framework is relevant; why generalizations are not possible; how the Dalits regard themselves; and how non-Dalits perceive the community. In sum, class may not be a useful tool for measuring or understanding the progress of Dalits unless we modify its definition to such an extent as to blur the distinction between caste and class—something that some Marxists have accomplished with their argument that caste is class in Indian terms. Ramkrishna Mukherjee argues: "Thus, it is that we should not look at caste as a 'new avatar.' . . . Class structure has cut across the caste hierarchy, forming new alliances and antagonisms. . . . Today, in India, caste in class depicts the reality, and not caste *per se* or caste and class."[33]

While measurable factors like education, professional status, and income can be employed to classify people into groups (classes), membership in a class depends not only on merit (one cannot become a doctor without a medical degree, for example) but also on acceptance by other members. This is not a new argument: historically, minorities in many countries suffered nonacceptance at one time or the other. For example, though Jews and Catholics were never subjected to violence in the United States—at least on the scale of the Dalits in India—they were not welcome into its hallowed spaces, either. The case of African Americans has more similarities with that of the Dalits. Ironically, in India, history does not always follow a linear progression; on cultural matters, people there tend to run in circles.

NOTES

The author is grateful to the two anonymous reviewers whose suggestions made this essay better than its previous version.

1. For the complexities of defining "class," see Patil, "Should 'Class' Be the Basis for Recognising Backwardness?," 2733; Stern, "Power in Modern India."

2. Demerath, Demerath, and Jodhka, "Interrogating Caste and Religion in India's Emerging Middle Class," 3813.

3. Stern, "Power in Modern India," 65–67.

4. Beteille, *Caste, Class, and Power*, 187.

5. Abraham, *Arrivals and Departures*, n.p.

6. R. Smith, "Anthropology and the Concept of Social Class," 467.

7. M. Srinivas, "An Obituary on Caste as a System," 459.

8. Driver, "Caste and Occupational Structure in Central India," 29.

9. Ibid., 29.

10. Kumar, Heath, and Heath, "Determinants of Social Mobility in India."

11. Ibid., 2987.

12. Kumar, Heath, and Heath, "Changing Patterns of Social Mobility."

13. Ibid., 4095–96. See also Pankaj, "Engaging with Discourse on Caste, Class and Politics in India," 338.

14. Krishna, "What Is Happening to Caste? A View from Some North Indian Villages."

15. Ibid., 1190.

16. Ibid., 1175.

17. Joshi, "'Ex-Untouchable,'" 221.

18. Mallick, "Affirmative Action and Elite Formation," 346.

19. Mahalingam, "Essentialism, Culture, and Power," 739.

20. Chowdhry, "'First Our Jobs Then Our Girls,'" 440–41.

21. Sarah Beth reports that the (Hindi) Dalit writers, a small but articulate group in the community, find themselves caught between their urban middle-class status and the Dalit identity that they proclaim through their autobiographies. See Beth, "Hindi Dalit Autobiography," 554.

22. Randeep Ramesh, "Untouchables in New Battle for Jobs," *Guardian*, October 2, 2004.

23. Karla Hoff and Priyanka Pandey report how the mere public revelation of "lower-caste" students' caste identity had adversely affected their performance, which is known as "stereotype threat" ("Discrimination, Social Identity, and Durable Inequalities," 208).

24. A. Deshpande, "Recasting Economic Inequality," 382.

25. Quoted in Morris, "Caste and the Evolution of the Industrial Workforce in India," 130.

26. Quoted in L. Jenkins, "Becoming Backward," 42.

27. Hossain and Moore, "Arguing for the Poor," 1.

28. Babu, "India's Liberalisation and the Dalits."

29. Joshi, "'Ex-Untouchable,'" 196.

30. For example, see Sundaram and Tendulkar, "Poverty among Social and Economic Groups in India in 1990s."

31. The Mala-Madiga rivalry was so intense that even efforts to rope in Ambedkar to bring about a reconciliation failed. See Mendelsohn and Vicziany, *The Untouchables*, 113.

32. Chakraborty, Babu, and Chakravorty, "Atrocities on Dalits," 2479.

33. Mukherjee, "Caste in Itself, Caste and Class, or Caste in Class," 1761.

10

From *Zaat* to *Qaum*:
Fluid Contours of the Ravi Dasi Identity in Punjab

SURINDER S. JODHKA

According to the popular view, caste is an integral part of Hindu social life, culture, and religious traditions. While inequality or even hierarchy may exist in other cultures, religions, and regions, caste is peculiar to the Hindu mind and its religious codes. The hierarchical structure of the *varna* system (an ancient Hindu classification of humankind into four groups: the Brahmins, the Kshatriyas, the Vaishyas, and the Shudras; outside the varna were the untouchables), is presumed to have existed since time immemorial. It continues to exist without much change over the centuries or regional variations across the south Asian subcontinent, where the Hindus live. Even when there is a recognition of the possibility of internal fluidity, such as through the process of Sanskritization, this textbook view of caste rarely doubts the essential unity of the system. Those at the top were always the Brahmans, and those at the bottom were always the untouchables. The agency for the system's reproduction, in this popular understanding, always rested with the Brahman, its primary ideologue and benefactor. This view has not only persisted for a long time but continues to be the most dominant view, even in the political life of contemporary India, irrespective of the larger ideological location—the Left, center, or Right.

Interestingly, this view persists despite voluminous evidence and widespread recognition of the fact that caste and caste-like structures have existed and continue to exist among non-Hindus in the subcontinent, even in the faith systems that have no essential role for the Brahmans in their ritual systems (such as Sikhism or Christianity), and even when Brahmans are simply not in the faith system (such as in south Asian Islam). Those who perform rituals in such faith systems do not come from a specific kinship community and do not occupy a fixed, high status. There is also enough evidence to suggest that the nature of the caste system varies significantly across the regions of the subcontinent, even within Hinduism. Like any other social reality, caste would have evolved as a part and parcel of the larger social formation. But caste is rarely seen as being in any way connected to the realities of agrarian systems, political regimes, or ecological landscapes that emerged over time.[1]

What we call today caste or the caste system would indeed have been influenced and shaped by the material histories of relevant regions and communities. How do we bring this factor into the study and analysis of change in contemporary India, particularly the study of the social order of caste? How could caste reproduce itself even in absence of the Brahman, its chief benefactor? In other words, how do we factor in the essential materiality of caste that survived and flourished irrespective of religious ideologies? How do we take into account its contestations in the modern and so-called premodern times? This chapter attempts to do so by looking at the social history of the Ravi Dasis of Punjab and the dynamics of the group's identity formation over a rather long period of time, with a focus on its contemporary construction by those who proudly identify themselves as Ravi Dasis, both in Punjab and in the diaspora.

Religion and Caste in Contemporary Punjab

Of all the states of the Indian union, Punjab has the highest proportion of scheduled castes (SCs) in its population. In contrast to the national average of around 16 percent, according to the 2001 census, nearly 29 percent of Punjab's population was listed as SCs. The SC population in Punjab has also been growing at a rate much higher than that of the rest of the state's population. Punjab has also been one of the more vibrant states of the country, socially, economically, and politically. Though it is no longer the richest state, it continues to be a prosperous area in terms of per capita income and other measurements of social development. It also has much lower rates of poverty and malnourishment than most other parts of the country. Though the Green Revolution was clearly biased in favor of the land-owning cultivating farmers—almost all of whom in Punjab were from the dominant upper castes—its benefits did trickle down to other groups in the local population.

Socially and politically also Punjab has been a vibrant region. In addition to its active involvement in the freedom movement, Punjab has witnessed some of the most powerful identity movements during the past century. Sociologically, the significance of Punjab also lies in the fact that it is on the periphery of India and is one of the few states where Hindus, who constitute nearly 80 percent of India's population, are a minority. Despite being non-Hindus, the "lower-caste" Sikhs of the state have the distinction of being included in the list of the SCs, a status that was not granted to their counterparts in the other minority communities—that is, Muslims and Christians. Even the Buddhists and Jains were not considered for such a status. Only beginning with the 1991 census have neo-Buddhist converts begun to be listed as SCs. According to the 1961 census of the entire SC population of India, 98.56 percent were Hindus, and the remaining 1.44 percent were Sikhs.[2]

In addition to widespread violence, the region's partition at the time of India's independence almost completely changed its demographic profile. Despite the popular image of Indian Punjab being a Sikh state, it was only in 1966, after its reorganization in response to a strong movement for a Punjabi-speaking province, that the Sikhs became a majority in the state. Punjab before partition was a much bigger province, in which Muslims outnumbered both the Hindus and the Sikhs. According to the 1911 census, in Punjab 50.86 percent of the population was Muslim and 36.35 percent was Hindu. Only around 12 percent had reported their religion to be Sikhism (Christians accounted for around 1 percent).

The population exchange that accompanied partition in 1947 changed the demographic profile of Punjab very significantly. Almost the entire Sikh and Hindu population of western Punjab crossed over to the Indian side, and the Muslims living on the Indian side left for Pakistan. Thus, in Punjab after partition, the Hindus came to constitute a majority. However, the Sikhs too gained in demographic terms. Their proportion of the population went up from around 12 percent to around 35 percent, and they became concentrated in specific districts of Punjab, constituting more than half of the population. When linguistic surveys were carried out to reorganize the provincial boundaries, Punjab was declared a bilingual state with the Sikh-dominated districts reported as Punjabi-speaking areas and the Hindu-dominated districts as Hindi-speaking areas.

The Sikh leaders (mostly upper caste) saw in the new demographic scenario the possibility of a Sikh-majority province. After a long-drawn-out struggle, Punjab was reorganized in 1966 by removing the Hindi-speaking areas: the southern districts were put together into the new state of Haryana, and Hindu-majority or Hindi-speaking hill districts were merged with Himachal Pradesh.

Though the demand for a separate Punjabi Suba (a majority Punjab state of Punjabi speakers) was articulated in linguistic terms, the protests were mostly carried out on communal lines, both by the Sikh Akalis and the Hindu leaders who were opposed to the idea of reorganization. Interestingly, the SC Sikhs also did not show any enthusiasm for the division of Punjab. They feared that the formation of a Sikh-majority province would further consolidate the power of the already dominant landowning Jat Sikhs, which would make their position in the rural society of Punjab even more vulnerable.[3] After the 1966 reorganization of Punjab, the Sikhs constituted nearly 60 percent of the population and the Hindus around 38 percent. Christians and Muslims were present in some pockets of the state, but each of those groups accounted for only around 1 percent of the population.

Dalit Assertion and Identity

Beginning in the early twentieth century, Punjab, particularly the eastern or Indian Punjab, has witnessed active Dalit politics. The trajectory of Dalit politics in Punjab can be located in the changing socioeconomic and political situation in the region after the establishment of colonial rule in the middle of the nineteenth century. Though British colonial rule came to Punjab late, its influence there grew quite rapidly. The British-established canal colonies helped in the growth of agriculture in the region. They laid a network of canals in the western and central districts of Punjab, taking water from its rivers to areas that depended almost exclusively on rainwater for irrigation. In addition, they established new settlements of farming communities in some of the western districts of Punjab (in present-day Pakistan). In some cases they also moved members of the cultivating castes from the central districts of Punjab to the western districts. These initiatives brought additional land under cultivation. Assured availability of canal water increased the productivity of land. Agriculture thus grew both extensively as well as intensively. Colonial rule also led to the development of urban centers. For example, the town of Jalandhar experienced significant growth during the colonial period after it was chosen as the site of a military cantonment for recruiting soldiers from the region. The colonial army provided new opportunities of employment to the children of Punjabi peasants and also opened up avenues for social mobility for a section of local Dalits, particularly the untouchable Chamars who worked with leather.

The cantonment increased demand for leather goods, particularly boots and shoes for the British army. As was the case elsewhere in the subcontinent, much of the leather trade in the region was controlled by Muslims. However, at the local or village level, it was the Chamars who supplied the raw animal skins. Some of them were quick to exploit the new opportunities being offered to them by the changing world. Not only did they move out of the village, but they also ventured out to other parts of the subcontinent and abroad—especially to the United States, Canada, and England. However, the local leather trade remained under the control of Muslims. In fact, two of the local Chamars tried to set up shop in Jalandhar but failed and had to create businesses in Calcutta instead. The social and economic mobility that some untouchables experienced during this period prepared the ground for political mobilizations of Dalits in the region.

The introduction of representational politics by the colonial rulers also produced a new grammar of communities in India. The colonial administrative structure employed new categories of social aggregation and classification. The British thought of the Indian population in terms of religious communities and looked at them accordingly in the process of governance. They "encouraged the members of each community to present their case in communitarian terms."[4] As is well known to students of Indian history, the colonial census and classifications of the population into categories that made sense to the alien rulers played a critical role in converting the fuzzy boundaries of difference into well-defined communities.[5] Though the British came to Punjab only around the middle of the nineteenth century, this process of new identity formations and restructuring of communities became pronounced in the region fairly early through social reform movements among the Hindus, Sikhs, and Muslims.[6]

The anxiety about numbers among the neoreligious elite of the Hindus and Sikhs also had important implications for the Punjabi Dalits. Through newly launched social reform movements, Hindu and Sikh leaders began to work with Dalits. The Arya Samaj in Punjab started a *shudhi* (purifying from defilement) movement in which they encouraged the untouchables to purify themselves and become part of mainstream Hinduism. The movement also encouraged Dalits to send their children to schools being run by the Arya Samaj. Similarly, Sikh reformers began to decry the caste system publicly, and it was mainly through a claim to castelessness that they argued for the distinctiveness of Sikhs from Hindus.[7]

It was in this context that the Ad Dharm (literally, ancient religion or faith) movement emerged in Punjab. Though the idea had already begun to take shape during the early 1920s, it took off only with the arrival of Mangoo Ram. Mangoo Ram was the son of an enterprising Chamar of Maguwal Village in the Hoshiarpur district of the Doaba subregion of Punjab. Like other Dalits in rural Punjab during the early nineteenth century, his family had to bear the stigma of untouchability and social exclusion. However, his father was very enterprising and had been able to make some money through the leather trade.

Like some others of his caste community, Mangoo Ram acquired a secular education in a school run by the Arya Samaj. Migration to the West had already begun in the Doaba subregion of Punjab as a desirable way to attain social and cultural mobility. Mangoo Ram's father accumulated some money and sent him to the United States in search of better-paying work. While in California, Mangoo Ram was influenced by the left-wing ideas of his contemporaries from Punjab and got involved with the Gadar movement. He came back to Punjab in 1925 with the goal of working with his own people. After his return, he set up a school for "lower-caste" children with the help of the Arya Samaj, but very soon he distanced himself from that movement and joined with some other members of his community who were trying to initiate an autonomous identity movement—the Ad Dharm movement—among the local Dalits.[8]

The Ad Dharm movement saw itself as a religious movement. Its proponents argued that the untouchables were a separate *qaum*, a distinct religious community similar to the Muslims, Hindus, and Sikhs, and should be treated as such by the colonial rulers. Invoking the then popular racial-origin theories of caste, they argued that Ad Dharm had always been the religion of the Dalits and that the qaum had existed from time immemorial.[9] Despite stiff opposition from the local Hindu leadership, the colonial census of 1931 listed the Ad Dharmis as a separate religious community.

Though it claimed the status of a separate religion, Ad Dharm did not evolve as a religious movement. The emphasis on its being a separate religion, a qaum, was to undermine the caste identity of a community and its autonomy from Hinduism. As a separate qaum, at least theoretically, Ad Dharmis dissolved their caste identity and were to be identified as a religious community. Thus, they were no longer positioned in the system of caste hierarchy which had presumably made them a part of Hinduism. The dissolution of their caste identity also made them equal to other qaums recognized by the colonial state, the Hindus, Muslims, and Sikhs. Mangoo Ram also expected to bring other untouchable communities into the fold of Ad Dharm and to help the movement emerge as a viable community at the regional level.

A total of 418,789 persons reported themselves as Ad Dharmis in the 1931 Punjab census, almost equal to the number of Christians in the province. The Ad Dharmis accounted for about 1.5 percent of the population of Punjab and around a tenth of its "lower-caste" population. Nearly 80 percent of the "lower castes" of Jalandhar and Hoshiarpur Districts reported themselves as Ad Dharmis.[10]

How were they religiously different from Hindus, Muslims, or Sikhs? The Ad Dharm movement succeeded in mobilizing the Chamars of the Doaba subregion and in instilling a new sense of confidence in them. Though the movement had emerged for purely political and instrumental reasons, its members began to evolve a religious worldview of their own that would distinguish them from Hindus. Though they did not identify themselves with the Sikh religion, they looked toward it for alternative sources of religious and ritual life. In any case, Dalits had never been given the status of full membership by the custodians of the Hindu religion in Punjab or elsewhere. Sikhism was easier for Dalits to engage with, not only because it theologically opposed the caste system, but also because the Sikhs' holy book, *Guru Granth*, included the writings of a Chamar saint, Sant Ravi Das. However, the Dalits chose not to convert to Sikhism and would have had reasons for doing so. The obvious reason for this would have been the hold of the upper-caste communities over the social organization of the Sikh community. Even when, theologically, Sikhism provided space to the Dalits, its social organization was influenced by the preexisting exclusionary practices of the region.

Much of the subaltern religiosity in Punjab had been syncretic in nature, consisting of *deras* (places of worship, often identified with an individual guru) and *dargahs* (Islamic shrines) of *sants* (saints), *babas* (ascetics), and *faqeers* (ascetic Hindu or Muslim monks). It was these shrines of the little traditions that made up the religious landscape of those living on the margins of Punjabi society in the early twentieth century. Among them were also the deras of Ravi Dasi sants, who were themselves from untouchable families but who had gained some amount of respectability in the wider society and were seen to possess spiritual prowess by their followers and admirers. It was these deras of the Ravi Dasi sants that emerged as sites of popular religious life for the Dalits of Punjab.

The Ad Dharmis today are among the most prosperous and educated of the Dalit communities in India and are far ahead of other Dalit communities in Punjab (see table 10.1).

TABLE 10.1 Percentages of Different Scheduled Caste (SC)
Communities in Punjab by Educational Level

SC	Below primary	Primary	Middle	Matric (tenth grade) / Intermediate (twelfth grade)	Postmatric diploma	Graduate and above
Ad Dharmi	21.0	30.7	18.7	25.8	0.7	3.0
Balmiki	30.9	33.5	17.2	16.8	0.2	1.3
Mazhabi	37.0	32.5	14.0	14.5	0.3	0.7
All	28.9	31.6	16.8	20.3	0.5	2.0

Source: Office of the Registrar General, India, "Punjab: Data Highlights: The Scheduled Castes."

However, despite its success, the movement could not maintain its momentum for very long and began to dissipate soon after its grand success in 1931. According to the popular understanding, the causes of the decline of Ad Dharm movement lay in its success. Its leaders joined mainstream politics. Mangoo Ram and some of his close comrades became members of the Punjab Legislative Assembly when the Ad Dharm movement finally merged with the emerging pan-Indian movement of the Dalits, taking over the caste issue. The Ad Dharm Mandal, a reformist Ravi Dasi sect, began to see itself as a social and religious organization and in 1946 decided to change its name to Ravi Das Mandal, "entrusting the political work to All India Scheduled Castes Federation in conformity with rest of India."[11]

From Ad Dharm to Ravi Dasi

A closer understanding of the Ad Dharm case would require a critical look at the evolution of the Indian state and the manner in which it dealt with caste and religion. The beginning of the decline of the Ad Dharm movement might be located in the famous Poona Pact of 1932 between Mahatma Gandhi and B. R. Ambedkar and the formation of Scheduled List in the Government of India Act in 1935. The grouping of SCs with Hindus left the Ad Dharm movement in Punjab with no choice but to accept the nationalist and official mode of classification. The Ad Dharmis had to forgo the benefits of reservations based on caste identity if they claimed a separate religious identity. Given the socioeconomic status of the community at that time, they chose the untouchable identity and reconciled themselves to the official classification. As a senior Dalit activist explained: "Ad Dharm lost its meaning after we got eight seats reserved for us when the elections were first held in the province. Our candidates won seven out of the eight seats. Mangoo Ram too was elected to the assembly during the next election, in the year 1945–46." Another activist put it more emphatically: "In 1931 we were recognized as a separate religion by the colonial census, but by the act of 1935 we became one of the scheduled castes, one among others in the same category. Communal award had recognized our autonomy, which had to be surrendered by B. R. Ambedkar under the Poona Pact. Under the Poona Pact we were given reservations, but only if we accepted [that we were] part of the Hindu religion. . . . However, even though we legally became a part of Hinduism, it did not stop discrimination against us. Even now it continues, though it is less pronounced and more subtle."

Though most of the Dalit respondents among the Ad Dharmis remembered the Ad Dharm movement with a sense of pride, some of them felt bad about its decline. They had no strong feelings for the movement or resentment at being grouped with Hindus. They could not locate any writings by its erstwhile leaders expressing distress or anger at its decline or attributing that to a conspiracy. The Ad Dharm movement and its leaders may also have been swayed by the mainstream or dominant politics of the time—that is, the freedom movement and its hegemonic influence. As one of our respondents, the president of the Ravi Das Trust, said to us: "At one time the Ad Dharm movement was very popular in Punjab. However, slowly, with the growing influence of Congress politics, its leaders started leaving. Master Balwanta Singh was the first to leave the Ad Dharm Mandal. He joined the Congress Party. Similarly, some other leaders also left the movement to become part of mainstream national politics. Eventually even Mangoo Ram joined the Congress Party. The movement was over." Those with more radical views on the Dalit question were swayed by Ambedkar and joined the Republican Party of India and the Scheduled Caste Federation, both set up by Ambedkar. Some of them eventually turned to Buddhism for spiritual autonomy and religious identity.

Equally important for its decline may be the fact that though the Ad Dharm movement articulated itself as a religious identity and demanded official recognition as a religious movement, it was essentially a political movement. As a prominent member of the community told us during an interview: "It had no holy book or scripture of its own, it had no rituals of its own, it had no pilgrimage places or sacred symbols. . . . How could it have survived as a religion?" While the Ad Dharmi identity simply became a designation of a

Hindu caste group for the purposes of official classification, the Chamars of Doaba did not really go back to Hinduism. Instead, they began to develop autonomous religious resources under the identity of Ravi Dasis.

As mentioned above, it was, in fact, during the Ad Dharm movement that the Ravi Dasi identity had begun to take shape. Leaders of the movement also saw that identity as their own resource. In 1971, long after dissolving the Ad Dharm Mandal and after having been in retirement for many years, Mangoo Ram summed up the achievement of the Ad Dharm movement in an interview with Mark Juergensmeyer, in which his focus was more on having given the local Dalits a new community and religious identity than on their political empowerment: "We helped give them a better life and made them into a *qaum*. We gave them *sants to believe in* and something to hope for" (emphasis added).[12] After having changed the movement's name to Ravi Das Mandal in 1946, members shifted their focus to social and religious matters. They had realized long before that to consolidate themselves as a separate qaum, they needed a religious system of their own that was different from Hinduism and Sikhism. However, to do that they chose a caste-based religious identity: "Chamar=Ad Dharmi=Ravi Dasi." Even though during its early days the Ad Dharm movement had aspired to bring all the formerly untouchable communities together into a new faith, the movement had appealed mostly to the Chamars of Doaba. After its listing as one of the SCs, it became obvious and official that the Ad Dharmis were a section of the Chamars. Sant Ravi Das appeared to be an obvious choice for the Ad Dharmis as a religious symbol for the community. Though he was born in Uttar Pradesh, he belonged to the Chamar caste. The fact that his writings were included in the Sikhs' holy book, *Guru Granth*, which had been compiled in Punjab and written in the local language, made Ravi Das even more effective and acceptable.[13]

Thus the Ad Dharm movement played a very important role in developing an autonomous political identity and consciousness among the Chamar Dalits of Punjab, and the movement's renaming itself as a religious body, the Ravi Das Mandal, in 1946 was an important turning point in the history of Dalit movements in Punjab. However, it is important to mention here that the Ravi Dasi religious identity had already begun to take shape, independently of the Ad Dharm movement in the region. In fact, some of the Ravi Dasi deras had played an active role in the late 1920s when Mangoo Ram was campaigning for separate religious status for Ad Dharmis. Mangoo Ram often visited the Ravi Dasi deras during this campaign.

Interestingly, even when the community reconciled itself to the idea of being grouped with Hindu SCs for census enumerations, the Ad Dharmi identity continued to be important for them. As many as 14.9 percent (1,047,280) of the 7,028,723 members of scs in Punjab were listed as Ad Dharmis in the 2001 census, substantially more than those who registered themselves as belonging to the Ad Dharmi qaum in 1931. In religious terms, as many as 59.9 percent of the members of Punjab scs enumerated themselves as Sikhs and 39.6 percent as Hindus. Only 0.5 percent declared their religion to be Buddhism.

Notwithstanding this official classification of all scs into the mainstream religions of the region, everyday religious life of the Punjab Dalits is marked by enormous diversity and plurality. In addition to the popular syncretic religious traditions that have long existed in the region, the Dalits in Punjab and elsewhere in India have also developed an urge for autonomous faith identities, particularly to get out of Hinduism. They view Hinduism as the source of their humiliating social position in the caste system. This urge became much stronger with the emergence of an educated middle class among them during the later phase of British colonial rule. The Ad Dharm movement of the 1920s was a clear example of this.

Sant Ravi Das

Ravi Das is believed to have been born in 1450 AD in the north Indian town of Banaras, in present-day Uttar Pradesh, in an untouchable caste, the Chamars (traditionally identified with leather work), and to have died in 1520.[14] Like many of his contemporaries, he travelled extensively, and had religious dialogues with saint poets, enlightened and holy persons of medieval times, in different parts of northern India. Over time he acquired the status of a saint. However, his claims to religious authority were frequently challenged by the local Brahmans, who complained about his sacrilegious behavior to the local rulers. His followers believe that every time the king summoned Ravi Das, he managed to convince the political authorities of his genuine spiritual powers through various miraculous acts. He is believed to have visited Punjab and met with Guru Nanak, founder of the Sikh faith, at least three times. He also gave most of his writings to Guru Nanak, which eventually became part of the Sikh holy book, *Guru Granth*.[15]

Though historians of Indian religions tend to associate Ravi Das with the Bhakti movement, a pan-Indian devotional cult, his ideas appear to be quite radical. He imagined his own utopia, a vision of an alternative society, that he articulated in his hymn "Begumpura"—a city without sorrows, "where there will be no distress, no tax, no restriction from going and coming, no fear."[16] More interestingly perhaps, his message is also increasingly being presented by his contemporary followers in a modern political language that foregrounds the question of caste oppression and his fight against the prevailing structures of authority and Brahmanical moral order. About the social milieu in which Ravi Das was born, his biographer Sat Pal Jassi (a Ravi Dasi) writes: "Since the advent of Vedic Age, caste system and untouchability have been prevalent in India. In passage of time, the socio-religious inhibitions became more strict and cruel. The untouchables were given an ignoble place. They were debarred from acquiring knowledge, own property and worship of God. . . . These conditions prevailed in India for more than 3000 years."[17] Locating Ravi Das in the "dark history" of caste oppression, Jassi presents him as a pioneering socialist thinker: "He was protagonist of equality, oneness of God, human rights and universal brotherhood. . . . He was a suave socio-religious reformer, a thinker, a theosophist, a humanist, a poet, a traveller, a pacifist and above all, a towering spiritual figure. . . . He was pioneer of socialistic thought and strengthened noble values."[18] Ravi Das's utopia was also significantly different from that presented in some of the later writings on a desirable India produced by people like Mahatma Gandhi. As Gail Omvedt rightly comments, Ravi Das "was the first to formulate an Indian version of utopia in his song 'Begumpura'. Begumpura, the 'city without sorrow', is a casteless, classless society; a modern society, one without a mention of temples; an urban society as contrasted with Gandhi's village utopia of *Ram Rjaya*."[19]

Though born into a Dalit family, Ravi Das indeed became a part of the larger movement of protest against Brahmanical control over people's social and religious life and was accepted as a leader across the entire region. His identification with Guru Nanak, who was from an upper caste, clearly proves this point. As mentioned above, Guru Nanak added works by Ravi Das—forty of his hymns and one couplet—to his collection of important writings of the times, which were eventually compiled into the *Guru Granth* by the fifth Sikh guru.

It is perhaps this connection with Guru Nanak and Sikhism that explains the emergence of many centers of Ravi Das in Punjab and not in Uttar Pradesh, where he was born. It was the inclusion of his writings in the *Guru Granth* that, in a sense, kept Ravi Das alive, albeit among the people of Punjab who revered that book—the Sikhs and others in the region. Though a separate community of Sikhs began to evolve quite early, with the emergence of Sikh movement, the Sikh gurus and *Guru Granth* have been revered by those who do not necessarily identify themselves as Sikhs.[20]

However, unlike the founder of the Sikh movement, Ravi Das did not develop a significant community of followers or appoint a successor. Though he developed a critique of the Brahmanical social order, in the absence of a community of followers he could not develop any kind of political ambitions. It was only in the twentieth century that a community of Ravi Dasis began to emerge, initially in Punjab and later in other parts of northern India. It was only with the loosening caste hierarchy and village social structure that an untouchable caste could begin to constitute itself as a separate religious community. The Chamars of Doaba were among the first in northern India to organize themselves under the name of the Ad Dharm movement. Ravi Das was rediscovered by them.

The Ravi Dasis Today

Though the message of Ravi Das had been integrated into the Sikh holy book and was routinely read and sung at the Sikh *gurudwaras* (Sikh places of worship) as part of the *gurbani* (religious singing), it was only in the early years of the twentieth century that separate Ravi Dasi deras began to emerge in Punjab. The reason for this sudden mushrooming of Ravi Dasi deras may be found in the growing prosperity of Chamars in the region after the British set up a cantonment in Jalandhar. Reform movements among the major religious communities of the Muslims, Hindus, and the Sikhs would have also played a role in opening up opportunities for secular education among them.

Perhaps the most important of the Guru Ravi Das deras in Punjab today is the dera located in village Ballan, around ten kilometers from Jalandhar. It is locally known as Dera Sachkhand Ballan. Though the dera was set up by Sant Pipal Dass sometime in the early twentieth century,[21] it is identified more with his son, Sant Sarwan Dass. In fact, among its followers, it is also known as Dera Sant Sarwan Dass. According to the popular myth narrated by various interviewees during the fieldwork, which we also found in published leaflets, the history of the dera could be summed up like this: Sant Sarwan Dass was born in a village called Gill Patti in Bhatinda District of Punjab. He lost his mother when he was five years old. To help his son overcome the loss, his father, Pipal Dass, decided to travel with him. After visiting a few places, they came to Ballan Village. The elder brother of Sarwan Dass had earlier lived in the same village. On the outskirts of Ballan, they found a pipal tree that was completely dry and dead. However, when Pipal Dass watered the tree, life returned to it, and its leaves turned green. This, for him, was an indication of the place being spiritually blessed. The tree also made the child

Sarwan Dass happy. The father and son decided to build a hut close to the tree and began to live there. After the death of his father in 1928, Sant Sarwan Dass expanded his activities. He opened a school and started teaching Gurumukhi (the script used for writing Punjabi) and the message of *Guru Granth* to young children. He also persuaded his followers to send their children to the school. "Parents who do not educate their children are their enemies," he used to tell his followers. Impressed with the work that Sant Sarwan Dass was doing in the village, a local landlord gave him one *kanal* (about one-fifth of an acre) of land close to the hut, where the dera was eventually constructed. Sarwan Dass remained head of the dera from October 11, 1928, until he died in June 1972. He was succeeded by Sant Hari Dass and Sant Garib Dass. The dera is currently headed by Sant Niranjan Dass.

Ravi Dasi as a Religious Identity

As mentioned above, the Ad Dharm movement rapidly declined after the signing of Poona Pact. Over the years it essentially acquired the status of a caste identity. In postindependence India, Ad Dharmis have been listed as members of a Hindu SC for Punjab. However, their attitude toward Hinduism has always been quite ambivalent. Given their status as untouchables in classical Hinduism, they could never feel comfortable with the idea of being Hindus. However, they also did not want to give up the possible benefits of being an SC in the new state system. Public-sector jobs have been an extremely effective source of upward mobility for individual Dalits in India.

Sikhism has been an attractive alternative for the Dalits of Punjab. A good number of them in fact joined the faith and identify themselves as Sikhs. However, the continued presence of caste differences in Sikhism and dominance of certain caste groups in religious affairs of the Sikhs gives Sikh Dalits the impression that they continued to be seen as less than equals.[22]

The alternative as seen by the neo-Dalits is autonomy. Ravi Dasi identity and the deras run by the gurus and babas of their own caste offer them that. The most important of these deras is the Dera Ballan.

The Dera and the Disciples

What makes the Dera Ballan popular with common Ravi Dasis? Why are they so committed to the dera? What is the reason for such close identification with their gurus? Is it purely as a spiritual quest that they visit the dera, or are they also motivated by more worldly pursuits? In addition to interviewing important functionaries of the dera, lay disciples were also sought to find answers to some of these questions.

Though its primary identity is religious, the dera at Ballan appears to be playing an active role in consolidating the caste community. A survey conducted by a scholar recently showed that those who visited the dera were all from the Chamar or Ad Dharmi caste.[23] The dera also gave them a sense of identity, and its opulence and grandeur made them feel proud. They looked at it as a symbol of prosperity and dignity. Although they are not rich, the dera may help them forget their poverty and marginality.

The interviewees and the lay disciples seemed to confirm this. Dalit empowerment, autonomy, and development were some of the common points that they underlined. While these ideals appeared to be purely secular, for the Ravi Dasi Dalits they were part and parcel of the religious movement. One man, for example, viewed the dera and growing influence of Ravi Das's teachings as symbolizing autonomy and empowerment of the Punjabi Dalits:

> I am a Chamar by caste. Earlier we were treated as untouchables. Things have changed. Earlier we were not even allowed to worship God. Sant Ravi Das's message was that even Chamars have the right to worship God. . . . Sant Ravi Das's worshippers can be from any community. I am from the Ravi Dasi community. I do not believe in caste. . . . . Earlier we used to worship Sant Ravi Das in a hidden way. But now we do in a respectable way.

The fact that the dera has not only confined its activities to religion and has started its own schools and hospitals as charitable institutions was evidence of Brahmanism being challenged by the Ravi Dasi movement. The same man said: "Schools and hospitals are being opened by the dera. I think that it has posed a serious challenge to Brahmanism. They [the upper castes] had barred us from getting educated, and today we have reached a stage where we can teach and provide education to our community." Another interviewee was even more articulate about caste discrimination and the role deras had played in Dalit empowerment, giving them a sense of dignity and autonomy: "We need the dera to make people aware of Sant Ravi Das. When we go to other *mandirs* (Hindu temples) and gurudwaras, there is psychological discrimination, if not physical. But here, because it is our community that manages everything, there is no discrimination at all. In fact, we feel a sense of pride that we are in our place of worship. We would not have needed a separate mandir or gurudwara had there been no discrimination. But Hindu society is divided on caste lines. Sant Ravi Das fought against it and for our dignity. So we worship Sant Ravi Das." Interestingly, it was not only the Hindu temples that Dalits were barred from entering. Even other deras in Punjab discriminated against Dalits. Yet another interviewee pointed to the fact that "earlier there was discrimination. That is why our people have opened our own deras. We do not discriminate. We respect all religions and communities. The other deras do not respect us. It is only in our own dera that we feel welcomed. Dera Beas, for example, is the biggest dera in Punjab, but they do not respect Dalits." It is not only Hindu society that treats Ravi Dasis badly—even the Jat Sikhs in rural areas discriminated against them and their religion. "Even when we keep the *Guru Granth* in our temples in the villages, no Jat will ever enter our temples," reported another interviewee in Ballan. Underlining the need for a separate and autonomous religion for Dalits and the fact that the dera was helping meet that need, he argued: "Every religion needs a guru. The dera has given our community a guru. The dera never gets involved with politics. However, when we need to fight for our rights, it unites the community. Our gurus have worked hard to keep the community united. They have stopped members of our community from going to other deras. They have opened schools and hospitals." References to caste and discrimination and the need for an autonomous religious system for the Dalit community were common in many other interviews as well. Equally common were the references to the emphasis that Ravi Dasi sants put on education. Not only did the disciples point to the schools opened by the dera, but many of them also referred to personal experiences of having been able to study only because they were able to get financial help from the dera sants or because of their persistence and motivation.

Though Dera Ballan is a religious center with a focus on preaching universalistic values and spirituality, it actively identifies itself with local Dalit issues and Dalit politics. Not only do the spiritual heads of the dera foreground Ravi Das's message of building a casteless society, they have also been actively identified with Dalit activism. Sant Sarwan Dass kept in active touch with Mangoo Ram during the Ad Dharm movement, and Mangoo Ram visited the dera to communicate his message to the Dalit masses of the region. During one of his visits to Delhi, he also met Ambedkar, who "showed great respect to Sant Sarwan Dass Ji."[24] In one of his letters to Ambedkar, Sant Sarwan Dass described him as "a great son of the community."[25] In the emerging national context, Dalit political leaders began to connect with their peers in other regions. Religious sants like Sant Sarwan Dass did the same.

The message of Ravi Das had thus far reached the Punjabi Dalits primarily through the Sikh holy book, the *Guru Granth*. However, the religious institutions of Sikhism were mostly controlled by "upper castes" among them.[26] The continued presence of caste differences and hierarchy in the region made Sant Sarwan Dass look for resources within the caste community to support further expansion of the dera's activities. Ravi Das was the obvious symbol for the Chamar Dalits to use in building an autonomous community of believers. Over the years they have also tried to distinguish themselves from the Sikhs. For example, they have replaced the Sikh Ek Onkar (which translates as "the One God") with their own symbol, the *har*. Though the format appears similar to those recited in Sikh gurudwaras, the Chamar Dalits have introduced subtle differences in the prayer as well. More recently, after the murder of a Ravi Dasi sant in Vienna, Austria, presumably by fundamentalist Sikhs, many of the Ravi Dasi deras have removed the *Guru Granth* from their religious centers and worship only a picture of Sant Ravi Das and read only the *bani* (poetry) composed by him. Writings of Ravi Das have also been compiled into a separate book.[27]

Dera Ballan has continued to be an important center of Dalit political activity in Punjab. Leaders and writers and other intellectuals of the community often meet at the dera to discuss emerging political and cultural challenges faced by the community of Ravi Dasis. Kanshi Ram, another leader of the Dalits of northern India, who belonged to Punjab and was born into a Ravi Dasi family, was a frequent visitor to the dera. He did so not only to pay his respect to the dera's chief, but also to discuss with other leaders of the community strategies for making Dalits more effective in politics.

The Diaspora Effect

The second, and perhaps more important and interesting phase in the history of the Ravi Das movement in Punjab began during the 1990s, with the phase of globalization. Along with other Punjabis, a large number of Chamars of the Doaba subregion had migrated to countries in the Western hemisphere during the 1950s and 1960s. There are no exact figures available, but—quoting the Indian consular office—Juergensmeyer claims that in the United Kingdom the "percentage of Scheduled Castes within the total Punjabi community was as high as 10 percent. The rest were largely Jat Sikhs."[28]

In the context of another country, with no systemic justification for caste ideology, Punjabi Dalits did not expect to be reminded of their low status in the caste hierarchy. While they did not have any such problems in the workplace or the urban public sphere in the United Kingdom, they often experienced caste prejudice when they tried to be part of the local Punjabi community in the diaspora. Juergensmeyer sums this up quite well:

> The Chamars, who came to Britain expecting to find life different, take offence at the upper caste Sikhs' attitude towards them. They earn as much as the Jat Sikhs, sometimes more, and occasionally find themselves placed by the British in command over them—a Chamar foreman superintending a Jat Sikh work crew—much to the displeasure of the latter. . . . . The Scheduled Castes can afford to act more bravely in Britain since they have now entered a new context for competing with the Jat Sikhs. In the Punjab the cards were stacked against them, but in Britain they have a fresh start, and the ideology of Ad Dharm has prepared them to take advantage of it.[29]

The migrant Dalits felt this bias in the gurudwaras, which were mostly controlled by the Jats and other upper-caste Sikhs. Given their numbers and position in the local economy, Dalits did not find it difficult to assert their rights to equal status and dignity. They began to set up their own autonomous associations in the name of Sant Ravi Das. The first two were created in Britain, in Birmingham and Wolverhampton, in 1956.[30] While in the first 20–25 years of their emigration, they simply built their own community organizations and separate gurudwaras wherever they could, over the years they also began to influence the homeland. The growing availability of new communication channels such as the Internet and satellite television during the early 1990s made it easier for them to renew an active relationship with Punjab and the Ravi Dasi community at home.

By the early 1990s, diaspora Dalits had also experienced considerable economic mobility, which made it easier for them to travel back home, and they began to do so more frequently. When they returned to India, they brought money for the deras, and this new money and diasporic energy played a very important role in the further growth of the movement. This was summed up well by a Dalit businessman who has been involved in mobilizing the Ravi Dasi sants into a pan-Indian association: "It is the brethren from the West who first understood the value of our deras and the need to strengthen them. They gave huge donations when they came to pay a visit. The number of visitors from abroad and the frequency of their visits also increased during the 1990s. They invited the local sants to their countries. All this gave a boost to the Ravi Dasi movement." Going beyond their immediate sphere of influence also provides a context to the current Ravi Dasi sants to mobilize the community at a global level. Traveling to the countries in Europe and North America where Punjabi Ravi Dasis have settled has almost become a regular affair for the religious leaders of different deras. Apart from collecting money for their activities in India, these visits also give a sense of connectivity to the Ravi Dasi diaspora as a community different from the Sikhs.

Over the past fifteen years or so, the dera at Ballan has expanded significantly. In 2007 a new building was inaugurated in which nearly twenty thousand people could be accommodated to listen to the teachings of Sant Ravi Das. It has a *langar* (communal kitchen) where two thousand people can eat together. Among other things, this hall has the technology to permit live telecasts and the recording of videocassettes. In collaboration with the Jalandhar channel of Doordarshan (a television network run by the Government of India) it broadcasts a program called *Amrit Bani* (holy songs) every Friday and Saturday morning.

Not only has the dera at Ballan expanded over the years, but deras, gurudwaras, and temples in the name of Sant Ravi Das have flourished in Punjab, particularly in the Doaba subregion, where Ad Dharmis and Chamars have been numerically predominant among the Dalits. There were six or seven major sants who can be considered as leaders of the community and more than 250 deras or gurudwaras dedicated to Sant Ravi Das in Punjab. Some of these deras have become quite affluent and influential. However, they are all patronized exclusively by the local Chamars and Ad Dharmis.

Conclusion

Writing about the Punjabi Dalits nearly four decades ago, Juergensmeyer characterized their social and economic position by using the phrase "cultures of deprivation." Though he did not see similarities between the situation of Punjabi Dalits and the slum-dwelling Mexican poor, mentioning Oscar Lewis's work on the "culture of poverty" seems quite obvious.[31] Unlike the poor in the Mexican slums, the Dalits were not simply poor. Their poverty was often reinforced by institutionalized prejudice, the caste system, and the symbolic order of Hinduism, which in turn also reinforced their poverty. It is this peculiar reality that makes it crucial for the Dalits to pursue not just a path out of economic poverty but also a struggle for cultural autonomy, and to seek a symbolic system that gives them a sense of self-esteem and dignity.

As discussed above, a group of the Dalits in Doaba subregion of Punjab began to experience social mobility and economic prosperity during the early twentieth century when a new secular economy was put in place by the

British colonial government. However, given the nature of their deprivation, the upwardly mobile Dalits soon realized the need for cultural resources that would give them dignity. Given the religious nature of the ideological power of caste, they could imagine alternatives only in religious modes. The Ad Dharm movement was the outcome of this first generation of upwardly mobile Dalits of Punjab.

Though the movement's main demand during its early phase was for the recognition and enumeration of Ad Dharmis as a separate religious group, it was not really a religious movement. As noted above, a prominent member of the community said that the movement "had no holy book or scripture of its own, it had no rituals of its own, it had no pilgrimage places or sacred symbols. . . . How could it have survived as a religion?" Indeed, when it came to actually working out a religious system, the Ad Dharmis of Doaba invariably went back to their caste identity or the available religious resources. The most attractive and easily available resource was Ravi Das and the Sikh holy book, *Guru Granth*. The Ad Dharmis even adopted Sikh rituals and ceremonies. Their assertion of autonomy through the Sikh religious text was easier for them in a region that had become dominated by Sikhism by the middle of the twentieth century.

However, the continued existence of the caste system in Punjabi culture and the agrarian economy of rural Punjab reinforced the Ad Dharmis' desire for a separate identity, the kind of identity that the Ad Dharm movement had promised them. Though it did not last for long, the movement was successful in instilling in the Chamar Dalits of Doaba a sense of autonomy and autonomous community.

Growing urbanization, migration, and the impact of the Green Revolution during the postindependence period only reinforced this process. The new capitalist agriculture nearly destroyed old structures of dependency and patronage. Not only did Dalits start dissociating themselves from the traditional caste occupations, but they also distanced themselves from the local agrarian economy. Even when they continued to live in a village, they acquired a sense of autonomy from the village community. Though they did not feel economically empowered in the absence of any radical land reforms, they were able to get away from the local power structure more easily. This newly acquired political agency and the newly emerging political and economic elite among them helped the Dalits to further consolidate their identity. Their quest for a separate religious identity began to be articulated through the Ravi Dasi deras. Identification with Ravi Dasi deras and building of separate Ravi Dasi gurudwaras in almost every village of Doaba acquired the shape of a social movement. Migration to urban centers in India and abroad and growing prosperity among a group of Ad Dharmis provided resources to sustain this movement.

Apart from the sants and religious heads of deras, who all came from within the caste community, leadership of this movement has been provided mostly by the mobile Dalits, those who were the first to get out of the traditional system of caste hierarchy and into urban occupations, the successful businessmen and professionals.

Over the years the Ravi Dasis have emerged as a strong religious community, a qaum. Though its center continues to be in Doaba, it has spread to other parts of Punjab, neighboring Haryana, Uttar Pradesh, and even to far off Maharashtra. This strength of the community is reinforced by the increasingly active involvement of the Ravi Dasi diaspora.

This transformation of a formerly untouchable caste (*zaat*) into a strong religious community (qaum) clearly has had several social and developmental effects on members of the community and Punjabi society at large. As it has been argued based on interviews with a cross section of people, one of the contributions of the dera most frequently referred to was the motivation it provided for education and the sense of dignity it gave to the community of formerly untouchable Chamars. The religious idiom seems also to play a very important role in "horizontal consolidation," to use M. N. Srinivas's terms.[32] In a democratic polity like that of India where communities have become important actors in electoral politics, a marginalized group of Dalits can only gain through such a process. While on the one hand their consolidation into a strong community enables them to open their own institutions (such as schools and hospitals) to provide a better life, on the other hand such a process of mobilization strengthens their bargaining capacity vis-à-vis the state and other sections of the civil society.

NOTES

1. Jodhka, *Caste*.
2. K. Suresh Singh, *The Scheduled Castes*, 10.
3. Nayar, *Minority Politics in the Punjab*, 50–51.
4. Grewal, "Changing Sikh Self-Image before Independence."
5. Breckenridge and van der Veer, *Orientalism and the Postcolonial Predicament*; Cohn, *Colonialism and Its Forms of Knowledge*; Dirks, *Castes of Mind*.
6. Fox, *Lions of Punjab*; Oberoi, *The Construction of Religious Boundaries*.
7. Jodhka, "Caste and Untouchability in Rural Punjab."
8. Juergensmeyer, *Religious Rebels in the Punjab*.

9. Ibid., 45.

10. Ibid., 77.

11. Ibid., 153.

12. Quoted in ibid., 155.

13. Some of the local Dalit leaders also believe that it was the Hindu nationalists who suggested Ravi Das as a possible religious symbol to the Chamars. One of them said: "In order to make sure that untouchables did not convert to Sikhism, Islam, or Christianity, the Arya Samajis propagated the symbol of Ravi Das among Chamars, Valmiki among the Chuhras, and Kabir among the Meghs. That's how they made sure that Dalits stayed within the Hindu fold." While this may be true, the image of Ravi Das as a Chamar had already been made available to the people of Punjab by the Sikh gurus.

14. Omvedt, *Seeking Begumpura*, 7.

15. This discussion is based on Jassi, *Holy Hymns and Miracles of Guru Ravi Das Ji*.

16. Quoted in Hawley and Juergensmeyer, *Songs of the Saints of India*, 32.

17. Jassi, *Holy Hymns and Miracles of Guru Ravi Das Ji*, 24.

18. Ibid., 25.

19. Omvedt, *Seeking Begumpura*, 7.

20. Oberoi, *The Construction of Religious Boundaries*.

21. Mark Juergensmeyer in his pioneer work on the Ad-Dharm movement writes: "When he [Sant Hiran Das] established his Ravi Das Sabha, in 1907, in village Hakim . . . several other *deras* including that of Sant Pipal Das, were founded soon afterward" (*Religious Rebels in the Punjab*, 87).

22. Jodhka, "Caste and Untouchability in Rural Punjab."

23. Charlene, "Dalits-Sikhs' Relation: A Contrasted Approach."

24. Quoted in "Sant Sarwan Dass Ji: A Great Visionary Sant," leaflet published by Sant Surinder Dass Bawa (n.d.).

25. Ibid.

26. Even though Sikhism decries the caste system, caste-based divisions and hierarchies have continued to survive among the Sikhs in Punjab. See Jodhka, "Sikhism and the Caste Question"; Judge and Bal, "Understanding the Paradox of Changes among Dalits in Punjab"; Puri, "The Scheduled Castes in the Sikh Community."

27. Jodhka, "The Ravi Dasis of Punjab."

28. Quoted in Juergensmeyer, *Religious Rebels in the Punjab*, 246.

29. Juergensmeyer, *Religious Rebels in the Punjab*, 247–48.

30. Ibid., 248.

31. Lewis, "The Culture of Poverty."

32. M. Srinivas, *Caste in Modern India and Other Essays*, 74–75.

BIBLIOGRAPHY

Abbasayulu, Y. B. *Scheduled Caste Elite: A Study of Scheduled Caste Elite in Andhra Pradesh*. Hyderabad: Osmania University, 1978.

Abraham, Abu. *Arrivals and Departures: Abu on Janata Rule*. Sahibabad: Tarang Paperbacks, 1983.

Aloysius, G. *Religion as Emancipatory Identity: A Buddhist Movement among the Tamils under Colonialisms*. New Delhi: New Age International, 1998.

Ambedkar, B. R. *Babasaheb Ambedkar: Writings and Speeches*. Vol. 6. Compiled by Vasant Moon. Mumbai: Department of Education, Government of Maharashtra, 1998.

———. Foreword to G. R. Pradhan, *Untouchable Workers of Bombay City*. Bombay: Karnatak, 1938: i–iv.

———. "On the Adoption of the Constitution." In *Thus Spoke Ambedkar: A Stake in the Nation*, edited by Bhagavan Das, 204–21. New Delhi: Navayana, 2010.

———. "States and Minorities." In *Babasaheb Ambedkar: Writings and Speeches*. Vol. 1. Compiled by Vasant Moon. Bombay: Education Department, Government of Maharashtra, Bombay, 1979.

———. *What Congress and Gandhi Have Done to the Untouchables*. Bombay: Thacker, 1945.

Amin, Shahid. Introduction to William Crooke, *A Glossary of North Indian Peasant Life*, edited by Shahid Amin, i–liv. Delhi: Oxford University Press, 1989.

Anand, Mulk Raj. *Untouchable*. London: Hutchinson International, 1935.

Anandhi, S. "Work, Caste, and Competing Masculinities: Notes from a Tamil Village." *Economic and Political Weekly* 37, no. 43 (2002): 4397–406.

Andhra Pradesh Civil Liberties Committee. *The Chunduru Carnage: August 6, 1991*. Vijayawada, 1991.

Anjaneyulu, Kodali, ed. *Andhrapradesh lo Gandhiji*. Hyderabad: Telugu Academy, 1978.

Apparao, Dhakarapu. *Akhila Bharatha Brahma Samajamu: Samkshiptha Charitra*. Hyderabad: self-published, 1980.

Aqida, Gurnam. *Kakh Kande: Nijh ton Hakikat vall*. Barnala: Vishavbharti Parkashan, 2007.

Aqida, Gurnam. "Baba Jeevan Singhji di Mahan Kurbani nu vi Nahin Samjhia Sikh dharm de akhouti thekedaran ne." *Indo-Punjab: Monthly Magazine* 1, no. 1 (January 2010).

Arifi, Naranjan. *Ranghrehtian da Itihas (Adi kal ton 1850 tak).* Amritsar: Literature House, 1993.

Arunima, G. *There Comes Papa: Colonialism and the Transformation of Matriliny in Kerala, Malabar C. 1850–1940.* Hyderabad: Orient Longman, 2003.

Ashok, Shamsher Singh. *Mazhabi Sikhan da Itihas.* 1987. Amritsar: Bhai Chatar Singh Jiwan Singh, 2nd revised edition, 2001.

Atkinson, Edwin T. *Statistical, Descriptive and Historical Account of the North-Western Provinces of India.* Vol. 3. Allahabad: North-Western Provinces and Oudh Government Press, 1883.

Ayrookuzhiel. *Swami Anand Thirth: Untouchability.* Delhi: ISPCK, 1987.

Babu, D. Shyam. "India's Liberalisation and the Dalits." Working paper, the Royal Institute of International Affairs, Asia Programme, London, August 2004.

Babu, D. Shyam, and Chandra Bhan Prasad. "Six Dalit Paradoxes." *Economic and Political Weekly* 44, no. 23 (2009): 22–25.

Bagul, Baburao. *Dalit Sahitya ajache Kranti Vidynana.* Nagpur: Buddhist Publishing House, 1978.

Bajpai, Rochana. "The Conceptual Vocabularies of Secularism and Minority Rights in India." *Journal of Political Ideologies* 7, no. 2 (2002): 179–98.

———. "Constituent Assembly Debates and Minority Rights." *Economic and Political Weekly* 35, nos. 21–22 (2000): 1837–48.

———. "Minority Rights in the Indian Constituent Assembly Debates, 1946–1949." Working paper, QEH Working Paper Series. December 1999. Accessed October 6, 2015. http://www3.qeh.ox.ac.uk/pdf/qehwp/qehwps30.pdf.

Balagopal, K. "Caste and Civil Rights' Movement in Andhra Pradesh." Lecture to members of the People's Democratic Front, at the National College, Bangalore, May 9, 1996.

———. *Probings in the Political Economy of Agrarian Classes and Conflicts.* Hyderabad: Perspectives, 1998.

———. "A Tangled Web: Subdivision of SC Reservations in AP." *Economic and Political Weekly* 35, no. 13 (2000): 1075–81.

———. "This Anti-Mandal Mania." *Economic and Political Weekly* 25, no. 40 (1990): 2231–34.

Bandyopadhyay, Sekhar. *Caste, Protest and Identity in Colonial India: The Namasudras of Bengal, 1872–1947.* London: Curzon, 1997.

Bardhan, Pranabh. *The Political Economy of Development in India.* New Delhi: Oxford University Press, 1998.

Barstow, A. E. *The Sikhs: An Ethnology.* 1928. Delhi: Low Price Publications, 1993.

Baxi, Upendra. "Emancipation as Justice: Babasaheb Ambedkar's Legacy and Vision."*Ambedkar and Social Justice.* Vol. 1. Publications Division, Government of India, 1992.

Beteille, Andre. *Caste, Class, and Power: Changing Patterns of Stratification in a Tanjore Village.* Bombay: Oxford University Press, 1966.

———. *Society and Politics in India*. New Delhi: Oxford University Press, 1997.

Beth, Sarah. "Hindi Dalit Autobiography: An Exploration of Identity." *Modern Asian Studies*, 41, no. 3 (2007): 545–74.

Bhagwati, Jagdish. "The Design of Indian Development." In *India's Economic Reforms and Development: Essays for Manmohan Singh*, edited by I. J. Ahluwalia and I. M. D. Little, 23–39. New Delhi: Oxford University Press, 1998.

Bharati, Sunita Reddy. "Dalit: A Term Asserting Unity." *Economic and Political Weekly* 37, no. 42 (2002): 4339–40.

Bharti, Anita. "Anyay ke Kilaaf Larna hai. . . ." *Yuddhrat Aam Aadmi* 87 (2007): 16–17.

———. "'Kafan' aur 'Dalit Stree-Vimarsh.'" *Sandhaan* (2004): 209–13.

———. "'Rangbhoomi-Dahan' aur Dalit-Asmita ka Prashan." *Apeksha* 10 (2005): 60–64.

Bhattacharya, Neeladri. "The Problem." *Seminar* 522 (2003). Accessed September 19, 2015. http://www.india-seminar.com/2003/522.htm.

Boas, H. J. *Report on the Eleventh Settlement of the Moradabad*. Allahabad: Superintendent Government Press United Provinces, 1909.

Bose, Ajoy. *Bahenji: A Political Biography of Mayawati*. New Delhi: Penguin, 2008.

Bourdieu, Pierre. *The Field of Cultural Production: Essays on Art and Literature*. Translated by Randall Johnson. Cambridge: Polity, 1993.

Breckenridge, C. A., and Peter van der Veer, eds. *Orientalism and the Postcolonial Predicament: Perspectives on South Asia*. Philadelphia: University of Pennsylvania Press, 1993.

Briggs, George. *The Chamars*. Oxford: Oxford University Press, 1920.

Brueck, Laura. "At the Intersection of Gender and Caste: Re-Scripting Rape in Dalit Feminist Narratives." In *South Asian Feminisms*, edited by Ania Loomba and Ritty Lukose, 224–44. Durham, NC: Duke University Press, 2012.

Brueck, Laura. *Writing Resistance*. New York: Columbia University Press, 2014.

Burns, Kathryn. *Into the Archive: Writing and Power in Colonial Peru*. Durham, NC: Duke University Press, 2010.

Calhoun, Craig, ed. *Habermas and the Public Sphere*. Cambridge, MA: MIT Press, 1990.

Cassan, Guilhem. "British Law and Caste Identity Manipulation in Colonial India: The Punjab Alienation of Land Act." October 18, 2010. Accessed July 4, 2015. http://www.econ.upf.edu/docs/seminars/cassan.pdf.

Census of India, 1881. Vol. 17, part 1: *Report, North West Provinces and Oudh*. Allahabad: North-West Provinces and Oudh Government Press, 1882.

Census of India, 1911. Vol. 15, part II. Allahabad: Superintendent of Government Press United Provinces, 1923.

Census of India, 1933. Vol. 23, part I: *H.E.H. the Nizam's Dominions (Hyderabad State)*. Hyderabad: Government Central Press, 1933.

Census of India, 1961. Vol. 15, part V. Delhi: Manager Publications Government of India, 1965.

Chakrabarty, Dipesh. *Provincializing Europe: Postcolonial Thought and Historical Difference*. Princeton, NJ: Princeton University Press, 2000.

———. *Rethinking Working-Class History: Bengal 1890–1940*. Princeton, NJ: Princeton University Press, 1989.

Chakraborty, Debashis, D. Shyam Babu, and Manashi Chakravorty. "Atrocities on Dalits: What the District Level Data Say on Society-State Complicity." *Economic and Political Weekly*, June 17–23, 2006, 2478–81.

Chakravarti, Uma. *Gendering Caste: Through a Feminist Lens*. Calcutta: Stree, 2003.

Chalam, K. S. "Caste Reservations and Equality of Opportunity in Education." *Economic and Political Weekly* 25, no. 41 (1990): 2333–39.

Chandavarkar, Rajnarayan. *The Origins of Industrial Capitalism in India: Business Strategies and the Working Classes in Bombay, 1900–1940*. Cambridge: Cambridge University Press, 1994.

Chandra, Kanchan. *Why Ethnic Parties Succeed: Patronage and Ethnic Headcounts in India*. New York: Cambridge University Press, 2004.

Charsley, Simon. "'Untouchable': What Is in a Name?" *Journal of Royal Anthropological Institute* 2, no. 1 (1996): 1–23.

Chatterjee, Partha. "Caste and Subaltern Consciousness." In *Subaltern Studies VI*, edited by Ranajit Guha. Delhi: Oxford University Press, 1989.

——. "Introduction: A Political History of Independent India." In *State and Politics in India*, edited by Partha Chatterjee, 1–39. Delhi: Oxford University Press, 1997.

——. *The Politics of the Governed: Reflections on Popular Politics in Most of the World*. New York: Columbia University Press, 2004.

——. "Secularism and Toleration." *Economic and Political Weekly* 29, no. 28 (1994): 1768–77.

Chentharassery, T. H. P. *Ayyankali*. Trivandrum: Prabhatam, 1979.

——. *Ayyankali: The First Dalit Leader*. Delhi: Navdin Prakashan Kendra, 1996.

——. *Pampady John Joseph*. Thiruvalla: Backward People's Development Corporation, 1989.

——. *Sree Kumara Guru Devan*. Trivandrum: Navodhanam, 1983.

Chhibber, Kesar Singh. *Bansavalinama Dasan Patshahian Ka*. Edited by Rattan Singh Jaggi. Chandigarh: Panjab University, 1972.

Chirakkarode, Paul. *Dalit Christhavar Keralathil*. Thiruvalla: Christhava Sahithya Samithi, 2000.

Chitnis, Suma. "Education for Equality—Case of Scheduled Castes in Higher Education." *Economic and Political Weekly* 7, nos. 31–33 (1972): 1675–81.

——. "Positive Discrimination in India with Reference to Education." In *From Independence to Statehood: Managing Ethnic Conflict in Five African and Asian States*, edited by B. Robert Goldmann and A. Jeyaratnam Wilson, 31–43. London: Frances Pinter, 1984.

Chowdhry, Prem. "'First Our Jobs Then Our Girls': The Dominant Caste Perceptions on the 'Rising' Dalits." *Modern Asian Studies* 43, no. 2 (2009): 437–79.

——. *The Veiled Women: Shifting Gender Equations in Rural Haryana, 1880–1990*. Delhi: Oxford University Press, 1994.

Clark, E. G. *Report on the Revision of Settlement of the Bharaich District, Oudh*. Lucknow, North-Western Provinces and Oudh Government Press, 1873.

Clough, Emma Rauschenbusch. *While Sewing Sandals: Tales of a Telugu Pariah Tribe*. 1899. New Delhi: Asian Educational Services, 2007.

Cohn, Bernard S. *An Anthropologist among the Historians and Other Essays*. Delhi: Oxford University Press, 1987.

———. *Colonialism and Its Forms of Knowledge: The British in India*. Princeton, NJ: Princeton University Press, 1996.

Collection of Papers Connected with an Inquiry into the Conditions of the Lower Classes of the Population, Especially in Agricultural Tracts, in the North-Western Provinces and Oudh, Instituted in 1887–1888. Allahabad: Northwestern Provinces and Oudh Government Press, 1888.

Collection of Papers Relating to the Conditions of the Tenancy and the Working of Present Rent Law in Oudh. Allahabad: North-Western Provinces and Oudh Government Press, 1883.

Comaroff, John, and Jean Comaroff. *Of Revelation and Revolution*. Vol. 2: *The Dialectics of Modernity on a South African Frontier*. Chicago: University of Chicago Press, 1997.

Corbridge, Stuart, and John Harriss. *Reinventing India: Liberalization, Hindu Nationalism and Popular Democracy*. Cambridge: Polity, 2000.

Crooke, William. *The Tribes and Castes of the North-Western Provinces and Oudh*. 4 vols. Calcutta: Superintendent of Government Printing, 1896.

Crosthwaite, C. H. T., and W. Neale. *Report of the Settlement of the Etawah District*. Allahabad: North-Western Provinces and Oudh Government Press, 1875.

Currie, Robert G. *Report on the Settlement of the Shahjehanpore District*. Allahabad: North-Western Provinces and Oudh Government Press, 1874.

Dalmia, Vasudha. *The Nationalization of Hindu Traditions: Bharatendu Harischandra and Nineteenth-Century Banaras*. Delhi: Oxford University Press, 1997.

———. "Vernacular Histories in Late Nineteenth-Century Banaras: Folklore, Puranas and the New Antiquarianism." *Indian Economic and Social History Review* 38, no. 1 (2001): 59–79.

Dangle, Arjun. "Dalit Literature, Past, Present, and Future." In *Poisoned Bread: Translations from Modern Marathi Dalit Literature*, edited by Arjun Dangle, 234–66. Hyderabad: Orient Longman, 1992.

Das, Sisir Kumar. "The Narratives of Suffering: Caste and the Underprivileged." In *Translating Caste*, edited by T. Basu, 150–80. New Delhi: Katha, 2002.

Deliege, Robert. *The World of the Untouchables: Paraiyars of Tamil Nadu*. Translated by David Philips. Delhi: Oxford University Press, 1997.

Demerath, Loren R., N. J. Demerath, and Surinder S. Jodhka. "Interrogating Caste and Religion in India's Emerging Middle Class." *Economic and Political Weekly* 41, no. 35 (2006): 3813–18.

Deshpande, Ashwini. "Recasting Economic Inequality." *Review of Social Economy* 63, no. 3 (2000): 381–99.

Deshpande, Prachi. "Caste as Maratha: Social Categories, Colonial Policy and Identity in Early Twentieth-Century Maharashtra," *Indian Economic and Social History Review* 41, no. 1 (2004): 7–32.

Deshpande, Satish. *Contemporary India: A Sociological View*. New Delhi: Penguin, 2004.

———. "Exclusive Inequalities: Merit, Caste and Discrimination in Indian Higher Education Today." *Economic and Political Weekly* 40, no. 24 (2006): 2434–44.

———. "Fashioning a Postcolonial Discipline: M. N. Srinivas." In *Anthropology in the East: Founders of Indian Sociology and Anthropology*, edited by Patricia Uberoi, 496–536. Delhi: Permanent Black, 2007.

Dharamveer. *Premchand: Samant ka Munshi*. Delhi: Vani Prakashan, 2005.

Dharwadker, Vinay. "Dalit Poetry in Marathi." *World Literature Today* 68, no. 2 (1994): 319–24.

Dherivala, Mohammad Azhar. "'Thakur ka Kua': Dalit Chetna ka Dastavej." *Apeksha* 8, (2004): 16–18.

Dietrich, Gabriele. "Dalit Movements and Women's Movements." In *Gender and Caste*, edited by Anupama Rao, 57–79. Delhi: Kali for Women, 2003.

Dirks, Nicholas. *Castes of Mind: Colonialism and the Making of Modern India*. Princeton, NJ: Princeton University Press, 2001.

Drake-Brockman, D. L. *Report on the Settlement Operations of the Saharanpur District, 1921*. Allahabad: Superintendent of Government Press, United Provinces, 1921.

Driver, Edwin D. "Caste and Occupational Structure in Central India." *Social Forces* 41, no. 1 (1962): 26–31.

Dumont, Louis. *Homo Hierarchicus: The Caste System and Its Implications*. Chicago: University of Chicago Press, 1998.

Dussel, Enrique. *Philosophy of Liberation*. Translated by Aquilina Martinez and Christine Morkovsky. New York: Orbis, 1985.

Evans, H. F. *Report on the Settlement of the Agra District, 1880*. Allahabad: North-Western Provinces and Oudh Government Press, 1880.

Foucault, Michel. "Governmentality." In *The Foucault Effect: Studies in Governmentality*, edited by Graham Burchell, Colin Gordon, and Peter Miller, 87–104. Chicago: University of Chicago Press, 1991.

Fox, Richard G., *Lions of Punjab: Culture in the Making*. Berkeley: University of California Press, 1985.

Fraser, Nancy. "Rethinking the Public Sphere: A Contribution to the Critique of Actually Existing Democracy." In *Habermas and the Public Sphere*, edited by Craig Calhoun, 110–24. Cambridge, MA: MIT Press, 1990.

Fremantle, S. H. *Report on the Second Settlement of the Rae Bareli*. Allahabad: North-Western Provinces and Oudh Government Press, 1898.

Fremantle, S. H. *Report on the Settlement of the District Bareilly, 1903*. Allahabad: Superintendent of Government Press, United Provinces, 1903.

Further Papers Relating to Under-Proprietary Rights and Rights of Cultivators in Oude. Calcutta: Foreign Department Press, 1867.

Gajarawala, Toral Jatin. "Some Time between Revisionist and Revolutionary: Unreading History in Dalit Litertaure." *PMLA* 126, no. 3 (2011): 575–91.

Galanter, Marc. *Competing Equalities: Law and the Backward Classes in India*. Berkeley: University of California Press, 1984.

Gandhi, Mahatma. *Collected Works of Mahatma Gandhi*. Vol. 70: *October 21, 1936–February 24, 1937*. 2nd rev. ed. New Delhi: Publications Division, Ministry of Information and Broadcasting, Government of India, 1969.

276 · BIBLIOGRAPHY

———. *The Penguin Gandhi Reader*. Edited by Rudrangshu Mukherjee. New Delhi: Penguin, 1993.

Gandiwind, Giani Nishan Singh, *Shaheed Baba Jiwan Singh: Jeevan, Rachna te Viakhia*. Amritsar: Bhai Chatar Singh Jeevan Singh, 2008.

Ganganiya, Ish. "'Rangbhoomi,' Gandhi, aur Ambedkarvadi-Vimarsh." *Apeksha* 10 (2005): 22–26.

Ganguly, Debjani. *Caste and Dalit Lifeworlds: Postcolonial Perspectives*. New Delhi: Orient Longman, 2008.

Gautam, M. B. *Bhagyodayam, Maadari Bhagya Reddy Varma: Life Sketch and Mission*. Hyderabad: Adi-Hindu Social Service League Trust, 1991.

Gharu, Gurdas Singh. *Pagdandian taun Jeevan Marg tak*. Jagmalera, Sirsa: Sant Ram Udasi Yaadgaari Prakashan, 2000.

Ghosh, Jayati. "Liberalization Debates." In *The Indian Economy: Major Debates since Independence*, edited by T. Byres, 295–334. New Delhi: Oxford University Press, 1998.

Ghosh, Partha. "Positive Discrimination in India: A Political Analysis." *Ethnic Studies Report* 15, no. 2 (1997): 135–72.

Gladstone, J. W. *Protestant Christianity and People's Movements in Kerala: A Study of Mass Movements in Relation to Neo-Hindu Socio-religious Movements in Kerala, 1850–1936*. Kerala: Seminary Publications, 1984.

Gopalankutty, K. "The Task of Transforming the Congress: Malabar, 1934–40." *Studies in History* 5, no. 2 (1989): 177–94.

Gorkhi, Prem. "Dhukhdi Dhooni Pharolani payee." *Lakeer*, January–March 1995, 23–29.

Gorringe, Hugo. *Untouchable Citizens: Dalit Movements and Democratisation in Tamil Nadu*. New Delhi: Sage, 2005.

Government of India. *National Commission for Scheduled Castes and Scheduled Tribes, Annual Reports: 1996–97 & 1997–98*. New Delhi: Government of India, 1997–98.

Grewal, J. S. "Brahmanizing the Tradition: Chhibber's Bansavalinama." In *The Khalsa: Sikh and Non-Sikh Perspectives*, 59–101. New Delhi: Manohar, 2004.

———. "Changing Sikh Self-Image before Independence." In *Self-Images Identity and Nationalism*, edited by P. C. Chatterjee, 187–200. Shimla: Indian Institution of Advanced Studies, 1989.

———. "Contest over the Sacred Space." In *The Sikhs: Ideology, Institutions, and Identity*, 229–60. New Delhi: Oxford University Press, 2009.

———. *Contesting Interpretations of the Sikh Tradition*. Delhi: Manohar, 1998.

Gupta, Charu. "Dalit Virangana and Reinvention of 1875." *Economic and Political Weekly* 42, no. 19 (2007): 1739–45.

———. "Feminine, Criminal, or Manly? Imaging Dalit Masculinities in Colonial India." *Indian Economic Social History Review* 47, no. 3 (2010): 309–42.

Gupta, Ranajit Das. *Labour and Working Class in Eastern India: Studies in Colonial History*. Calcutta: K. P. Bagchi, 1994.

Guru, Gopal. "Dalit Movement in Mainstream Sociology." *Economic and Political Weekly* 28, no. 14 (1993): 570–73.

———. "Dalits in Pursuit of Modernity." In *India: Another Millennium?*, edited by Romila Thapar, 123–36. New Delhi: Viking, 2000.

———. "Dalit Women Talk Differently." *Economic and Political Weekly* 30, nos. 40–41 (1995): 2548–49.

———. "Introduction: Theorizing Humiliation." In *Humiliation: Claims and Context*, edited by Gopal Guru, 1–22. New Delhi: Oxford University Press, 2009.

———. "The Language of Dalit-Bahujan Political Discourse." In *Dalit Identity and Politics*, edited by Ghanshyam Shah, 96–107. New Delhi: Sage, 2001.

———. "The Politics of Naming." *Seminar* 478, November 1998: 14–18.

———. "Rejection of Rejection: Foregrounding Self-Respect." In *Humiliation: Claims and Context*, edited by Gopal Guru, 209–25. New Delhi: Oxford University Press, 2009.

———. "A Subsidised Notion of Democracy." *Economic and Political Weekly* 37, no. 1 (2002): 39–41.

Habib, Irfan, translated. "An Account of the Sikhs, 1808 from Ghulam Ali Khan, Imadus Saadat." In *Sikh History from Persian Sources*, edited by J. S. Grewal and Irfan Habib, 212–17. New Delhi: Tulika, 2001.

Hans, Raj Kumar. "Rich Heritage of Punjabi Dalit Literature and Its Exclusion from Histories." *Beyond Borders* 6, nos. 1–2 (2010): 73–81.

———. "Sant Poet Wazir Singh: A Window for Reimagining Nineteenth Century Punjab." *Journal of Punjab Studies* 20, nos. 1–2 (2013): 135–58.

Hardiman, David. *The Coming of the Devi: Adviasi Assertion in Western India*. Delhi: Oxford University Press, 1987.

Harishchandra, Bharatendu. "Aggarwaloin ki Utpatti." 1871. In *Bharatendu Granthavali: Tisra Bhag*, edited by Brajratnadas, 5–12. Benares: Nagri Pracharini Sabha, 1954.

———. "Khatriyon ki Utpatti." 1873. In *Bharatendu Granthavali: Tisra Bhag*, edited by Brajratnadas, 247–60. Benares: Nagri Pracharini Sabha, 1954.

Harlow, Barbara. *Resistance Literature*. New York: Methuen, 1987.

Hawley, J. S., and M. Juergensmeyer. *Songs of the Saints of India*. Delhi: Oxford University Press, 1988.

Hoff, Karla, and Priyanka Pandey. "Discrimination, Social Identity, and Durable Inequalities." *American Economic Review* 96, no. 2 (2006): 206–11.

Hooper, J. *Report of the Settlement of the Basti District*. Allahabad: North-Western Provinces and Oudh Government Press, 1891.

Hugel, Baron Charles. *Travels in Kashmir and Panjab, Containing a Particular Account of the Government and Character of the Sikhs*, with notes by T. B. Jervis. 1845. Delhi: Low Price Publishers, 2000.

Human Rights Watch. *Broken People: Caste Violence against India's "Untouchables."* New York: Human Rights Watch, 1999.

Hunt, W. S. *The Anglican Church in Travancore and Cochin, 1816–1916*. Vol. 1. Kottayam: Church Missionary Society, 1920.

Ilaiah, Kancha. "Caste in a New Mould." *Biblio*, November 1996.

———. *Why I Am Not a Hindu: A Sudra Critique of Hindutva Philosophy, Culture, and Political Economy*. Calcutta: Samya Prakashan, 1996.

Impey, W. H. L. *Report on the Settlement of the Jhansi District, 1893*. Allahabad: North-Western Provinces and Oudh Government Press, 1893.

Irschick, Eugene. *Politics and Social Conflict in South India: The Non-Brahmin Movement and Tamil Separatism, 1916–1929.* Berkeley: University of California Press, 1969.

Jaaware, Aniket. "Eating and Eating with the Dalit: A Reconsideration Touching upon Marathi Poetry." In *Indian Poetry: Modernism and After,* edited by K. Satchidanandan, 262–93. New Delhi: Sahitya Akademi, 2001.

Jaffrelot, Christophe. *India's Silent Revolution: The Rise of the Lower Castes.* London: Hurst, 1999.

Jassi, Sat Pal. *Holy Hymns and Miracles of Guru Ravi Das Ji.* Jalandhar: Shri Guru Ravi Das Janam Asthan Public Charitable Trust, 2001.

Jatav, Mangal. *Shree 108 Swami Achhutanand ji ka Jeevan Parichay.* Gawlior; Saraswati Press, 1997.

Jeffrey, Robin. *The Decline of Nayar Dominance in Society and Politics in Travancore 1847–1908.* Delhi: Manohar, 1994.

Jency, T. "Contemporary Dalit Mobilization for Land." MPhil thesis, Mahatma Gandhi University, 2009.

Jenkins, Laura. "Becoming Backward: Preferential Policies and Religious Minorities in India." *Commonwealth & Comparative Politics* 39, no. 1 (2001): 32–50.

Jenkins, Rob. *Democratic Politics and Economic Reforms in India.* Cambridge: Cambridge University Press, 1999.

Jha, Shefali. "Representation and Its Epiphanies: A Reading of Constituent Assembly Debates." *Economic and Political Weekly* 39, no. 39 (2004): 4357–60.

———. "Secularism in the Constituent Assembly Debates, 1946–1950." *Economic and Political Weekly* 37, no. 30 (2002): 3175–80.

Jodhka, Surinder. *Caste.* New Delhi: Oxford University Press, 2012.

———. "Caste and Untouchability in Rural Punjab." *Economic and Political Weekly* 37, no. 19 (2002): 1813–23.

———. "Dissociation, Distancing and Autonomy: Caste and Untouchability in Rural Punjab." In *Dalits in Regional Context,* edited by Harish Puri, 62–99. Jaipur: Rawat, 2004.

———. "The Ravi Dasis of Punjab: Global Contours of Caste and Religious Strife." *Economic and Political Weekly* 44, no. 24 (2009).

———. "Sikhism and the Caste Question: Dalits and Their Politics in Contemporary Punjab." In *Caste in Question: Identity or Hierarchy,* edited by Dipankar Gupta, 165–92. New Delhi: Sage, 2004.

Jodhka, Surinder, and Avinash Kumar. "Internal Classification of Scheduled Castes: The Punjab Story." *Economic and Political Weekly* 42, no. 43 (2007): 20–23.

Jogdand, P. G. "Reservations in Private Sector—Legislation in Maharashtra." *Economic and Political Weekly* 39, no. 39 (2004): 3444–46.

Joseph, John. *Memorial Submitted to the Honourable Members of the British Parliament.* Trivandrum: Anantha Rama Varma, 1935.

Joshi, Barbara R. "'Ex-Untouchable': Problems, Progress, and Policies in Indian Social Change." *Pacific Affairs* 53, no. 2 (1980): 193–222.

Judge, Paramjit. "Religion, Caste, and Communalism in Punjab." *Sociological Bulletin* 51, no. 2 (2002), 175–94.

———. "Hierarchical Differentiation among Dalits." *Economic and Political Weekly* 38, no. 28 (2003): 2990–91.

Judge, Paramjit, and G. Bal. "Understanding the Paradox of Changes among Dalits in Punjab." *Economic and Political Weekly* 43, no. 41 (2008): 49–55.

Juergensmeyer, Mark. *Religious Rebels in the Punjab: The Social Vision of Untouchables.* Delhi: Ajanta, 1988.

Juergensmeyer, Mark, and N. Gerald Barrier, ed. *Sikh Studies: Comparative Perspectives on a Changing Tradition.* Berkeley, CA: Graduate Theological Union, 1979.

Kamalasanan, N. K. *Kuttanadum karshakathozhilali Prasthanavum.* Kottayam: DC, 1993.

Kangazha, Vijayan. *Sree Kumara Guru Devan: Biography.* Trichur: Upavasam, 1978.

Kannabiran, Vasanth, and Kalpana Kannabiran. "Caste and Gender: Understanding the Dynamics of Power and Violence." In *Gender and Caste*, edited by Anupama Rao, 249–60. New Delhi: Kali for Women, 2003.

Kardam, Jaiprakash. "Sahitya men dogalaapan nahi chalega." *Apeksha* 10 (2005): 88.

Kateb, George. "The Moral Distinctiveness of Representative Democracy." *Ethics* 91, no. 3 (1981): 357–74.

Kaviraj, Sudipta. "Democracy and Social Inequality." In *Transforming India: Social and Political Dynamics of Democracy*, edited by Francine R. Frankel, Zoya Hasan, Rajeev Bhargava, and Balveer Arora, 89–119. New Delhi: Oxford University Press.

———. Introduction to *Politics in India*, edited by Sudipta Kaviraj, 1–36. New Delhi: Oxford University Press, 1997.

Kerr, Ian J. "British Relationships with the Golden Temple, 1849–90." *Indian Economic and Social History Review* 21, no. 2 (1984): 139–51.

Khairmode, C. B. *Babasaheb Ambedkaranche Charitra.* Mumbai: Maharashtra Rajya Sahitya and Sanskruti Mandal, 1990.

Khaitan, Tarunabh. "Transcending Reservations: A Paradigm Shift in the Debate on Equality." *Economic and Political Weekly* 43, no. 38 (2008): 8–12.

Khare, R. S. *The Untouchable as Himself: Ideology, Identity and Pragmatism among the Lucknow Chamars.* Cambridge: Cambridge University Press, 1984.

Kooiman, Dick. *Conversion and Social Equality in India: The London Missionary Society in South Travancore in the 19th Century.* Delhi: Manohar, 1989.

Koshy, Ninan. *Caste in Kerala Churches.* Bangalore: Christian Institute for the Study of Religion and Society, 1968.

Kothari, Rajni. "Rise of the Dalits and the Renewed Debate on Caste." In *State and Politics in India*, edited by Partha Chatterjee, 439–58. New Delhi: Oxford University Press, 1998.

Krishna, Anirudh. "What Is Happening to Caste? A View from Some North Indian Villages." *Journal of Asian Studies* 62, no. 4 (2003): 1175–90.

Kumar, Dharma. *Land and Caste in South India: Agricultural Labour in the Madras Presidency during the Nineteenth Century.* Cambridge: Cambridge University Press, 1965.

Kumar, Pradeep. "Reservations within Reservations: The Real Dalit-Bahujans." *Economic and Political Weekly* 36, no. 37 (2001): 3505–7.

Kumar, Radha. *The History of Doing: An Illustrated Account of Movements for Women's Rights and Feminism in India 1800–1990*. New Delhi: Zubaan, 1993.

Kumar, Sanjay, Anthony Heath, and Oliver Heath, "Changing Patterns of Social Mobility: Some Trends over Time." *Economic and Political Weekly* 37, no. 40 (2002): 4091–96.

Kundu, Amitabh. "Report of the Expert Group on Diversity Index." *Report of the Expert Group on Diversity Index*. Accessed on 20 September 2015. http://www.minorityaffairs.gov.in/sites/upload_files/moma/files/pdfs/di_expgrp.pdf.

Kusuman, K. K. *Slavery in Travancore*. Trivandrum: Kerala Historical Society, 1973.

Kymlicka, Will. "Three Forms of Group-Differentiated Citizenship in Canada." In *Democracy and Difference: Contesting the Boundaries of the Political*, edited by Seyla Benhabib, 153–70. Princeton, NJ: Princeton University Press, 1996.

Lakshminarasaiah, G., and Tripuraneni Srinivas, eds. *Chikkanavutunna Pata: Dalita Kavitvam*. Vijayawada: Kavitvam Prachuranalu, 1995.

Lakshminarasaiah, G., and Tripuraneni Srinivas, eds. *Padunekkina Pata: Dalit Kavitvam*. Vijayawada: Kavitvam Prachuranalu, 1996.

Lari, Z. H. *Constituent Assembly Debates: Official Report*. Vol. 7. Delhi: Lok Sabha Secretariat, 1948.

Lewis, Oscar. "The Culture of Poverty." *Scientific American* 215 (October 1966): 19–25.

———. *Five Families: Mexican Case Studies in the Culture of Poverty*. New York: Mentor, 1959.

Liddle, Joanna, and Rama Joshi. *Daughters of Independence: Gender, Caste and Class in India*. New Delhi: Kali for Women, 1986.

Limbale, Sharankumar. *Towards an Aesthetic of Dalit Literature: History, Controversies, and Considerations*. Translated by Alok Mukerjee. New Delhi: Orient Longman, 2004.

Ludden, David. "Introduction: A Brief History of Subalternity in South Asia." In *Reading Subaltern Studies: Critical History, Contesting Meaning, and the Globalization of South Asia*, edited by David Ludden, 1–42. New Delhi: Permanent Black, 2001.

Lynch, Owen. *The Politics of Untouchability: Social Mobility and Social Change in a City of India*. New York: Columbia University Press, 1969.

Macauliffe, Max Arthur. *The Sikh Religion: Its Gurus, Sacred Writings and Authors*. Vol. 2. 1909. Delhi: Oxford University Press, 1963.

Madhusudanarao, T. *Kavitvam-Chaitanyam: Sahitya Vimarsa Vyasalu*. Andhra Pradesh: Viplavarachayitala Sangham, 2006.

Mahalingam, Ramaswami. "Essentialism, Culture, and Power: Representation of Social Class." *Journal of Social Issues* 59, no. 4 (2003): 733–49.

Mahar, J. Michael. "Agents of Dharma in a North Indian Village." In *The Untouchables in Contemporary India*, edited by J. Michael Mahar, 17–35. Tucson: University of Arizona Press, 1972.

Malcolm, John. *Sketch of the Sikhs: A Singular Nation, Who Inhabits the Provinces of Penjab*. 1812. New Delhi: Asian Education Services, 1986.

Malhotra, Anshu. "Living and Defining Caste: The Life and Writing of *Giani Ditt Singh / Sant Ditta Ram*." *Journal of Punjab Studies* 20, nos. 1–2 (2013): 159–91.

Mallick, Ross. "Affirmative Action and Elite Formation: An Untouchable Family History." *Ethnohistory* 44, no. 2 (1997): 345–74.

Mann, Gurinder. *The Making of Sikh Scripture*. New Delhi: Oxford University Press, 2001.

Marenco, Ethne. *The Transformation of Sikh Society*. New Delhi: Heritage, 1976.

Mariot, Alan. "Dalit or Harijan? Self-Naming by Scheduled Caste Interviewees." *Economic and Political Weekly* 38, no. 36 (2003): 3751–54.

Mayaram, Shail, M. S. S. Pandian, and Ajay Skaria, eds. *Subaltern Studies XII: Muslims, Dalits and Fabrication of History*. Delhi: Permanent Black, 2005.

McLeod, W. H. "The Sikh Concept of Caste." In *Essays in Sikh History, Tradition, and Society*, 175–86. New Delhi: Oxford University Press, 2007.

———. "Sikhs and Castes." In *Textures of the Sikh Past: New Historical Perspectives*, edited by Tony Ballantyne, 104–31. New Delhi: Oxford University Press, 2007.

Mehra, Usha. *Report: National Commission to Examine the Issue of Subcategorization of Scheduled Castes in Andhra Pradesh*. Hyderabad: Government of Andhra Pradesh, 2008.

Mendelsohn, Oliver, and Marika Vicziany. *The Untouchables: Subordination, Poverty and the State in Modern India*. Cambridge: Cambridge University Press, 1998.

Menon, Dilip. *Caste, Nationalism and Communism in South India Malabar, 1900–1948*. Cambridge: Cambridge University Press, 1994.

Menon, P. K. K. *The History of Freedom Movement in Kerala*. Vol. 2: *1885–1938*. Trivandrum: Department of Cultural Publications, 2001.

Moffatt, Michael. *An Untouchable Community of South India: Structure and Consensus*. Princeton, NJ: Princeton University Press, 1979.

Mohan, Sanal. "Dalit Discourse and the Evolving New Self: Contest and Strategies," *Review of Development and Change* 4, no. 1 (1999): 1–24.

———. "Imagining Equality: Modernity and Social Transformation of Lower Castes in Colonial Kerala." PhD diss., Mahatma Gandhi University, 2005.

———. "Religion, Social Space and Identity: The Prathyaksha Raksha Daiva Sabha and the Making of Cultural Boundaries in 20th Century Kerala." *South Asia* 28, no. 1 (2005): 35–63.

Moon, Vasant. *Growing Up Untouchable in India: A Dalit Autobiography*. Translated by Gail Omvedt. Lanham, MD: Rowman and Littlefield, 2000.

More, M. S. *The Social Context for an Ideology: Ambedkar's Political and Social Thought*. New Delhi: Sage Publications, 1993.

Morris, David. "Caste and the Evolution of the Industrial Workforce in India." *Proceedings of the American Philosophical Society* 104, no. 2 (1960): 124–33.

Mowli, V. Chandra. *Theirs Is the Kingdom of God: "Jogin" Girl-Child Labour Studies*. New Delhi: Sterling, 1992.

Mudie, R. F. *Report on the Settlement and Record Operations in District Agra*. Allahabad: Superintendent of Government Press, United Provinces, 1930.

Mudiraj, K. Krishnaswamy. *Pictorial Hyderabad*. Vol. 2. Hyderabad: Chandrakanth, 1934.

Mukherjee, Ramkrishna. "Caste in Itself, Caste and Class, or Caste in Class." *Economic and Political Weekly* 34, no. 27 (1999): 1759–61.

Murphy, Anne. "Materializing Sikh Pasts." *Sikh Formations* 1, no. 2 (2005): 175–200.

Nagaraj, D. R. *The Flaming Feet and Other Essays: The Dalit Movement in India*. Edited by P. D. C. Shobi. 2nd rev. ed. Ranikhet: Permanent Black, 2011.

Namboodiripad, E. M. S. *Em Esinte Sampurnakritikal*. Trivandrum: Chinthi, 1999.

Namishray, Mohan Dass. *Apne-Apne Pinjare: Ek Dalit ki Atamakatha*. 1996, 3rd rev. ed. New Delhi: Vani Prakashan, 2006.

Narayan, Badri. "Reactivating the Past, Memories of 1857." *Economic and Political Weekly* 42, no. 19 (2007): 1734–38.

Narayana Rao, Velcheru. "Sahityanni Sahityanga Choose Vallu Kavali." Special issue on contemporary literature, edited by Devulapalli Amar, *Prajatantra*, 2002: 19–29.

———. *Twentieth Century Telugu Poetry: An Anthology*. New Delhi: Oxford University Press, 2002.

Navaria, Ajay. *Yes Sir*. New Delhi: Samyik Prakashan, 2012.

Nayar, B. R. *Minority Politics in the Punjab*. Princeton, NJ: Princeton University Press, 1966.

Nehru, Jawaharlal. *The Discovery of India*. 1946. Delhi: Oxford University Press, 1981.

Nigam, Aditya. "Secularism, Modernity, Nation: Epistemology of the Dalit Critique." *Economic and Political Weekly* 35, no. 48 (2000): 4256–68.

Ninan, K. I. *Sabhacharitra Vichinthanangal-Anglican Kalaghattam*. Thiruvalla: Christhava Sahithya Samithy, 1997.

Nirbhay, Hari Singh. *Mazhabi Sikhan di Jaddo-jaihad*. Amritsar: Baba Jeevan Singh Mazhbi Dal, 1975.

Nizam Rashtra Prathamandhra Maha Sabha. *Presidential Address of Suravaram Pratapa Reddy and the Resolutions*. Hyderabad-Deccan: Shyama Sundara Mudrakshara Shala, 1930.

Oberoi, Harjot. *The Construction of Religious Boundaries*. Oxford: Oxford University Press, 1994.

Office of the Registrar General, India. "Punjab: Data Highlights: The Scheduled Castes." Accessed July 10, 2015. http://censusindia.gov.in/Tables_Published/SCST /dh_sc_punjab.pdf.

O'Hanlon, Rosalind. *Caste, Conflict, Ideology: Mahatma Jotirao Phule and Low Caste Protest in Nineteenth Century Western India*. Cambridge, Cambridge University Press, 1985.

Oman, John Campbell. *Cults, Customs and Superstitions of India*. 1908. Delhi: Vishal, 1972.

Omvedt, Gail. "Capitalism and Globalization, and Dalits and Adivasi." *Economic and Political Weekly* 40, no. 47 (2005): 4881–85.

———. "The Great Globalization Debate." Paper presented at the Indian Institute of Advance Study, Shimla, October 16, 2008.

———. *Seeking Begumpura: The Social Vision of Anticaste Intellectuals*. New Delhi: Navayana, 2008.

———. "'Twice-Born' Riot against Democracy." *Economic and Political Weekly* 25, no. 39 (1990): 2195–201.

Orsini, Francesca. *The Hindi Public Sphere: 1920–1940*. New Delhi: Oxford University Press, 2002.

Pai, Sudha. *Dalit Assertion and the Unfinished Democratic Revolution: The Bahujan Samaj Party in Uttar Pradesh*. Delhi: Sage, 2002.

Pandey, Geetanjali. *Between Two Worlds: An Intellectual Biography of Premchand*. Delhi: Manohar, 1989.

Pandey, Gyanendra. *The Construction of Communalism in Colonial North India*. Delhi: Oxford University Press, 1990.

Panikkar, K. N. *Against Lord and State: Religion and Peasant Uprising in Malabar 1836–1921*. Delhi: Oxford University Press, 1989.

Pankaj, Ashok K. "Engaging with Discourse on Caste, Class and Politics in India." *South Asia Research* 27, no. 3 (2007): 333–53.

Pant, Rashmi. "The Cognitive Status of Caste in Colonial Ethnography: A Review of Some Literature on the North-Western Provinces and Oudh." *Indian Economic and Social History Review* 24, no. 2 (1987): 145–62.

Parekh, Bhiku. *Gandhi's Political Philosophy*. Delhi: Ajanta, 1989.

Patil, Sharad. "Should 'Class' Be the Basis for Recognising Backwardness?" *Economic and Political Weekly* 25, no. 50 (1990): 2733–44.

Pawar, Urmila. "What Has the Dalit Movement Offered to Women?" In *At Crossroads: Dalit Movement Today*, edited by Sandeep Pendse, 83–94. Mumbai: Vikas Adhyayan Kendra, 1994.

Pawar, Urmila, and Meenakshi Moon. *We Also Made History: Women in the Ambedkarite Movement*. Translated by Wandana Sonalkar. New Delhi: Zubaan, 2008.

Pendse, Sandeep, ed. *At Crossroads: Dalit Movement Today*. Mumbai: Vikas Adhyayan Kendra, 1994.

Phillips, Anne. *Engendering Democracy*. Cambridge: Polity, 2005.

———. *The Politics of Presence*. Oxford: Clarendon Press of Oxford University Press, 1995.

Pillai, T. Sivasankara. *Scavenger's Son*. Translated by R. E. Asher. New Delhi: Orient Paperbacks, 1975.

Pitkin, Hanna. *The Concept of Representation*. Berkeley: University of California Press, 1967.

Pollock, Sheldon. "The Ramayana: Myth and Romance?" In *The Ramayana of Valmiki: An Epic of Ancient India*, vol. 3: *Aranyakanda*, edited by Robert Goldman; introduction, translation, and annotation by Sheldon Pollock, 10–15. Princeton, NJ: Princeton University Press, 1991.

Prasad, Kalekuri. *Dalita Udyanam—Dalita Sahityodyamam*. Hyderabad: Sakshi, 1989.

Prasad, Mata. *Jhompri Se Rajbhavan*. New Delhi: Naman Prakashan, 2002.

Prashad, Vijay. *Untouchable Freedom: A Social History of a Dalit Community*. Delhi: Oxford University Press, 2000.

Pratt, Mary Louise. *Imperial Eyes: Travel Writing and Transculturation*. New York: Routledge, 1992.

Premi, Kusum K. "Educational Opportunities for the Scheduled Castes: Role of Protective Discrimination in Equalization." *Economic and Political Weekly* 9, nos. 45–46 (1974): 1902–10.

Puri, Harish. "The Scheduled Castes in the Sikh Community: A Historical Perspective." *Economic and Political Weekly* 34, no. 36 (1999): 2693–701.

Pushpendra. "Dalit Assertion through Electoral Politics." *Economic and Political Weekly* 34, no. 36 (1999): 2609–18.

Raghavaiah, Jai Prakash. *Basel Mission Industries in Malabar and South Canara 1834–1914*. Delhi: Gyan, 1990.

Raghuvanshi, U. B. S. *Shree Chanvar Purana*. Kanpur: Commercial Press, no date.

Raina, C. R. "Basel Mission and Social Change in Malabar." MPhil thesis, University of Calicut, 1988.

Raj, Kaviyuoor K. C. *Chennaikkalude Idayil Kunjadukal*. Ettumanoor: KK, 1966.

Rajan, Baby and Babu Rajan. *Thiruvithamkur Prathyaksha Raksha Daiva Sabha Charithram Poikail Yohannanu Sesham*. Ettumanoor: G. J. Printers, 1994.

Ram, Pandit Bakshi. *Mera Jeevan Sangharash*. Jalandhar: Punjab Pradesh Balmik Sabha, 1983.

Ram, Ronki. "Untouchability, Dalit Consciousness, and the Ad Dharm Movement in Punjab." *Contributions to Indian Sociology* 38, no. 3 (2004): 323–49.

Ramaswamy, U. "Education and Inequality." *Economic and Political Weekly* 20, no. 36 (1985): 1523–28.

——. "Preference and Progress: The Scheduled Castes." *Economic and Political Weekly* 19, no. 30 (1984): 1214–17.

——. "Protection and Inequality among Backward Groups." *Economic and Political Weekly* 21, no. 19 (1986): 399–403.

Rammohan, K. T. "Material Processes and Developmentalism: Interpreting Economic Change in Colonial Tiruvitamkur 1800–1945." PhD diss., Centre for Development Studies, 1996.

Ramulu, B. S. *Gabbilam* 1, no. 2 (1995).

——. *Sahitya Charitrani Kottachooputo Tiragarayali: Telangana Perspective*. Hyderabad: Vishala Sahitya Akademi, 2005.

Rao, Anupama. *The Caste Question: Dalits and the Politics of Modern India*. Berkeley: University of California Press, 2009.

——. Introduction to *Gender and Caste*, 1–48. New Delhi: Kali for Women, 2003.

Rao, Madapati. *Telangana Andhrodhyamamu*. Vols. 1 and 2. Hyderabad: Andhra Granthamala, 1950.

Rao, N. Sudhakar. "The Structure of South Indian Untouchable Castes: A View." In *Dalit Identity and Politics*, edited by Ghanshyam Shah, 74–96. New Delhi: Sage, 2001.

Ravikumar. "Re-Reading Periyar." *Seminar* 558 (February 2006). Accessed September 20, 2015. http://www.india-seminar.com/cd8899/cd_frame8899.html.

——. *Venomous Touch: Notes on Caste, Culture, and Politics*. Kolkata: Samya Prakashan, 2009.

Rawat, Ramnarayan. "Occupation, Dignity, and Space: The Rise of Dalit Studies," *History Compass* 11, no. 12 (2013): 20157–67.

———. *Reconsidering Untouchability: Chamars and Dalit History in North India.* Bloomington: Indiana University Press, 2011.

Rawls, John. "Justice as Fairness." In *Contemporary Political Philosophy: An Anthology*, edited by Robert Goodin and Philip Pettit: 185–200. Oxford: Blackwell, 2006.

Reddy, Deepa. "The Ethnicity of Caste." *Anthropological Quarterly* 78, no. 3 (2005): 543–84.

Reddy, Suravaram. *Rajah Bahadur Venkata Rami Reddy Jeevitha Chartra.* Hyderabad: Reddy Sangham, 1939.

Rege, Sharmila. *Dalit Studies as Pedagogical Practice: Claiming More Than Just a "Little Place" in the Academia.* Chennai: Madras Institute of Development Studies, 2006.

———. *Writing Caste/Writing Gender: Reading Dalit Women's Testimonios.* New Delhi: Zubaan, 2006.

Reid, J. R. *Report on the Settlement Operations in the District of Azamgarh.* Allahabad: North-Western Provinces and Oudh Government Press, 1881.

Report of the National Commission for Religious and Linguistic Minorities. New Delhi: Government of India, 2007.

Report of the Reforms Committee-1938. Hyderabad-Deccan: Government Central Press, 1938.

Rodrigues, Edward. "Dalit Struggle for Recognition within Indian Sociology." In *The Practice of Sociology*, edited by Maitrayee Chaudhuri, 221–57. Hyderabad: Orient Longman, 2003.

Rosenbloom, David. *Federal Equal Employment Opportunity, Politics and Public Personnel Administration.* New York: Praeger, 1977.

Rudolph, Lloyd I., and Susanne H. Rudolph. *The Modernity of Tradition: Political Development in India.* 3rd ed. Hyderabad: Orient Longman, 1999.

Sachar, Rajinder. *Report on Social, Economic and Educational Status of the Muslim Community of India.* New Delhi: Government of India, 2006.

Sagar, Pandit Sunderlal. *Yadav Jivan.* Agra: Shree Jatav Mahasabha, 1929.

Sambasivarao. "Yadhatadha saampradaya Dhrukpatham to Dalita Sahityodyama viplava Dhrukpaathaniki pottu kudaradu." In *Dalitarananninadam*, edited by Sambasivarao, 13. Hyderabad: Edureeta, 2005.

Samithi, Grandha Rachana. *Sree Kumara Devan.* Ettumanoor: R. K., 1983.

Saradamoni, K. *Emergence of a Slave Caste: Pulayas of Kerala.* New Delhi: Peoples Publishing House, 1980.

Sarkar, Sumit. *Beyond Nationalist Frames: Postmodernism, Hindu Fundamentalism, History.* Bloomington: Indiana University Press, 2002.

———. "Indian Democracy: The Historical Inheritance." In *India's Successful Democracy*, edited by Atul Kohli, 23–46. Cambridge: Cambridge University Press, 2001.

———. "The Limits of Nationalism." *Seminar* 522 (February 2003). Accessed September 16, 2015. http://www.india-seminar.com/2003/522/522%20sumit%20sarkar.htm.

———. "The Return of Labour to South Asian History." *Historical Materialism* 12, no. 3 (2004): 285–313.

———. *Writing Social History*. Delhi: Oxford University Press, 1999.

Sarojini, Regani. "The Movement for the Social and Cultural Revival of Telangana in the Erstwhile Hyderabad State." In *Aspects of Deccan History*, edited by V. K. Bawa. Hyderabad: Institute of Asian Studies, 1975.

Saseendran, Kallara, ed. *Dalit Saradhikal Theeyathikalilude: Oru Nakhha Chitram*. Mundakkayam: Ambedkar Bhavan, 1999.

Satyanarayana, K. "Dalit Reconfiguration of Caste: Representation, Identity and Politics." *Critical Quarterly* 56, no. 3 (2014): 46–61.

———. "Dalit Studies as a New Perspective in the Indian Academia." In *Dalit Studies in Higher Education: Vision and Challenges*, edited by Arun Kumar, 81–95. Delhi: Deshkal, 2005.

Satyanarayana, K., and Susie Tharu. *No Alphabet in Sight: New Dalit Writing from South India (Dossier 1: Tamil and Malayalam)*. Delhi: Penguin, 2011.

Satyanarayana, S. V. *Dalitavada Vivadalu*. Hyderabad: Vishalandhra, 2000.

Satyasodhana. *Reservationlu Madigalakem Chesindi*. Ongole: Madiga Hakkula Porata Samiti Publications, 1995.

Schomer, Karine, and W. H. McLeod, eds. *The Sants: Studies in a Devotional Tradition of India*. Delhi: Motilal Banarsidas, 1987.

Scott, David. *Conscripts of Modernity: The Tragedy of Colonial Enlightenment*. Durham, NC: Duke University Press, 2004.

Seetal, Sohan Singh. *The Sikh Misals and the Punjab*. Ludhiana: Lahore Book Shop, 1981.

Sekhar, C. R. *Dalita Shakthini Antamondinche Rajakeeya kutra Vargeekarana: Paavulugaa Marina Dandora Nayakulu*. Hyderabad: Bahujana Vijnana Kendram, 2005.

Shah, A. M. "The 'Dalit' Category and Its Differentiation." *Economic and Political Weekly* 37, no. 42 (2002): 1317–18.

Shah, Ghanshyam. "Consequences of Reservations." In *The Politics of Backwardness: Reservation Policy in India*, edited by V. Pai Panandiker, 240–55. New Delhi: Konark, 1997.

Shah, Vimal P., and Tara Patel. *Who Goes to College? Scheduled Caste/Tribe Post-Matric Scholars in Gujarat*. Ahmedabad: Rochana Prakashan, 1977.

Sharan, Awadhendra. "From Caste to Category: Colonial Knowledge Practices and the Depressed/Scheduled Castes of Bihar." *Indian Economic and Social History Review* 40, no. 3 (2003): 279–310.

Sharma, S. K. *Social Movements and Social Change: A Study of Arya Samaj and Untouchables in Punjab*. Delhi: B. R. Publishing, 1985.

Sharma, Sri Ram. *Punjab in Ferment*. New Delhi: S. Chand, 1971.

Siddiqi, Majid. *Agrarian Unrest in Northern India: The United Provinces, 1918–1922*. Delhi: Vikas, 1978.

Sikhamani. *The Black Rainbow: Dalit Poems in Telugu*. Translated by Kiranmayi et al. Hyderabad: Milinda, 2000.

———. *Dalitasahityatatvam*. Hyderabad: Literary Circle, 1998.

Singh, Baldev. *Panjwan Sahibjada*. Ludhiana: Chetna Prakashan, 2005.

Singh, Bhai Pratap. *Jaat Paat te Chhut-Chhaat sambandhi Gurmat Sidhant*. Amritsar: Shiromani Gurdwara Parbandhak Committee, 1933.

Singh, Ganda. *Life of Banda Singh Bahadur*. Amritsar: Khalsa College, 1935.

Singh, Giani Udham. *Guru ka Beta: Itihas Shahid Baba Jeevan Singh*. Amritsar: Jeevan Lehar, 1968.

Singh, Gurmukh. *Bhai Jaita Ji: Jiwan te Rachna*. Amritsar: Literature House, 2003.

Singh, Indera Pal. "Caste in a Sikh Village." In *Caste among Non-Hindus in India*, edited by Harjinder Singh, 66–83. Delhi: National Publishing House, 1977.

Singh, Ishar. *Sikh Ithas de Visre Panne*. Chandigarh: Lokgeet Prakashan, 2005.

Singh, Jagmohan, ed. *Shahid Bhagat Singh ate uhna de Sathian dian Likhtan*. Ludhiana: Chetna Parkashan, 2005.

Singh, K. Suresh. *The Scheduled Castes (People of India, National Series Volume II)*. Delhi: Oxford University Press, 1995.

Singh, Khushwant. *The Sikhs*. London: George Allen and Unwin, 1953.

Singh, Rajpal. *Achhutanand Harihar*. Delhi: RajLaxmi Prakashan, 2003.

Singh, Satnam. *Chamar Jati ka Gauravshali Aitihas*. Delhi: Samyak Prakashan, 2009.

Singh, Sohan. *Banda the Brave*. Lahore: Bhai Narain Singh Gyani, 1915.

Smith, Raymond. "Anthropology and the Concept of Social Class." *Annual Review of Anthropology* 13 (1984): 467–97.

Smith, T. E. *Report on the Revision of Settlement in the District of Aligarh*. Allahabad: North-Western Provinces and Oudh Government Press, 1882.

South Indian Gospel Association. Booklet. Kottayam: V. E., no date.

Srinivas, K. "Dalita Suryodaya Kavita." Satishchander, *Panchamavedam*, 79–84.

Srinivas, K. "Rendu Prapancha Yudhala Madhya Telugu Sahityam: Telanganalo Sahitya Punarvikasam 1919–1939." PhD diss., Potti Sriramulu Telugu University, 2001.

Srinivas, M. N. *Caste in Modern India and Other Essays*. Bombay: Media Promoter and Publishers, 1962.

———. "An Obituary on Caste as a System." *Economic and Political Weekly* 38, no. 5 (2003): 455–59.

Srinivas, Panthukala, dir. *Dandora Dagapadda Gunde Chappudu*. 2006. DVD.

Srinivasulu, K. "Caste, Class and Social Articulation in Andhra Pradesh: Mapping Differential Regional Trajectories." London: Overseas Development Institute, September 2002. Accessed June 27, 2015. http://www.odi.org.uk/publications/working_papers/wp179.pdf.

Statistical, Descriptive and Historical Account of the North-Western Provinces of India. Vol. 9. Allahabad: North-Western Provinces and Oudh Government Press, 1883.

Steedman, Carolyn. *Dust: The Archive and Cultural History*. New Brunswick, NJ: Rutgers University Press, 2002.

Steinbach, Henry. *The Punjaub: Being a Brief Account of the Country of the Sikhs*. 1846. Karachi, Pakistan: Oxford University Press, 1976.

Stern, Henri. "Power in Modern India: Caste or Class? An Approach and Case Study." *Contributions to Indian Sociology* 13, no. 1 (1979): 61–84.

Stoker, B. T. *Assessment Report of Tahsil Khurja of the Bulandshahr District*. Allahabad: North-Western Provinces and Oudh Government Press, 1889.

———. *Report on the Settlement of Land Revenue in the Bulandshahr District, 1891*. Allahabad: North-Western Provinces and Oudh Government Press, 1892.

Stoler, Ann. *Along the Archival Grain: Epistemic Anxieties and Colonial Common Sense*. Princeton, NJ: Princeton University Press, 2009.

Sudhakar, Yendluri. "Drumbeat." *Little Magazine* 6, no. 495 (2007).

———. *Nalladraksha Pandiri: Darky: A Bilingual Anthology of Poems*. Secunderabad: J. J. Publications, 2002.

Sundaram, K., and Suresh D. Tendulkar. "Poverty among Social and Economic Groups in India in 1990s." *Economic and Political Weekly* 38, no. 50 (2003): 5263–76.

Sunstein, C. R. "Preferences and Politics." *Philosophy and Public Affairs* 20, no. 1 (1991): 3–34.

Suryavansh Kshatriya Jaiswar Sabha. Lahore: Bombay Machine Press, 1923.

Taylor, Charles. "The Politics of Recognition." In Charles Taylor, *Multiculturalism*, with commentary by K. Anthony Appiah, Jürgen Habermas, Steven C. Rockefeller, Michael Walzer, and Susan Wolf; edited and introduced by Amy Gutmann, 25–73. Expanded paperback ed. Princeton, NJ: Princeton University Press, 1994.

Teltumbde, Anand. "Reverting to the Original Vision of Reservation." *Economic and Political Weekly* 42, no. 25 (2007): 2383–85.

———. "State Market and Development of Dalits." In *Atrophy of Dalit Politics: Intervention I*, edited by Gopal Guru, 79–102. Mumbai: Vikas Adhyayan Kendra, 2005.

Tendulkar, Dinanath. *Mahatma: Life of Mohandas Karamchand Gandhi*. Vol. 6. New Delhi: Publication Division, Government of India, 1953.

Thapar, Romila. *Cultural Pasts: Essays in Early Indian History*. Delhi: Oxford University Press, 2000.

Tharakan, P. K. Michael. "History as Development Experience: Desegregated and Deconstructed Analysis of Kerala." PhD diss., Mahatma Gandhi University, Kottayam, 1977.

Tharu, Susie, et al. "Reservations and Return to Politics." *Economic and Political Weekly* 42, no. 49 (2007): 39–45.

Thorat, Vimal. "'Manusmriti' ka Taalibaani vistaar." *Yuddhrat Aam Aadmi* 87 (2007): 12–15.

Thulaseedharan, Assary. *Colonialism, Princely States and Struggle for Liberation: Travancore (1938–1948)*. New Delhi: APH Publishing House, 2009.

Thurston, Edgar, and K. R. Rangachari. *Castes and Tribes of Southern India*. 9 vols. Madras: Government Press, 1909.

Uberoi, J. P. S. *Religion, Civil Society and the State: A Study of Sikhism*. Delhi: Oxford University Press, 1996.

Uberoi, Patricia, Satish Deshpande, and Nandini Sundar. "Introduction: The Professionalisation of Indian Anthropology and Sociology: People, Places, and Institutions." In *Anthropology in the East: Founders of Indian Sociology and Anthropology*, edited by Patricia Uberoi, Nandini Sundar, and Satish Deshpande, 1–105. Delhi: Permanent Black, 2007.

Upadhya, Carol. "The Idea of Indian Society: G. S. Ghurye and the Making of Indian Sociology." In *Anthropology in the East: Founders of Indian Sociology and Anthropology*, edited by Patricia Uberoi, 194–255. Delhi: Permanent Black, 2007.

Valmiki, Omprakash. *Dalit Sahitya ka Soundarya Shastra*. Delhi: Radhakrishna, 2001.

———. *Joothan: An Untouchable's Life*. Translated by Arun Prabha Mukherjee. New York: Columbia University Press, 2003.

———. "Premchand: Sandarbh Dalit Vimarsh." *Teesra Paksh* 14–15 (2004): 25–32.

Van der Veer, Peter, ed. *Conversion to Modernities: The Globalization of Christianity*. New York: Routledge, 1995.

Varshney, Ashutosh. "Mass Politics or Elite Politics? India's Economic Reforms in Comparative Perspective." In *India in the Era of Economic Reforms*, edited by Jeffrey D. Sachs, Ashutosh Varshney, and Nirupama Bajpai: 249–57. New Delhi: Oxford University Press, 1999.

Venkatswamy, P. R. *Our Struggle for Emancipation*. Secunderabad: Universal Art Printers, 1955.

Viplava Shityodyamam (1970–1999). Viplava Rachayitala Sangham. Nellore, 1996.

Virdi, S. L. *Punjab da Dalit Itihas*. Phagwara: Dalit Sahit Academy, 2000.

Vivek, Pushpa. "Dalit Striyan Sabak sikhane ka hausla Rakhti hain." *Yuddhrat Aam Aadmi* 87 (2007): 40–41.

Viyougi, Nandlal. *Ambedkar ki Awaz arthat Achhutoin ka Federation*. Allahabad: Jagriti, 1949.

Walia, Rashpal. "The Problem of Untouchability among Sikhs in Punjab with Special Reference to Mazhabi Sikhs." PhD diss., Punjab University, 1993.

Wangmay, Samagar. *Mahatma Jotirao Phule*. Mumbai: Maharashtra Sahitya Sanskruti Mandal, 1998.

Wankhade, G. G. "Educational Inequalities among Scheduled Castes in Maharashtra." *Economic and Political Weekly* 36, no. 18 (2001): 1553–58.

Warid, Muhammad Shafi. "Banda Bahadur and His Followers from Muhammad Shafi 'Warid." Translated by Irfan Habib. In *Sikh History from Persian Sources: Translations of Major Texts*, edited by J. S. Grewal and Irfan Habib, 160–62. New Delhi: Tulika, 2001.

Webster, John C. B. *The Dalit Christians: A History*. 3rd ed. Delhi: Indian Society for Promoting Christian Knowledge, 2000.

———. "The Dalit Sikhs: A History?" In *Textures of the Sikh Past: New Historical Perspectives*, edited by Tony Ballantyne, 132–54. New Delhi: Oxford University Press, 2007.

Weiner, Myron. "The Political Consequences of Preferential Policies: India in Comparative Perspective." In *The Indian Paradox: Essays in Indian Politics*, edited by Ashutosh Varshney, 151–75. New Delhi: Sage, 1989.

William, Melissa. *Voice, Trust and Memory: Marginalized Groups and the Failing of Liberal Representation*. Princeton, NJ: Princeton University Press, 1999.

Wiser, William, and Charlotte Wiser. *Behind the Mud Walls*. New York: R. R. Smith, 1930.

Wright, F. N. *Report of the Settlement of the Cawnpore District*. Allahabad: North-Western Provinces and Oudh Government Press, 1878.

Yadvendu, Ramnarain. *Yaduvansh ka Aitihas*. Agra: Navyug Sahitya Niketan, 1942.

Young, Iris. "Polity and Group Difference: A Critique of the Ideal of Universal Citizenship." *Ethics* 99 (1989): 250–74.

Zelliot, Eleanor. *Doctor Bahasaheb Ambedkar and the Untouchable Movement*. New Delhi: Blumoon Books, 2004.

CONTRIBUTORS

D. SHYAM BABU is a senior fellow at the Centre for Policy Research, in New Delhi. In collaboration with Devesh Kapur and Chandra Bhan Prasad, he has completed a study of the phenomenon of Dalit entrepreneurs. He is a coauthor of *Defying the Odds: The Rise of Dalit Entrepreneurs* (2014).

LAURA BRUECK is an associate professor of Hindi literature and South Asian studies at Northwestern University. She is the author of *Writing Resistance: The Rhetorical Imagination of Hindi Dalit Literature* (2014). She has also published *Unclaimed Terrain* (2013), a collection of translations of short stories by the Delhi-based author Ajay Navaria.

SAMBAIAH GUNDIMEDA is an assistant professor in the School of Policy and Governance at Azim Premji University, in Bengaluru, India. He is currently a fellow at the Nehru Memorial Museum and Library, in New Delhi, and working on his second book, tentatively titled "Dalits and the Public Sphere in Contemporary India." His first book, *Dalit Politics in Contemporary India*, is forthcoming.

GOPAL GURU is a professor in the Center for Political Studies, Jawaharlal Nehru University, New Delhi. A nationally recognized public intellectual of India, he is the author of a number of books and scores of articles on contemporary Indian politics and political thought. Most recently he has coauthored, with Sundar Surrakai, *The Cracked Mirror: An Indian Debate on Experience and Theory* (2012).

RAJ KUMAR HANS is a professor of history at the Maharaja Sayajirao University, in Baroda, India. His book, *History of Punjabi Dalit Literature*, is forthcoming. He is also the author of an essay in *Devotion and Dissent in Indian History*.

CHINNAIAH JANGAM is an assistant professor of history at Carleton University, in Canada. He is finishing a book titled *Meanings from the Margins: Dalits and the Making of Modern India 1900–50*. His most recent article, "Desecrating the Sacred Taste: The Making of Gurram Jashua—the Father of Dalit Literature in Telugu," was published in the *Indian Economic and Social History Review*, April–June, 2014.

SURINDER S. JODHKA is a professor of sociology at the Jawaharlal Nehru University, in New Delhi. A recipient of the Indian Council for Social Science Research-Amartya Sen Award for Distinguished Social Scientists in 2012, he has published widely on the subjects of rural and agrarian change, social and economic dynamics of caste, and social or cultural identities. Most recently he has published *Caste in Contemporary India* (2015).

P. SANAL MOHAN is an associate professor in the School of Social Sciences, Mahatma Gandhi University, in Kottayam, India. Currently a fellow of the Social Science Research Council, in New York, he is working on Dalit Christian prayers and prayer practices in Kerala, as part of the council's program called "Religion and the Public Sphere." He is the author of *Modernity of Slavery: Struggles against Caste Inequality in Colonial Kerala* (2015).

RAMNARAYAN S. RAWAT is an associate professor of history at the University of Delaware. He is the author of *Reconsidering Untouchability: Chamars and Dalit History in North India* (2011). He is currently working on his second book, "Parallel Publics: A New History of Indian Democracy," which has been supported by the American Institute of Indian Studies senior research fellowship (2008–2009), American Council of Learned Societies' Charles Ryskamp fellowship, 2013 (2015–16) and the Smuts fellowship (2014–15) at the University of Cambridge.

K. SATYANARAYANA is a professor in the Department of Cultural Studies at the English and Foreign Language University, in Hyderabad, India. Most recently he has coedited with Susie Tharu two volumes of new Dalit writing: *No Alphabet in Sight* (2011) and *Steel Nibs Are Sprouting* (2013). He is currently working on a book project titled "Literature, Modernity and the Lens of Caste: Dalit Literature, 1970–2010."

INDEX

Abraham Issac, Paradi, 79

Achhutanand, Swami, 8, 17–18, 22, 63, 69–70

"Achhut da Sawal" (Bhagat Singh), 148

Adhasthitha Navodhana Munnani, 97–98

Adi-Andhra Mahasabha, 128

Adi-Andhras, 108, 110, 124, 125, 202–3, 211

Adi-Dharm/Ad Dharma movement, 13, 22, 147–48, 253–57, 263, 267

Adi-Dravidas, 108, 110

Adi-Hindu Mahasabha, 22, 63

Adi-Hindu Press, 111

Adi-Hindus, 108–9, 114, 115

Adi-Karnatakas, 108

Adi-Maharashtrians, 108

Adi Tamilzhar Peravai, 5

Adivasis, 155, 216

affirmative action. *See* scheduled caste (SC) reservations

"Aggarwaloin ki Utpatti" (Harischandra), 66–67

agricultural work (*krishi karya*), 53, 94, 210–11

Aiyangar, Aravamdu, 115. *See also* Constitutional Reforms Committee

alcohol addiction, 113

All India Scheduled Castes Federation, 255

Aloysius, G., 8, 15

Ambedkar, B. R., 5, 8, 12, 17–18, 105, 161, 163, 170, 223; Bhagya Reddy on, 113; critique of Gandhism, 8, 10, 120, 125–26, 188; on Dalit citizenship, 164; on Dalit consciousness, 187, 188; establishment of Republican Party, 47; Hindus on, 43; on Indian nationalism, 21, 32, 39, 205; *Manusmriti* burning, 189; on minority status, 204; on modern India, 34;

moral editing by, 46; Poona Pact, 255–56; on purity/pollution ideology, 34, 38; rediscovery of, 163; on Sikhism, 132–33, 144–45; on social discrimination, 204–5; on study of Untouchables, 25; on urban migration, 241; on *varna* model, 28n29

Ambedkar Youth, 5

Amin, Shahid, 57

Anand, Mulk Raj, 9

Anandhi, S., 194

Andhra Jana Sangh, 106

Andhra Maha Sabha, 118, 119, 120

Andhra Pradesh, 5, 24–25, 161–62, 202, 217, 218–19, 221, 241

Andhra Pradesh Civil Liberties Committee (APCLC), 164

Andhra Pradesh Viplava Rachayitala Sangham (Virasam), 155, 157, 160, 162

Andhra Rashtra Adi-Andhra Mahajana Sabha, 118, 119, 120, 123, 124, 126

Anglican missionaries, 75, 81, 84, 90

Anupama Rao, 7, 15, 105, 182

APCLC. *See* Andhra Pradesh Civil Liberties Committee

Apeksha (journal), 186, 191

"Apology, An" (Sikhamani), 167–69

A. P. Viplava Rachayitala Sangham (Virasam). *See* Andhra Pradesh Viplava Rachayitala Sangham

Aqida, Gurnam, 146

Arif, Sadhu Daya Singh, 140

Arifi, Naranjan, 132, 136, 138, 141

Arjun, 137

Arunatara (journal), 169

Aryans, 66, 108
Arya Samaj, 69–70, 117, 143–44, 252–53
Asan, Krishnadi, 87
Ashok, Shamsher Singh, 136
Audaiah, M. L., 110
Audinarayana, Prathipati, 123, 124–25
Awadh Kisan Sabha, 57, 61–62
Ayyankali, 21, 76, 79, 83–87, 96–97
Ayyappan, Sahodaran, 80

Babu, Shyam, 245–46
Bagul, Baburao, 20
Bahiskrut Bharat, 34, 36, 37–39, 43
Bahiskrut Bharat (newspaper), 34
Bahujan Samaj Party (BSP), 4, 5–6, 35–36,
    40–47, 59, 163, 235–36
Balagopal, K., 4, 162, 164, 222
Balaramaiah, Matari, 119
Bali, King (mythical figure), 34
Balmukund, Rai, 108, 110, 117
Banda Bahadur, 139
Bansavalinama Dasan Patshahian ka (Chhib-
    ber), 141
Barstow, A. E., 143
Barton, William, 111
Basavanna, 16
Basel Evangelical Mission, 82
Baviskar, B. S., 13
Bayly, Susan, 105
BDSA. *See* Bharatiya Dalit Sahitya Akademi
"Begumpura" (Ravi Das), 258–59
belonging, national, 35
Beteille, Andre, 13, 208, 234
Bhagyanagar Patrika (newspaper), 111–13, 120
Bhagyayya, Maadari. *See* Bhagya Reddy
    Varma
Bhai Jaita, 135–36, 137–38, 140
Bhakti movement, 258
Bhangis, 203
Bharatiya Dalit Sahitya Akademi (BDSA),
    180–81
Bharatiya Janata Party, 36, 41, 82, 98
Bharti, Anita, 189–91, 195, 196
Bhattacharya, Neeladri, 11
Bose, Subhas Chandra, 1
Bourdieu, Pierre, 86
Brahmans/Brahmins, 9, 18, 55, 248–49;
    capitalism and, 39; colonialism and, 105;

in Congress Party, 37; influence of, 15, 227;
    practices in Sikhism, 23, 141–47
Brahma Pathyaksha Raksha Dharma Pari-
    palana, 79
Brahmo Samaj, 110, 117
*Brief View of the Caste System of the Northern-
    Western Provinces and Oudh* (Nesfield), 67
British Raj, 146–47
BSP. *See* Bahujan Samaj Party
Buddhism, 15, 22, 256
Bujangadasu, Mangalagiri, 125
Burns, Kathryn, 58

capitalism and Brahmanism, 39
castes: *avarna*, 18; vs. class, 233–39, 246; con-
    sciousness, 14, 38; histories, 65; inequities,
    ix–x, 5, 6–7, 8, 11, 13; modernization of, 13;
    politics of, 166; reassertion of, 239–41; Sikh-
    ism on, 134–36; slave, 75–77, 81; subaltern,
    14–15; *varna* model, 9, 55–56. *See also*
    scheduled caste (SC) reservations; *specific
    castes*
Castes of Mind (Dirks), 55
census and surveys, 55–56, 58, 114, 250
Central Adi-Hindu Social Service League, 22,
    108, 109, 114–16, 117–18, 119, 121. *See also*
    Manya Sangham
Chakraborty, Debashis, 245–46
Chakravorty, Manashi, 245–46
Chamar Jati ka Gauravshali Aitihas (Singh), 65
Chamars, 12, 13, 22, 53–55, 57, 59–64, 203, 209,
    242–43, 257, 258, 267; Dalit, use of term, 181;
    Dalit agenda and, 64–71. *See also* Dalits
Chand (newspaper), 69
Chandar, Satish, 169–71
Chandra, Kanchan, 32
Chandragupta (Mauryan Emperor), 66
Chanjan, P. C., 87
Chatterjee, Partha, 3–4, 14, 165
Chattopadhyaya, Aghorinath, 110
Chenchudasu, Mangalagiri, 125
Chengara, 97
Chentharassery, T. H. P., 84
Cheramar Daiva Sabha, 91
Cheramar Mahajana Sabha, 76, 79, 90, 96
Cheramar Sangham, 97
Chhibber, Kesar Singh, 141
Chitharaiah, Ch., 119

Chitnis, Suma, 209
Chothi, Vellikkara, 79
Chowdhry, Prem, 241
Christianity, 22; Dalit, 23, 77–81, 98, 170, 243–44; missionaries, 75–77, 84, 90, 202; Syrian, 23, 75, 80, 84, 87, 90–92. *See also* Anglican missionaries
Christ symbol, 170
Church Missionary Society (CMS), 78, 91
Church of South India, 91–92
citizenship, 33–34, 164–65, 234
civil society: Dalit movements and, 74–76, 79–80, 88–90, 98, 109–10, 268; patriotism and, 38; vs. political society, 165. *See also* Puruskrut Bharat
class vs. caste, 233–39, 242–45, 246
CMS. *See* Church Missionary Society
Cochin Praja Mandalam, 76
Cohn, Bernard, 12, 55
colonial archives, 56–58, 71
colonialism: backwardness and, 10; Brahmanism and, 105; divide and rule policy, 13, 22; Hindu dominance and, 18; modernity and, 2–3, 10, 15–16, 15–17, 20–21, 26, 75, 80, 99; multiple locations and, 77; nationalism and, 36; racism of, 39; sociology of, 55–56, 58–59, 70
Comaroff, Jean, 75
Comaroff, John, 75
Communist Party of India (CPI), 92, 94–95
Congress Party, 4, 18, 21, 37, 41–42, 47, 82, 92, 256
Constituent Assembly, 25; Ambedkar speech, 46
Constitutional Reforms Committee, 115
Constitution of India: Ambedkar's role in, 43; on minority status, 204–6; on political rights, 22; reforms, 115–17; on SC reservations, 4, 13, 26n6, 96, 162, 204–6
contact zone, use of term, 78
Corfield, B. C., 91
Council of Dalit Christians, 98
CPI. *See* Communist Party of India
Criminal Intelligence Department reports, 65
Crooke, William, 57
cultural capital, use of term, 86
Cust, Robert Needham, 142

Dalit activism: of Bhagya Reddy, 109–17; civil society and, 74–76, 79–80, 88–90, 98,

109–10, 268; critique, 164–66, 175; Hyderabad constitutional reforms, 115–17; literary sphere, 180–84; major concerns, 225; on mass killings, 161–62, 165, 168–69, 245–46; poetry on, 166–75; politics of caste in, 166; post-independence, 95–98, 99; pride and, 241; in Punjab, 251–55; rise of, 5, 11, 20, 105–7; on SC reservations, 202, 204–6, 211–22, 227; in Sikhism, 136–40, 254, 261; social space and, 21, 74–75, 79, 86, 88, 98; study of, 12–13, 21, 70
Dalit Christians, The (Webster), 136
Dalit consciousness (*chetnā*), 2, 10, 20, 47, 58, 79, 99, 106, 109, 140, 184, 186–90, 192, 193, 195–97
Dalit feminism, 4, 7, 15, 177n24, 184, 192–97
Dalit Kala Mandali, 163
Dalit Mahasabha, 5, 161–62
Dalit Panthers of India, 5, 6; of Maharashtra, 47
Dalit Rachayitala, Kalakarula, Medhavula Ikya Vedika (Darakame), 163
Dalits: caste vs. class, 233–39; contemporary context, 1–8; diaspora, 7, 23, 264–66, 268; dignity of, 2–3, 17, 24, 26; Hindi, 21, 24; humiliation of, 1–3, 17, 26; identities, 11–12, 32; India's independence and, 32–33; marginalization of, 31; middle classes, 25, 44, 46, 166, 208–9, 241; minority status, 204–6; Sikhs, 23; stereotypes of, 4, 9, 18; Tamil, 8, 15; use of term, 2, 181–82, 203. *See also* specific communities
Dalit Sahitya ka Soundarya Shastra (Valmiki), 187
Dalit saints, 12, 16. *See also* specific saints
Dalit Sangarsh Samiti, 5
Dalit studies: conferences, 27n19; emergence of, 3, 4, 7; frameworks, 9, 19–20; recognition of, 31
"Dalit Women Talk Differently" (Guru), 7
Dandora debate, 216–22; unity and uniformity in, 222–25
Dangle, Arjun, 20
Darakame. *See* Dalit Rachayitala, Kalakarula, Medhavula Ikya Vedika
Das, Sisir Kumar, 199n8
Das, Veena, 13
Demerath, Loren, 234
Demerath, N. J., 234

Depressed Classes, 203
Dera Sachkhand Ballan/Dera Sant Sarwan Dass, 260, 261–64
Deshpande, Ashwini, 243
Deshpande, Prachi, 59
Deshpande, Satish, 214
Devendrudu, Naralasetti, 122, 123, 125
Dharamveer, 184, 192–97
dharma and authority, 14
Dharmanna, Kusuma, 8, 108, 122
Dheds, 32, 203
Dherivala, Mohammad, 190
Dietrich, Gabriele, 194, 197
dignity, 2–3, 17, 24, 26
Dil, Lal Singh, 148
Dirks, Nicholas, 55–56
Discovery of India, The (Nehru), 37
Diwans, 86–87
Doms, 12
Dos Santos, Francis Xavier, 107
Dravidian movement, 5, 15
"Drumbeat" (Sudhakar), 172–74
Dufferin Report, 57
Dumont, Louis, 11
Dussel, Enrique, 133

economic liberalization, 7
education: Adi-Hindus and, 109, 111; citizenship and, 164–65; economic independence and, 104–5; missionaries and, 202; modernization and, 127; right to, 83–85; SC reservations and, 4, 24–25, 162, 202, 206–9, 211–12, 217, 234, 245, 255
Edureeta (journal), 163
Egerton, Robert, 142
Ekalavya (journal), 163
Ek Onkar, Sikh, 264
Ellis, Francis, 56
embedded histories, 66
employment: colonial army and, 251–52; modernization and, 127; public, 104, 112, 208, 214–16, 217; SC reservations and, 4, 24–25, 162, 202, 206–9, 211–12, 227, 234, 241
ethical relativism, 45–46
exclusion: of academic Dalits, 4–5; of Dalits from temples, 19; nationalism and, 2; practices of, 20; untouchability and, 19
Ezhavas, 79–80, 82

Fanah-dar-Makan (Arif), 140
Farid, Sheikh, 133
feminism. *See* Dalit feminism
"Fifth Note" (Satish Chandar), 170–71
forced labor, 119–20
Forster, E. M., 243
fragmentation, 38
Fraser, Nancy, 159
freedom, struggle for, 9; Ad Dharm movement and, 256; Dalit consciousness and, 187; nationalism and, 37–39; in Punjab region, 250; slave castes and, 81

Gabbilam (journal), 163
Gadar movement, 253
Gaddar, 160
Gajarawala, Toral, 193, 200n16
Galanter, Marc, 214
Gandhi, Mahatma, 1, 2, 11, 21, 121, 184, 259; Ambedkar critique of, 8, 10, 120, 125–26, 188; Harijan ideology, 2, 9–10, 20, 95; on nationalism, 37; in nationalist politics, 120–26; Poona Pact, 255–56; on untouchability, 243; in Vaikom Satyagraha, 93
Gangaiah, Rayudu, 122, 123
Garib Dass, Sant, 261
Gender and Caste (Anupama Rao), 7
gender inequity, 24
Ghai, Kavi Dhanna Singh, 138
Gheba, Tara Singh, 138–39
Ghulam Ali Khan, 139–40
Ghurye, G. S., 11
globalization, 34
Godavari Keratalu (journal), 163
Golden Temple, 140, 142, 144
Gopalan, A. K., 93
Gopalan, Laha, 103n83
Gorhki, Prem, 145–46
Gouda Saraswata, 95
Government of India Act (1935), 255
Govindacharyulu, Atmakuri, 125
Great Rebellion of 1857, 34, 39–40, 55–56
Green Revolution, 165, 249–50, 267
Grewal, J. S., 141
Guardian (newspaper), 242
Guha, Ranajit, 14
Gujjars, 236
Gupta, Charu, 32, 193–94

Guru, Gopal, 2, 7, 10, 13, 15, 16, 203
Guru, Narayana, 79–81, 82, 85, 92, 95
Guru Granth Sahib, 22, 133, 254, 257, 258, 259, 261, 264, 267
Guru Nanak, 134–35, 258, 259
Guruvayur Satyagraha, 93

Habermas, Jürgen, 159
Hanumantha Rao, Madapati, 106, 117, 121
Hanumantha Rao, Nallapati, 122
Hardiman, David, 68–69
Hari Dass, Sant, 261
Harijan ideology, 2, 9–10, 20, 95
Harischandra, Bharatendu, 66–67
Harlow, Barbara, 199–200n13
Heath, Anthony, 238
Heath, Oliver, 238
Heer (Waris Shah), 140
Hindus: on Ambedkar, 43; colonial dominance by, 18; in Congress Party, 37; contradictory roles of, 39; discriminatory practices by, 2, 6–7, 13, 19, 89, 208; Hindutva politics, 43, 223; practices in Sikhism, 141–47; in Punjab, 250; reform activities, 117–18
Holeyas, 209
Hooper, J., 59–60
Hossain, Naomi, 244–45
Hugel, Charles, 141–42
humiliation, 1–3, 17, 26, 42–43
Hyderabad constitutional reforms, 115–17

identity: caste, 24, 165, 167; Dalit, 11–12, 32, 155, 166–67, 171, 174, 181–82, 198, 234, 236–37, 251–55, 257–58, 267; *dhed*, 32
Ilaiah, Kancha, 197
illiteracy, 107
inclusion (*sarvajan*), 35–36, 40–47
Indian Dalit Federation, 97
Indian Express (newspaper), 235
Indian Institutes of Technology, 208
Indian National Congress, 76, 93
Internet, rise of, 7
Iyer, C. P. Ramaswai, 96

Jacobite Church, 81
Jagan Mitra Mandali, 107
Jain, Seth Lalji Meghji, 108
Janamma, 88

Jassi, Sat Pal, 259
Jatav, Ram Dayal, 63
Jatav Mahasabha, 53
Jatavs, 53–54, 63–64, 65, 70
jati, 14
Jatiyas, 53–54
Jatt Sikhs, 23, 132, 145, 147, 251, 265
Jeeva Raksha Jnan Pracharak Mandali, 111, 117
Jodhka, Surinder, 22, 234
John Joseph, Pampady, 76, 79, 90, 96
Joint Political Congress, 96
Joseph, T. S., 92
Joshi, Barbara, 239, 245
Juergensmeyer, Mark, 157, 264–65, 266

Kakinada Congress, 92
Kaleshwara Rao, Ayyadevara, 125
Kannabiran, Kalpana, 194
Kannabiran, Vasanth, 194
Karamchedu massacre (1985), 161–62
Kardam, Jaiprakash, 190
Karunakaran, K., 95
Kaviraj, Sudipta, 203
Kelappan, K., 93
Kempu, Claude, 126
Kerala, 5, 74, 81–82
Kerala Harijan Federation, 97
Kerala Pulayar Maha Sabha, 97
Keshav Rao, 108, 110
Khalsa, 134
Khalsa Sewak (newspaper), 144–45
Khare, R. S., 13
"Khatriyon ki Utpatti" (Harischandra), 66
Khattris, 66
kinship, 56, 82–83, 249
Komaram Bheem (Sahu), 155
Kothari, Rajni, 4
Krishna, Anirudh, 238–39
Krishna, Manda, 174
Krishnaiah, Chunduru, 123
Kishna Rao, Baji, 110, 120
Krupakar, 174, 223
Kshatriyas, 9, 55, 65–66, 248
Kumar, Sanjay, 238
Kumara Guru Devan. *See* Yohannan, Poikayil
Kurmaiah, Vemula, 122, 124, 126

land revenue records, 56–57, 65, 70–71
land rights (*mirasi*), 56, 60–61
Lari, Z. H., 228n16
Laxminarayana, Unnava, 121, 123
leatherworkers, 57, 63–64, 65, 222, 251–52, 258.
  See also Chamars
Lewis, Oscar, 266
Limbale, Sharankumar, 186–87
literacy, 75, 207
Lokur, B. N., Committee, 209, 210
Ludden, David, 29n72
Lynch, Owen, 13

Mackenzie, Colin, 55
Madhavan, T. K., 92
Madhavanar, K., 93
Madhusudanarao, T., 160
Madiga Dandora, 223–24, 225
Madiga Reservation Porata Samiti (MRPS), 5,
  172, 173, 202–3, 216–17, 223, 227
Madigas, 12, 24, 114–15, 117, 121, 127–28, 163,
  173–74, 202–3, 210–22, 241. *See also* Adi-
  Hindus; Dandora debate
Mahars, 12, 189, 203, 209
Mailrapporten, 58
Mala Mahanadu (MMN), 203, 211, 213–14, 216,
  219–22, 223–24, 225, 227
Malas, 12, 24, 106, 114–15, 117, 121, 127–28, 163,
  173–74, 202–3, 209, 211–22, 241. *See also*
  Adi-Hindus; Dandora debate
Malaviya, Madan Mohan, 69
Malayali Memorial, 80
Mallela, Venkatarao, 219
Mallesha Rao, Gurakula, 119
Mandal, B. P., 4
Mandal Commission Report, 4, 5, 6, 8, 13,
  23–24, 162
Mandali, Jananatya, 160
Mangs, 209
Mansingh, Seth Sitaram, 63
Manu Dharma, 170, 224
Manusmriti, 12, 18, 189, 197
Manya Sangham, 107–8, 109. *See also* Central
  Adi-Hindu Social Service League
Marathas, 59
Marxist historiography, 76–77
masculinity, 193–94, 196–97, 198
Masterjee, 163

Matam, Brahma Nishta, 85
Maurya, B. P., 210
Mayawati, 43, 235
Mazhabis, 136, 138, 209
McLeod, W. H., 134, 135
Meghwal, Kusum, 195
"Mera bharat mahan" (my India is great)
  slogan, 37–38
MMN. *See* Mala Mahanadu
modernity: colonial, 2–3, 10, 15–16, 20–21,
  26, 75, 80, 99; Dalits and, 16, 81–92, 94, 99,
  127, 162, 165, 179n71; Hinduism and, 19; in
  Kerala society, 74, 81–83; nationalist project,
  13, 16
Moon, Vasant, 58
Moore, Mike, 244–45
MRPS. *See* Madiga Reservation Porata Samiti
Mudaliar, Ranganatha, 123
Mukherjee, Arun Prabha, 187
Mukherjee, Ramkrishna, 246
Murthi, Vellanki Krishna, 123
Muthaiah, J. S., 107

Nagaraj, D. R., 16
Naik, Waman Ramachandra, 110, 119, 121
Nairs, 80, 84
Nalapu (journal), 163
Nallapati Rao, Hanumantha, 123
Namasudras, 12, 14–15
Namishray, Mohan Dass, 58, 188–89
Nandanar, 16
Nandy, Ashish, 37
Narayan, Badri, 32
Narayana Rao, Velcheru, 156–61
National Commission for Scheduled Castes
  and Scheduled Tribes, 208
National Coordination Committee for SC
  Christians, 24
National Council of Education Research and
  Training (NCERT), 180, 181, 183
National Democratic Alliance, 43
National Election Study, 238
National Federation of Dalit Women (NFDW),
  6, 194
nationalism: Dalits and, 33–39; exclusion and,
  2; of pan-Indian elite, 13; secular, 13; social
  equality and, 47; Telugu, 112, 118–20
Navaria, Ajay, 184

Naxalite movement, 148
NCERT. *See* National Council of Education Research and Training
Nehru, Jawaharlal, 1, 11, 37
Neiyyer, K. S., 136
Nesfield, J. C., 67
NFDW. *See* National Federation of Dalit Women
Niranjan Dass, Sant, 261
Nizam's territory, 105–6, 110–11, 114, 115, 118–19
Nizam Andhra, 118

OBCs. *See* Other Backward Classes
O'Hanlon, Rosalind, 12–13, 105
Oman, John Campbell, 142
Omvedt, Gail, 4, 32, 259
Other Backward Classes (OBCs), 162, 239
Oudh Rent Acts (1868, 1886), 62

Padmarao, Katti, 161–62
Palars, 209
Pallans, 12
Pampady John Joseph. *See* John Joseph, Pampady
Pandey, Geetanjali, 199n10
Pandey, Gyanendra, 63
pangat, 134–35
pan-Indian elite, 13
Paraiyans, 12
Parayar Mahajana Sangham, 79
Parayars, 209
Parekh, Bhiku, 37
Pasis, 12, 61–64
patriarchy, 6–7, 15, 197
Pawar, Urmila, 15
Periyar, 5
Phillips, Anne, 214, 224
Phule, Jotirao, 12–13, 34, 105, 163
Pillai, P. Krishna, 93
Pillai, Sivasankara, 9
Pipal Dass, Sant, 260
police intelligence reports, 65, 68, 70
Pollock, Sheldon, 67
Poona Pact (1932), 188, 255–56
Popular Legislature, 96
Popular Legislature of Travancore, 79, 89
Prabuddha Bharat, 34
Pradhan, G. R., 25
Praja Rajyam Party, 240

Prasad, Chandrabhan, 208
Prasad, Mata, 1–2, 17
Prasad, Rajendra, 1
Prasad, Vara, 221–22
Prashuram, 66
Pratap (newspaper), 69
Prathyaksha Raksha Daiva Sabha (PRDS), 76, 79, 87–88, 99
Pratt, Mary Louise, 78
PRDS. *See* Prathyaksha Raksha Daiva Sabha
Premchand, Munshi, 24, 180–81, 183; critique of, 184–91, 198; feminism and, 192–97
Premi, Kusum K., 209
public sphere: Dalit, 161–63, 165; defined, 159; Telugu, 156–61, 171
Pudiya Tamilazham, 6
Pulaya Maha Sabha, 87
Punjab, 249–51
Punjab Darpan (newspaper), 143–44
Punjab Land Alienation Act (1901), 147
purity/pollution ideology, 34, 38
Puruskrut Bharat, 34, 36, 37–39, 43, 47

Raghavender Rao Rao, 108
Raghubansia family, 65
Raghuvanshi, U. B. S., 65
Rai, Lala Lajpat, 1
Rajalingam, K., 110
Ram, H. S. Venkat, 107
Ram, Jagjivan, 17–18
Ram, Kanshi, 264
Ram, Mangoo, 13, 17, 22, 147, 253–55, 256–57, 263
Ram, Pandit Bakshi, 145
Ram, Seth Jivan, 63
Ramachandra, Baba, 62–63
Ramachandra Rao, Guduru, 122, 123, 125
Ramadasias, 209
Ramakrishnaiah, Baddela, 123
Ramaswamy, Arigay, 110, 121, 127
Ramaswayi, E. V. *See* Periyar
Ramji Rao, Vermuri, 122
Ram Rajya, 37, 259
Ranga, N. G., 123
Rangaiah, Gorantla, 113
Ranganath Mishra Commission, 98
Rangaswamy, Jala, 122
Rangbhūmi (Premchand), 180–81, 183, 184, 190–91

Ranghreta, Bir Singh, 138
Ranghretas, 136–37, 138
Rao, P. V., 219–20
Ravi Das, Sant, 16, 22–23, 254, 258–61, 263–64,
    266, 267
Ravi Dasis, 250, 255–58, 261–66, 268
Ravi Das Mandal, 255, 257
Rawat, Ramnarayan, 15
Reddy, Bahadur Venkata Rama, 110
Reddy, Bhagya. See Bhagya Reddy Varma
Reddy, Ravi Narayan, 120
Reddy, Suravaram Pratapa, 106
Rege, Sharmila, 15, 19, 194
Reporter, R. E., 108
Report of the Settlement of the Basti District
    (Hooper), 59–60
Republican Party of India, 47, 256
reservations. See scheduled caste (SC)
    reservations
Rodinson, Maxime, 199–200n13
Rosenbloom, David, 215
Rudolph, Lloyd, 13
Rudolph, Susanne, 13

Sadhu Jana Christiya Sangham, 91
Sadhu Jana Paripalana Sangham (SJPS), 21, 76,
    79, 83, 86–87, 93–94, 99
Sagar, Sunderlal, 53–54, 59, 65, 69
Sahu, 155
Samajwadi Party, 6, 163
sangat, 134–35
Sanskritization model, 10, 11, 16, 25, 248
Sarathi, 176n6
Sarkar, Sumit, 8
sarvajan model, 35–36, 40–47
Sarwan Dass, Sant, 260–61, 264
Sastri, Kesavan, 96
Satnamis, 14–15
Satya Sodhak, 163
scavenger figure (bhangi), 9, 243
Scheduled Caste and Scheduled Tribe (Pre-
    vention of Atrocities) Act (1989), 181
Scheduled Caste Employees' Welfare Associa-
    tions, 163
Scheduled Caste Federation, 256
scheduled caste (SC) reservations, 4; caste
    divisions/identity and, 165, 173, 209–10,
    233–34, 240, 255–56; categorization debate,

211–16, 227; Constitution of India on, 4, 13,
    26n6, 96, 162, 204–6; Dalit demand for, 98,
    156, 161, 162, 174, 202–3, 207, 211–22, 225,
    227; justification for, 204–6; literacy rate
    and, 207; opposition to, 28n42, 162, 208,
    219, 226, 230n50, 231n67; in private sector,
    225–26; representation and, 205–6, 211–14,
    216, 218, 219; social justice and, 204, 226
Schumacher, Michael, 237
Second Backward Classes Commission, 4
segregation, 14, 38, 75, 91
Sekhar, C. R., 213
Separate Administration Movement, 92
Seshaiah, Walthati, 107
settlement reports, 59–64
SGPC. See Shiromani Gurudwara Prabandhak
    Committee
Shah, A. M., 13
Shama Rao, 110
sharma, 117
Shiromani Gurudwara Prabandhak Commit-
    tee (SGPC), 137, 145
Shivaram, H. S., 107
Sree Narayana Dharma Pariplana (SNDP),
    74, 80
"Shroud, The" (Premchand), 184, 185–86, 187,
    192–97, 198
shudhi (purifying) movement, 252
Shudras, 9, 55, 66, 248
Sidhanar Service Society, 97
Sikhamani, 166–69, 171
Sikhism: Brahmanization of, 23, 141–47; Dalit
    initiatives in, 136–40, 254, 261; egalitarian-
    ism and caste in, 132–36, 147; independence
    of, 138; Jatt, 23, 132, 145, 147, 251, 265; misals,
    138–39; origin of term, 133; in Punjab,
    250–51, 253–54; Sanatan, 141; scholarly lit-
    erature on, 131–32; on untouchability, 132,
    134–36, 141
Singh, Aalam, 138
Singh, Balwanta, 256
Singh, Bhagat Lakshman, 143, 148
Singh, Bhai Pratap, 144
Singh, Charat, 138
Singh, Chet, 151n70
Singh, Dhakkar, 138
Singh, Dharam, 138
Singh, Diani Ditt, 140

Singh, Garja, 138
Singh, Gobind, 23, 133, 134, 137–38, 139, 144
Singh, Gulab, 138–39
Singh, Jiwan, 135. *See also* Bhai Jaita
Singh, Khushwant, 143
Singh, Man, 138
Singh, Nigahi, 138
Singh, Ranjit, 140, 141, 146
Singh, Sardar Amar, 144–45
Singh, Satnam, 65
Singh, Wazir, 140
Singh Sabha movement, 23, 140, 142–43
sjps. *See* Sadhu Jana Paripalana Sangham
slave labor, 75–76, 77, 81, 85
sndp. *See* Sree Narayana Dharma Pariplana
social justice: Dalit literature and, 191; representation and, 205–6, 213, 214, 216, 219; sc reservations and, 204, 225–26; structural injustice and, 215
social space: Dalit movements and, 21, 74–75, 79, 86, 88, 98; globalization and, 32
Sri Gur Katha (Bhai Jaita), 135–36, 137–38, 140
Sri Krishna Devaraya Andhra Basha Nilayam, 106
Srinivas, K., 155
Srinivas, M. N., 10, 11, 13, 237, 268
Srinivasulu, K., 162, 163
Sri Raja Raja Narendra Andhra Basha Nilayam, 106
Sri Sri, 24
Statistical, Descriptive and Historical Account of the North-Western Provinces of India, 65, 67
Steedman, Carolyn, 58
"Steel Nibs Are Sprouting, The" (Sikhamani), 171
Steinbach, Henry, 141
Stern, Henri, 234
Stoker, B. T., 64
Stoler, Ann, 57–58
subalternity: publics, concept of, 165; studies project, 13–14; use of term, 13–14
Subbaiah, Thiruvakolluri Venkata, 123
Subba Rao, Undru, 122
Subhadra, Jupaka, 224
Sudhakar, Yendluri, 172–74
Sukumaran, Kallara, 95, 97
Sumanakshar, Sohanpal, 180–81, 186, 188

Suryanarayana, Athili, 125
Suryavansh Kshatriya Jaiswar Sabha, 65
Swami, Sadananda, 85
swaraj, 205

Tagore, Rabindranath, 11
Tamil Nadu, 5, 38
Tandon, Purshottam Das, 69
Tharakam, Bojja, 161–62
taxes, agricultural, 64
Taylor, Charles, 2
Teertha, Swami Ananda, 95
Telegu: nationalism, 112, 118–20; publics, 156–61, 171, 216
Telugu Desam Party, 162
Telugulu Kavita Viplavala Swaroopam (Narayana Rao), 156
temple entry movements, 69, 82, 85–86, 92–93, 95, 122, 125
Thass, Iyothee, 8, 15, 17–18
Thennindian Suvishesha Sangham, 91
Thorat, Vimal, 196–97
Tiyyas, 82
Tottiyute Makan (Pillai), 9
Towards an Aesthetic of Dalit Literature (Limbale), 186–87
Travancore State Congress, 76

Uberoi, J. P. S., 133
Udasi, Ram, 148
United Progressive Alliance, 242
University Grants Commission, 7–8
untouchability: abolition of, 234; exclusion and, 19, 55; as Hindu caste problem, 243; in Sikhism, 3, 132, 134–36, 141; struggles against, 8, 10–11, 23. *See also* Dalit consciousness; Dalits
Untouchable (Anand), 9
Untouchables in Contemporary India, The, 12
Untouchable Workers of Bombay City (Pradhan), 25
Uttar Pradesh (up), 5–6, 22, 35, 40–41, 42–45, 53–54, 69, 209, 235–36

Vadas (neighborhoods), 34, 171, 173
Vadhyar, Haris, 85
Vadhyar, V. J. Thomas, 85
Vaghela, Arvind, 242

Vaikom Satyagraha, 92–93
Vaishyas, 9, 55, 248
Vallon, K. P., 87
Valmiki, Omprakash, 187–88
Valmikis, 242–43
Varan (varna), 135
Varma, Bhagya Reddy, 8, 17–18, 21–22, 106–7, 127; activism of, 109–17; on Ambedkar, 113; Dalit organizations and, 108–9; ideological foundation, 120–22; publications, 111–12, 121; on Telugu Nationalism, 118–20
Varma, T. Dhanakoti, 108
varna model, 9, 55–56, 58, 248
Vattappara, Stephan, 92
Vedanta, Adviata, 80
Vedic rituals, 70
Veeraswamy, Kusuma, 123
vegetarianism, 70
Vellars, 56
Venkaiah, Sundru, 122, 123
Venkatramaiah, Kusuma, 122
Venkat Rao, B. S., 115
Venkatswamy, P. R., 106, 117, 123
Vietnam War, 168
Virasam. *See* Andhra Pradesh Viplava Rachay-itala Sangham
Virdi, S. L., 136
Vivek, Pushpa, 195, 196
Viyougi, Nandlal, 21

Warid, Muhammad Shafi, 139
Waris Shah, 140
Webster, John, 136
Wellinker, N. G., 108, 110
Western ethnocentrism, 234
What Congress and Gandhi Have Done to the Untouchables (Ambedkar), 10
William Barton Boys School, 111
women: autobiography genre, 196; Dalit power structure and, 46; as heroes, 39–40; in politics, 6; reservation benefits and, 220; violence against, 15, 24, 192–98. *See also* Dalit feminism
World Conference Against Racism, Racial Discrimination, Xenophobia and Racial Intolerance (Durban, 1980), 4, 7

Yaduvansh (Yadvendu), 63
Yadvendu, Ramnarain, 63, 65, 69
Yes Sir (Navaria), 184
Yohannan, Njaliyakuzhi Simon, 88
Yohannan, Poyikayil, 23, 76, 78, 79, 87–89
Youth League of Ambedkarites, 115–16
Yuddhrat Aam Aadmi (journal), 195

Zelliot, Eleanor, 12, 105
Zindagi Bilas (Arif), 140